AF516353

UPROOTING AND SOCIAL CHANGE

Uprooting and Social Change

The Role of Refugees in Development

STEPHEN L. KELLER

Foreword by
M.S. RANDHAWA

MANOHAR
2023

First published 1975
Reprinted 2021, 2023

© Stephen L. Keller, 1975

All rights reserved. No part of this publication may be reproduced or transmitted, in any form or by any means, without prior permission of the author and the publisher.

ISBN 978-93-88540-96-4

Published by
Ajay Kumar Jain *for*
Manohar Publishers & Distributors
4753/23 Ansari Road, Daryaganj
New Delhi 110 002

Printed at
Replika Press Pvt. Ltd.

TO MY PARENTS

Foreword

The Partition of India on 15 August, 1947 led to the creation of a new country, Pakistan. Its western and eastern wings were separated by a long distance. The father of Pakistan, Muhammad Ali Jinnah, demanded an 800-mile corridor through India to link East Pakistan with West Pakistan. This fantastic demand was not accepted. West Pakistan included Sind, North-West Frontier Province, Baluchistan, Bahawalpur and sixteen prosperous districts of Punjab including the famous canal colonies. The canal colonies were developed by the skill and stamina of the Sikh farmers who had to migrate from the districts of Amritsar, Gurdaspur, Jullundur, Hoshiarpur and Ludhiana which are in Indian Punjab. On the creation of Pakistan the Hindu-Sikh population felt that it could not stay in that country with honour. The entire Hindu-Sikh population of West Pakistan, about 5 million, was soon on the move after 15 August. As the railway trains were attacked most of the migration was in the form of bullock-cart caravans or in foot convoys. Arrangements were made by the Government of India for feeding these convoys during transit. Truck-loads of parched gram, wheat floor and *gur* accompanied the convoys. All the roads leading from Pakistan to India were choked with men, women and children as well as bullock-carts and cattle. On all the roads a seething mass of humanity stretched over many miles all moving towards India urged onwards by a relentless destiny. It was an awe-inspiring spectacle the kind of which had not been seen for centuries in human history. When they reached India they were given shelter in colonies of tents, the refugee camps.

East Punjab was much poorer as compared with West Pakistan. As a result of the partition, East Punjab obtained control over the waters of three out of five rivers of the united Punjab and obtained about 45 per cent of the population, 38 per cent of the area, and 31 per cent of the income of the united province. West Punjab, on the other hand, includes about 55 per cent of the population, 62 per cent of the area and controls about 69 per cent of the income of the old province. It has retained the important canals and about 70 per cent of the fertile canal-irrigated tracts of the undivided province as well as the huge revenues earned therefrom. It possesses important forests and mineral resources and a large number of exclusive industries, e.g., rubber-goods, surgical instruments, sports goods, resin, etc., and has inherited all the shisham plantations and the lion's share of the province's integrated system of communications. It had been fortunate also in getting the only university as well as the principal educational, medical, technical, veterinary, and agricultural institutions of the province. West Punjab had, therefore, emerged comparatively bigger, richer and more food-producing and had a density of just 256.5 square miles as compared with 338 in East Punjab. Of the irrigated area of the undivided province, only 26 per cent was situated in East Punjab, while considerable deficit existed in wheat and rice.

After the refugees had rested for some time in camps a plan was made for their distribution in districts. The colonists had already gone back to their ancestral villages and were supported by their relatives. As against an area of 67 lakh acres of land abandoned by the Hindu-Sikh land-owners in West Pakistan, only 47 lakh acres were available in East Punjab. The gap in area was not bad enough but the position was actually much worse when we consider the factors like fertility of soil and means of irrigation. The Hindu-Sikh land-owners left 43 lakh acres of irrigated land as against 13 lakh acres of irrigated land left by the Muslims. Out of the irrigated area left in West Pakistan by the Hindu-Sikh refugees, 22 lakh acres were perennially irrigated as against only 4 lakh acres of such land left by the Muslims in East Punjab.

The land left by the Muslims was allotted to the refugee land-owners under a scheme of graded cuts. Upto 10 acres of land the rate of cut was 25 per cent and in the case of holdings of above 40 acres it was from 55 per cent to 95 per cent. As a result, a good deal of levelling took place and large landlordism was abolished.

After the allotment of land a number of schemes for agricultural development were taken up. Garden colonies were established over an area of 20,000 acres to make up the loss in gardens. It may be mentioned that all citrus orchards were in the canal colonies of West Pakistan. In the garden colonies the land was consolidated on a priority basis; electricity was supplied for electrifying tubewells and loans were liberally granted for purchase of tractors. In some cases, *pacca* approach roads were also provided. Apart from the garden colonies most of the farmers were given loans in kind in the form of agricultural implements, pump sets and tractors. This work was completed in 1950, and within six months agriculture in Indian Punjab showed a marked improvement.

In the Green Revolution which took place in India with the introduction of Mexican strains of wheat evolved by Dr. N. E. Borlaug in 1966 it is in the areas where the Punjab refugees had settled that most tangible results have accrued. Punjab, Haryana, Terai districts of Uttar Pradesh are the Green Revolution areas of India. It is the refugee farmers who have played an outstanding role in the acceptance of new agriculture. In these areas, tractors, tubewells, use of fertilizers and plant protection chemicals are widespread. This is mainly due to the fact that the refugee farmers are progressive. They were faced with a challenge and they met it by their stamina and capacity for hard work. It should, however, also not be ignored that as compared with the small holdings of non-refugee villages, most of them have viable holdings with an average of 10 to 20 acres. On holdings which are in that range it is possible to adopt mechanized cultivation. It need hardly be mentioned that tractors and threshers have played a crucial role in the Green Revolution, and it is among the refugee farmers that the use of machinery is the largest.

It may further be mentioned that if the Government of India had not dealt with the problem on an emergency basis, and had not given such a generous financial support, the results would have been different. Land was allotted with speed and all facilities for agricultural development were provided to the refugee farmers and they produced results.

So far, this great event of the partition of India and the exodus of population and their rehabilitation had not attracted the attention of western scholars. I am glad that Dr Keller has studied this problem in great detail. In this book, Dr Keller has attempted to delineate some of the more enduring consequences of trauma of partition in an attempt to see how individual traits, taken in the mass, have consequences on the economic, political and social systems. He approached the problems by examining how refugees saw their own experiences. He has tried to integrate their views with analytical work by psychologists who have studied the refugees.

This is a study of great importance and I am sure that it could be consulted with profit in many countries.

Kharar
(Near Chandigarh),
19 August, 1973

M.S. RANDHAWA
Vice-Chancellor
Punjab Agricultural University

Introduction

During the fiftees and early sixties India was the scene of exciting social science research as scholars from many quarters sought to understand better the processes of social change and economic development. Much of this scholarly activity involved the creative adaptation of theories and research methods developed in other settings. Very frequently the results demonstrated that presumed scientific generalizations did not apply in the Indian case, and thus there arose a need for more modesty about "general theories" and a deeper understanding of Indian society. Against this intellectual background Stephen L. Keller's study, *Uprooting and Social Change : The Role of Refugees in Development*, stands out sharply, for this remarkable piece of scholarship represents the rare case in which a field study conducted in India has produced a general theory which now calls for testing in other situations.

It is appropriate that the study of the psychology of refugees should begin in the subcontinent because in the region there are some 25 million permanent refugees, and if the people who have experienced temporary dislocations are added, the number nearly doubles. Elsewhere in the world, there have also been massive flows of refugees since World War II : the division of Europe forced hundreds of thousands to leave their homes in Poland and East Germany and move to the west; the establishment of Israel produced the Arab refugee camps; and the historical events in mainland China, Tibet, Cuba and several parts of Africa created further homeless people.

In the face of this widespread phenomenon of political events uprooting whole populations of unsuspecting and often politically unawakened peoples and casting them into new identities, it is hard to understand why there have not been more serious attempts to investigate and theorize about the political psychology of refugees. Usually the social sciences are alert to the large problems of social life. It is, therefore, exceedingly strange that there should have been such insensitivity about the traumas people experience when their world is shattered by political forces far beyond their control and they are forced to seek new existences in alien settings. Possibly the explanation lies in the fact that so many leading intellectuals in so many parts of the world have in their family backgrounds the experiences of the refugee.

Whatever the explanation, now that this omission in scholarship is being corrected, we are fortunate to have as an intellectual guide a scholar who combines rigour and reverence for truth with human understanding and compassion. Professor Keller demonstrates a remarkable capacity to empathize in his mind to observations of changes in their personalities. He reports not only their sufferings but also how they appear to have become more aggressive, more prone to risk-taking, more economically and politically active than those who were spared the shock of losing their worlds.

By combining studies of how people have reacted to great physical disasters and his own interview data, Professor Keller arrives at a dynamic model of the refugee experience. He notes that the political refugee tends to pass through several stages : first he is likely to be benumbed by events, semi-paralysed and grief stricken; then he may begin to have feelings of guilt for having somehow survived while loved ones have died; these feelings of guilt lead to wonderment as to why he should have been spared, which in turn makes him sense that somehow he must be special, possessed of a charmed life, may be better and more deserving of life than others. Initially he is appreciative of all who aided and supported him, but in time he turns hostile towards those he feels have not done as much for him as they should have. In the end the refugee seems to come out of his experience a more aggressive person. In some cases this leads to a greater tendency toward physical violence. In others it leads to economic and political risk-taking, a willingness to take the chances necessary to get ahead in life.

Few social science studies have captured through interviewing as vivid a portrayal of the dynamics of both historical and individual psychological processes as appear in this book. Through long and patient interviews with scores of humble people, Professor Keller has captured not only the human dimension of great historical events but also the greatness of individual psychological change. A careful reading of this book can teach much about India. It also raises a host of questions which can only be answered when there has been comparable research on refugees in other cultural settings. Stephen Keller has identified and opened a new field of study, and it is greatly to be hoped that other studies will follow. The study of political socialization which has focussed for so long on the experiences of childhood and youth now needs to be balanced by studies of the changes in adulthood which can come from being uprooted by the harshness of politics. Subsequent studies may expand our knowledge of this important subject, but this study will remain a model of how rigorous empirical research can be wedded to the building of theory and the expansion of human understanding.

LUCIAN W. PYE

Preface

Because of radical shifts in the realities of international power and the burgeoning of communications channels in the past two decades the people of the more developed nations have been forced to focus their interest on the hitherto remote areas now known as "emerging," "developing," and "new." For the layman the exposure has been spotty, but even he, because of the pervasiveness of modern communications media, could not help but be aware of secession in Nigeria, war in Laos, guerrilla movements in Latin America, and the emergence of Bangla Desh. For intellectuals, and social scientists in particular, the emerging areas were the object of a more conscious, less passive interest. In general it could be said that we have been attracted to the new nations for a number of reasons, not least among which is the desire to empirically examine the theories of predecessors in an attempt to determine whether any universal truths exist in the field of social, political, and economic change. Daniel Lerner in *The Passing of Traditional Society* says "What the West is...the Middle East seeks to become" (p. 47). In part *our* fascination with the developing areas could be similarly phrased : "What they are, we once were." To use a rather cold-blooded metaphor, the developing areas present the social scientist with a unique laboratory where the bare bones of abstract theories can be clothed with the solid flesh of empirical data. Indeed this is the scientific method exemplified : just as the physicists' theories often outrun their ability to empirically test them, so have the social scientists until very recently. Now, newly refined techniques of survey research, funds for area studies and field work, and high-speed computational devices have developed concurrently with the dissolution of colonial empires making the study of development a great deal more practicable than it had been.

But if mere curiosity had been the sole rationale for the study of people and institutions in the third world, social science would indeed be guilty of the callousness of which it is accused by members of the radical community. In an age in which even the most despotic regimes proclaim themselves "democratic" and in which everyone pays at least lip service to the rights of man and equality of opportunity for all, the poverty and squalidness of the lives of two-thirds of the world's people are an affront to the dignity of all men that demands recognition and redress. If we in the economically more prosperous nations can understand why certain areas develop while others do not, perhaps what we discover in one area can help decision makers in others to form policies that will allow their people to take part in the abundance of modern life.

Over the years since World War II the scholarly focus on the developing areas has followed a number of paths. We have seen descriptive ethnographic accounts, historical analyses, structural-functional models and psychological approaches. Most recently there has been a growth in combining the insights gained by specific disciplines into an interdisciplinary approach to the problems of development. This study of the refugees of north India is such an interdisciplinary effort, one that attempts to integrate insights gained in historical, anthropological, psychological, and political studies into an explanation of some specific recent happenings in the Punjab-Haryana region. Indeed, dealing with a subject like refugees we are forced to be more catholic in our approach, for despite the fact that in the refugees from West Pakistan we find a group that is numerically significant enough to be a nation (there are more Punjabi refugees than the population of seventy-five independent nations) the existence of a refugee group identity is often overlooked by foreign observers. This oversight is the result of refugees being fairly evenly distributed over Punjab and Haryana and because the refugees are outwardly indistinguishable from their non-refugee neighbours. Yet the refugees are an important group, not only in terms of the self-image of the refugees themselves but because their presence is often correlated with political, social, and economic change. And, if one wishes to understand the relationship between refugees and change, he must examine the interrelationships between the refugees' lives today and their earlier experiences, the history of the region, the political forces and government actions of the past century, the forms and structures in which social and political life is embedded and, overarching and influencing all the culture of India.

But in examining Punjabi refugees and their contributions to economic and political change I hope that other social scientists will not view this work as a particularistic study of a specific group. In a sense the refugee is the epitome of the transitional man, a man whose roots have been torn out of the soil of his traditional life. We may, by studying his experiences and his position today, be able to learn not only about the effects of sudden and drastic change but also about what we may expect from the more gradual forms of social change : modernization of agriculture, industrialization, and urbanization. One could say that for the refugees the time period of normal social change has been compressed. What we learn from the refugee may be used to help non-refugees over a painful transition in the future.

This study will delineate the types of people who have at various times been called refugees and select the type which appears to be numerically, socially, and politically most significant today. It will then attempt briefly to describe the refugee experience of two particular groups : Punjabi Hindus and Sikhs. It will discuss the psychological states undergone by these people and the symptoms (the "refugee syndrome") which develop. From the general psychological orientation some hypotheses will be raised and tested using data gathered from a sample of Punjabi and Haryanvi refugees and a matched sample of non-refugees. Specifically we will examine those perceptions, sentiments, and attitudes which, taken in the mass, constitute the political culture and then shift direction to look at economic development in an attempt to see whether or not the refugees have helped or impeded India's push to modernization.

In a venture encompassing as many disciplines as this one and traversing uncharted areas it sometimes becomes necessary to take diversions, the purposes of which are not immediately apparent. At this point then let us explain what follows. Chapter I is a general introduction to the world refugee scene. Chapter II is an attempt to place the partition of India, the event that created twelve million refugees, in an historic context before going on to the individual and societal consequences of that historic event. Chapter III develops a model of the refugee experience. Wherever possible the refugees' own words are used to describe what they underwent, felt and thought during the uprooting of 1947. In general the model is presented as the sequential development of certain outlooks and behaviours. Naturally, because situational and individual factors may cause crucial and differential offshoots there are a few instances where perfect sequentiality has been abandoned to show the parallel growth of different traits in different refugees. Although the chapter deals heavily with the transformations in individual outlook and behaviour that occur *during* the period between uprooting and resettlement the most important sections are those dealing with residual states, especially the enduring characteristics of a sense of guilt and a sense of invulnerability. Believing that these two traits help to account for the oft-noted correspondence between areas of refugee resettlement and both violence and "progressive" behaviour we attempt in later chapters to see whether the refugees (or any particular sub-group of refugees) are more aggressive and progressive than similar non-refugees. Before doing this, however, we went back to the literature that dealt with the people of Punjab before partition to show that to a large degree the aggressiveness and progressiveness now noted was generally not found by foreign observers. A discussion of this can be found in Chapter IV. Chapter V deals with the political cultures of Punjab and Haryana and examines the similarities between the two groups—refugees and non-refugees—regarding elements of the political culture that have in the past been associated with aggressive behaviour: a concern with power, a conflictual world view, and authoritarianism, along with a brief discussion of the relationship between the mass media in the Punjab-Haryana region and political development in the area. Chapter VI analyses the greater progressiveness of the refugees and attempts to show how this trait is closely related to aggressiveness, both having as a crucial element a sense of relative invulnerability that frees the individual to take risks. Chapter VII outlines the conclusions based on the description and analysis of the data gathered in filed research during 1967-68.

Any research project of this nature is the product not only of its author but those who furnished help and encouragement over the long gestation period. I am deeply grateful to the Foreign Area Fellowship Program of the Social Science Research Council and the American Council of Learned Societies for generously providing the funds that made the entire project possible. In addition to the financing of the field research, the Foreign Area Training Program also most kindly provided a six-month grant for the study of Hindi and area studies at the University of Chicago prior to my departure for India and a three-month grant for the study of Punjabi in India. Upon my return they once again generously came to my aid with a write-up grant.

I also owe a debt of gratitude to the Office of Education of the United States Government for a National Defense Foreign Language Fellowship in Hindi for the summer of 1965 at the University of Wisconsin.

The South Asia Language and Area Centre employed me during the academic year 1968-69 as a Teaching Intern while writing the dissertation and also provided me with some greatly appreciated financial aid and access to the University of Chicago Computation Center. The Memorial University of Newfoundland graciously helped to defray some of the costs of production of the final form of the dissertation.

To my *gurus* at the Massachusetts Institute of Technology I owe a tremendous debt of gratitude. Without the intellectual stimulation and encouragement of Professors Lucian Pye, Myron Weiner, Frederick Frey, and Daniel Lerner this project could not have been completed. But my debt to them runs far beyond this project for it was they who awakened me to the inherent drama of the process of development and the necessity to go beyond the traditional confines of political science to the interface where political science, sociology, psychology, and anthropology meet.

In India, the help extended by Professor Victor D'Souza, Head of the Department of Sociology at Punjab University was greatly appreciated. Dr. R. P. Bambah, Director of the Centre for Advanced Study in Mathematics at Punjab University kindly consented to my request to use the computation facilities of the Centre for preliminary data processing. Sardar Narinder Singh of the Punjab Government was of great importance in furnishing his unique insights as well as by introducing me to a number of extremely knowledgeable officials and political leaders. Finally, the final work could not have been done without the unflagging efforts of my Chief Research Assistant Mr. Bam Dev Sharda. His devotion to truth and his immense energy helped me from the earliest days of translating the questionnaire through the pre-test and the entire data gathering phases. On the home front Mr.

Gobind Singh Bist, general factotum of the household, helped our entire party keep body and soul together and in so doing made the field experience a pleasant one.

I am deeply indebted to the South Asian Language and Area Center at the University of Chicago and especially to Professors Lloyd and Susanne Rudolph for their kindness and the interest they showed in the project upon my return from India. A special debt of gratitude is owed to Professor Marvin Zonis of the University of Chicago who more than anyone, through his patience, encouragement and the many suggestions he made during the data processing and the initial stages of the write-up, furnished the moral support and intellectual challenge that encourages diligence. John Iannantuoni of the University of Chicago Computation Center, who helped to impose order on the chaos of a seemingly infinite mass of data, also gets a large vote of thanks.

But all the efforts put into the project by myself and all the aforementioned people would have come to nought without the patience and cooperation of the members of the sample. The 126 villagers, townspeople, and city dwellers often did not know when they began how tedious a long interview schedule can be. Despite the fact that all were subjected to several sittings that sometimes totalled ten hours in duration, often in 115° heat, most retained their good humour and many became close friends. In choosing the sample I was glad to receive the advice of two former Directors General of Relief and Rehabilitation, Tarlok Singh, I.C.S. and M. S. Randhawa, I.C.S. as well as the cooperation of R. L. Anand of the India Census.

Carole Boehme was of inestimable assistance in the preparation and editing of the manuscript for publication. Without her cheerful help and constructive suggestions this book would not have been completed.

Finally I must acknowledge the person who was with the project from its inception to its completion: my wife Martha Keller. Her support, suggestions and criticisms were a major force behind the project and without her none of this would have been possible.

STEPHEN L. KELLER

Contents

CHAPTER I

Refugees : An Introductory Survey

Between the enormous fluted Ionic columns
There seeps from heavily jowled or hawk-like foreign faces
The guttural sorrow of the refugees.
—Louis Macneice

A refugee is a man who votes with his feet.
—Lenin

With creation of many new nations following World War II has come a large increase in the number of people defined as refugees. With each passing year the number seems to grow. The refugees of the Congo, Palestine, Hong Kong, and India have been joined by similar groups in Nigeria, East Africa, and Vietnam; indeed, there is hardly a country of the world without some refugees. Until recently little work has been done to examine refugees at all. The issue of whether a common refugee political culture exists either trans-nationally or within a single nation has received no attention. The questions: Do the refugees perceive of their roles in politics and society differently than their non-refugee countrymen; do refugees share certain attitudes towards government, their neighbours, and political, social, and economic life, have not been asked.[1] Since no real systematic study of refugees has been done, the roots of their sentiments and the behaviour which can be expected to stem from their sentiments in the future have of course likewise been ignored.

One reason for the neglect of the refugee problem is the fact that no coherent theory of the effects of adult trauma on political behaviour has emerged to match that of Erikson, Hagen, and Pye regarding the traumata of youth and adolescence.[2] Indeed, for literature regarding adult trauma and its effect on attitudes one must leave the realm of political science completely and turn to psychology and sociology where a long tradition of study exists.[3] Secondly, because adult trauma is generally a more individual phenomenon, seldom as widely shared as the mass child rearing practices of a society, it may be difficult to isolate, still more difficult to achieve comparability between various traumata, and in most cases all but impossible to assess their effect on individual personalities and attitudes. Is a five-alarm fire equivalent to an earthquake in the psychological stress it places on its victim ? These circumstances have, in the past, militated towards a general reluctance to study and even to recognize political effects of trauma.[4] Nevertheless, if we accept the notion that trauma affects personality and that personality is one determinant of political attitudes and behaviour[5] we must recognize that a large group of people, the refugees, as a result of having undergone some of the most severe trauma imaginable, probably have been psychically scarred. It is difficult to ignore the conclusion that these people are likely to be very different than they were before they became refugees and from those people who did not undergo similar trials. With upwards of 24.5 million refugees in Asia, a rapidly rising number in Africa and a newly augmented group in the Middle East compounding the already difficult tasks of creating workable polities and peaceful territories, the importance of this work cannot be overemphasized.[6] And, if 24.5 million seems insignificant in the vast populations of Asia it must be remembered that the refugees are clustered and concentrated in small areas. A few countries now may even have refugee majorities. Another reason for study is the high degree of congruence which some observers have noted between areas of high refugee concentration : (a) subsequent political unrest, (b) interpersonal violence, and (c) economic development. When speaking of the correspondence noted between refugeeism and both interpersonal aggression and political instability we do not mean merely to say that where there is violence there are refugees since refugees, by definition, are those people who flee from an area because of violence or the threat of it. (For a more detailed discussion of who can be called a refugee see the section of this chapter "Refugees : A Typology"). What is meant by these observers is that many years after the flight and resettlement, those areas in which a lot of refugees have settled are responsible for a disproportionate amount of the violence occurring in that society. The implication is that the refugees are responsible for it.[7] Moreover, the refugees are seen not only as being more aggressive following their trials than their non-refugee fellows but also more aggressive than they themselves had been before. On a larger scale this interpersonal aggression may be at the root of the political instability and disorders in many of the same areas, although here especially one must be careful to determine antecedent conditions.[8] The third correlation has been less noted than the previous ones although one does find occasional references to it. This is the relationship between refugeeism and both economic development and social change.[9] In the chapters that follow I will attempt to see whether the correlations between the characteristics do exist for one particular group of refugees and if so what the possible roots of the correlations might be.

Despite the timidity of the political scientists in exploring what appears to be such a rich lode, much of the groundwork for such studies does exist, having been done by sociologists and psychologists concerned with the rehabilitation of concentration camp victims, the adaptation of immigrants, the effects of natural disaster and exposure to the atomic bomb. Some studies mention aggression and hatred as effects of the victim's ordeal but none treats the subject centrally.[10] No study that I know of relates refugeeism and economic development. Because of this dearth of material I have been forced to modify the work of the disaster and A-bomb studies, attempted to integrate them and then introduced new data, hypotheses, and conclusions gained during field research in Punjab and Haryana states of India to describe the refugee experience and its consequences.

Refugees : A Typology

In reading the literature on refugees one is immediately struck by some very basic imprecisions. Even in estimates of the number of refugees, wide variations exist: some rehabilitation officials, who stop considering a person a refugee once he has a job or a home outside a resettlement camp, are able to state with confidence that only 1,900 refugees still exist in Europe.[11] But almost simultaneously the International Refugee Organization claimed that 16 million of the world total of 40 million refugees were to be found in Europe.[12] The truth, then and now, as in most cases, lies somewhere in between the two extreme statements; some refugees by virtue of certain basic personality characteristics have overcome the trauma and reintegrated themselves into community life but, as the psychologists point out, merely having become a refugee under the circumstances usually attending present-day political upheavals has such a deep effect on personality that most people who have undergone uprooting and resettlement bear the psychic scars and related altered behaviour for the remainder of their lives.[13] While there is this disagreement over numbers, no one would argue the point that recent political developments are generating refugees at a rate faster than even the most basic rehabilitation work can keep pace with. Hence it is not too risky to state that refugeeism is on the increase throughout the world, especially in those areas often referred to as "under-developed", particularly where the underdevelopment coincides with recent shifts in political relationships. Further, it is likely that within the next few years the number of refugees in the developing areas will increase sharply. Even if peace is restored in Vietnam, large numbers of the uprooted will persist for years.[14] Israel's 1967 victory in the "six-day war" forced her to assume control of 900,000 people in the Gaza Strip and West Bank of whom over 500,000 were already refugees.[15] Three hundred thousand more Arabs fled eastward into Jordan, many of them becoming in the process second- and third-time refugees.[16] Ethnic Chinese in Southeast Asia are facing events which in other contexts have been the prelude to expulsion or persecution leading to flight of minority groups. In Africa tribal tensions force large numbers of people across international frontiers each month.[17] These prognostications are likely to be conservative in their estimate of the increments which could accrue to an already large world refugee population for refugeeism is most often unpredictable. To some extent many tensions go unnoticed until they break into open conflict, but even when their danger is recognized, officials tend to minimize the potentials for mass transfers of populations; a minimization which in the past has often proved a critical factor in the misfortunes which occurred afterwards.

Another factor promoting cloudiness in the literature is an indiscriminate use of the term "refugee" to describe a variety of people with a broad spectrum of past experiences. In fact, the more one reads the more one becomes confused. For this reason it is desirable to develop a typology of refugeeism based on a number of variables. First, and probably most important, is the cause of dislocation. Second is the degree of understanding the individual has of his move and the forces acting on him. The understanding may be of proximate causes or larger social forces. Related to this is the amount of warning he has had and the mental preparations he has been able to make. Third is the degree of violence he encounters in his shift. And fourth is the speed with which he is resettled. When the typology has been developed one immediately becomes aware of certain basic changes which have taken place over the past thirty years both in the nature of refugeeism and the characteristics of those people designated as refugees.[18]

The various literature on refugees covers three broad types of individuals: those who have become refugees due to economic causes, those who became refugees due to war, and those who owe their refugee status to political, religious, or ethnic reasons.

The first class, the economic refugees, encompasses most of the original immigrants to this country and more recently, the Puerto Ricans. It also covers much of the internal migration that is occurring in the developing nations today. Despite the negative motivation of escape from the general privations of their native land, the cause of the displacement can be described as positive motivation or a desire for economic betterment. The actual travel is felt to be more of an adventure than an escape. In almost all cases the move is voluntary, made after long planning in the hope and belief that the new environment will be more hospitable than the old.[19] Since in most cases death is not the alternative to migration and violence does not attend it, these people suffer little or no psychic damage. Trauma, at least in the move, is not severe, and if one is unhappy in his new surroundings (the resettlement aspect), he always retains the option of returning to his old home. For this reason, and because at least since World War II the trend of legislation in the world has reduced this once great flow to a trickle, we will not concern ourselves with this class which might better be referred to as economic immigrants than as refugees.[20]

The second class, war "refugees", includes those made homeless by war and who have not yet been resettled. The displacement, sometimes voluntary, sometimes not, is negatively motivated: it is necessary to flee if one's safety is to be guaranteed. Some agencies break this group into 'internal' and 'external' refugees. Shortly after the initiation of war, one can find many homeless wandering about the scene of conflict without food, shelter, or livelihood. If the conflict persists long enough and they manage to survive, they reach safety behind the lines of one of the combatants. This is usually in a city because the countryside has been ravaged. In a milieu which would be strange to them even had its entire social and economic life not been disrupted by war, they quickly become literally 'demoralized', living by their wits to obtain the minimum required for survival. They perform all those services essential in wartime. For the military command they become intelligence gatherers, for the troops procurers, for the civilians the middle men in what is often a thriving black market situation. There are the internal refugees. The best example of them today can be found in Vietnam.

External refugees are those who, during or shortly after the time of conflict, migrate to a new homeland or are relocated by the authorities beyond the boundaries of their state. They too undergo great misfortunes and share many of the experiences of the internal refugee.

The degree of understanding the people of these two groups can bring to bear on the events may be considerable or slight. Likewise their mental preparation for the event may be great or small depending on the social and cultural setting. However, although violence may be severe, it is seldom aimed at them; rather they are incidental targets, pawns in a larger game. This may be small comfort to victims and survivors but it may significantly affect how they comprehend the conflict. If they are accidental casualties, there may be an inability to see any meaning or system in the punishment which may make it difficult for them to develop any comprehensive understanding of the events. The internal and external groups' suffering is extremely great for at least the duration of the war. Shifting fronts may make a man a refugee several times over and with each uprooting there is likely to be some attrition of property and family members. Both groups usually find their situations improved, if not remedied, with the restoration of peace. Thus, although it is likely that trauma often exists in both these groups, little data is available on them because at the reestablishment of peace they often return to their homes and merge with returning soldiers and those lucky ones who, having stayed behind through the fighting, still managed to survive. And before this, while they are still displaced, it is often hazardous, if not impossible, for non combatant researchers to contact them.

It should be emphasized that the distinction between "internal" and "external" refugees of this sort is an extremely artificial one, of concern only to rehabilitation workers. This is immediately apparent when one recognizes the fact that in a traditional or transitional society a man may not be very aware of frontiers and areas of authority. And since, in this study, we are interested in "subjective man," we will in the future eliminate the distinction and refer to this entire group as war evacuees.

The third class of refugees, the one with which my research has dealt, is a relatively new one: those people who, as the result of a new government or new policies find themselves a threatened minority in a hostile environment merely because of some characteristic of their identity. It may be that their ethnic or religious community is out of harmony with a new governing majority or because of certain political beliefs held by some members of the community. Because of this dissonance, they leave that environment for safer shores. Included in this group are expellees such as the Tamils of Ceylon soon due to return to India and those affected by the Greek-Bulgarian-Turkish repatriation schemes of the 1920's. Much larger by far, however, is that group made up of those who flee what they fear will be a new, oppressive government (possibly dominated by traditional rivals) or an ineffectual government unable or unwilling to protect their minority rights from a hostile majority. Examples of the former are the refugees of the Indian subcontinent and the Middle East; of the latter, those of the Congo. This new type of refugeeism's major characteristic is the violence attending the transplantation. That it has occurred in the newly independent nations, where until recently most people lived in ralative peace, is not surprising. In the past, if one felt threatened by traditional enemies, he and his people moved to the next village or attacked these enemies first. In either case the amount and scale of violence and the distance one party fled was very limited, if only because of technological backwardness. In areas of colonial penetration the foreign power enforced its peace and much of this insecurity did not even exist. However, the colonial powers may have been playing up communal differences for their own ends and however much this may have intensified the hostility of later generations of the communities, the colonialists did believe deeply that the heaviest portion of the white man's burden, the achievement of which they could boast most proudly, was the imposition of law and order.

Since boundaries in the colonial realms seldom approximated any sort of linguistic or ethnic reality, groups often found themselves split and, due to the vagaries of a Home Office, intermixed with enemies. That national loyalties never arose in most of these areas to supplant the parochial ones based on religion and tribe merely added to the belief of those in the nationalist-independence movements that nationality and nationhood were synonymous. Those of a different "nationality" could not, by definition, be part of the nation. And nationality to them and to most political scientists of the early twentieth century meant what we would call ethnic group or community. Since such people were of a different nation, they belonged across the river with their own kind and, since there were generations-old grudges to be settled, independence came to be looked upon by all concerned as a new day of the long knives, when the dominant "nation", through its government, would have licence to massacre. The only difference from the old, pre-colonial days was that modern communications methods and technology, introduced by the colonial power to enforce the peace, were now in the service of inhumanity, allowing atavistic brutality and violence to increase its scope beyond the village to the tribal, ethnic, and national levels.

A typical chronological arrangement of such a period can be delineated. Very often with the approach of independence tensions which have existed between parochial groups for years suddenly reach the breaking point. Conflict bursts into the open and threatens the preservation of life. Fearing the worst and often experiencing it, most of the minority community pick up and leave as fast as they could. They generally head for some territoriy they view as safer, often a neighbouring country where their group rules. In their flight there are almost always physical clashes with the now dominant community with life and property as the stakes. Those who escape unscathed, with families intact, are luckier than most but even they are now paupers without land or livelihood in a new country. Others, needless to say, have more difficult trials in their flight. Even when physically safe on the "right" side of the border the new refugee is either interned in a refugee camp or left to fend for himself. More on this later.

Another basic difference of these people from the refugees of the past is that it is a core element of their identity that is the root of all their troubles.[21] It is because they are bedouin or Bakongo that they are undergoing such undreamt of misfortune. Since very soon after the beginning of troubles they come to realize that they are *the* target and that they are the target because of what or who they are, their understanding, at least of the proximate causes of their misfortune, is consequently greater than that of the war evacuees. Yet precisely because as traditional rather than transitional or modern people a much greater part of their self image is based on their identity of being a Bakongo, an Ibo, or a bedouin, the new refugeeism is likely to be damaging psychologically.

The new nations are mainly underdeveloped. Those fleeing to them, coming from traditional-transitional societies, are unlikely to being any utilizable skills with them and government resources, already strained by the removal of colonial capital and ambitious development schemes, have to be stretched still further. (Contrast this with the European refugee case: of the displaced persons who entered the United States following World War II over 50 per cent had more than nine years of schooling and 71 per cent had utilizable skills. Theodor Heuss, the President of West Germany, was able to say in the 1950's that the Federal Republic welcomed refugees because refugees brought skills.)[22] Requiring (and expecting) a great deal of care, they get little. Overworked, newly established relief officials can't be as sympathetic as they might be and funds are short. The refugees become dissatisfied with all those who are supposed to be taking care of them. Where there has been an earlier relationship with parental aspects of government, these lose their nurturant aspect as the parent figure becomes distant and cold. With the new relationships forced upon them by life in a refugee camp there comes a distorted awareness of what government and normal social life really are and how inadequate these are for solution of their problems.

Despite the above mentioned considerations, not all the changes which have occurred in the nature of refugeeism have made for more difficult mental trials. Most of the new refugees are moving within a traditional or at best a transitional world. National borders and central governments are distant, almost mythical things. As a result of these factors there is less discontinuity in the immediate environment and conditions of life before and after the uprooting, depending of course on the nature or lack of the rehabilitation effort. Hence there is correspondingly less mental strain for the Indian peasant or the Tibetan shepherd than there was for the Polish peasant coming from Europe to America.[23] Life in the new surroundings, once he leaves the refugee camp, is apt to differ little from the old, peaceful pre-refugee days; the same language is spoken, the same customs observed, and the same values shared. Perhaps even more important, when the transitional refugee reaches his new homeland he can feel secure; he is in a place where his group is dominant and often in control of the government. By his ethnicity, he is automatically a citizen and hence avoids what Europeans considered to be the worst aspect of refugeeism: statelessness.[24] While this doesn't matter much to the traditionals who are, by definition, parochial, they too are back where people like themselves are in a comforting majority.

This three-fold typology, it should be emphasized, is only for the sake of convenience. In any nation there may be more than one type of refugee (Korea and Vietnam both have the second and third types, Australia has the first and third, Holland and Israel have all three). Even among one refugee ethnic group, depending on their motivation and time of departure, different types can be found. Thus Jews who fled Germany in the 1930's were of the third group while those who waited too long and still managed to survive became the second. Other "mixed" types are of course possible. Recently there has been a resurgence of the second type, the war evacuee of the external variety, traditional people who, because of enemy occupation of their territory, are forced to flee to more or less inhospitable or unsympathetic areas. The Nigerian civil war had the effect of forcing many Ibos into a precarious life in the jungle, and the Chinese subjugation of Tibet has sent thousands of Khampas and Tibetans into the hilly regions of India. The Vietnam war alone has created approximately five million refugees. Nevertheless the largest number of refugees (and the group most susceptible to increase) would be those of the third type, and it is with this group that I will concern myself in the pages to follow. Naturally, many of the things I will say will to some extent fit the other types as well, especially the internal war evacuee, but the hypotheses which will emerge and the data to test them should be considered valid for only the third type until further research can be done.

I have noted that refugees can be found in many areas of the world. In selecting a country in which to do research on them directly a number of considerations arose. It was felt desirable that aside from the country being a fairly significant one and presenting a favourable research climate, it should also have a large number of refugees of long standing whose refugee experiences would not only be typical of the general refugee experience but also be internally varied enough so that the weight of several factors leading to a refugee psyche, if one existed, could be assessed. Another condition for the selection of a locale in which to do the field research was availability of good documentation of the events before and during the exodus. India fulfilled all these criteria. Moreover, India, already sheltering ten or fifteen million refugees, promises to have a great many more before very long. With the independence and/or economic reforms of many nations of Africa and Asia the Indians who have for generations dominated trade in them will be forced to return. This has already occurred in Burma and Uganda, is in process in Kenya, and could occur in Singapore, Malaysia, and some nations of East Africa. Ceylon intends to repatriate over 500,000 Tamils (mainly labourers) resident in that country. India until very recently also received a steady flow of Hindu refugees from what was then East Bengal and is a haven for more than 50,000 Tibetans who fled from their country when it was overrun by the Chinese. Thus the conditions for future comparative research are most favourable in India. The Punjab-Haryana region north of Delhi was selected as the area most likely to furnish data to test our hypotheses.

REFERENCES

1. In any given country having refugees there are a number of possible relationships between the refugee and non-refugee political cultures :

(i) The refugees of the country share in a trans-national political culture which is distinct from the non-refugee political culture of that country.

(ii) The refugees of the country differ from the non-refugees in the quality of their perceptions, attitudes, etc. in a pattern which may not be duplicated elsewhere.

(iii) The refugees of the country may deviate from the non-refugees with regard to the intensity of some traits and responses in a way consistent with other refugee cultures.

(iv) The intensity may vary as above but the pattern may not be duplicated elsewhere.

(v) There may be no difference between the refugee and non-refugee political cultures within the country, i.e. there is no refugee political culture present.

2. Everett Hagen, *On the Theory of Social Change*, Homewood Ill.: Dorsey, 1962; Lucian Pye, *Politics, Personality, and Nation Building*, New Haven : Yale University Press, 1962; Erik H. Erikson, *Childhood and Society*, New York: Norton, 1950.

3. In sociology Durkheim, Cooley, Thomas and Znaniecki, and Blumer have all been concerned with the effects of social disorganization and its relationship to individual disorganization. All psychologists since Freud have been concerned with the effects of trauma. Allport lists it as one of the four mechanisms by which attitudes are formed. G.W. Allport, "Attitudes", in *Handbook of Social Psychology*, ed. by C. Murchison, New York: Oxford University Press, 1935. A notable addition to the literature has been Robert J. Lifton's *Death in Life: Survivors of Hiroshima*, New York: Random House, 1967.

4. Herbert Hyman in his *Political Socialization*, Glencoe, Ill.: Free Press, 1959, uses Allport's scheme but decides trauma has little or no effect on political attitudes. He uses data mainly on American youth who have experienced little wide scale trauma and his neglect of this important area is questionable.

5. T. F. Adorno, *et. al.*, *The Authoritarian Personality*, New York: Harpers, 1950; Everett Hagen, *op. cit.*; Pye, *op. cit.*

6. The figure of 24.5 million is contained in one of the best descriptive accounts of the refugee problem, Joseph B. Schechtman's *The Refugee in the World*: *Displacement and Integration*, New York : A. S. Barnes, 1963, p. xiv. The estimate includes only residents of Asia or the Middle East displaced between 1945 and publication date and as such underestimates the world problem seriously.

7. For example, see "Pattern of Murders in Karnal," *The Tribune* (Ambala), August 17, 1967, which quotes a state government police official as saying that refugees are responsible for most of the murders in the district. A list of five "typical" murders of the previous month shows that the murders are committed by normal citizens and not by criminal elements or ruffians.

8. Probably the clearest case of overlap between large numbers

of refugees and political instability has been in Burundi, formerly part of the Belgian colony of Ruanda-Urundi. Before independence had been granted by the Belgians but after their intention had been voiced, the numerically superior but heretofore politically subjected Bahutus rose up against their Watusi masters in Ruanda (later to become the independent nation of Rwanda). In the carnage that ensued 100,000 Watusis were killed and 200,000 fled to neighbouring countries, among whom were 100,000 who reached safely as refugees in the new nation of Burundi. Their effect on the political life of the new nation has been, to say the least, electric. One premier was killed before independence; another who had held office only eight days was killed in January 1965; eighty-six persons, including all the officers of both houses of Parliament, were killed in a short but effective bloodbath tied to an attempted *coup d'etat*; a fourth premier was shot but survived (he lost office shortly after); and the King or Mwame was deposed. All the shootings with the exception of the executions are alleged to have been carried out by Watusi refugees and the executions were related to the Watusi's drive for power. (*Africa Report*, February, 1966, and various issues of *The New York Times* during December, 1965, January and February, 1966).

9. The reports on economic development relate more to refugees in Western countries than to those in the underdeveloped world. Every so often an article such as "Cuban Negro Refugees in Miami Find 'Open Doors' to Prosperity," (*New York Times*, October 28, 1968), or "Hungarian Refugees of 1956 Revolution Find Success in U.S.," (*The New York Times*, Oct. 20, 1968), appears in the press. While such cases are mainly from the West there are impressive hints that the phenomenon of success orientation, achievement motivation, or whatever, exists among refugees in whom there was little indication of the characteristic prior to their uprooting. Thus we find the Punjab-Haryana region of India with its close to 40 per cent refugees the centre of small scale industry, improved cropping and poultry raising in India. The Punjab region of Pakistan has been similarly progressive. I have been told by officials of the U.S. Agency for International Development that Tibetan refugees in India with no experience or training are making their way into entrepreneurial activities—and have been successful at them.

10. Works indircctly touching on the issue of aggression and hostility include Gardner Murphy, *In the Minds of Men*, New

York : Basic Books, 1953, p. 192; Henri Stern, "The Aftermath of Bėlsen," in *Flight and Resettlement*, ed. by H. B. M. Murphy, Paris: UNESCO, 1955; Miriam L. Gaertner, "A Comparison of Refugee and Non-Refugee Immigrants to New York City," in Murphy, *op. cit.*, pp. 99-112. One political scientist and one writer on refugee affairs have likewise treated the issue peripherally, mentioning the aggressive characteristics of some refugees. The political science work is John George Stoessinger, *The Refugee and the World Community*, Minneapolis: University of Minnesota Press, 1956. The other is Schechtman, *op. cit.* Both the latter works consider aggression only in the refugee camp situation and call for the need for rehabilitation rather than internment.

11. Dr. Elfan Rees, adviser on refugee affairs to the World Council of Churches, recently gave this figure in a sermon at Riverside Church, reported in *The New York Times* of November 23, 1964.

12. Schechtman, *op. cit.*, p. xi. The magnitude of this number can best be appreciated when one learns that the total number of immigrants to the United States from 1790 to 1950 was only 41 million. All figures relating to refugees must however be viewed with caution. The unreliability of statistics becomes evident when one considers that the agency most concerned with refugees, the United Nations High Commission for Refugees, by restricting its definition to economic and political criteria (one must be incapable of earning one's livelihood and have crossed an international frontier) eliminates resettled refugees and those in Vietnam and Biafra (Middle Eastern refugees fall under the provenance of another U.N. agency, the United Nations Relief and Works Agency) thus giving the very low figure of 3.5 million in thirty countries. (From "Friend of the Friendless," *The New York Times*, November 19, 1968.) For other estimates see the reports of the United States Committee for Refugees, Inc., a private agency. They found 11 million in 1967—an estimate that would have to be increased for today. Also see reports of the International Rescue Committee or the many church groups involved in refugee relief (one publishes a newsletter, *World Vision Frontline News*, in Pasadena) about its activities in Vietnam. The U.S. State Department using unclear criteria lists the following as refugees :

Pakistani Hindus in India	1,000,000
Indian Moslems in Pakistan	500,000
Vietnamese in South Vietnam	800,000

Laotians	300,000
Angolans, scattered in the Congo	260,000
Rwandans, scattered	160,000
South Sudanese in six other African countries	130,000
Tibetans in India and Nepal	60,000
Guinians in Senegal	55,000
Congolese in other countries	57,500

The official quoted went on to say that the 700,000 refugees who fled from the new state of Israel had at that time almost doubled to 1,300,000. ("State Department's Wine Asks : Why Doesn't Refugee Problem Make News?" *Overseas Press Bulletin*, XXI, No. 41, October 29, 1966, p. 1. Another source of data is the United States Senate Subcommittee on Refugee Affairs headed by Senator Edward Kennedy.)

13. Murphy, *op. cit.*

14. The United States and South Vietnamese governments even using the narrowest possible definition (resident in camps) admit to 1.2 million refugees (*The New York Times*, February 9, 1969). Other agencies estimate that one-third the agrarian population has been displaced (*Tribune*, October 20, 1967). As has been pointed out by others none of the official figures include the more than one million Catholics and anti-communists who fled the north in 1954 or the two million villagers who, in search of safety have left their native villages.

15. *Statesman*, June 19, 1967.

16. *Statesman*, July 8, 1967; *Hindustan Times*, August 9, 1967.

17. *Statesman*, October 11, 1967.

18. Others have suggested classifying refugees as to whether they have been uprooted as a result of mass flight, mass expulsion, or mass deportation or by the ostensible reason for persecution : religious, political, economic or military factors. Such an approach does not appear fruitful because causes and identities often overlap. For such an approach see K.V. Muller, *et. al.*, *Weggis Report 1960*, Augsburg, 1961.

19. The host country often tried to dispel this utopian dream. See *Messages for Newcomers* published by the North American Civic League for Immigrants, 1916. The booklet for immigrants stated, "America has no more to offer lazy and stupid people than has Europe. Her prizes are for those who burn to secure an honourable success."

20. In Europe particularly we see a new phenomenon: the temporary economic migrant, the man who is invited to a country to provide labour for the factories but who is generally not given the opportunity to become a citizen. Under such programmes there are Turks, Italians, and Slavs in all of the more industrialized countries of northwest Europe. The worker must return to his native land either when his job ends or after a fixed period of time. His position is only slightly more permanent than those Mexican farm workers imported into California to harvest crops. In countries with less formally marked or guarded frontiers the border crossing of job hunters can often lead to or exacerbate existing tensions as in the "Soccer War" of June-July 1969 between Honduras and Salvador. For an interesting discussion of the politics of the internal economic migrant see Myron Weiner, "Urbanization and Political Extremism: An Hypothesis Tested," *Civilizations*, XVII, No. 7, 1964, pp. 1-7. For a discussion of the American immigrant's life including his politics see Oscar Handlin, *The Uprooted*, Boston: Little-Brown, 1951.

21. The Jews of Hitler's era who escaped from Germany were the first of the new large-scale refugees of this type but they, unlike their traditional counterparts of today, were modern people with identities founded on a much broader base.

22. Cited in Elfan Rees, *We Strangers and Afraid*, New York: Carnegie Endowment for World Peace, 1959.

23. A. T. Thomas and F. Znaniecki, *The Polish Peasant in Europe and America*, New York: Knopf, 1927, found the cause of individual disintegration of Polish immigrants was that their values were not congruent with the values of American society and that the influence of existing social rules of behaviour over the individual had decreased.

24. The literature on European refugees all refer to this. Almost every book and article includes Aristotle's observation that a stateless person must be either a god or a beast and the Russian maxim that a man is made of three parts: a body, a soul, and a passport.

CHAPTER II

The Roots of Partition

History concocts itself out of insignificances.

—Hiller B. Zobel

On June 3, 1947 His Majesty's Government announced that India would be partitioned seventy-two days later into what were to become the independent nations of India and Pakistan. The statement, at least at that late date, was greeted by almost all parties as the only feasible solution to the communal bitterness and mounting violence of the preceding few years. Partition was to dissipate the internal tensions which had been building up since the breakdown of the Non-Cooperation Movement of the 1920's. The tensions had been snowballing since 1940. In that year the Muslim League in its Lahore Declaration demanded autonomy for areas of the subcontinent in which Muslims were in majority. Now their demand was to be met. The outcome of partition is well known: in the communal rioting that immediately followed the division, up to one million people perished. When it was over, seven and a half million Hindu and Sikh refugees had joined a truncated India and six million Muslims had fled to the new state of Pakistan. In their flight many lost their entire property and countless others were beaten, tortured raped, and killed by members of the opposing community. Many historians and others have concerned themselves with the causes of the great division—a division which had been voiced merely as a sort of vague chimera some seventeen years earlier by Mohammed Iqbal, the poet laureate of the Muslims, but never fully accepted by his people until the mid-1940's. Most historians, as is their wont, tend to see inevitability in most events and the partition of the Empire is no exception. When one considers inevitability he must account for it in some way and several explanations have been put forth to account for the fission of India. For convenience I have given these explanations the following labels: The Two-Nation explanation, the Backwardness explanation (and its close relation, the Time-Lag explanation), the Class-Warfare or Economic Determinism explanation, the Divide-and-Rule explanation, and a variety of Personal Devil explanations. I will describe the major premises of each of these briefly and then discuss their validity.

The Two-Nation Explanation

The Two-Nation explanation states that partition was inevitable because of inherent differences between Hindus and Muslims. As two distinct nations the Hindus and Muslims, the champions of this explanation claim, are as oil and water which, although capable of being stirred up, can never truly mix. Their arguments cite religious, social, cultural, and philosophical differences between the two groups as evidence of their incompatibility. A prime factor is that the Indian Muslims are seen to be descended from the invaders who swept through the Khyber Pass in the first half of this millennium and felt to be racially distinct from their neighbouring Hindus. They, the Muslims, as conquerors, were reluctant to mix and kept themselves separated from their Hindu vassals. In addition Islam and Hinduism are seen to be religions of such different types as to make conflict inevitable. One modern proponent of this argument puts it this way :

> The code of ethics involved in the various forms of Hinduism is extremely elastic...The code of ethics in the Muslim faith is rigid, concrete and written. The Hindu faith is, in a sense, an essentially negative one...The Muslim faith, on the other hand, is extremely positive...Those are sharp differences in basic belief. It is not unnatural that those differences would be reflected in monumental differences in modes of life...The most striking difference between the two groups, as far as mode of life is concerned, is, however the fact that Hindu society is a caste society. The Muslims do not recognize caste on a religious basis. Indeed, the Muslim faith goes to the opposite extreme...Theoretically at least, Muslim society is relatively simple. Hindu society is enormously complex.[1]

Arguments like this one go on to describe how these differences also exist in residence, economic standing (more on this later), and sources of wealth, and how all these differences help to generate conflict situations which grow into riots when either party has any group activity such as a religious procession. Although the quotation was written at the time of partition the views expressed are fairly similar to those made by government officials in the last part of the nineteenth century. Without getting into "divide-and-rule" theories at this point it should be noted that such views were quite influential in forming the attitudes of the early Muslim political elite. Sir Syed Ahmad Khan made the following rather harsh reply to a proposal for Hindu-Muslim unity in the Congress :

> I do not understand what the words "National Congress" mean. Is it supposed that the different castes and creeds living in India belong to one nation, or can become a nation, and their aims and aspirations be one and the same? I think it is quite impossible, and when it is impossible there can be no such thing as a National Congress, nor can it be of equal benefit to all peoples... I object to every Congress in any shape or form whatever which regards India as one nation.[2]

Thus all differences were at an early date considered irreconcilable by the first political leader of the Muslim community. Advocates of this argument believe the above quotation to be as true of 1947 as it was seen to be of 1888.

The Backwardness Explanation

Of all explanations the Backwardness and Time-Lag explanations are perhaps the most popular today. They can be summed up quite concisely but to appreciate the full flavour one must go to the original. For example, after the British conquest of Muslim areas of India :

> Muslim peasants of course shared in the general improvement in conditions. But the Muslim upper and middle classes, in town or country, were in very different circumstances. For centuries they had been a ruling class...courtiers, soldiers, judges, administrators. The fortunate ones had commanded armies and ruled Provinces and stood at the right hand of kings and emperors. All had enjoyed in some measure the prerogatives and perquisites of rulers.

> All these material advantages of political ascendancy were now enjoyed by the British, and if there were Muslims who had the inclination to turn to other fields of activity and the qualifications required to make good in them, they found, as we have noted, Hindus already in possession of trade, commerce and the professions. In addition to the decline in their material fortunes, Muslims had the mortification of playing second fiddle to the despised Hindus in political importance and influence with the British rulers of India. This rankled perhaps more than anything else. The reversal of fortune was so crushing that the members of the Muslim community seemed stunned by it. Wrapping themselves in the fatalism of their creed, they sulked in the corner, watching apathetically and with impartial distaste their new rulers and their former subjects, infidels both and supplanters as well.
>
> This apathy in a quarter of the inhabitants of the country could not last for ever. But it was not until almost the last quarter of the nineteenth century that there were signs of a Muslim renaissance. For this revival the chief credit must go to Sir Syed Ahmad Khan, a man of vision and a leader who, in spite of the opposition to the old school of conservatives, captured the imagination of the rising generation of Muslims. He had a threefold programme: Social reform...Western education, and friendship with the British. The second item of the programme was urgent...the connection between education and power was too obvious to be ignored. "When Hindu clerks were being promoted to posts in which they could give orders, when even policemen were chosen because they were good at their books, it was clearly wise for Muslims to reconsider their attitude to the new education."[3]

Ram Gopal gives particulars of the rise of the Hindus during the early days of the Raj emphasizing the role of the Permanent Settlement and the dispute over what was to be the official language of administration.[4] Others have shown that indeed *some* Hindus did make out well at the expense of *some* Muslims.[5]

The issue of backwardness was stressed in all dealings with Government and by 1885 Ameer Ali's Mohammedan Civil Service Association had gotten this concession in the form of a resolution from the Governor-General-in-Council :

> There are a large number of appointments the gift of which lies in the hands of the local Governments, the High Courts,

> or local officers. The Governor-General-in-Council desires that in those provinces where Mohammedans do not receive their full share of state employment, the local Governments and the High Courts will endeavour to redress this inequality as opportunity offers, and will impress on subordinate officers the importance of attending to this in their selection for appointments of the class referred to. The subject of the extent to which Mohammedans are employed under Government might usefully be noticed in the annual reports of the provincial administration.[6]

Wilfred Cantwell Smith argues that the late start mentioned above did not affect the type of politics employed by the Muslims but that it did have profound implications for nationalist politics in general. That is to say that for every stage in the growth of Hindu nationalism he finds a corresponding stage of Muslim nationalist politics but that these came after approximately a fifteen year lapse. This time lapse is viewed as the critical factor in dividing the communities further for by the time the Muslims were petitioning peaceably, the Hindus engaging in extremism, saw the Muslims as collaborators. At every stage in this precarious climb toward political influence each group misunderstood the actions of the other. Meanwhile British concessions to the Muslims produced a sort of Hindu backlash with each Muslim success engendering greater and greater Hindu ill-feeling. The culmination was the formation and growth of the Hindu Mahasabha and similar organizations aimed, at least partly, at "keeping the Muslims in their place."

Because of the fact that the Muslims (at least some of them) were concerned not merely with catching up but with regaining their previous eminence, they felt that a special position had to be found either within or without the Indian Union where the Muslim "nation" could once again relive the glories of the Islamic state. The recognition that in the democratic twentieth century, with only twenty-five per cent of the population of the subcontinent they could never hope to rule a united India brought forth once again all the cries of incipient Hindu domination and the need for a separate Muslim state.

Economic Explanations

Economic arguments rely heavily on Marxist principles. One class, either Hindu money-lenders or Muslim Zamindars, exploit and grind down the peasants and tenants of the opposite community. Usually this type of relationship is seen as the direct result of the upheavals within society caused by the advent of the British—before the British India was Elysium.[7] Exploitation naturally generates class consciousness and hostility which can only find its outlet in class warfare (or partition). Since the economic relationships and identities correspond so clearly in people's minds with religious identities the difference becomes cloudy and the hostility diffuses to all members of the other community. With such theories having been endorsed by such a notable as Nehru many others began to see the poor lot of the Indian peasant as the direct result of oppression from above. Where communal differences existed between rulers and ruled it was believed that the inevitable class war would be religious in form (since most peasants are usually not too "up" on their dialectical materialism). Because many occupations were outside the pale of caste for Hindus and many others were prescribed by the Koran for Muslims the issue was made still more complicated by even denying each group the choice of being exploited by its fellows in certain occupational spheres. Of course in its most extreme form the argument is seldom spelled out in detail. Nevertheless in a few cases the documentation is impressive that economic forces in certain areas created political alignments which tended to coincide with religious divisions. But as we shall see the alignment was often not the predicted one.

The Divide-and-Rule Explanation

The Divide-and-Rule explanation hypothesizes that India's partition comes as a direct result of a conscious British policy of dividing the two major groups within the society (three if you include the Sikhs) and playing them off against each other. Congress wallahs of the pre-Independence eras (and some individuals even today) felt almost every British act to be aimed at favouring one side in order to foster the hostility of the other, thereby preventing united action against the Raj. Ram Gopal discusses the grounds for such arguments at length and although he doesn't believe divide-and-rule tactics to be the prime factor leading to later difficulties he still believes them to be significant. He quotes a letter to *The Times* from Lord Olivier, Secretary of State for India in 1926 :

No one with any close acquaintance of Indian affairs will be

> prepared to deny that on the whole there is a predominant bias in British officials in India in favour of the Muslim community, partly on the ground of closer sympathy but more largely as a make-weight against Hindu nationalism.[8]

Ram Gopal goes on:

> For many years, far-sighted Englishmen had been warning the British rulers that Indian unity would prove disastrous to their rule. Sir John Seeley, writing in *The Expansion of England,* observed that 'so long as the populations have not formed the habit of criticising their Government, whatever it be, and of rebelling against it, the Government of India from England is possible, and there is nothing miraculous about it. But if the state of things should alter, if by any chance the population should be welded into a single nationality, then I do not say we ought to begin to fear for our dominion; I say we ought to cease at once to hope it.'[9]

Going back still further we find that the policy was not new even if the actors were. Elphinstone in a Minute of 1859 suggested: "*Divide et Impera* was the old Roman motto, and it should be ours."[10] Sixteen years earlier Ellenborough had stressed the need for the use of communalism if India was to be kept: "I cannot close my eyes to the belief that the race (Mohammedan) is fundamentally hostile to us and our true policy is to reconciliate the Hindus."[11]

Around the turn of the century much of the brain of the Aligarh movement was supplied by the English principals of the Muslim College, Beck, Morrison, and Archibald, all of whom did all they could to prevent their wards from making common cause with the predominantly Hindu Congress. The seeds they planted bore fruit for in 1906, shortly after the formation of the Muslim League, Nawab Waqar-ul-Mulk told the students at Aligarh: "God forbid, if the British rule disappears from India, Hindus will lord over it; and we will be in constant danger of our life, property, honour. The only way for the Muslims to escape this danger is to help in the continuance of the British rule."[12]

The literature gives many examples of such a policy including congratulatory notes to officials for splitting the two communities. In 1909 not only were the Muslims given a separate electorate but they were given the direct franchise, something which the Congress had been petitioning for and agitating for for years and which was still withheld from them. Naturally such concessions as this and the Communal Award of 1932 stimulated a Hindu backlash and indeed it is between 1930 and partition that communal feeling runs highest as demonstrated by countless disturbances and riots. With each passing year the unrest grew more severe until partition was the only alternative to civil war.

Personal Devil Explanations

Personal Devil and Personal Devil Explanations are frequently utilized by journalists as explanations of any unpleasant historical event. The partition of India is no exception. One reason for this is that journalists generally do not have a great deal of familiarity with the social or cultural systems in which they work and perhaps not even much knowledge of the historical background of the events about which they are reporting. Thus it becomes very easy to see almost any event in terms of individual actors, especially if one has been conditioned for his entire working life, as most journalists have, to report on the interrelationships of various actors. It might be said that they develop an occupational disease, a sort of professional myopia. Probably the most widely publicized "explanation" of partition, that of Leonard Mosley, fits into this category very neatly.[13] He finds Viscount Mountbatten to be the prime villain, a manipulator of people, either twisting the Congress politicos around his fingers or isolating those whom he could not manipulate. Actually Mosley's main accusation against Mountbatten is not so much this manipulation as that being in a great hurry to return to the Navy to fulfil his father's dashed ambitions. Mountbatten pushed partition through when it, or at least its high cost in lives, might have been avoided. Others come off only slightly better at Mosley's hand: Wavell a sincere but inarticulate fumbler lost in the machinations of the Congress and especially those of Gandhi; Gandhi who chose to be ambiguous to Wavell when a little clarity might have saved a great many lives later; Nehru who by reneging on the Cabinet Mission proposals to which he was bound caused the final breakdown of the Congress-Muslim League detente; Jinnah and Suhrawardy for calling for Direct Action day and implementing it. In fact about the only person who comes out of Mosley's book unscathed is V. P. Menon, architect of the final proposal (but who can hardly be considered one of the responsible decision makers before the last stages of negotiations.)

There is another class of writers which conjures up personal devils: these are the participants themselves. Being intimately involved in complex events over a long period of time, as indeed the actors within the Independence movement were, the personalities of other participants as well as their own come to take on crucial significance (as indeed they do in the actual interpersonal relationships). Here the case for personal devils can be made much more strongly but one must be on guard to discern hostilities antedating the events being described. For example, Maulana Azad has few kind words for Sardar Patel.[14] But can it be decided on the basis of Azad's book that uncomplimentary remarks about Patel's actions in earlier periods stem from what Azad thought of Patel's role in the partition or is it more likely that two so very different men may have been in perpetual conflict over ends and means for many years ?

Every actor has his own cast of heroes and knaves: Unfortunately for analysis the heroes are all too often the authors themselves and the knaves their rivals for power. Nehru blames it all on the failure-cum-opportunist Jinnah who would do anything for a place in the history books; Jinnah blames it on Nehru "who like all Hindus tried to get seventeen annas for a rupee" and Gandhi, "that naked Hindu revivalist"; Azad includes as villains (although on a lesser plane than Patel) Liaquat Ali Khan for trying to embarrass Congress as Finance Minister of the Interim Government, Gandhi for making Jinnah the leader of the Muslims by calling him *Qaid-i-Azam* (Great Leader) and thus conferring status upon him, and even his friend Jawaharlal for not making sufficient concessions to the League in 1937 over the U.P. ministry. In fact Azad appears to be the only blame free individual in his book (although he does blame himself for not serving another term as Congress President from which position he believes that he would have been able to prevent partition).

There is as little consensus among the historians as among the individuals involved: some see the Aligarh group, others see the interpreters of Iqbal, and still others save all their ammunition for Jinnah.[15] It should be noted, however, that none of these see individuals as the only or even the primary cause as do the journalists and politicians.

Discussion

How well do the component parts of the models correspond to reality? First of all the Two-Nation argument: Were the Hindus and Muslims of India so different as to make peaceful integration impossible? Before going into actual cases let us examine the general frame of the argument. It soon becomes apparent when one breaks down the premises that they are skirting the thin edge of circularity: India was partitioned; incompatible peoples (or nations) living amidst one another must eventually split or be engulfed in civil war. Therefore since India was partitioned the peoples within it must have been different and incompatible. Thus partition becomes the indicator of incompatibility which in turn causes partition. Despite these difficulties such logic can be a powerful tool in the hands of an irresponsible or extremely dedicated nationalist prepared and able to show that peaceful coexistence is impossible—but it doesn't make the argument any more valid. Towards the end of united India, Jinnah did show this, probably not by design but nonetheless effectively, by calling for Direct Action Day. In the bloodshed that ensued 5,000 died. Nevertheless until actual life and limb were in danger many, if not a majority of Indian Muslims considered themselves to be Indians and were hostile to the idea of Pakistan.

Disregarding the difficulties inherent in deciding how different two groups must be to be considered separate nationalities we must still face the issue of whether or not the Hindus and Muslims were distinct groups. Clearly the answer is no. When the British arrived there was no one nation of India and no one nation of either Hindus or Muslims. While communications may have broadened the ties of individuals and subgroups of each community, neither religious group was homogeneous. Within each religion there was the diversity for which India is known but little of the supposedly complementary unity. In any area Muslim and Hindu peasants were much more like each other than either was to his co-religionist who was a zamindar or bania moneylender. This was because despite claims to the contrary the mass of Muslims were not descended from the invaders who had come from the northwest but were in actuality the descendants of Hindu peasants who had been converted either by the sword or from lower caste groups seeking the equality promised by Islam. The former types were found in Punjab and Sind and the latter in U.P., Bihar, and Bengal. Because of these roots and because in most areas Hindu and Muslim peasants, or at least villages, were interspersed, many customs, practices, and historical memories were shared by the two groups. So much so as to make them indistinguishable to the untrained eye.[16] In the towns, of course, the cleavages were more clear and indeed the towns were where most of the communal violence of the nineteen-twenties, thirties, and forties took place until the great holocaust brought on during and after the endgame manoeuvring. Likewise, at the elite level differences were sharp but it is important to realize that neither community was unified or even capable of being unified into a cohesive mass. The Hindu elite was split into the "respectable natives" and the Congress; the latter was fragmented in the early days between so-called extremists and moderates, later into rural and urban, labour and management, socialist and capitalist, and who knows how many other divisions. The Muslim elite was at first split over Syed Ahmad Khan's proposals; they were split into Sunnis and Shias and also into those who claimed ancestry of Persian, Mughal, Afghan, Turkoman, and Pathan invaders. In fact the Muslim elite, centered in U.P., was divided in so many ways it found it possible to agree on only one thing: that the Muslims of Bengal, coming almost entirely from low caste Hindu converts had not made any social, economic, or educational progress from their previously debased state. And, because they were poor, uneducated and of low status the Bengali Muslim could not in any sense be considered the equal of the U.P. elite. But, despite this feeling of superiority the Bengali Muslim, at least in the abstract, was at the core of elite Muslim demands to the British. The elite, through the Muslim League, always pointed to the backwardness of their poor relations in Bengal in order to wring concessions from Government. This may appear inconsistent but rhetoric and objective should not be confused. One demanded concessions for the Bengalis but the actual concessions were always aimed at benefiting the elite themselves. This point will be clarified below. The Hindu and Muslim elites were, if it is true, not able to find a common ground but was this due more to their being members of two nations than to their having different economic interests and views of political life?

> Men of the Aligarh school mainly represented the aristocratic and middle classes of Muslims, and the Congress did not interest them when it talked of the poverty and degradation of the

peasantry, the exacting salt and forest laws, and the oppression of the poor by the bureaucracy.[17]

The general splits which still exist in India and Pakistan existed then in both communities: there were urban and rural Hindus and urban and rural Muslims. There were western educated and uneducated in both groups. There were traditional and modern people, landlords and tenants, activists and moderates, religious elements in the traditional sense and secular groups. There was no Indian nation, there were not two nations, there was only a very complex and fragmented society which happened to have one particularly complex cleavage.

Refutation of the Backwardness and Time-Lag explanations depends upon the heterogeneity of the Muslim community. Neither the U.P. elite nor the Bengali peasant had been pushed down specifically as Muslims. In the upheavals that attended the coming of British law many people lost and many gained. In the 1880's Sir Syed Ahmad Khan, claiming that the Muslims were backward by presenting the Muslim groups as homogeneous and at the level of the poor Bengali, demanded and got special compensatory action by Government. In actuality Sir Syed's own group, the U.P. Muslims, had not done too badly under the British. That they had not sulked in their tents is shown by statistics.

> Up to 1838, the Muslims in service were almost as numerous as the English put together, the proportion being six Muslims to seven Hindus and Englishmen together. Even as late as 1851, after the English became the official language, the Muslims stoutly held their own, and equalled the combined number of Hindu and English pleaders...[18]

The situation did not change in the second half of the century although some people claimed that the Muslim elite did not take advantage of Western education to the same extent as the Hindus and as a result were not able to rise as high as the Hindu elite during this period. In fact a certain Rev. B. H. Bailey was able to report that although Muslims accounted for only about a tenth of the population of the North-West Provinces where the Muslim elite was centered, they numbered about one-fourth the total number of students attending school and colleges in the province.[19]

Despite this the Muslim League kept pointing to the wretched Bengali as good cause for extra favours, education, and representation. Since for part of this period the seat of Government was Calcutta the picture the League presented rang true to the British and in the late nineteenth and in the twentieth century compensatory legislation put the Muslim elite in a still better position relative to his Hindu counterpart. Furthermore, it is interesting to note that the spectre of Hindu domination raised as a justification for separate privileges and later for the partition never really had any basis in fact: It was areas with Muslim majorities in which the Muslims were the worst-off element of the population while in minority areas they enjoyed a higher standard of living than the Hindus.

Economic explanations are quite plausible but as has been noted earlier they fit only in certain localized areas : parts of Punjab and Bengal as well as what is now Kerala. But even in these areas the facts are unclear: For example, in Punjab class warfare on religious lines did not emerge. Rather a coalition of rural agricultural elements, mainly Muslim and Sikh but with some Hindus, emerged as the Unionist party. The Unionists were powerful enough to dominate the political scene for over two decades keeping both the Congress and the Muslim League out until they were defeated in the 1946 elections partly because of the death of two important leaders. Indeed if economic theories are considered important it is hard to explain why the Sikhs did not opt for Pakistan. In most other parts of the country, while the peasantry was unmercifully squeezed, it was squeezed by its own fellows.

Divide-and-Rule explanations contain at least a grain of truth but while it is undeniable that earlier Viceroys such as Curzon and Minto saw the Muslims as a counterweight to the Congress Hindus and manipulated communal differences to their own ends, most of the later Viceroys, especially those coming toward the end of the Raj, saw the necessity for unity in the subcontinent. Some lower officials may have introduced irritants or aggravated grievances between the two communities but the acknowledged official policy of His Majesty's Government was the generation and preservation of unity and integration.[20] While it could be agreed that earlier deeds had later effects it must be noted that it was after the aforementioned divide-and-rule tactics (during the teens and twenties of this century) that the greatest degree of Hindu-Muslim amity and cooperation came about. From the rulers' point of view Great Britain's proudest claim with regard to India was that she had brought unity to a multitude of fragmentary states and peace to an anarchic and chaotic land. All development had been done on an all-India basis and partition would vitiate many of the advantages which had accrued from British rule. The canal colonies of the Punjab would end up in Pakistan but the headworks controlling the water needed for their survival would be in India. The Indian Army would be torn apart. With all this it hardly seems likely that the British could have desired partition.

Personal Devil explanations are more difficult to refute without access to the individuals and the archives but they too have their difficulties. Who does one believe when everyone involved is picked by someone else as the major malefactor. That all the allegations probably contain some truth makes the task impossible. Certainly the actors made mistakes, acted imprudently and perhaps even basely at times but this is human nature and it is hard to say what would have been different had a new set of actors been installed at the negotiations.

What then are the causes, seeds, roots, or what have you of partition ?

Conclusions

If none of the traditional explanations are satisfactory can a better one be found? Before going into this it should be mentioned that unitary "explanations" of historical or social events are almost certain to be too simple—human beings and social groups are far too complex to have their actions analyzed by looking at single causes. Social, historical, and economic forces, conscious and unconscious motives, form and move individuals and groups in ways that they may not even be aware of. Now, while I assign causality to two particular factors, I still believe that many other individuals, groups, and forces played important roles.

Of the two crucial factors one is cultural and the other historical. Neither is sufficient without the other as an explanation of what happened in 1947 and perhaps both still need to be bolstered by certain sub-factors from the previously mentioned theories.

The cultural factor might be called the "zero-sum syndrome" and is found in many areas of the world in which scarcity exists. The name has been taken from games theory. In these areas all life is seen to be a zero-sum game with any player's gains equalled out by another's losses. Individuals and groups compete for the scarce outputs of the political, economic, and social systems with a view that anyone else's success is "taking the bread out of my children's mouths." Whether such an attitude derives from or contributes to a profound distrust need not concern us but this deep distrust does permeate all social relations and fosters a "hurry-up" attitude toward getting as much as you can for yourself now in order to keep the other fellow from getting it first.[21] And, since all the other players are governed by the same rules and perceptions and can be expected to act in similar ways to maximize *their* own ends such a course of action may be prudent. The whole round of life in the villages and towns of many countries including India revolves about such an image of the world.[22] Looking at this pervasive mistrust among larger units or at the societal level it could be said that at least in one sense it was not that Hindus and Muslims were so different as to be two distinct "nations" but rather that they were so similar, sharing so many attitudes and outlooks about competition that conflict became inevitable. It is likely that mistrust is not a sentiment held only by the masses; the great distrust among the various negotiators at Delhi and Simla (*vide* Jinnah's remark about Nehru quoted above) shows that such feelings were not lacking at higher levels of the political pyramid. But such distrust and the accompanying jockeying for a larger slice of the pie would not have been critical in an expanding political arena. It was the slowness and heavy-handedness of the British (the historical factor) which compounded the difficulty of finding an acceptable solution. The British were not able to convince the Indian actors that the size of the slice was less important than the size of the pie itself. This was a result of their having made all reforms and changes in such large and discrete jumps rather than in gradual steps. This type of policy made distrust the rock on which any chance for compromise had to break. For example, if the participants could have been convinced that constitutional development was a constant or even a frequent, gradual thing rather than a decennial occurrence, the stakes at each step would not have been perceived as being so great. One could have afforded to lose skirmishes for position and come back the following year for another go. But with the ante so high all parties had to push without restraint.

So far Hindus and Muslims or Congress and the League have not been mentioned. Where do they fit into the "zero-sum and historical factors" argument ? As noted the Muslims had for some time been looking for their place in the sun via special concessions from the British—but they wanted to stay within the Indian Union, at least in the early days. Petitioning as such was all right during this period but two things led to a great change in Muslim politics and both can be traced to Gandhi's transformation of the Congress into a mass movement. First the patrician Jinnah withdrew from what he considered to be a motley rabble. Nehru claimed this was because after the rise of Gandhi, Jinnah realized he could never be a power within the Congress, but Jinnah did have a deep aversion to mass, agitational politics. The irony of this is that because of the zero-sum mentality and the recognition that changes were infrequent the second outcome of the transformation of Congress was Jinnah's realization that the Muslim League too had to be converted to a mass movement : (a) to give him legitimacy in the eyes of the British, and (b) to combat Congress at the polls and in negotiations. (Congress claimed to be the voice of the entire population including Muslims.) The difficulty was that the Muslim League had no tradition of grass roots activity. (The Aligarh movement, it will be remembered, was strictly for the aristocracy.) The population had to be mobilized if Jinnah was to place any weight behind his demands. He succeeded but only by enlisting the aid of the *ulema* and making the entire issue religious and communal and introducing the religious fanaticism of the divines.

With a mass organization and some bargaining power Jinnah went to the British Government, then personified in the Simon Commission. Since the stakes were so high—by 1927 it had been ten years since the last reform had been proposed and it might be another ten before the next one—Jinnah went to the Commission with a list of demands, determined to bid high and be a hard bargainer.[23] The Commission rejected Jinnah's proposals as impractical and illogical (one was to make Urdu the national language) but in a few years the Government had made a complete *volte face* with the Communal Award. Jinnah cannot have expected all his demands to have been met. Some were patently window dressing to be traded away as a gesture of goodwill. It must have come as a very pleasant surprise when Government yielded on almost all points. After this success he changed his mode of action and always demanded a high, if not unreasonable price for any co-operation on his part. The wildest demands were held onto tenaciously until the last possible moment before they were discarded with a flourish. Toward the end he was demanding an 800-mile corridor between East Bengal and West Punjab. It has been said that Jinnah was repeatedly surprised by the concessions he wrung from Government. This may or may not be true but on one issue most observers agree he was surprised : this was the demand for Pakistan (which some people feel he didn't even want until the very end). This point can be argued but the fact is that by this time the movement had gotten away from him. He was seventy years old and the young turks in his movement were restive. In a sort of Gresham's law of politics demagogy had driven out statesmanship. Jinnah could have said with a great deal more truth than Gandhi : "There go my people, I must hurry up and catch them for I am their leader." He was in the position of having to run hard to stand still.

Of course there were other factors at work as well : Nehru's reneging on the Cabinet Mission proposals was probably the greatest single blow to unity but it is doubtful that such unity could have lasted very long anyhow at that late date. Even if it had been able to endure, a united India would have been a weak federated conglomeration with little power of effective action.

While near the end partition probably could not have been avoided, the horrors which attended it certainly could have been. Some have argued that if, instead of seventy-two days, a year had been allowed for division of the services and assets of the nation, the army could have been reorganized in order to effectively quell the disturbances which were bound to result from partition. Penderel Moon and others dispute this view and believe that since earlier work hadn't been done, delay would have caused even worse trials.[24] That no one had thought about population transfers testifies to the lack of planning and hastiness of action on all sides. None of the leading politicians involved in the decisions was from Bengal or Punjab. They didn't know the temper of the people and didn't have the time or inclination to listen to those who could have predicted the outcome of partition. Therefore all involved must carry a share of the responsibility for the carnage that followed their decisions even if, to a large extent, their decisions were controlled by larger forces.

Perhaps partition was not inevitable but without a great deal more prescience by all concerned regarding the effects of their actions it is hard to see how it could have been avoided after 1932. If the British had allowed gradual political development after 1909 rather than giving big concessions which were too little and too late anyway they might possibly, and only possibly, have gotten the vision of Congress and the League to encompass the pie rather than just the slice.

REFERENCES

1. Robert A. Smith, *Divided India*, New York: McGraw-Hill 1947, pp. 139 ff. Smith's views are presented for their conciseness and typicality rather than for their objective "truth" of course. Indeed we now know from the work of Imtiaz Ahmad and others that Muslim society in north India is fully as complex as that of the Hindus.

2. Ram Gopal, *Indian Muslims : A Political History*, London : Asia, 1959, p 67.

3. Sir Frederick Puckle, "The Pakistan Doctrine : Its Origins and Power," *Foreign Affairs* Vol. XXIV, April, 1946, pp. 532 ff., and quoted in Robert A. Smith, *op. cit.*, pp. 147 ff.

4. Ram Gopal, *op. cit.*, pp 15 ff.

5. For the socio-economic changes that resulted from the British entry on the scene see Bernard Cohn. "The Initial British Impact on India," *Journal of Asian Studies*, Vol. XIX, 1960, pp. 418-431; Ramakrishna Mukherjee, *The Dynamics of a Rural Society*, Berlin : Akademie Verlag, 1957; N. V. Sovani, "British Impact on India," in Guy S. Metraux and Francois Crouzet, *The New Asia*, New York : New American Library, 1965.

6. Ram Gopal, *op. cit.*, p. 54.

7. Ramakrishna Mukherjee, *op. cit.*, for one type of this argument.

8. Ram Gopal, *op. cit.*, p. 46.

9. *Ibid.*, p. 47.

10. *Ibid.*, p. 46.

11. *Ibid.*

12. *Ibid.*, p 101.

13. Leonard Mosley, *The Last Days of the British Raj*, London :

Weidenfeld and Nicolson, 1961.

14. Abul Kalam Azad, *India Wins Freedom*, Bombay : Orient Longmans, 1960.

15. Examples of those blaming individual actors are many. Ram Gopal, *op. cit.*, is an articulate spokesman for those who blame the Aligarh group. Robert A. Smith, *op. cit.*, is one critic of Iqbal, and Sir Percival Spear in his *India*, Ann Arbor : University of Michigan Press, 1961, places a great deal of the blame on Jinnah.

16. Imtiaz Ahmed's forthcoming book on Muslims in villages in U.P. makes this point forcefully.

17. Ram Gopal, *op. cit.*, p. 74.

18. *Ibid.*, p. 27. Since this chapter was written Anil Seal in his *Emergence of Indian Nationalism*, Cambridge : The University Press, 1971, has presented even more data refuting backwardness and time-lag explanations. See especially Chapter 7, "The Muslim Breakaway," pp. 298-340.

19. *Ibid.*, p 33.

20. See Penderel Moon, *Divide and Quit*, Berkeley: University of California Press, 1962, for a brief description of how such acts were carried out locally in the Punjab.

21. See Erik H. Erikson, *Childhood and Society*, New York: Norton, 1950, for an interesting discussion of the psychological roots of basic trust-mistrust.

22. Richard Fox has described the political and social effects of such attitudes among the trading castes of a small town in eastern Uttar Pradesh. See his *From Zamindar to Ballot Box*, Ithaca: Cornell, 1969. For a discussion of the role of trust in the politics and life of a southern Italian village see Edward Banfield. *The Moral Basis of a Backward Society*, Glencoe: Free Press, 1958.

23. For a good run-down on demands made by Jinnah and the League and the unreasonableness of many of them see B. R. Ambedkar, *Pakistan, or the Partition of India*, Bombay: Thacker, 1946, especially pp. 239-261.

24. Moon, *op. cit.*

CHAPTER III

The Stages of Refugeeism

O Friend of sorrow,
Look at the Punjab.
The village square heaped with corpses,
The Chenab flooded with blood!

* * *

Song is crushed in every throat;
Every spinning wheel's thread is snapped;
Friends parted from one another;
The hum of spinning wheels fell silent.

—Amrita Pritam

The solution finally agreed upon may have been the best possible one but it was not a good one. Each group was hopelessly intermixed in the other's territory making any non-patchwork settlement impossible. There were no districts of what is now Pakistan that were without some Hindus. There were often a sizable minority and in some cases, like Karachi, a majority. Each group in the Punjab would, regardless of settlement, have had to leave large minority pockets within the other's territory. The best possible solution, that drawn up by Sir Cyril Radcliffe, the British chairman of the mixed partition commission, left 27 per cent of Punjab's Muslims in Indian territory and 32.5 per cent of the non-Muslims (Hindus and Sikhs) in what was to become Pakistan. The Sikh community was equally divided. Almost instantaneously, local majorities had been transformed into threatened minorities totalling upwards of five million people on each side. No thought had been given to the transfer of population.

In early 1947, violence broke out in Lahore. Each side tried to force the other out of the city in order to claim the state capital as part of its portion of the soon-to-be-divided Punjab. In three and a half months, 3,200 people were killed and well over 100,000 non-Muslims fled eastward. Passions were aroused in the rest of the state by these first refugees and a rash of tit-for-tat killing and massacre ensued. Those who had remained behind in opposition territory (the early refugees were almost entirely Lahoreans) fled in terror :

> The minorities, in most cases, did not even try to hold onto their 'pockets'. Like a lightning flash, it came to them that the game was up; everything seemed alien to them, the civil administration, the police and the army; even their houses frightened them as a potential prison or a slaughter house; the assassin's knife was receiving a fresh edge on the stone; the fire-raising brigade might be at the door any minute. As the instinct of self-preservation was roused, the attachment to earthly possessions suddenly became atrophied. The definition of a secular state and the charters of minority rights were just dangerous nonsense to those who felt themselves in deadly peril.[1]

Their exodus was truly remarkable. Foot convoys of 40,000 individuals each covered an average of 150 miles in its march. (One convoy contained 800,000 people and was forty-five miles long.) Many died of exhaustion and were left by the roadside by their families in their haste to escape. Convoys of this type and the small family caravans were attacked frequently by local marauders; women and children were abducted and food supplies frequently failed. Often if a Hindu or Sikh convoy encountered a Muslim convoy headed in the opposite direction, a miniature war broke out with thousands being killed. Refugees who came by rail underwent similarly chilling experiences. Trains with fantastic numbers of people hanging onto their sides and tops were scraped clear by *goondas* (hooligans) waiting for them to pass by. Both sides discovered or invented previously undreamt of horrors to impose on their new enemies. Persons fleeing alone faced even more terrifying trials.

When it was all over, almost 7.5 million Hindus and Sikhs had entered the Indian Union from West Punjab and about six million Muslims had left. Perhaps one million died in the transfer.[2] The fact that these Hindus and Sikhs had reached safety in India did not mean that their troubles were over however. Some difficulties ensued over resettlement and eighty-five camps, whose total population ranged up to one million, were set up in the post-World War II European tradition. The nature and amount of property left behind on each side and the previous communal division of labour also played a large part in the difficulty of resettlement.[3] But the Government of India in the first test of its competence did a remarkable job in rehabilitating the refugees.[4]

In talking of millions of people, hundreds of miles, and scores of camps, much of the sense of what was undergone at the individual level becomes blurred. This chapter will endeavour to trace the personal aspects of the refugee experience; what the refugee feels and does when threat, violence, and flight become part of his life. The language of the chapter is couched in general terms because many of the reactions are common to refugees anywhere in the traditional world. Where an element is of particular significance to Indians or Punjabis, it has been noted.

Earlier Study of Refugees

Almost all of the psychological literature relating to refugees has been concerned with problems found among two groups: Europeans emigrating to other European countries or the United States or those resident in refugee or relocation camps. Virtually nothing exists for any of the refugee groups formed since World War II. The reason for this imbalance was the great wave of revulsion experienced by the world after that war when it was discovered what the conflict had created in terms of hardship and misery. Huge numbers of refugees, forced out of their countries because of German relocations or post-war Communist takeovers, as well as former residents of concentration camps were all in the process of seeking new homes in what they hoped would be more secure surroundings. Homeless wanderers were everywhere in Europe. The conscience of the world was aroused and in an attempt to make some sort of amends for our fellow man's cruelty studies of refugees and what could be done to help them were initiated. Most of the relief programmes precipitated by these studies have long since stopped but the stream of books and papers related to all aspects of the refugee problem flowed on long after their cessation. Despite the fact that one informed scholar was able to describe this literature as,

> ...an excursion into what is still largely *terra incognita*...either of a highly emotional, polemical nature sadly lacking in objectivity, or merely statistical with little attempt at analysis...[5]

it did help to provide many insights and represented an interest and concern which unfortunately one finds lacking today. That such a large amount of literature was produced then makes the dearth of materials on today's refugees even more disappointing. But the world is no longer quite as shocked by the horrors of refugeeism as it was in the 1940's (although if anything, today's refugees are much worse off than their predecessors). With nuclear annihilation a possibility, with a most horrible war being fought in the jungles of a far-off country, with racial strife at home, people do not want to be reminded of man's bestiality any further. The Congo, India, and Biafra are far off geographically. Psychologically they are more distant than the moon to the American public. Scholars are no more interested than the laymen: psychologists have other, more interesting, less politically sensitive objects to study...and they are closer at hand. The disregard for the plight of the refugees stems perhaps from the fact that man's injustice to his neighbour is now considered one of the uglier faces of life which, if we avert our gaze, will vanish. That these new nations (where most of the world's refugees are found), being undeveloped, have few psychologists to tackle the problems of their own people is viewed as unfortunate, but aside from a rare warning few people really care and still fewer are doing anything to present the problem to the world.

Others have felt that refugees and what can be done to aid them should be taken more seriously:

> The danger in the existence of such people is two-fold; first, and more obviously, their ever-increasing numbers threaten our political life, our human artifice, the world which is the result of our common and coordinated effort in much the same, perhaps even more terrifying, way as the wild elements of nature once threatened the existence of man-made cities and country-sides. Deadly danger to any civilization is no longer likely to come from without. Nature has been mastered and no barbarians threaten to destroy what they cannot understand, as the Mongo-

> lians threatened Europe for centuries. Even the emergence of totalitarian governments is a phenomenon within, not outside, our civilization. The danger is that a global, universally interrelated civilization may produce barbarians from its own midst by forcing millions of people into conditions which, despite all appearances are the conditions of savages.[6]

But the appeals have fallen largely on deaf ears. Further on the relationship between refugeeism and aggression will be discussed, but let it suffice to say that the lack of interest in refugees is surprising when one considers the often observed correlations between areas of refugee concentration and public disorder and violence, to say nothing of the aggressive acts and stances of such refugee newsmakers as Sirhan Sirhan, General Ky, the Miami Cubans, and the assassins of a number of public figures in Africa.[7]

What happens during the actual trauma of becoming a refugee? There is little direct information of this other than such vague statements, made by refugees long after the fact, as, "It was like a nightmare." Two refugees with psychological training in two quite dissimilar books liken it to that ultimate of traumas: being born, an emergence from what was supposed to be a safe, warm, hospitable environment to a cold, hositile one, to a cutting of the umbilical cord tying oneself to a secure past.[8] Other than these scanty descriptions there have been no reports on how the refugee felt during his uprooting, flight, and resettlement.

Articles and books written some time after the event have had the value of showing which latent attitudes emerge and what these imply in terms of the prospects for readjustment. However they do not show what brings these attitudes or the personality variables associated with them into being. In order to really study the psychological effects of great trauma, specifically the refugee case, the original hypotheses of this work had to be developed from studies of natural disaster victims. I leaned especially heavily on Martha Wolfenstein's *Disaster : A Psychological Essay*.[9] At that time it seemed that there were grounds for considering refugees similar to victims of various other calamities. John Walker Powell of the University of Maryland Psychiatric Institute defines disaster as :

> The impinging upon a structured community, or one of its sections, or an external force capable of destroying human life or

> its resources for survival, on a scale wide enough to excite public alarm, to disrupt normal patterns of behaviour, and to impair or overload any of the central services necessary to the conduct of normal affairs or to the prevention or alleviation of suffering and loss...usually the term disaster refers to an episode with tragic consequences to a substantial portion of the population.[10]

Form and Nosow use a much broader definition: "...a condition in which the established social life of a community or other type of social organization abruptly ceases to operate."[11] Refugees can certainly be fit under either rubric. More important, looking at the circumstances at an individual level, the refugees, like the disaster victims, are "objects rather than free subjects of a given...situation which is in no way of their own making and which they have no choice but to bear."[12] More recently Robert Jay Lifton has shown how similar the conditions of *hibakusha* (atomic bomb survivors) are to both groups.[13] In time of war they were non-combatants living far from the battlefront. Although aware of the war, they were totally unprepared for the calamity about to engulf them. Needless to say there are likewise strong differences between disaster victims, refugees, and *hibakusha* but they all are to some degree faced with the same effects of an obscure cause beyond their comprehension: homelessness, death, injury, and loss of property. Refugees of course undergo a geographical uprooting which prevents their returning home after the shock. By comprehension of cause I refer here not to the proximate causes of the injury or homelessness (a tornado, an A-bomb, a Muslim attack) which the victim usually understands quite well after only a short time, but to an answer to the question, "Why me?", an attempt to find meaning in misfortune. Moreover all three types of events are often looked upon by their victims in the same way. It is obvious that war evacuees have many of the above characteristics. However since they are difficult to interview in wartime and to locate in peacetime, and because they differ in terms of the four variables used to define refugees, they will not be considered here. In the following sections the stages and mental states through which a refugee passes will be described. The general theoretical aspects were first developed from the disaster studies. Recently, in light of the findings of field research in which seventy-three refugees of varied background were subjected to a questionnaire, psychological tests, and a long open ended interview about their experiences at the time of partition, they have been slightly modified. The quotations of the actual experiences of the respondents are followed by an asterisk and their respondent number. Quotes from other sources are noted conventionally.

The Early Stage : Reaction to Threat

When threat impinges on his peaceful world, the individual may react in several different ways. People who have studied natural disaster see four elements that determine how people evaluate the threat of extreme danger.

These are:

1. A statistical measure of threat, i.e. the amount of loss to be incurred if the threat should materialize multiplied by the probability of its materialization. Of course the arithmetic is unconscious.
2. The imminence of the threat.
3. Whether effective countermeasures are available and to what extent they can be expected to protect the evaluator.
4. The cost in time and money to activate the countermeasures.[14]

The most commonly mentioned reaction among the respondents interviewed in this project in Punjab and Haryana was a sort of disbelief that they could be affected by the impending disaster. One after another we hear that the respondents could not believe harm could befall them, even where advance notice came from officials or the media.

> We heard about partition through the papers but we thought that this division would not disturb us. The people would continue living as they always had. (*011)
> We used to hear the news from the newspapers that we would have to come to India but we never thought it would come true. We heard it while we were harvesting the wheat. Even with such news we sowed our *kharif* (winter) crops and didn't bother to sell our *rabi* (summer). We thought that agriculturists could never leave their lands. (*063)

In most cases one brush with death was sufficient to change such opinions but for many there was a failure to perceive the threat, a form of denial of the danger by ignoring it. This denial appears to be a maintenance of the residual sense of invulnerability and omnipotence which, in greatly attenuated form, we all retain from childhood. The obverse of this, a sense of complete impotence and vulnerability, will be discussed below. In such cases the denial persisted for individuals and whole communities until the escalation of violence reached such a pitch that a threshold of awareness was reached where one could no longer deny and survive. Even so the threshold was amazingly high in some cases :

> We were in Settlement 485, Tehsil Samundri. That was a Muslim village. A canal passed about a furlong from the village. Every day we could see human bodies and bloody water in that canal but we kept on working. About a month earlier we had heard word about the formation of Pakistan but that hadn't really affected us. The canal sight made us a little uneasy but that is all. The Muslims did'nt speak to us. (*017)
>
> We sent our brothers on a bullock cart from Settlement 7, Karmaliwala, to Settlement 4, Kasowal, and I was left alone. When my father returned from town he got angry with me for sending the cart along with my brothers. I told him that I had heard of the danger of violence and that all were to assemble in Montgomery. Nevertheless he insisted that I bring them back. I went to get them. (*021)
>
> Rumours spread that we had to leave the area because Pakistan had been created. An old Muslim lady kept telling us that it would be best for us to leave for India soon but we, thinking she was after our property, didn't take her seriously. When *Id* came, we knew she had told the truth. (*048)

Besides denial and disbelief there were other reasons for late start on the road to India. Partly from inertia, almost everyone tried to carry on, at least for some time, with the normal routine of life.

> We heard from the newspapers, even before August 15 (1947) that the country was to be divided. I went to Lahore (earlier that year) to see relations and even then I saw that some villages were being burnt. Even so in that year I took land on contract

> in two villages. I was to get the receipts of the deposited money from Sargodha. I stayed on. A Muslim clerk in the D.C.'s court told me that I had better flee lest I be killed. He explained that it was now Pakistan. In spite of this I stayed on. I even made further deposits of Rs. 6,000 and Rs. 3,000 to the Revenue Officer without troubling myself over a receipt. I thought all this upset was temporary and I ploughed the lands and got the seeds sown quickly. I stayed on for three more months but not long enough for the harvest. (*065)

Some like the above case succeeded in their self-delusion for several months but they too finally had to relinquish the hope for a return to pre-threat life as all relationships disintegrated around them. Even then many saw their flight as temporary :

> In our village there were fifty per cent Hindus (and Sikhs) and fifty per cent Muslims. We didn't bother to take anything with us. We thought that as in earlier history the rule had changed but not the public. So we were hopeful of coming back after some time. Why take anything ? We did lock our doors but never guessed that the houses would be burned as we later learned. (*013)

There were other reasons for staying on as well. Profit was one :

> We never thought in terms of making money but since we had expected trouble we had put aside wheat and other grains. The persons who didn't have much purchased it. There were some people we thought cowards because they sold off their grain (at a loss) and ran for this side (India) but this was beneficial to us since with the extra profits we could buy ammunition. (*002)

Others were reluctant to leave the lands of their ancestors or the standing crops. In many cases the people were encouraged by the authorities to carry on "business as usual." Most disregarded the advice but a few were lulled into a sense of security which was soon shattered.

> Before we left there radios were broadcasting. When Jinnah said that Pakistan had been created the news came from Lahore.

Before that there was the news that although Pakistan had been created the Muslims there in India would live there (in India) and the Hindus and Sikhs on the Pakistan side could stay on in Pakistan. But Jinnah said it could not be allowed and that each man should come to within his own boundaries. It was after this that we started. (*016)

Firstly the Muslim Police Sub-Inspector told us we should sit easy and that no one would turn us out. But when the final announcement was made he showed his inability (to protect us) and we moved the next day. (*008)

When the conflict started we were at Hoti. The Nawab of Hoti was Akbar Khan. In the city there were big gates. In the villages around there were only about five per cent Hindus and Sikhs. In 1946, late in the year, when the Hindus and Sikhs of the villages began to feel unsafe, the Nawab called them to the city. We also came at his call. For all our safety he put private guards with rifles on the big gates. He said that the Hindus and Sikhs are "our old friends" and the Muslims would not do any harm to them. But later when he felt that there was danger to the city, he begged our pardon and asked us to go to India. (*028)

I'd decided to live on in Pakistan in obedience to the commands of Gandhiji. I stayed on in my house in Lahore until the 14th of August, 1947. I was all alone (with my immediate family). Every Hindu had left the locality. My younger son went upstairs and found that the next house was on fire and that Muslim mobs were plundering the adjacent houses. At this point we had no option but to leave. (*035)

When the partition of the country came into being, I was residing in Lahore at Kila Lachman Singh's *mohalla.* There were attacks there but no one ever thought they would have to leave their native homes. And on the other side Indians leaders were also saying that wherever a man was he should keep on staying there so that the economic structure of both countries should not suffer...People who had the information through the press relied on the assurances of their leaders and did not leave their homes...I went to visit a relative with a view to returning after a little while. But the tension got so much worse that wherever a man went he was stuck there...he became immobile...as violence spread. (*073)

> We were about twenty-five families living as a Hindu (and Sikh) village. We were the tenants of a Muslim zamindar. When the trouble started, he asked us to move into his big house lest the Muslims kill us. We all went with our bag and baggage—including cattle. Next morning some 3,000 Muslims collected outside his house to kill us. At first we hoped that he would save us but seeing the mob of Muslims he too changed. He came riding on a horse and wearing a gun on his shoulder and said that we should either become Muslims or he would kill us all with his gun. Then we thought that we should collect all the womenfolk in a room and burn them. Then we should fight with the Muslims and kill some of them and be killed rather than become Muslims. But all that was a ruse of his. He came in and advised us that he would cut our hair and tell the mob that we had become Muslims in order to save our lives. We reluctantly agreed and cut our hair ourselves to save our lives and the lives of our children...We stayed on for twenty-five days in constant danger (of exposure) before we got away. (*059)

It is interesting to note that in each case mentioned (and not only the examples cited) the reassurances were given by holders of paternal roles. In India the father is the stern protector, who in return for obedience and respect, is bound to provide safety for children.[15] In the Indian family the father's power (if he is head of the household) is, if not absolute, considerably greater than his American counterpart's. But aside from his power, the entire tone of the father-son relationship is charged with the son's reliance on the father, a sort of abdication of all responsibility by the son. This is not to say that the father is a distant figure respected mainly for his authoritarianism. He is, in addition to being the protector, the provider of all necessities of life. In asking the Punjabis about the men they admired most ("What two men, living or dead, do you admire most and why?") a striking thing about the responses was the frequency with which they chose their own fathers (12.3 per cent, the second greatest response only exceeded by Guru Nanak). When they chose other individuals, their reasons were again couched in paternal imagery : "Gandhi...He was a father to his people"; Guru Nanak...All the people were his children"; "Guru Gobind Singh...He protected the weak and the poor as if they were his own."

In Punjab and other areas of north India government has always been characterized as *ma-baap* (mother-father).[16] As *ma-baap* it is duty bound to provide a rich, warm, nurturant relationship (the *ma* part) as well as paternal protection from the dangers of life (the *baap* part) occasionally punishing wrongdoers. Unquestionably, throughout history in the subcontinent the *baap* aspect, stern protector who in return for obedience provides safety, has been more important in everyday life. This is not to minimize the *ma* aspect however. In hard times, especially in times of famine or flood, the government becomes maternal in its care of its children. How well the government played the maternal role in the case of partition will be discussed below.

As might be expected, when the father can no longer protect, the father-son relationship breaks down as the son is left without any other meaningful protective relationship. The realization that powers previously thought to be omnipotent are now impotent even in their own behalf can be shattering. What is even more shattering than the failure of the protector is that the assailants often appear in the guise of the paternal power. Soldiers and police, politicians and government officials either turn their backs on their wards or join in the scourging.[17] With all this there comes upon the victim an awareness that that most chilling fear of childhood, of being abandoned by loving parents and being helpless in attempting to preserve his well-being and satisfy his own needs, has actually come true. It has been expressed thus :

> The feeling of abandonment and impotence in connection with lowered physical resistance makes the mercilessness of the enemy appear as an overwhelming unconscious command : You shall give up resistance, you shall despise yourself, you shall die.[18]

Or as one of Lifton's *hibakusha* put it, he himself was ordered by God to die.[19] The enemy now of course is not an individual or nation ; rather it is an entire world gone mad, a malevolent universe personified :

> I saw human corpses lying there. The people said that they were of Muslims who had been killed there. Though I was only a child, I was thinking that if even a single man were to die in our family the entire village would go into grief. Yet here I don't

know why they are killing and slaughtering so many people and not even feeling or weeping. (*034)

Not only has he been abandoned by his protectors but he is in real trouble. When violence does intrude upon his world, the first impression of the victim is what has been called the "ground-zero" effect :[20] The individual believes himself to be at the centre of violence, at the point of application of all the destructive forces which threaten his world.[21] Regardless of whether he considers himself the sole target, he believes himself to be the focal one. In their recollections of what they felt during the early incidents of their uprooting, the respondents repeatedly bring forth the imagery of centrality, of being surrounded by huge numbers of the enemy as well as by other hostile elemental forces. While this must have actually occurred in some cases in others it is clearly implausible. One house in a *mohalla* could not be surrounded, nor could the terrified man who stayed hidden in an underground room for five days be aware of being encircled. The refugee's conception of himself as the focus of all disaster persists in stories of how the rain clouds travelled over *his* caravan for over three weeks, flooding *his* route. Cholera was worst in *his* section of the temporary camps and the fiercest Muslims were the ones attacking *him*. One respondent told of Muslim gangs converging on *his* camp to poison the wells. Where the refugee has good fortune it is clearly the result of a mistake and the forces of trouble can be expected to zero in on him again.

Then we (our village) got our turn to board the train. We got first chance. The chances were fixed by drawing of lots. But since we were still very much afraid of being killed by the police we preferred to wait a little longer and some other villages took our turn. No one on that train survived. Then no train came for five days. In the draw we again got our turn first of all. We were still afraid of being killed by the Muslims. The women, children, and the aged were provided space in the compartments and the young people took their seats on top of the bogies. The train was ready to go at 2.00 p.m. but it did not start until 4.00 p.m. The military who were guarding us did not let the Muslim crowd come near the train at the railway station. The train was running very fast. The drivers wanted to take the

> train into Lahore before dawn. They had a plan to kill us all there but because there was only a single track, our train had to stop for others to pass. As a result, day broke on the way and we were saved again. (*021)
>
> The raiders were still looting the Gojra camp so I returned immediately. I could not see the caravan camp. We were anxious over its fate. A big Pakistani military officer came and ordered that all men from the caravan camp should be taken outside.
>
> The machine guns were set up on all sides. In the meanwhile the D.C. of the District who had been away to Lahore came back. He asked the caravan campers why they were standing on the road and they told him the whole story. He ordered everyone to go back to the caravan camp. He fixed a special C.I.D. police force instead of the military to guard them...We were also taken to the camp. The injured were given first aid in the caravan camp. After two days an airplane threw posters to us saying that unless we got military aid from India we should not move. Rations were also sent from India in the form of rice, etc. but then cholera spread in the camp and many died. (*064)

Emerging from the feeling of centrality, impotence, and vulnerability is a mental state similar to that of abandonment : one in which the individual's resolution of his relationships with supernatural powers is called into question.

Some people feel that they have a sort of contract with the powers of the universe in which they agree to behave properly in return for divine protection. The fact that disaster has occurred is proof that the powers have broken their part of the bargain thus entitling the human contractor to do the same. Seeing the entire social matrix disintegrating, these people, in times of extreme stress, ignore warnings to flee and either live riotously or break all societal rules. Of course, they, alongwith the unreconciled "it can't happen here" type, often have to pay the ultimate price for their misperception.

Another type of refugee, very numerous, is one who looks upon the disaster as a punishment by the gods.[22] Especially in traditional societies there is a great dependence upon protective powers. One will try hard to please them and to secure their protection through charms, worship, and ritual and, for fear of punishment, one will also try to hold down any rebellious tendencies towards them.[23] Disaster shows the victim that gods as well as men do not love him, that they have seen through his false front, recognized his baser nature, and found him unworthy of love. This reinforces the earlier feeling of abandonment. In most cases, and especially in those people having a strong demand for love and recognition, the violence directed at the individual is likely to be seen as punishment *a la* the parent-child model. But the punishment is unjust and undeserved and this generates the resentment and rebellion which *are* worthy of punishment. As violence mounts he has direct evidence of retribution for his misdeeds and hateful thoughts. Often the fact that he has received punishment is proof enough that he has sinned. A spiral of rebellion-punishment is set in motion, the internal rebelliousness inextricably entwined with the external violence. Since in refugeeism there is usually a progression of misfortune from localized trouble through mass violence to flight involving the risks of travel, disease, and natural obstacles, at each step the rebellious tendencies become greater, thereby triggering the greater punishments which seem to come inevitable.

A few people, in an effort to integrate their experiences with their religious beliefs, saw the entire thing as a test by god. Indeed the theme is a common one in Indian literature, folklore, and history and is apparently present in some form in all parts of the sub-continent. The stories of the job-like Maharaja Hariscandra of Bengal, the patient crow of the Tulsi Das *Ramayana*, and the young sons of Guru Gobind Singh, walled up alive by a Moghul governor, are well known in present-day India. A few older respondents took a slightly different approach. They were saved by god, not tested or scourged by him. One man claimed that he owed his life to the fact that he had thrown himself on god's will at an especially critical moment.

The Middle Stage : Extreme Danger and Flight

It is at this point that the refugees begin to react differently from one another. One victim, to escape the ever expanding spiral of rebellion-punishment, displaces his aggression to more convenient, less powerful figures. In such cases the minority may look for pockets where their group is relatively strong and attack the members of the oppressor community, here at last trapped as a minority. Similarly there are accounts of thousands being killed with the outbreak of miniature wars when caravans fleeing from India and Pakistan encountered one another. One respondent told of an attack on his caravan :

> Later we were again attacked by the Muslim block military (probably police). During the battle a girl from the camp was drawing water from a well when some people (Muslims) who had been hiding near there took her away. The campers were enraged. Then they saw the horses of the raiders—they (the campers) stole the mares and took them to the camp. It was all they could do. (*002)

In many cases the spiral or even a single catastrophe leads directly to what has become known as the disaster syndrome : that state of dazed or stunned blankness so often noted after natural disaster. Those victims who survive the immediate calamity quickly emerge from this state. If they have loved ones, they may be carried along by them until they recover. If they have no relatives or friends to help them or if they take too long to recover, they may be caught. Here it would be wise to point out a fundamental difference between disaster and refugeeism. Disasters such as cyclones and floods generally strike only once in a location. (Of course they may strike again in later years but the emphasis here is on the single trial rather than the series of increasingly horrible events.) Thus, in a natural disaster the victim, once he has removed himself or been removed to safety, has a chance to recover without facing further threat. Like a special case of disaster victim, the flood victim sitting dazed on a rooftop with the water rising about him, the refugee must rouse himself or be roused. Like the man atop the house the key factor in survival is time. The fact that his would-be-rescuers are also in jeopardy and must save themselves as well makes his situation still more precarious. He may, in his dazed state, be too much of a burden and as a result be left on the wayside. Leaving a relative or a loved one may in fact be the only way to save oneself. The consequences of such an act for the survivor will be discussed in a later section.

It is probable that the dazed condition stems from an overloading of those circuits of the mind concerned with providing appropriate responses to new situation. The stimuli here are few, undreamed of dangers each coming close on the heels of the previous one. As the circuits break down the respondent may go into his dazed state. But, to carry the switchboard model a little further, the overloading of the circuits may lead to a lot of "wrong numbers" or clearly inappropriate responses to the danger stimuli; inappropriate in the sense that behaviour in danger situations should be directed toward the goal of preservation of life, either one's own or that of a loved one. Here are the statements of two respondents on their reactions in situations of great danger. The boy who had been ordered by his father to bring back his brothers' reports that after leaving :

> I got a lift on someone's bicycle. On the way we saw Iqbal Nagar town burning. The Muslims were doing it. It was from there that I was to get a train. No one was in the station to issue the tickets. The stationmaster wasn't there either. I never travelled without (a ticket) before but I had to travel without this time because I could not get the ticket. I was very much afraid of being ticketless. (*021)

The fear of death had prompted him to send his brothers away but in a far more dangerous situation, in a town that at that very moment was being burned and looted by a Muslim mob, his main concern is that he may be caught by the authorities for travelling without a ticket.

The businessman who stayed on in Lahore in deference to Gandhi's wishes tells of an outing he made from the relative safety of the refugee camp. After going to the hospital to search for the body of his brother-in-law he goes on :

> ...the moment I entered the hospital I found that twelve Sikh young men all shot and dead were displayed on the footpath. These young men were shot on the morning of the fifteenth on Shish Mahal Road when they were trying to reach the refugee camp. (*035)

After finding the body of his brother-in-law and trying futilely to get permission to perform the last rites he decided to go to his shop:

> I saw dead bodies of one of my neighbours lying on the Fleming Road. As I proceeded further, a young man came out of a shop

> with a curved dagger. I don't know what happened to me. On seeing him I laughed loudly and to my surprise the young man also smiled and re-entered the shop. Perhaps he took me for a Muslim and spared my life. I am a fool—I sometimes became so fearless—immune, that one day without telling anybody I slipped out and, walking slowly as if there were nothing in the city and as if I were immune to everything, went deep into the Muslim area in Dabi Bazaar, Mochi Gate. After roaming about I called on a Muslim friend of mine. I knocked on his door. He looked down from the second story and saw me standing at his door. He rushed down, opened the door, took me in and asked, "How did you come to this place ?" I told him that I was just out looking at the madness of human beings; how little faith men have in religion, goodness, and the Lord. He heard me, served me tea but was very much amazed at my madness. He called at least seven Muslim neighbours and requested them to escort me safely to the main road. I saw shops burning, property looted, women being raped, and children being killed. (*035)

Others, when attacked by raiding parties, thought not of fighting back but rather of denying the fruits of victory to the enemy. Killing one's wife, daughters, and sisters to save their honour happened in many cases and this was as indicative of a desperation stand—a display to the enemy of the firm resolve to fight to the death as denial of the fruits of victory. We hear also of besieged people who did not fight when attacked but who burned their luggage and bullock carts instead.

It may be that the more alone a person is, the more extreme the form of the inappropriate behaviour is likely to be.[24] One respondent whose mother had been left behind in Pakistan returned to search for her several times. A widower, he left his two small children alone in a hut by the roadside in Delhi. At a time when tensions were very high, after having, through his own foolhardiness, been arrested twice as a spy on previous returns, he finds his mother and brings her to Lahore. Unable to gain her release from Pakistan, he decides to sneak out of the camp with her to go to the city. Once there, he goes directly to the High Commissioner for Refugees office to sit in *dharna* in order to shame him into granting her release.

Partly the inappropriateness of certain actions appears to represent a form of detachment from the events going on about oneself. This "third person view" manifests itself in the threatened individual's acting in ways appropriate for normal life but extremely risky in times of social upheaval or natural disaster. Despite the protestations of the businessman to the contrary, his actions did not stem from "fearlessness" but rather from his detached state of mind : "I don't know what happened to me..."

Merely escaping from the intolerable situation at one's home does not bring relief to the refugee as it does to the disaster victim. In fact one might liken the refugee to a victim of a protracted disaster, one which might last months.[25] Furthermore not only may the danger be correspondingly greater on the road than at home and the trials come at more rapid intervals, but the range of possible misfortunes is broadened, often considerably. The perils of being in a caravan in those days were by no means negligible :

> After passing the headworks we saw thousands of human corpses. There was such a bad smell there that it was difficult even to pass them. A person told us that a day before, a caravan of Hindus and Sikhs were killed and those corpses were of those unfortunate refugees. After that, in Patoke and Sacha Sauda area, cholera broke out and about 100-200 persons used to die every day. When we were near Kasur City, my maternal uncle, who was with us then, fell prey to this disease. We tried to save his life...but could not get a doctor there. (*041)
>
> We came to a village at the bank of the Beas river. The people of five or six villages assembled there. Muslims escorted by their military attacked our camp with guns. Some 4,000 persons were killed there. The Muslims took away certain women from the camp. After a while the military brought some of the women back but some were never traced. Some of the women died by drowning themselves. The remaining persons crossed the river by swimming or by hiding and coming in the boats later. (*046)
>
> The river was rising and the water (reached where we had camped). Some 4,000-6,000 persons (Hindus and Sikhs) assembled in that place. The Muslims attacked us there. They killed many with guns and spears. They were on horses. Women and children were also killed there. We fled to the nearby jungle. Two of the sons of my brother, my mother-in-law, and some eight or nine of our relatives were killed there. (*048)

> We went in the caravan. Some forty or fifty more carts came. The last one-third were stopped and attacked. Only a few of them could escape back to the previous camp. Among those were two carts from my village. Those people left the carts and escaped but one young married girl alongwith her jewelry was taken captive and brought to a house where there were four or five more women. An old Muslim woman was guarding them in the house. The young girl bribed her with jewelry and at midnight she jumped out, crossed the canal by swimming, and reached the caravan camp. All were inspired by her bravery. (*064)

But just reaching one of the way-station camps where caravans rested and regrouped was not to achieve safety. One was often in as great danger as on the road.

> But before leaving they (the military) looted the camp of money and material. The persons who were to safeguard the camp looted it! Apart from this the *goondas* from the villages were brought. They used to stab anyone who went out of school premises. At least 3,000 persons were killed that night in that camp. No distinction of either Hindu or Sikh was made. In the morning dead bodies were seen on all sides but nobody dared to go out of his shelter. The military jeeps took all the dead bodies and threw them in Lower Chenab Canal which was one and a half miles from Akalgarh. No one worried about the dead. The military wrote in their diaries that no Hindus were left in the camp and ran away.
>
> For three days no one was there to take care of the camp or the town. So everything happened in those three days; whatever the Muslims wanted they looted or whatever they wanted to do they did. On the evening of the third day Maratha military, who were posted near there, reached us. (*075)

Despite the horrors undergone, there were beneficial aspects to being in flight as compared to waiting at home for the axe to fall. Once more one became actor, in many cases he regained the status of subject rather than object and was able to respond effectively to the dangers around him.

> We stayed at Burianwal for the night. Some got the train. All those who boarded the train were massacred on the way. Where we were, one Muslim woman and two men came in the night. They threw a bomb at us and three or four persons were killed. Some of us got hold of these Muslim persons and we killed them all. (*068)

Even where one could not strike back directly the respondents remark that just being able to move toward India could give a great sense of well-being and efficacy. Moreover the feeling of centrality and direct punishment is attenuated as one flees and comes into contact with other people in flight. The refugee finds that they too have been threatened and punished. All of these new-found comrades share at least one characteristic with him: the cause of their refugeeism i.e. their communal identity. In the Punjabi case it is religious; in other areas of the world it may be linguistic, tribal, or ethnic. This *enosis*, this coming together, eases the refugee's mind and dilutes the uncomfortable rebellion-guilt feelings. It allows him to embrace the psychically more comforting notion of collective or communal guilt which is quickly diluted to the model of the cursed family where he and others are being punished not for what they have done but for someone else's sins. Since it frequently happened that the authorities on one side held a fleeing *jatha* (caravan) hostage for the safe passage of one coming in opposite direction, the view is not an entirely unreasonable one. In many cases this view of the situation leads to a deep sense of injustice, a rage that one who is blame-free is suffering so much for someone else, a someone else who may be so distant in space and time as to be unrecognizable.

While simple flight can help to restore the individual's sense of efficacy, being part of a caravan large enough to be capable of defending itself can go still further in this direction. Louise Pinsky recognized after World War II that "no matter how severe the trauma it becomes bearable if it is shared by others. The sense of homogeneity that it produces would seem to act like a catalytic agent against utter despair and hopelessness."[26] The idea of a corporate identity, aside from being a useful legal fiction, has some basis in fact in a *jatha*. From the descriptions of their own *jathas* it would seem that these had certain personalities and capacities for action which would be impossible in an individual in the same conditions. These group personalities differed from one *jatha* to the next. From the accounts we hear of *jathas* which "ran scared", others which turned and fought, still others which through guile and craft managed to elude the clutches of the enemy. A dynamic *jathedar* and a combination of fortuitous circumstances could not only bring an entire convoy through without incident but create a feeling of unity and cooperation that could lead to decisive defensive action instead of panic and disaster.

On the other hand, being part of a large group can dilute the individual's responsibility to his fellow man :

> We were attacked again. When they started using spears we ducked under a moving cart. Only three of six in our party did this. I don't know what happened to the other three. We walked or crawled about 150 yards under the moving cart when we saw fifty young men of our caravan engaged in hand to hand combat with the Muslims. But we didn't go to their aid. We passed them (still under the carts) and never learned their fate. (*064)

Often the welfare of one's fellow travellers was forgotten if one had the resources to buy escape or even temporary relief.

> The surviving persons crossed the river by swimming or by hiding and coming in the boats...Some rich landlords crossed the river by boats. They had brought money with them and paid Rs. 1,000 to a Muslim who took them and some others and left (them) on the Indian side of the border without caring for (the safety of) the persons coming afterwards. (*046)

It should not be forgotten that many refugees did not come in the large *jathas* or joined them fairly late in the exodus. They too had troubles,

> We started towards Jarhanwala where we reached after seven or eight days. When we were camping there, the Pakistan military attacked us at about 6.30 p.m. and the firing continued for three hours. By that time Indian military came and seeing them, the attackers stopped the firing. So we were saved from the clutches of death. (*041)
>
> We stopped at night but the Muslim leaders of the village asked

> us not to leave at night. The next day they escorted our small caravan with guns. They rode on horseback. On the way we met some Muslims who were beating drums and shouting that we should be killed but the Muslims who were escorting us told them not to do so or they (our Muslim friends) would open fire on them. So we went ahead. At the railway station of Mandi Hira Singh we saw a train carrying Muslim refugees coming from Amritsar. There was blood flowing out of the train and the rail track was filled with blood. The women's breasts had been cut off, their noses were cut off, and many men and women had been killed. The Muslims wanted to take revenge. We felt sorry over the misfortune of the Muslim refugees who suffered the cruelty of our Sikh brothers in India...and we were always in fear that we would fall victim to the Muslims who wanted to take revenge. But the Muslims who were escorting us saved us. (*051)

but in the main the refugees joined the caravans as quickly as possible for the comfort of safety in numbers.

Reaching Safety

But comfort and safety, it should be emphasized, were not guaranteed by numbers even if they did grant the escapee a sense of efficacy. Especially in the latter days of the exodus the attackers realized that more was to be gained by attacking the large, easily located camps or the jam-packed railroad trains than by searching out isolated pockets of slow movers. As a result, the trauma was likely to be drawn out from the first incidence of violence to even the places where one might have expected to feel secure : the large, supposedly well-guarded camps. Still further on, on the last steps of the journey the risks and stresses were also great. On the very border of one's new homeland, while crossing into India, gangs of *goondas* waited to annihilate the wayfarers.

> It was decided (by someone in charge) that we should not go to India via Lahore but via a more southern route. It should have been only a two hour journey but that train took from early morning until after dark. We reached the border which at that place was at the river. The train stopped before the bridge. The people took their own luggage off; there were no coolies there. Some

> Muslims arrived and charged two rupees per box to take the luggage but they would only take it halfway across because the bridge was half in India and half in Pakistan. It was terrible to see all these fatigued people struggling to get their stuff across... even young girls dragging their luggage with the help of their scarves...There were many corpses; a naked lady near the canal; a horse and a man bleeding and dying. (*073)

With the crossing however, came the feeling that one had reached the promised land. Many of the survivors were immediately interned by the Government of India in any one of the eighty rehabilitation or relocation camps. Life in camps was likely to be a dreadful experience for the refugees. Many of the inhabitants of the camps were mentally disturbed by the events of the preceding several months and as Margaret Parton put it in a dispatch to *The New York Herald Tribune*, they "frequently...work(ed) against the welfare of the whole."[27] Add to the mentally disturbed the criminal elements desirous of preying upon them and the other helpless refugees and the situation becomes quite volatile.[28] At this peak, during late 1947 and early 1948, the camps had a population of approximately one million people. Many individuals, however, declined to go to the camps. There were three types of people who decided not to go to a camp. First, there were people who had relatives living on the Indian side. Many of the older inhabitants of the canal colonies had migrated from East Punjab in the early years of the century. Whole families had not gone; rather the youngest sons, for whom the amount of land held by the family in East Punjab would have been insufficient, went, leaving older brothers and parents behind. In most cases close ties were retained and frequent visits were made in the ensuing years. Furthermore, castes in the Punjab prior to this colonization tended to be localized in specific districts. For this reason many of the young colonists and their children married inhabitants of their old home districts. Thus to many of these people coming to India was seen as more of a return than a flight to a new land.

A second group declining camp life were those who felt they were well enough off in terms of what they had been able to salvage to make out on their own. The third type were those others who in their flight had become separated from members of their families and preferred to move around searching for their loved ones.

Many of those interned on arrival left the camps at the earliest possible date.

Only about a fourth of the sample stayed in actual refugee camps upon their arrival in India. Most found the camps too crowded and if they had any resources, tried to settle down to pull themselves and their families together after the ordeal they had just been through. Few were able to put down roots. Almost a third (31.9%) were forced to move from their original settlement within six months of their arrival. A larger number (34.8%) managed to stay for periods up to three years but then had to move either because they received land resettlement grants or because the land they had settled on was granted to other refugees. About one-third (31.9%) either found a place in a village in which they had relatives or were tenacious enough to carve out a livelihood in a new locale.

On the Indian side inside and outside the camps there was violence also. Muslims were being attacked by Hindus and Sikhs. In many cases they offered strong resistance as had the uprooted on the other side of the border. As a result, even for Hindus and Sikhs it was very difficult to feel oneself safe in India outside a camp.

> I came to Ludhiana by train in search of my family. From there I went to my ancestral village, Dhanaur, about nine miles away. My grand-father had gone to the canal colonies of Lyallpur in 1887. I wasn't able to get any information about my family at Dhanaur. The trains in Punjab were not running then so I had to walk the nine miles back to Ludhiana. It was dangerous moving alone then; rioting was going on in the Indian villages. Pakistani military were guarding the caravans of Muslims going to Pakistan and if they saw any Hindu or Sikh near them they would shoot him. Whenever I felt in danger I hid behind trees. I got to Ludhiana on the fifth of September, the first day that Muslims left the city (in an organized fashion). The police didn't allow me to enter the city but I had to reach the station. I did and when I got there, there were a lot of Muslims assembled there. Then three or four bombs were thrown by the Hindus and Sikhs there. I managed to escape and fled to the bus stand. I don't know how many were killed there. (*036)

From there he managed to get to his wife's village but although he found her and the other members of his family, it turned out that he was not out of difficulty yet.

> Every night we could hear firing. Whenever we heard it, we were frightened and felt that we couldn't even be sure of our safety on the Indian side. We were thinking all along that we were out of one danger and into another one (from the frying pan into the fire). We hid in that village for three or four days and daily heard rumours that the Muslims were going to attack it. Neither we nor the Jats of that village had any weapons...It was even more unsafe than it had been at Lyallpur (in Pakistan). (*036)

Despite this post-partition violence, sooner or later the countryside started to settle down. People were able to assess their circumstances and start on the road to recovery. It is at this point that several psychological states of special import begin to take shape. Actually, some of the attitudes and sentiments which will be discussed originate in either the initial or flight stages but it is not until the relative peace of having reached safety that the refugee starts to voice these consciously and begins (a) to formulate them in a systematic way in his mind and (b) to realize that many others feel the same way about what has happened.

As the refugee approaches and attains safety, the cursed-family model of being punished for someone else's sins undergoes a marvellous transformation. The view grows that those who survive are, by definition, the only ones worthy of salvation. The refugee has passed from states of guilt at his rebellious tendencies through the feeling of being blame-free and punished for someone else's misdeeds to a sense of positive virtue as the cause of his preservation.[29] Conversely survival becomes the proof of virtue. In the refugee case, where benefits frequently accrued to others coincidental with the refugee's sacrifices (as in the creation of new states like India and Pakistan) the refugees begin to look upon themselves as the creators of such benefits. They, so the argument goes, are the true fathers of their country without whose hardships nothing would have come about. Politicians come to be resented as usurpers of the refugees' claim to fame and gratitude. Perhaps also because the politicians may be seen as the instigators of all the troubles which have led to this point, they are resented even more. The argument is occasionally even carried out to its limits : anything bad which came out of partition can be blamed on the British or the individual actors in the negotiations but the benefits are the creation of the refugee alone.

But alongwith the feeling that the virtuous have been saved is the knowledge that one has not been particularly virtuous. In many cases he has even acted basely in order to survive. Furthermore the refugee knows of many incidences of virtuous people not surviving...indeed it was often their virtue that was their undoing. Where one has lost members of one's family, especially young children who are generally considered innocent, the gnawing self accusation that one has survived not through virtue or even through chance but at the expense of the innocent develops. Even where one has not experienced a direct loss he is likely to develop guilt symptoms. Almost the entire literature on people who have survived various calamities documents the existence of survival guilt and the growth of a belief that one might have done more to help others in their need.

Among refugees the various types of guilt are dealt with in several ways. The two most common means of dealing with the problem of ambivalence over survival are by an almost manic activity and by the "closing-off" or "D. P. apathy" discussed widely in the literature.[30] The initial reactions to "survivor guilt", apathy and manic activity, are merely the first, not the only ones. Leo Eitinger of the University of Oslo found that more than twenty years after their release, survivors of Nazi concentration camps remained "possessed by anxieties and panics."[31]

The respondent who had become separated from his mother went first to Amritsar and alternated between periods of extremely hard work and guilt feelings about having rescued himself while having left her behind in enemy territory. He had been a medium size shopkeeper in Pakistan but on the Indian side he was nothing. All he had managed to salvage from his previous life was his immediate family and a little less than 1,000 rupees. Taking a job as a bicycle mechanic, he threw himself into his work thoroughly. His employers, amazed and delighted by his diligence, decided to promote him. But he recognized that this period was one of adjustment, of finding himself, rather than a permanent sort of thing.

> They told me they would give me Rs. 90 per month (twenty more than he was then getting) but I told them that I had never served (another person) in my life and that though I was doing it

now it was because I had to remain busy. I wholly expected to adjust myself so that I would be able to find independent work in the future and when the proper time came for me, I would leave them even if I would be making less in that (new) job...But in four months there I never forgot about my mother although I could not get any word of her. The government was resettling people in Panipat and Kurukshetra but I had to wait for my mother so I could not get an allocation. I left Amritsar for Delhi in search of any kind of manual work. On the little balance I had, I started preparing confectionary. I was successful...Then I gave that up and found a small shop in Sadar Bazaar. (*075)

Then one day some friends forced him to take some time off and accompany them to the cinema. The theme of the picture forced him to look at that which he had been avoiding through constant work:

> The picture's theme was parents. (My friends) hadn't planned it that way but that was how it turned out. They were happy but I became sadder and sadder and my mind became thirsty for my mother. The next day after thinking all night, I knew what to do. I got up early in the morning and went to the courts and applied for a permit to visit Pakistan. (*075)

He went to Pakistan and while he failed to locate his mother on this attempt, he had resolved his conflicts to some extent. He had recognized earlier that his frantic activity was somehow related to his having left his mother behind ("But... I never forgot about my mother") but now he had actually tried to do something. The theme of the picture continued to prey upon his mind until he went back to Pakistan again, located his mother and after many additional trials, succeeded in bringing her to India. It is significant that he recognized his frenzied activity as related to his guilt over having left his mother behind and that once this had been recognized he was able to slow down his pace. He was still tormented by his guilt feelings but was able to focus his energies on relieving their root cause rather than merely masking their existence with work.

Frenzied activity was not possible for those who found themselves in relocation camps. For them and for many others who didn't get to camps there was another adaptive mechanism that emerged upon reaching safety. This is the analogue of that most widely discussed and chilling symptom found among survivors of the concentration camps : D. P. apathy, a withdrawal from all the stimuli that could cause anxiety and/or guilt. Almost every study following World War II noted its existence, some in eloquent language :

> It is the silence of the churchyard. Large parts of the personality seem to have died. Much can be revived, but in many there will always be white spots, just like the white spots on the map of a bombed city.[32]

This apathy is often so deep that truly frightening incidents are recounted about people who are not aware of being alive or dead. Since they are amidst all this death they come to feel or sense that perhaps they are dead. Many of our respondents mentioned the fact that for a period after reaching the Indian side they were "out of commission". All accounts agree that the loss of the capacity to feel deeply stems from the trauma. Lifton sees "psychic numbing" as a defence against both death anxiety and death guilt. In his view, the extreme case of it follows this logic : "I almost died...I should have died...May be I did die, or at least I am not really alive; or if I am alive it is impure of me to be so...anything I do which affirms life is also impure and an insult to the dead who alone are pure."[33] Although Lifton feels that the anomic withdrawal is due to violence and death imagery other interpretations are also possible. Starting from Durkheim's characterization of anomie as utter apathy founded upon a wholesale suppression of anxiety we can shift to a classic American study. The loss of capacity to feel deeply was noted among Polish immigrants almost two generations ago by Thomas and Znaniecki who found that social disorganization played a major part in the resulting anomie. Lifton's emphasis is not incompatible with the earlier works in that it is the brush with death that makes the symptom so much more widespread among survivors than among immigrants. In fact Durkheim's thesis was that, when social regulation of the individual is upset and his view of the world broadened intolerably, conditions for anomie exist. It is certainly likely that the brush with death, the element of risk and chance involved in escape, has broadened the refugees world in such a way. Significantly, life in the camps symbolizes and actually represents social disorganization *par excellence*.[34] While an artificial community has been created by the authorities it is clearly an imposed system aimed at replacing what the refugee must feel is irreplaceable : the sense of community and solidarity of the pre-partition days.

We know from Freud's work in *Beyond the Pleasure Principle* that traumatic events need to be "exercised." In many cases this exorcism consists of a continued need to relive the experiences mentally or talk about them in an attempt to master them. Wolfenstein found the same to be true in the case of disaster victims and our experience bears out the fact for refugees.[35] Indeed, the refugees themselves often recognized the therapeutic value of discussing their trauma. Occasionally the experience was so painful that the respondent would weep but insist on continuing the interview to completion. It soon became apparent that we were not the first "therapists" but that the refugees had already discovered the process. Otherwise there would be no way to explain how refugees too young to have clear memories of the events of 1947 were able to tell stories of those days in great detail, stories which differed only superficially from those of other older members of their families. Such a performance was taken as an indication that the story had been told and retold many times in the family. Then it is probably true that those least able to build up their resistance to the event by recalling it would become the most apathetic.

> It may have been part of a general loss of capacity to feel deeply, in people whose experiences had caused them almost more anguish than they could bear. It may be that in repressing emotions, too terrible to remember, other emotions had been affected by the repressive mechanism. It did seem that the affectional responses had suffered and it is possible that they may have been crowded out by their polarity of hatred.[36]

And if we include as emotions too terrible to remember guilt at what one did or did not do under stress, we may be able to see why some people do not dare to feel. Gardner Murphy cites studies of an Austrian "unemployed village" and the unemployed of Warsaw which found that after an initial period of frantic activity searching for a job most of the people receiving inadequate and impersonal relief became completely withdrawn and apathetic "not having even the stamina to read, seek amusement, or to think."[37] He found that providing meaningful work within the camps he visited ensured that apathy did not develop. From his work it would appear that such non-guilt-related apathy is subject to several variables : the relationships that can be hypothesized are :

1. The refugee may be in a camp for a long period and apathetic as a result.
2. He may be in a camp for a long time but because of occupational therapy not become apathetic.
3. He may be in and out of the camp so quickly that apathy cannot take root.

To my knowledge no one has done extensive work on overall extreme apathy, whether trauma or camp induced, although Lifton has commented on apathy in specific areas.[38]

It is very hard to ascertain whether an individual was in a state of "D. P. apathy" twenty years earlier. It is less difficult to measure apathy in an individual at the moment of the interview although there are still methodological problems to be faced. One of the difficulties in determining whether a refugee was apathetic upon his arrival in India is how to measure the concept. I believe one indicator of this apathy was that the respondents tended to tell shorter, less personal stories about the time of partition. Their accounts tended to be more historical and they had to be reminded that it was their experiences in which we were interested. Further, they tended to skip large periods of time, probably because the events of the apathetic period were not imprinted very sharply on their minds. This use of a lack of data to recognize a trait (albeit a negative one like apathy) is somewhat unsatisfactory but there are two other factors which were noted. First, some refugees remembered their feelings as a sort of dreamy, trance-like state. Second, other members of the respondents' families in *their* therapeutic retelling of the events of 1947 told and retold to those very people who had been apathetic how they had been. Thus there was some indication that something similar to D.P. apathy existed in the refugees of the sample. But the apathy of the World War II survivor, described as :

...a generalized attitude of helplessness, a loss of initiative and

> self-confidence. Many of the refugees have the feeling that they can do nothing on their own, that they always need outside help, and more important, that it is unquestionably due them.[39]

did not develop in the Punjab case. A little earlier it was hinted that this parasitism seems to develop where the refugees feel that their suffering created some good such as the creation of a state or the "purification" of the nation. The relationship between individual loss, community benefit, and individual dependence appears to be a universal one among survivors. Punjabi refugees were no exception to the rule. The feeling was that "we have suffered for India and now India owes us something." In those heady days of the early independence period this feeling was to some extent granted legitimacy by policy makers. Wolfenstein recognized that those who have suffered extraordinary assaults, whether they succumb or survive, are apt to seem more noble than ordinary people and to evoke the admiration and love which are the due of superior beings.[40] Partly because of this official recognition, but more importantly because there was land available for immediate refugee resettlement (land evacuated by Muslims who fled to Pakistan), it was possible for something to be done for the newcomers. Thus the characterization of World War II refugees as "parasites" hardened into the mentality of a frustrated infant to whom all is owing[41] was to a large extent not duplicated in the Punjab. Because of the pre-partition land arrangement and distribution of wealth in Bengal, the Bengali Hindu refugee could not be resettled on the land as easily as his western counterpart. As a result it appears that the Bengali, who in many cases still is living in refugee camps (although they are no longer "officially" camps), did lapse into this more infantile, dependent state.[42] Before going any further into dependency it would be useful to examine the attitudes which refugees have about their losses.

It is said that the longest laugh ever recorded on radio was on the Jack Benny show when, in a skit, a holdup man accosted the notoriously parsimonious Benny with the words, "Your money or your life." A long pause ensued after which Benny replied, "I'm thinking it over." This humour may seem a little macabre when applied to refugees, some of whom literally had to make that very choice, but the point does exemplify the way the refugee looks at his losses.

> I went twice with the Muslim military as I had gone with the Hindu military (to escort minority pockets to safety). From one village we brought forty-seven families consisting of about 300 men, women, and children to the camp. But when we went into the village and the soldiers saw the wealth of the households, they demanded money for the safe conduct. Otherwise they would not have taken them and all would have been killed. They paid Rs. 3,000 gladly and put themselves into the hands of the military. (*075).

We have already spoken of refugees who decided to stay on a little longer in an attempt to make a profit on the instability around them. Sooner or later anyone attempting to remain is either forced to evacuate the area or be killed. When he has reached safety he at first feels that no matter how great his losses, he has managed to preserve his life, and the material goods left behind were the price paid for this.

> At that time I was of the opinion that we hadn't come off so badly. For example, I thought that we had come off better than the Muslims who had gone to Pakistan because we had carts (to make our trip easier) while they had to go on foot. This is because (all the people on this side) had small land holdings and could not afford carts. (*001).

With the passage of time however these feelings of gratification and relief change as the survivor shifts his frame of reference from those who are worse off than himself to those who are better off. Thankfulness that one is not worse off changes to bitterness with the awareness of how much worse off one is than he was before.

Also, the spontaneous sympathy and gifts of his new neighbours (if he is not living in a camp), never very great, taper off with time as these people once again become involved in their own affairs. In many cases the local people even become hostile to the refugees. This occurred for two reasons. First, non-refugees harbour their own guilt feelings about the refugees. They, in many cases, are felt to have survived by abandoning others or by not being true to their faith and dying like martyrs. (See *Residual States : Guilt* below) Often the refugees themselves feel this way. To the non-refugee (and the guilt-ridden refugee) such sinful behaviour is not to be rewarded but punished. At the same time however, the non-refugee is not sure how he himself would have acted in similar circumstances. Given the choice between one's faith and one's life would one choose the path of martyrdom and sacrifice ?

On a more concrete level, the refugees, shortly after their arrival, were allocated the lands of the Muslim evacuees on a temporary basis. Although the temporariness of the resettlement was made explicit by the government it did not take too much intelligence to know that in the long run it would be the refugees and not the non-refugees who received this property. Since in many cases the non-refugees, in the expectation of receiving these lands, had driven out the Muslim agriculturists in pogroms similar to those on the other side of the border, they were not pleased at the influx of refugee agriculturists.[43] Second, to the non-refugee the refugee was someone who had survived at someone else's expense and this attempt to get land was seen as further evidence of their moral depravity : This greed was more than an attempt to get something for nothing, it was an attempt to get what they, the non-refugees, had fought and killed for. The non-refugee's guilt at harbouring ill feelings for the refugees who had undergone so much is heightened by his guilt of what he himself did during partition. The guilt however is not sufficient to inhibit the hostility he feels toward the refugees. Even at the family level where some relatives were refugees and others not, the hostility sometimes emerged and became overt aggression.

> We slept on the road at night. One of my relatives was employed at Jullundur and he took notice of us and requested that we stay with (his family). Hesitatingly we accepted. On the third day a priest visited the house. In our presence my relative's wife told him that she was sick of guests after they had stayed two or three days. On hearing this we had to rethink our position and find another place for shelter. But by that time I had exhausted those ten rupees (all that he had been able to salvage from Pakistan) and I had no option but to stay on another week with them. It was the second week in September (at this point the respondent broke down and wept as he had at other trying parts of his narrative). It was raining heavily when we were told that we could no longer stay in their house. We were asked to quit and our bedding and the little clothing, all we had, one small box,

were put out in the open. (*035)

One of our elders, my uncle, came to the Indian side early. He was waiting for us in our ancestral village. Someone there told him that not even a single child had escaped from Chak Number 4, Karsawal (where we were living). He died right there of the shock and we couldn't even come to know of his death. Even if we had known we could not have done anything because we didn't have the money to travel. (The respondent and his family were stuck for three weeks in the bus stand of a town about sixty miles distant because they did not have the fare to travel on. Finally they managed to borrow some money from another refugee relative)...we went to Kurali and from there we went on foot (about five miles). Then we went to the place where our uncle had died and spent a night there. We sent before some ornaments (jewelry) including a gold medal won by one of my three uncles who had served in the military. They opened the little box before us but in it was only *gram dal* (a pulse grain). They had already removed the ornaments from it and had refilled it with *gram dal*. The ornaments were worth Rs. 10,000 if we take present prices. In this way our own relatives cheated us. Then we went to our ancestral village, Cherian. There we found the lock of our house broken. We found out that after our uncle's death the relatives with whom we had been living and who had cheated us of the ornaments, came to the village, broke the lock of our house, and took away whatever was available there. We broke relations with them. (*021)

If relatives cannot be trusted who can be ?

To quantify some of the statements made about the relationships between refugees and non-refugees a number of more structured questions were asked during the interview schedule section of the project. When asked whether local people (non-refugees) had been helpful and sympathetic when they (the refugees) had arrived, about two-thirds (63.7%) of the refugees felt they had not. Only about one-third felt that they had been received "properly" by the locals. Moreover, despite the fact that the locals had not acted well toward them initially, most of the refugees felt that following the reception period relations had deteriorated still further. It is difficult to imagine such a state of affairs persisting for very long in a community as tightly interwoven as the Indian village and indeed, in time, an uneasy *modus vivendi* emerged. The language used to describe the way in which accommodation has been reached is instructive. Thirty per cent (30.4%) claim that things have improved "because we have come to know them and their ways." Another tenth (11.6%) say it is because they have learned to cooperate. Only 4.3 per cent said that they had come to like the local people although a fairly large number (21.7%) felt that the rapprochement had come about from the local people coming to like the refugees. More than one-fourth of the refugees (29.0%) refused to answer this question, a larger proportion than for almost any other item. It may be too strong to put it that "They may like us but we still don't trust them" but the fact is that refugee-non-refugee relations are still strained. In the first village studied the factional leadership (here meant as all those who are not coerced because of economic dependence to take the part of their patrons) corresponded almost perfectly with the refugee-non-refugee distinction. The refugees controlled the *panchayat* but the non-refugees ran the co-operative society. In the second village the refugees dominated the economic life entirely (which they saw as entirely fitting) but there was evidence of high levels of covert hostility from non-refugees who would pass on malicious gossip to me about important refugees. Occasionally this hostility would come into the open as a non-refugee would tip off the police about some illegal distilling that a refugee might be doing. The cleavage within the third village was also refugee versus non-refugee but was not examined in detail because of high level of tension between the two groups over a recent case of child molestation.

To a refugee harbouring his own guilt feelings hostile actions by local people or relatives may serve to bring release in that he, who already feels unappreciated and unloved, now can actively feel hostility to someone for what that person is doing to him. Rather than turning his anger inward now he has a target, convenient and worthy of being blamed.

Robinson has observed that in the case of disaster there is a common cycle which the relationships between survivors and non-victim benefactors follow:

1. "the spontaneous reception" period, a happy few days;
2. some occasional frictions;
3. a trial-and-error effort at adjustment;

4. a *modus vivendi* that endured a few weeks;
5. the outbreak of exacerbating tensions that continued day after day.[44]

In general, the refugee-non-refugee relationship follows the paradigm although the tensions of stage five were, as has been noted, more extreme because of the competition for Muslim evacuee property.

Lifton remarks that in Hiroshima there was what he found to be a surprising lack of hostility to targets which he expected it to be directed, most notably the United States.[45] He attributes this to the rapidity of the blow which the *hibakusha* suffered which made formulation impossible at the moment of trauma. The refugees are somewhat similar to this in that they did not have time to formulate their hatred against the persecuting groups and a similar inability to generate strong feelings against those who were directly responsible for the violence. Many respondents made a point of telling how, when the madness descended on the countryside, they had been saved by Muslims. It was the madness which was responsible (some respondents blamed Pakistan or Jinnah), not the Muslims of the countryside who were merely its instruments. But now the refugee has a target for the rage within him. Since he has already felt these people to be unappreciative of his sacrifice, they are now worthy of his sympathy. He will make it without them, preferably at their expense.[46]

The Refugee and the Elements

Earlier the breakdown of traditionally unvarying systems and the way in which the refugee perceives the breakdown was discussed in terms of the trials of the trip, the role of former neighbours, the supplicant-donor relationship, all concerned with interpersonal dealings. The refugee, however, was also sorely tried by the elements. For the refugees the unreliability of laws of nature were an added physical and psychological trial.

Peasants live close to nature. In general their relationship to the elements is one of recognizing elemental power and showing their own deference to the elements as superior powers. Shrines recognized as housing such powers abound in the North Indian countryside. But now, and earlier, in flight, the refugee is in a strange countryside and often moving too fast to take the time to find the shrine of the appropriate elements. And besides, such worship is important when one is an agriculturist, not when one is fleeing for his life. During 1947 the retribution for their fickleness was brought home to the refugees. In August the rains were more severe than normal; the widespread flooding often cut off escape routes and served as what must have been seen as an accomplice to the brutality of the opposite community. It was not until late in September 1947 that the rains abated. In the meantime, and even before the land had dried out, the refugees were frequently forced to live without proper shelter. The Punjab peasant had always been in close contact with nature; now he was forced into an even closer relationship. But the relationship was no longer a two-sided one where he could expect both benefits and difficulties from the vagaries of nature. Only hardship could be expected and the most one could hope for was to be left alone.

Gradually these sentiments lose some of their hold on the refugee. As with the disaster victim the mistrust of the elements and belief in their malevolence becomes diluted as one begins to realize how bad it all might have been. Gradually he comes to feel that his testing or scourging is over. While a fear of recurrence that "they will be back to finish me off"[47] persists for some time and sometimes permanently, the refugee slowly regains his feeling that since he survived, things could have been worse. Wolfenstein sees in her disaster victims the opposite reaction, what she calls "the rise and fall of the post disaster utopia." The Punjabi refugees, probably because of the swift relief and rehabilitation measures of the state and central governments, was able to a degree to regain a confidence in the beneficence of the larger social matrix.

Nurturance and Government

A distinctive feature of the survivor psyche is the fear, anger, and resentment generated by the relief efforts of others. Lifton has expanded the discussion of this symptom and argued that the resentment and rage is aimed at what the survivor sees as "counterfeit nurturance"; nurturance seen as not originating from genuine sympathy or a desire to help but directed at confirming the survivor's helplessness, weakness, and humiliation.[48] Such feelings about nurturance are, however, not free of ambivalence. If the nurturance, however much resented, is not received, the lack augments the feeling of abandonment which has plagued the refugee since his original brush with violence. The step from ambivalent feelings about nurturance to similar attitudes towards the nurturing agents is a short one. Although in the early stages of rehabilitation observers have seen these agents to be sympathetic members of neighbouring communities, we have already noted that relations between refugees and non-refugees are, in the main, likely to be strained for other reasons. For the refugees the function of providing nurturance or rehabilitation must be undertaken by the government. The non-refugees are viewed darkly as those who are ungrateful for the sacrifices made in their behalf by the refugees. Attitudes toward government are more complex.

As relations between refugees and local people become less cordial, the refugees turn to government for the performance of the nurturance function. Since all efforts at rehabilitation from mere feeding to final resettlement take time to organize, the refugees for at least a short period will be in a sort of limbo where they are left to their own devices. During this period, being on their own without any of the forms of community life to which they have been accustomed and without sustenance, many of the constraints on the individual which allow social systems to function are likely to disappear. Literally demoralization occurs as the strong oppress the weak, and those having even the most meagre necessities find themselves with almost infinite power.[49] Fortunately in Punjab such a period was very short because of the availability of Muslim land on which refugees could be resettled and a number of other factors : First, government mechanisms for the care of refugees were rapidly created, partly through the government's being able to enlist the help of organized groups already concerned with social welfare functions. The Shiromani Gurdwara Prabandhak Committee, the Arya Samaj, the various Christian missionary groups all contributed funds and workers to help government meet the crisis. The government closed schools and colleges to furnish living space for the refugees. College and university students were given academic credit for their work in helping refugees. As a result the refugees of Punjab did not have to endure some of the privations and degradation to which refugees in other areas have been subjected. Nor was there any long period during which the refugee could feel that no one cared whether he lived or died.

Despite this, the performance of the government employees and the social workers suffered from one of the chronic problems of a transitional society—how to bridge the gap between the semi-elite bureaucrat and the rural, or even urban, traditional member of the public. While to outsiders, and to the elite and bureaucrats themselves, all the efforts being made at the time are clearly beneficial, the refugee finds the tight-fisted, impersonal bureaucrat no substitute for the benevolent traditional methods of welfare to which he is accustomed. Here is no *biradari* offering a loan because of its obligations to its members; here is no landlord giving food or clothing to his constituents. Instead there is a man who dresses and speaks differently than the refugees and almost invariably conveys to him a sense of suspicion at stories of how badly off he is and how much he has lost. That the individual who is supposed to maintain him is called a "Refugee Administrator" or bears a similar title reinforces the refugee's suspicion that help emanating from his office is counterfeit nurturance. The man helps refugees because they are helpless. To get this help they must display their helplessness and show how incapable they are of taking care of themselves. From the administrator's point of view he must develop a protective sheathing against the possibility of becoming too sympathetic. One cannot accede to all demands; he must shield himself from the emotional involvement inherent in such a nurturance role. But such an attitude almost inevitably conveys to the refugee a sense of suspicion of the truthfulness of refugees' stories of how much they have lost. If he will not believe the truth, the only solution for the refugee is to inflate the story of his losses. By doing so he must not only confirm his actual weakness but accentuate it. The administrator begins to see all claims as exaggerated and spiral of suspicion and resentment continues. A fairly common theme, undoubtedly exaggerated, among the refugees of this project was that they had not only received a *pie* (1/256 of an old rupee) but had even refused it. Despite the statement of having refused aid (which was assumed to be hyperbole) about four-fifths of the refugee sample (79.7%) felt that the government had helped them upon their arrival. But a large number (30.4%) felt that the government that had originally been so beneficent (or at least helpful) changed for the worse before very long.

Naturally, not everyone resented the quantity or quality of the government relief effort. For many the distribution of grain, cooking oil, soap, and other necessities proved to be the key to survival and was appreciated as such. Many refugees living in camps received these goods for years after their exodus until they were resettled. Others, generally the more powerful elements of the society, managed to make the system work in their favour, often gaining great benefits through the mechanism of refugee rehabilitation. Nevertheless, for many especially the formerlyl anded groups, what was desired was not what were seen as debilitating relief measures. There is a Punjabi proverb, "To keep your honour do not even ask for water". Going so far as to request counterfeit nurturance was felt to lead to undue dependence upon a government which had already failed them in their time of need. What was really desired was a chance to be independent. This could be achieved by receiving an allocation of a plot of land registered in their names. An allocation of land was not felt to be a form of nurturance but was a form of compensation for what they had left behind in Pakistan. Interestingly enough the government recognized the distinction between the right to receive subsistence grants and the right to receive compensation for losses. As soon as the countryside became relatively stabilized the government set to work to grant Muslim evacuee land to Hindu and Sikh refugees who immediately started farming it.[50]

The basic problem which the government had to face in granting land to refugees was a policy one : Should this opportunity be taken to distribute land to the landless at the expense of the big landlords or should distribution be aimed at restoring the *status quo ante* of Pakistan. The socialists and landlords argued the issue and petitioned government for some time. Finally a plan was put forward that met some of the demands of both groups. A graduated series of land cuts would be made so that smallholders would receive a larger percentage of their losses than would large *zamindars.* Cuts were necessary because East Punjab had less agricultural land than West Punjab. Specifically, the land left on the Indian side by fleeing Muslims was only seventy per cent of that abandoned by Hindus and Sikhs coming from Pakistan. Furthermore, the land on the Indian side was markedly inferior to that on the Pakistani side and variations in the quality of land on the Indian side made the allocation still more complex. It was only through an ingenious system which took into account the quality of land when calculating the "standard acreage" that the problem was made amenable to solution. When allowances were made for productivity of land, the proportion declined to only sixty-two per cent. This meant that if proportional cuts had been made, each refugee peasant would have had to accept a cut in acreage of between a third and a half. Since the majority of peasants were smallholders, such a solution would have created great strains on their ability to subsist.[51] In practice the "graduated cut" system did not work too terribly badly but the refugees, too close to the scene to understand the problems involved, were often left unsatisfied. The fact that any compensation that a government or international agency may try to make will almost always be less than the refugee's losses (and to his eyes far less than his due) is important, but perhaps even more significant to a traditional Indian are certain sentiments about the relationship between the suppli-cant and the donor. A recurrent theme in the interviews was that demands, if made long enough and persistently enough, have to be acceded to. In other words a supplicant expects to be able to approach any power figure or nurturant figure with the feeling that requests, demands, and boons will be granted, assuming that the supplicant is willing to invest sufficient energy. Certainly any foreigner who has been to India has seen the extreme behavioural manifestation of this in the not-to-be-denied beggar. That it exists in other forms of social interaction, and perhaps more importantly in the cognitive structure given to social relations, is not surprising. Our respondents saw many examples of this principle at work :

> (On the causes of partition:) It was a long standing demand by the Muslims that Pakistan be created so the British had to accede. (*039)
>
> (On getting help to escape to a refugee camp:) I met this officer and demanded that he escort me. He didn't want to but I would not let him go without doing this. Finally he agreed. (*035)

But the local people are not disposed to grant the wishes of the refugees except in the immediate period after the refugees' arrival and the state is unable to meet all the refugees' demands and unwilling to assume through its servants the very personal nurturant role to which the traditional person has been socialized throughout his life. Another system, previously seen as unchanging, has broken down.

Combining the sentiments about the quality of governmental nurturance which the refugee has with his earlier ideas about the protective powers of government and adding them to the refugee's new perspective of looking to those better off than himself (rather than to those worse off), it is easy to understand how he begins to feel that others are getting more than their share and that this is probably due to corruption, deceit, and chicanery. The feeling is unfortunately sometimes justified. That refugees in flight are often made aware that while the rich are often attacked they are also likely to have the resources necessary to purchase survival has already been discussed. Because of the dangers to himself, the refugee in flight does not formulate these ideas into any coherent system. But now, after safety has been reached, the average refugee sees the rich refugee as getting more than his share. The rich refugee in turn sees the poor refugee as trying to get benefits at his expense. The feelings of both are tightly intertwined with the ambivalence over counterfeit nurturance. Each resents the special care based on his refugee identity and at the same time is jealous of those who make the system work for their own personal benefit.[52]

For a person who has undergone so much in deprivation and suffering it is hard to explain that this, the promised for which his epic flight was made, cannot or will not satisfy all his demands. The suspicion that government and its servants, local people, and even his fellow refugees, are trying to cheat him, he who has done so much for the country, even created it, can change the short-lived regressive dependent attitude to one of generalized mistrust and hostility, especially among younger refugees. That so many refugees already have negative feelings towards government, as we have noted, merely accentuates the hostility. Such hostility has been recognized in many of the disaster and concentration camp studies of the past twenty years. Many writers have seen this hostility to government and authority as against both the authority of the persecuting power and the new host power, e.g.:

> What becomes of the lopsided ego? Can it be that we were all acting out the never dissolved conflict of our childhood entailed in "giving in"? Is it possible that our parents of the past were translated into the horrible enemy-authority, and that in thwarting him by escaping death, we actually took our final revenge on the resented early authority?[53]

Nevertheless, Lifton found that most of the hostility felt by the *hibakusha* was not directed against the United States but against the pre-war and wartime Japanese governments.[54] This is similar to the USSBS finding that Germans, Britons, and Japanese who had been subjected to aerial bombing during World War II voiced hostility not only at those who were dropping the bombs on them but also towards their own leaders for not providing sufficient protection.[55] Robinson notes that after the South Amboy fire, local people blamed their own officials for "letting it happen."[56] In this respect the Indians interviewed in this project were not entirely consistent with their predecessors in misfortune. Like the earlier cases they too were unwilling to find fault with their own long departed and by now revered leaders—Gandhi, Nehru, and Patel. Such was not always the case. Just before Gandhi was assassinated, police officials in Delhi were afraid that a rising of refugees enraged at the concessions to Pakistan that Gandhi had forced on the Congress leaders, would lead not only to the massacre of those Muslims who had stayed behind but to attempts on Gandhi's life.[57] That some refugees were implicated in the successful assassination as well as the earlier, unsuccessful bomb attempt shows how well grounded the fears of the officials were. Why this change in attitudes towards the leaders of the Independence movement which had such enormous consequences for the individual, the subcontinent, and perhaps the world? Mainly I believe it can be attributed to one of the mechanisms by which inconsistency of attitudes are resolved in the minds of men.[58] The Punjabi refugee was brought in and made not only a citizen but to some extent was recognized as the founder of the country. In the years that followed, every politician at the centre and state level publicly recognized the debt the country owed to the refugees. Moreover the debt kept increasing. Not only had they been the founders but they also turned out in three wars, one with China and two with Pakistan, to be the protectors of the nation. Further, as time passed they were pointed out as the most progressive and therefore admirable to the rest of India and to the world. Not only were they responsible for the India of the present but they *were* the India of the future. Gradually a Punjabi consciousness was transformed from one of disdain for the rest of India for not being like Punjabis to an attitude of "we are the true Indians of the future."[59] As the true Indians they adopted all the Indian political hagiolatry, including the veneration of the early Congress leaders for whom they had so little use during their lives.[60] At the same time they adopted the demonology of these same nationalists. More than a third of the respondents (36.2%) blamed the British for the partition and ensuing troubles and about one-sixth

(16.0%) felt that Jinnah and the League leaders were to blame. While the refugee feels that his Government may not have been responsible for partition and the resultant catastrophic events he does not necessarily like it. When he reached safety, as we have seen, he had to work intimately with its machinery to gain some compensation for his losses and this familiarity as the saying goes did breed resentment as well as contempt.

Wolfenstein notes that the post-disaster resentment of authority is aimed less at the evil parent figures who have inflicted the damage than at the good parent figures who, after all is done, are supposed to make everything all right again.[61] Gardner Murphy and Eduard Bakis also have recognized the hostility to government as aimed towards a father symbol.[62] Certainly the identification of governmental care with parental care is not too farfetched. Murphy also has noted an obvious but often overlooked point : that this hostility to a father figure may bring on severe guilt feelings which augment the persisting survivor-guilt feelings.

If guilt is considered as rage aimed inwards it is possible to conceptualize that some of the hostility of the refugee to others in the society may represent the displacement of an intolerable emotion (aggressive sentiments to a parent and/or aggression inward) to safer, more suitable targets: unsympathetic, unappreciative new neighbours. To some extent it may be focussed on the old neighbours who drove him from his old home or the nation which they represent, but in general the targets will be "enemies" which are handy to the refugee : minority groups, evil sorcerors, etc.

Along with displacement there often occurs a projection of similar sentiments to other groups. Although earlier studies have generally not examined this point it seems that some of the paranoia exhibited by refugees in the sample, which appears to be a significant segment of their personality, represents such a mechanism. This point will be amplified later.

On the other hand the generalized mistrust and hostility which the refugee carries within himself may lead to a form of avoidance behaviour, a desire to go it alone without regard for the opinions of society. Such refugees in their individualism may find release for their aggressive tendencies through socially acceptable if not approved acts. They might become hard working "loners" in a workshop or farm environment but they are more likely to become the solitary worker in a one-man operation. Another possible channel for such sentiments which could not be investigated in the research was the path of religious mendicancy.

Gradually the tone of normal life is restored. Over a period ranging from weeks to years the refugee becomes integrated in the mesh of a larger community. Those who have been residents of camps leave them for new homes or else the camps themselves are transformed into suburban settlements or self-sustaining villages. Some of those who stayed with relatives on their arrival move on or become new members of pre-existing households. In many cases the symbiotic relationships of the *jajmani* system are restored as landholders and their previous tenants or artisans become reunited. To a large degree the identity of the refugee as a victim recedes and he becomes the member of a larger group having the common identity of being refugees. For a number of reasons this new group identity becomes very important to the refugee. First, refugees can, through concerted action, act as a lobby to gain certain concessions from government. Second, being concentrated in certain areas, they become politically important. Any candidate in such an area must appeal to them. Third, there is a sense of shared experience. "We've been through the worst together and know what life is really like. Everyone else is an outsider who can't possibly share the same emotions as we do." Fourth, replacing the Muslims in villages, they come to control large blocks of land. The power resultant from land flows naturally to them. Since the basic cleavages in Punjabi villages have always been over land, a new group with a common identity entering the scene polarizes the non-refugees into a competing opposition group.

Thus "non-refugee" to a certain extent becomes a new group identity as well. I was struck, in the villages and towns in which I visited and lived, by how well the new refugee and non-refugee identities had weathered the strains of the twenty years since partition,[63] so much so that it would be safe to hypothesize that wherever refugees and their families make up thirty and seventy per cent of the agricultural population the inevitable factions will be those of refugees and non-refugees. Below this range the refugees are likely to join existing factions because of their lack of relative strength and above it they are likely to be split within themselves. In urban settings the situation is more complex. Certain of the bazaars in most north Indian towns have been taken over entirely by refugees.[64] They have not merely replaced Muslims who left (Muslims were generally not in trade in East Punjab) but displaced Hindu *baniyas* by hard work as well as by cleverness and progressive business practices. Their activities have in some cases led directly to conflict as local traders feel their businesses threatened by the newcomers.[65] The question of the unity of urban and town-dwelling refugees is complicated by the fact that refugees do vote with other refugees against non-refugees but that they are often divided among themselves. In the 1968 midterm election in Haryana a good many candidates were referred to as "refugee candidates." This referred not only to the fact that they themselves were refugees but that their entire support was based on the refugee electorate. Unfortunately for many of them the concentration of refugees in certain wards or towns meant that two or three of a six candidate competition for office might be refugees. As a result some of the benefits (and some of the threats) of refugee unity which might have been achieved were wasted.

Having discussed the changes resulting from early stages of refugeeism, it is necessary to look at what appear to be enduring characteristics of the refugee personality, characteristics which are felt to grow directly from these changes previously noted.

Residual States : Invulnerability

If a refugee identity remains important, does this mean that the hostility to non-refugees which developed after arrival in India is retained ? The only answer to this is that refugees still look upon non-refugees as different than themselves. The converse is also true. But although mistrust and hostility do still exist between the two groups most respondents reported that refugees had been as they put it, "integrated into society." Actually what appears to have happened is that the non-refugees have to a large extent been inducted into aspects of refugee culture. When asked whether refugees had had any effect on local life, both refugees and non-refugees repeatedly cited the changes introduced by the refugees in the areas of diet, clothing styles, farming practices and language.

But refugees change also after the initial period. These changes do not seem to have stemmed from their connection with non-refugees however. Rather the changes were spontaneous and probably due to the refugee experience. Most significant among these changes was the often noted refugee characteristic of being willing to take risks. The willingness to start anew was noted years ago in studies of natural disaster victims in this country but at that time it was thought to be a uniquely American characteristic related to American views of "luck."

> Closely related to the feeling of having been lucky is the readiness to start all over again. Instead of brooding about their losses people turn their heads to...getting life reorganized.[66]

Since the same behaviour patterns have been noted for Hindu and Sikh refugees, the trait must be more than simple a facet of American "national character." I believe that it is tied to a much hinted at but little discussed concept : the belief in one's invulnerability. Twenty years ago Louise Pinsky, in writing of children who survived the death camps, observed, "They reached rock bottom and nothing they may have encountered afterwards could baffle them : but she was too close to the event to see the persistence of this outlook or where it might lead.[67] Wolfenstein in another context came close to the issue but backed off : She felt that having weathered extreme shock could give some people a feeling of release from the normal constraints of life.

> The powers have shot their bolt...One sacrifice...buys immunity to further hazards. Having survived the disaster one may feel the sense of confidence in one's invulnerability strengthened.[68]

Probably one of the reasons for Wolfenstein's caution was her allegiance to earlier disaster studies which had brought up the concept of "subjective near miss." She discusses this but perhaps realizing how close the discussion comes to circularity (Victims who feel vulnerable are those who have had a subjective near miss. Subjective near misses are those feelings of centrality and vulnerability which some individuals develop when disaster strikes.), she bakes off without pushing the implications of her statement to their limits.

Miss Wolfenstein's view that people feel that they are starting with a clean slate is a valid one. They are able to feel that they owe nothing to supernatural powers; if anything the reverse is the case. Later she retreats a little from her earlier statement on invulnerability and dilutes it :

> A disastrous event does not make one see one's life in a tragic perspective. Rather one reminds oneself of the many good things one has had which certainly outweigh the present misfortune... If one recalls past hardships it is to remind oneself how one was able to surmount them. One not only feels good about having survived but confident in one's capacity to cope with difficulties... The emphasis is on one's strength and resilience in being able to take things, one's activity and resourcefulness in recouping one's situation.[69]

Such an analysis is neither strong enough nor does it go far enough to describe the mental state of the victim. Rather than merely feeling that lightning cannot strike twice and that he might as well start over, the survivor feels he has been through the worst that can be done to him. Whatever punishments he may deserve in the future are nothing compared to the scourging he has already received. Miss Wolfenstein's failure to link the eagerness to start anew with the feeling of immunity and invulnerability that develops in many survivors is a minor flaw in her important work.

It was precisely having undergone the extreme suffering that generates the sense of invulnerability that in its initial form is manifested by a strong desire to start all over again. But starting over involves only a relatively short time period when large governmental inputs are being introduced to the system. Even after this period is over and the refugee has started anew he retains his sense of invulnerability. To exercise this sense he pushes on the unwritten constraints of his culture and society. Where others dare not tread he strides fearlessly. As one of the Punjabis put it :

> We've been through so much; what more can happen to us ? No one can do anything to us that can be more terrible than has already occurred. Why should we be afraid ? Once everything was taken from us (in partition) and we have come back from our pennilessness to prosperity. If we lose it all again we could do it once more. (*035)

By their suffering they have become invulnerable—or at least their invulnerability has been proven. They can undertake ventures heretofore undreamed of : commerce with far off provinces, trips to foreign lands, business ventures, aggressive combats. The proverb,

"Run as far and as fast as you wish; you will reach only that which is ordained," has been forgotten.

Despite the willingness to take risks and the desire for respectable work and self-sufficiency, the task of rehabilitating oneself was not an easy one. The local people were, if not hostile, unsympathetic and the government aid did not go far enough. Not one of the refugees, in designating the changes that had occurred in his life on this side of the border (as contrasted with his life in West Punjab), remarked that he was materially better off than he had been on the other side of the border—although almost every non-refugee observer would describe many of them as such. Although the refugees cannot see themselves as better off they have managed to erase the stain of counterfeit nurturance and become self-sufficient once again. Only 4.3 per cent of the sample felt that they had not regained a degree of economic independence characterized as self-sufficiency and these were all old men. The road to this condition

TABLE 3.1

Refugees' Views of Time to reach Self-sufficiency

Less than six months	8.7 %
Six months to a year	4.3
One year to three years	21.7
Three years to five years	18.8
Five years to ten years	17.4
Ten years to fifteen years	20.3
Fifteen years to twenty years	2.9
Still not self-sufficient	4.3
DK	1.5
	100.0 %
	(N=69)

was a difficult one however. It took many years of hard work on one's own land and on that of others to repay the debts one had incurred. For members of trading communities it often meant working as a street peddler until one could scrape together enough capital to start a shop. For artisans it meant years of working as a hired labourer until one could set out on one's own as a small manufacturer. Although the work was hard, one did regain his self-respect through such efforts, but it was not an overnight process for the individual involved.

Disaster studies of the sentiment generally are concerned with the United States and other developed areas and as such miss the significance of such sentiments in the underdeveloped world.

Indeed one of the consistent complaints about the underdeveloped nations is that the attitudes of the inhabitants preclude risk-taking on their part. As a result, entrepreneurs do not emerge and economies stagnate. If the cautiousness of prospective entrepreneurial classes can be overcome, these arguments go on, then the energies and capital required for economic development will be released leading to rapid growth.[70]

Among the refugees interviewed in this project risk-taking appeared to be common. It was especially marked regarding occupations. Most refugees settled down to their earlier occupations but a significant number undertook new occupations and set up new enterprises. In examining the interview schedule data on occupational mobility among the refugee sample it was surprising to note the number of different jobs the respondents had had. The classificatory system used enumerated type and sphere of work. Type refers to whether the work was unskilled labour, skilled labour, cultivation of one's own land, white collar work, management, etc. while sphere refers to agriculture, industry, government, etc. Thus having had separate employers but having done the same job (as many labourers in India do) would not be counted toward occupational mobility; to be counted as having had two jobs one would have to have changed the type of work or the sphere of work. Thus agricultural labour was not considered equivalent to cultivation of one's own land but neither was it considered equivalent to unskilled labour in an urban *daftar* (office) or unskilled industrial labour.

TABLE 3.2

Occupational Mobility

Holding second job	26.0%
Having had other job in past	50.7
Having had two or more other jobs in past	17.8
Having served in military	5.5
	(N=73)

The table shows that more than a fourth of the sample "moonlight." Half have held other jobs in the past and about a third of these have held two or more jobs.

Many of the refugees went far afield to Bengal to drive taxis or start transport companies, to Delhi to start businesses, or to Uttar Pradesh to clear virgin land. Of those who stayed in the Punjab-Haryana area many started small workshops. Sleepy towns before partition were transformed into booming industrial centres. Almost all of the transformation can be credited to the refugees and the risk-taking which grows from their sense of invulnerability. This will be discussed in more detail in a later chapter.

Residual States : Guilt

From the preceding discussion of the mental states through which a refugee passes as he flees to and reaches safety, it is fair to say that the refugee experience does indeed closely resemble the model posited by the disaster and atomic bomb studies. There are of course significant differences : disaster and atomic bombs strike without much warning, the refugees in some cases knew for months that something drastic was going to happen. Refugeeism is also different in that it falls somewhere between the disaster which strikes and recedes quickly and the atomic bomb which, because of the long term danger of radiation-effects has been called a "continuous and unresolvable encounter with death."[71] There is a long, continuous brush with death for the refugee but in most cases this lasts a few months rather than the seventeen years of the Hiroshima victims Lifton wrote of. As such the events were well in the past for all the refugees in Punjab and Haryana. This is not to say however that the refugee's cares are over once he leaves a refugee camp, takes a permanent job, or is given land. Many of the stages through which the refugee passes in his exodus leave a residue of psychic scar tissue and continue into his present-day life to affect his perceptions, values, and attitudes.[72] It is possible to hypothesize on the basis of Lifton's work about certain characteristics which may emerge *after* reaching safety.

In many cases, especially where a loved one was lost, there is guilt merely at having survived. Survivor guilt has been widely discussed elsewhere. Indeed one of the universal themes in the literature of survivors and refugees appears to be guilt. We have already commented on Lifton's analysis of what he has called "guilt over survival priority."[73] Lifton's work is consonant with that of Niederland.[74] S. A. Prins, a psychologist who is also a refugee

(World War II vintage), has written that all individuals in flight in his generation "expressed unconsciously a deep self hatred."[75] Prins believes that the guilt stems from rebellion against parental authority and the superego rather than from ambivalence over survival priority. It is significant that, although he disagrees with other psychologists on the etiology of guilt, he recognizes its presence. Stefi Pedersen, in the same volume, properly recognizes that escapees whose friends had been captured and sent to concentration camps subjected themselves to extreme self torture.[76] Robinson, in discussing natural disaster, believes that survival guilt, where the individual tortures himself over what he might have done to save others who did not survive, can swell to the point where the person feels he must commit suicide.[77] Many studies have shown how enduring this guilt is.[78] If survival guilt is a universal reaction among survivors which persists in full or attenuated form for the remainder of the survivor's life, the question arises whether there are particularly Indian factors that may intensify or mitigate the effects of this universal form of guilt.

We have seen above the importance of the parent-child relationship, the emphasis of which is on protection granted by the father in return for respect and obedience. In fathers or heads of households responsible for the safety of relatives and yet unable to provide such safety the guilt my be unbearable. A Hindi proverb puts it thus :

> Sorrow for a dead father lasts six months;
> Sorrow for a dead mother a year;
> Sorrow for a wife until a second wife arrives;
> But sorrow for a dead son for ever.

A Ludhiana businessman who stayed behind in Pakistan for several months saving others repeatedly wept during our interview and blamed himself for not having saved some relatives for whom he felt himself morally responsible.

> Another reason for my staying on in Pakistan was that my son, father, mother, sister, and two of my daughters as well as my brother and all his family were stranded in Okara (about 100 miles away), District Montgomery, and no arrangements were being made (for their safety by the authorities). I managed to get

> a telephone connection with them. One *Jatha* started from Okara (at this point the respondent broke down and wept as he had done repeatedly throughout the interview. When asked repeatedly if he would like to be excused he insisted that we carry on, almost as if he saw this session as a therapeutic one) but it never reached the Indian side. It was all finished on the way and all I had done was to telephone. Moreover my brother-in-law, who was a clerk in Lahore, tried to leave Lahore. On the way to the station he and a colleague accompanying him were shot. (*035)

An agriculturist who had made a long trip from the western reaches of the state to the comparative safety of a refugee camp told of waiting for safe transport for the last leg of the exodus to India.

> We stayed there for two months. The first month passed easily. Then the Muslims brought their military in a train. Our camp had been constructed on both sides of the railway line. They brought that train right into the middle of it, right into our midst and then fired on both sides. They kept up firing for about a half hour and thousands were killed there. Five of my nephews were killed in that firing because panic broke out and they tried to run away. Two of them were in their teens and three were little kids. We lay down so we were saved. They stopped firing finally and went away. What could we have done. We thought that our death was certain even if we had done nothing. (*053)

A town dweller who only barely escaped several times tells of an incident that occurred in his flight :

> I said that we should bring this lady (another woman who had become separated from her family) with us. When I said this my aunt broke out in tears and said that her son had been left in a locked room (at their bungalow, many miles away). They had had a big bungalow. When the trouble began, in order to save their lives, they split up and lived in different houses. They had been very rich. In the confusion at the time of their rescue and escape they had forgotten him. (*073)

Several people either reached safety or happened to be on the Indian side of the frontier when the troubles began. A blacksmith, after an initial feeling of relief at being safe, decided to go to the Pakistani side to search for his sister. His tale reads like an odyssey. Many times he was in danger of immediate death. He killed at least once. Yet his guilt at having left his sister helpless in the midst of enemies forced him on. Among north Indians the relationship between brothers and sisters is a particularly close one, with the brother acting as the protector of the sister's honour.[79] After marriage he is often the only link between her old home and the conjugal home. Frequently he must intervene in her new family's affairs to keep her from being mistreated. In any event when a woman needs a protector she will turn first to her brother and only later to her husband. The actual closeness of the relationship is formally symbolized by the festival of *Raksha Bandhan* when sisters give their brothers a fancy wrist band in exchange for protection for the coming year. Although recently the boons demanded have been broadened to include a cash payment by the brother to the sister, the entire emphasis of the holiday is the protection given by the brother or surrogate.[80] In times of danger if one is unable to guarantee the safety and honour of the girl, it is the brother's duty to kill her before she falls into enemy hands and dishonour. Failing in such a duty not only brings dishonour to the brother and sister involved but disgraces the entire family. In North India where Muslim influence had the effect of emphasizing chastity before marriage and seclusion (*purdah*) throughout life, a girl is considered particularly vulnerable. It is up to her brother to maintain her virtue and honour. There is only one relationship warmer in its affect than the brother-sister one: that is the tie between mother and son.[81] Earlier the strong ties between father and children were seen to be of a rather cool nature. The very terms used for the relationships are almost devoid of any sense of personalness : obedience, respect, protection. On the other hand the mother-son relationship is unquestionably the warmest of all possible ones. The very application of the term mother to those elements of Indian life which are most nurturant and significant to the individual points this up. We have Mother Ganges, Mother Cow, the Mother-Goddess, and most recently Mother-India. Even before his sister, a son owes all allegiance to his mother. Any son who fails to provide for his mother in her old age is doomed to the lowest pits of hell. A son owes all to his mother and must answer her every demand.

The old North Indian proverb,

> For the good of a family, a member may be abandoned;
> For the good of a town, a family may be abandoned;
> For the good of a state, a town may be abandoned;
> For the good of your soul, all you own may be abandoned.

does not comfort the survivor for he can never be sure that his abandonment of others was necessary. Hence a residual condition of both doubt and guilt remain to cloud his life.

Identity Guilt

In Chapter I, an outstanding characteristic of the new refugeeism was seen to be its basis in group identity. Because a man is a Watusi, or a Sikh, or a Chinese he is persecuted and driven from his home. Where the individual has few other cross-cutting facets to his individual identity we might expect his identity problems to be highly significant. That the people on the receiving end of the violence see it in the same light is not surprising. In this case it is because they are Hindus and Sikhs that they are experiencing all the troubles of the times.[82] This was frequently made clear to the victims by their oppressors :

> On the fifteenth of August, 1947 when freedom was given, we heard that it had been published in the newspapers that the Hindus were to go to India and the Muslims would come to Pakistan. The fighting started. The Muslims attacked us because we were Hindus. They told us that we could convert to Islam or they would kill... us. We were 140 men, women, and children. What were we to do? So we took our luggage on our heads (and set out for India). (*023)
>
> We saw Hindus going to India. We thought we had better come to India because all the others were coming...In Pakistan we were thinking ourselves unsafe and could not help thinking of death constantly. The Muslims asked us to turn ourselves into Muslims but we could not do such a thing and we refused. (*024)

We have already heard of the group of Sikhs protected by a Muslim *zamindar* which deceived an attacking mob by pretending to be converted. The cutting of their hair, the removal of the most visible symbol of their group identity, was embarked upon only after serious soul-searching even when it was clear that refusal to do so would have led to certain death. In this case it is not even that they denied their religion, for in their hearts the people knew that they were not actually converting, but that they were merely publicly denying their religion in order to survive the holocaust. For Sikhs, whose personal religious life is so firmly grounded in the five symbols of the *khalsa* enjoined as mandatory for all Sikhs by Guru Gobind Singh, such a renunciation could be expected to be extremely difficult.[83] At the same time it was their very visibility which made their position most dangerous. One of the respondents, a Hindu, reported that the persecutors not only hated the Sikhs more than the Hindus but placed a higher price on their heads.[84] But regardless of the reasons for this differential price policy the Sikhs saw themselves, because of their Sikh-ness, as especially picked out for trouble.

When an individual did take the path of conversion in order to survive, his crime was thought to be quite serious. After great difficulty one respondent managed to find his lost mother, sister, and brother-in-law in Pakistan.

> A coolie was also travelling in that bogie (of the train). From our conversation he came to know that I had been waiting and searching for my mother. It turned out that he knew my brother-in-law... He told me that at first they had come to the camp but after considering their land and property, had gone back. They gave preference to their land and property instead of their religion ! I was apalled and shocked at this but what could I do ? So I thought, "let them do whatever they want, I will have nothing to do with them hereafter (I will ostracize them)," but it would be terrible to leave my mother in such a situation. (*075)

For many if not most of the refugees, death was considered preferable to becoming a Muslim and denying one's identity :

> When the police[85] arrested us we knew that they would demand that we become Muslims or be killed. But we had decided to be killed rather than become Muslims because one must die one day or the other but one must never sacrifice his honour. (*048)

Of course that respondent and all others we interviewed escaped, but there were tragedies. One respondent, sobbing, told the following story. In a similar situation :

> People thought that when our honour is being spoiled it is better to die. Since the military had guns and ammunition and the people had none they (the people) started the massacre of their own daughters. Thirty-seven girls were killed in a quarter hour by striking their necks with the edges of bricks. It was very weird...there every girl was demanding of her father or brother that she be killed first...When the military saw this scene, that we had killed our own daughters and that heaps of bodies were lying all around, they thought that (we were so desperate) that they could not escape death at our hands. (*075)

A denial of one's religion, the fundamental aspect of identity in the Punjab, engendered deep guilt in the respondents who spoke of this. Many said that although they had been rather lax about practices before partition, they now visited the temple or *gurudwara* more frequently. For Sikhs, whose religion is very tightly tied to the idea of martyrdom for the faith, the guilt was particularly oppressive. Guru Gobind Singh's sons, to say nothing of other martyrs such as the ninth Guru, Teg Bahadur, had gladly embraced death in particularly repellent forms rather than accede to the demands of their Moghul captors that they become apostates.[86] The Golden Temple in Amritsar, which could be likened to St. Peter's in its importance to Sikhs, has a museum which graphically not only depicts in paintings the martyrdom but even displays some of the torture instruments of the day. Thus with every visit to Amritsar or the various *gurudwaras* erected on the sites of the martyrdoms the devotee is reminded of how he, in a similar situation, failed to follow the example of the Gurus. And since from early childhood he has been taught that they are the objects most worthy of respect, he comes to see himself as unworthy of it.[87] Summarizing, the refugee has been attacked because of his identity. All the violence about him stems from the fact that he is different than his oppressors. His oppressors give him the option of erasing this difference and saving his life. But his religious identity is too precious; he cannot do it. What he can do however is to try for the best of all possible solutions: remaining true to his religion "inside" while externally denying it and embracing the identity of the oppressor.[88] While this does save his life he is, especially if he is a Sikh, constantly reminded of his failure to reach the standards of integrity expected of a devotee. Thus he is now assailed by the very religion he underwent such trials for.

Among such people the contradictions might be faced differently. In our group some Sikhs embraced the faith more fervently than they had before, even following the Akali Dal party's brand of "Sikh Power," a lightly disguised movement aimed at purifying Sikhism and cleaning up the backsliders. Others, feeling they had already deviated so far from the path of the Gurus, went whole hog. Some had shaved off their beards entirely and many trimmed them. A higher percentage of Sikh refugees mentioning guilt-producing identity conflicts had taken up smoking (a prohibited act under Sikhism) than among those who either did not mention such situations or were non-refugees.

With regard to Hindus it is much more difficult to make any firm statements. First of all, virtually no act is prohibited to Hindus (with the obvious exception of killing cows) and no external feature exists to differentiate them from Muslims if they chose to wear either Muslim or western dress.[89] Furthermore as far as I know there is little virtue in religious martyrdom in any of the Hindu epics or in the tales told to children.[90] Thus claiming to be Muslim or to having been converted would be expected to create less severe internal stresses. On the basis of our sample, however, I feel that the Hindu refugees conformed less to the Sanskritic ideal than did the Hindu non-refugees. More ate eggs and meat and a good number partook of alcohol. It must of course be remembered that the area of Punjab now in Pakistan, that is, the area from which they came, was long noted for its comparative laxity in the following of such norms, perhaps as a result of a strong Muslim influence or the reform influence of Sikhism. Therefore it would be risky to state that identity crises have produced this effect.

Guilt has been described as anger directed inward.[91] Anger has been recognized as the intervening variable between frustration and aggression.[92] If anger directed inward acts also as an intervening variable one would expect those having high guilt levels to aggress against themselves either as masochists or suicides. Although data is extremely difficult to obtain. Robinson believes that survivor guilt can swell to such extreme proportions that it can lead to the ultimate act of aggression against the self : suicide.[93] Berkowitz, not dealing with survivors or refugees, similarly states: "...it is clear that many suicides are extreme attacks upon the self arising from guilt and self blame."[94] There is a high incidence of suicide in some areas where refugees have settled,[95] but at the time of the field research there was no way of comparing this rate with other areas or determining whether refugees account for a disproportionate number of suicides in those areas in which they are found. One interesting point, however, is that unlike other areas of India, men, whom we hypothesized would feel survivor guilt more severely than women, account for more suicides than women.[96]

Although early studies of aggression simplistically hypothesized clearcut relationships between frustration and aggression we now know that the kinkages are extremely complex.[97] If aggressive sentiments directed at others are subject to mutation into projection, displacement, repression, etc., there is little reason to doubt that aggressive sentiments directed inwards can also be transformed and redirected. Such an explanation becomes even more persuasive when one reads that in the past suicide and masochism have been seen as last resorts when, because of extreme inhibition through fear of punishment, the self was the only target against which one could aggress. We are hypothesizing a reverse course. The refugee, we have seen, is not afraid of punishment. Indeed he is invulnerable and can let loose on his surroundings all the self-loathing bottled up within him.

Before going into the concept of aggression, which is an extremely complex one, (to which an entire chapter will be devoted), let us discuss projection and paranoia which, as more familiar concepts do not require as extensive treatment. Projection of hostile sentiments can result in paranoia, the feeling that others are aggressing against one. Lifton tells us that Harry Stack Sullivan saw paranoia as a transformation of the distressing notion "I have something wrong with me" into the only slightly less distressing "He does something to me."[98] The notion of having "something wrong" with him is not a new one to the refugee. First of all he has long realized that he has been victimized because of an innate characteristic, his identity as a Hindu or Sikh. What he is has proven to be more significant in his life than who he is. Second, once he reaches safety, he takes on another hated identity and becomes a "refugee." As a refugee he must cope with the counterfeit nurturance which tries to reaffirm his helplessness. Today psychiatry emphasizes the relationship between paranoid states and severe dependency conflicts.[99] The ambivalence of the refugee over counterfeit nurturance is such a dependency conflict. Once again the refugee finds that through no fault of his own a label has been appended to him which will determine whether he will receive the sustenance necessary for life or not. To live, at least in the immediate period he must embrace the hated identity and become totally dependent. Individual merit has nothing to do with his case. Even the once comforting notions of caste cannot save him from the degradation of the title "refugee" if he is to gain sustenance. Rage that has been diffused becomes concentrated and focussed during this reception period. For a while he wants to kill not only those he sees as responsible for his troubles but perhaps everyone he comes into contact with. These sentiments in most cases are short lived and a transformation takes place. Delusions that others want to kill him through nurturance develop. Lifton goes on to note that the mistrust commented on earlier represents a meeting ground between the oft-made artificial distinctions between paranoia and depression[100] with their "characteristic" behavioural results: murder and suicide. We too note the close relationship of these two states stemming from guilt.

The internal states of the refugee can be summed up as follows: Feeling guilty about survival priority, or for having been untrue to his religious identity, or for having had rebellious tendencies during flight, the refugee will harbour aggressive sentiments toward himself. Through the mechanism of projection of the hatred he feels for himself he comes to feel that everyone hates him and is aggressing against him.

If projection is linked to paranoia, displacement is linked to aggression and scapegoating. Since aggression among the invulnerable is punishment free they may act with impunity, retargeting the aggression they wish to commit against themselves to other, safer objects. A later chapter will examine the nature of aggression and how the concept has been used and measured in the past.

The open-ended interviews on refugee experience were not structured enough to allow an estimation of individual aggressiveness or paranoia. Yet I wanted to see whether such traits actually did exist and whether they would explain the oft-noted correlations between refugee presence and interpersonal aggression. Attitudes about economic life were felt to be an important element not uncovered during the open-ended interview. The open-ended interview, being an account of what the respondent thought, felt, and did during his flight from West Punjab 1947, had not been undergone by any non-refugees. To at least partly validate the statements made in this chapter would require a comparison of refugee attitudes with those of non-refugees. To achieve this comparability and to gain more data with greater precision a formal questionnaire was administered to seventy-three refugees and fifty-three non-refugees. Later chapters will discuss the problems encountered and the conclusions reached in this portion of the research.

Summary

It would be wise at this point to summarize this rather lengthy chapter. The stages of refugeeism may be divided into three phases : warning and impact, flight, and resettlement and return to normal life. In each of these the individual must cope with different issues not the least important of which is survival.

In the warning and impact period, the victim must first of all recognize and assess the threat, then decide when to leave, and re-evaluate his relations with protective powers. From the initial impact until he joins a caravan, he is apt to see himself as a target for the wrath of the world, abandoned by all who might save him. At this point, as danger intensifies, those who are less able to cope with it become dazed or act inappropriately. Whether he is alone in flight or in a group one regains some of the sense that he can act with effect. As one joins larger groups the feeling of centrality is replaced by one of collective guilt but this is soon dissipated as a sense of resentment and rage develops.

After crossing to safety one must obtain sustenance or die.[101] The "post-disaster utopia" flies by faster for the refugee than it does for the disaster victim because he is in direct competition with the local non-refugees for the goods and land left behind by the Muslims. On the other hand subsistence from government is resented as "counterfeit nurturance" and a mistrust of government officials develops. For those refugees interned on arrival the horror of life in the camps leads them to flee the camps as rapidly as possible. Despite the reluctance to accept subsistence grants, aid aimed at restitution or compensation that could put a man back on his feet is received with gratitude.

As people are able to start working again the sense of efficacy first regenerated by joining a caravan grows. Work also helps dissipate the apathy caused by guilt over rebellious tendencies. In the resettlement period the refugee has time to think about his situation. Needing to blame someone for his plight, he assails the leaders of his own country. Soon however, since he is a model for the nation and those whom *he* admires at least pay lip service to the memories of Gandhi, he reduces dissonance and shifts the blame from his own leaders to the leaders of the country that drove him out and to the now impotent British.

During the resettlement phase a number of developments occur that endure long after the refugee has reestablished himself. Foremost among these is the sense of invulnerability that grows as the refugee realizes that he has come through it all safely. This sense of invulnerability manifests itself in a heightened willingness to take risks (although to the invulnerable man there is no risk). In an economy of scarcity where others do not share these sentiments about risk-taking such attitudes may lead to individual gain and community-wide economic development. The second long-lasting effect of flight and its associated trauma is guilt. Guilt may result from having survived where others did not and/or from not living up to ideals of one's religion. Guilt is seen as anger directed inward and is capable of undergoing those transformations which normal anger may, including a change into aggression which may be outward or inward. The two major outcomes of the refugee experience then are the sense of invulnerability and the sense of guilt that emerge after safety has been reached. Both can be seen as intervening variables: the former leading to risk-taking and the latter to aggressive behaviour.

REFERENCES

1. Joseph B. Schechtman, *The Refugee in the World,* New York: A. S. Barnes, 1963, quoting J. Nanda, p. 101.

2. *Ibid.*, p. 108. Schechtman summarizes the conflicting estimates of casualties. Estimates of deaths in partition disorders range from Nehru's deliberately low estimate (to maintain peace) of twenty to thirty thousand killed to the official estimates of the govern-

ments involved. The Pakistani authorities claimed one million *Muslims* had been killed or abducted while Indian authorities, using a ten per cent of population transferred rule of thumb, felt at least one million deaths were attributable to partition.

3. The West Punjab with its 5.3 million cultivable acres includes the rich canal colonies that had given the name "breadbasket of India" to the state. The East Punjab, on the other hand, had only 4.1 million semi-arid, unirrigated, and generally poorer acres. Before partition the Muslims had been mainly artisans and agricultural labourers while the Hindus were shopkeepers and landlords and the Sikhs cultivators. Hindus had left behind 51,000 shops, Muslims 17,000.

4. See Tarlok Singh, *Rural Resettlement in Punjab*, Mimeo, July, 1950 for the problems which seniormost officials in charge of refugeeism had to face. For a discussion of local problems of rehabilitation see Ravi Vermani, *Partition and its Social Problems in East Punjab*, unpublished M. A. thesis, Madras School of Social Work, 1957. Also of interest are M. S. Randhawa, *Out of the Ashes*, Bombay: C. N. Raman, (1954), and the actual resettlement manual for officials: Tarlok Singh, *Land Resettlement Manual*, Simla: Government of Punjab, 1952.

5. John G. Stoessinger, *The Refugee and the World Community*, Minneapolis : University of Minnesota Press, 1956, p. 189.

6. Hannah Arendt, *The Origins of Totalitarianism*, New York : Harcourt Brace, 1951, p. 298.

7. There is no scarcity of news items dealing with crime and violence identify the aggressive actor(s) as a refugee. Thus we find : "Tibetans in India Attack Chinese," *New York Times*, December 31, 1968; "S. I. Ferry Rider Stabbed to Death as Result of Feud," *New York Times*, February 6, 1969; "3,000 Angry Cuban Exiles Besiege Playboy Club," *New York Times*, November 7, 1966; "Yugoslav Feud in West Germany Grows Bolder," *New York Times*, September 13, 1966; "Irked by Argentine Red Tape Pensioner Kills Welfare Clerk," *New York Times*, February 12, 1965. For a report closer to the area of this research see "Pattern of Murders in Karnal," *The Tribune* (Ambala), August 17, 1967.

8. K. C. Cirtautas, *The Refugee : A Psychological Study*, Boston: Meador, 1957, and S. A. Prins, "The Individual in Flight," in H. B. M. Murphy, *et al.*, *Flight and Resettlement*, Paris : UNESCO, 1955.

9. Martha Wolfenstein, *Disaster : A Psychological Essay*, Glencoe: Free Press, 1957.

10. John Walker Powell quoted in Donald B. Robinson, *The Face of Disaster*, New York : Doubleday, 1959, p. 39. Powell has devised a taxonomy of disasters based on whether the impact is single or prolonged, limited or extensive in effect, with or without warning (pp. 43 ff.). The case of refugees generally would be one of prolonged or repetitive impact, extensive effects but giving its victims some warning if they are alert.

11. William H. Form and Sigmund Nosow, *Community in Disaster*, New York: Harpers, 1958, p. 11.

12. Schechtman, *op. cit.*, p. 369.

13. Robert Jay Lifton, *Death in Life : Survivors of Hiroshima*, New York: Random House, 1967. For a more journalistic account of what occurred at the instant of atomic bomb impact see Frank W. Chinnock, *Nagasaki : The Forgotten Bomb*, New York: World, 1969.

14. I have paraphrased the elements cited by Robinson in *op. cit.*

15. For descriptions of the tone of relationships within Hindu families see Aline Ross, *The Hindu Family in its Urban Setting*, Toronto: University of Toronto Press, 1961, and Irawati Karve, *Kinship Organization in India,* Bombay: Asia, 1965.

16. Although in recent years the docility and dependence of the general population has come under attack by the authorities as "ma-baapism" the concept is very much alive and one still hears the term in a non-pejorative sense.

17. Penderel Moon, *Divide and Quit*, Berkeley: University of California Press, 1962.

18. S. Pedersen, "Reaching Safety," in Murphy, *op. cit.*, p. 35.

19. Lifton, *op. cit.*, p. 383.

20. Wolfenstein, *op. cit.*, pp. 51-56.

21. This seems to have been the universal reaction among atomic bomb victims at Nagasaki as well. See Chinnock, *op. cit.*

22. Robinson, *op. cit.*, pp. 183 ff. and Wolfenstein, *op. cit.*, p. 200.

23. See Everett Hagen, *On the Theory of Social Change*, Homewood : The Dorsey Press, 1962, for the relationship between child rearing and views of the supernatural, pp. 123-182.

24. Wolfenstein believes that separation from loved ones is a critical variable in the subsequent post-disaster readjustment and

that one of the most common syndromes among victims is "separation anxiety." Wolfenstein, *op. cit.*, p. 157.

25. One point which may be missed in our exposition is that in most cases the actual time in motion was relatively short. But few people came directly and with the breakdown of all services there were long delays at every stage of the journey. At consolidation points camps were set up where the refugees languished sometimes for months before getting their turn to make the final dash for safety. It often turned out that one was no safer waiting than he had been in travelling. Rather, one became more visible and the attacking forces multiplied. At the same time the boredom and unchanging daily cycle of life in the camp magnified the strains of living under the threat of death.

26. Louise Pinsky in Murphy, *op. cit.*, p. 56.

27. Margaret Parton, "India's Great Migration," *New York Herald Tribune*, December 13, 1947.

28. For some idea of how demoralizing life in a refugee camp could become see J. S. Bright, *Scandals of a Refugee Camp*, New Delhi : Tagore Memorial Publications, 1948: Balwant Singh Anand, *Cruel Interlude*, Bombay : Asia, 1961.

29. See Robinson, *op. cit.*, p. 185.

30. For a discussion of "D.P. Apathy" see Eduard Bakis, "D.P. Apathy," in Murphy, *op. cit.*, pp. 76-88. For the analogous concepts in natural disaster see Wolfenstein, *op. cit.*, Part III, "Aftermath." Lifton found the same characteristic among *hibakusha* and termed it "closing off" or "psychic numbing." Lifton, *op.cit.*, pp. 500 ff.

31. "Psychiatrist Stresses Trauma of Nazi Camps," *New York Times*, December 1, 1966. Other observers, Lifton most eloquently, have remarked on the persistence of survivor guilt.

32. Pedersen, *op. cit.*, p. 39.

33. Lifton, *op. cit.*, p. 504.

34. See Anand, *op. cit.*, and Bright, *op. cit.*

35. Wolfenstein, *op. cit.*, p. 168.

36. M. Gaertner, "A Comparison of Refugee and Non-Refugee Immigrants to New York City," in Murphy, *op. cit.*, p. 104.

37. Gardner Murphy, *In the Minds of Men*, New York : Basic Books, 1953, p. 193.

38. Lifton, *op. cit.*, sections on "Closing Off," pp. 500 ff.

39. Stoessinger, *op. cit.*, p. 193.

40. Wolfenstein, *op. cit.*, p. 191.

41. H. Stern, "The Aftermath of Belsen," in Murphy, *op. cit.*, p. 70.

42. I hope in further research to show that such indeed is the case and that differences between Punjabi and Bengali refugees are more due to this facet of resettlement than to "inherent" differences between Bengalis and Punjabis.

43. The pogroms on both sides of the border, while couched in religio-political terms, were in large measure aimed at the seizure of property of the minority group. This was especially so where the conflict was confined to the inhabitants of a single village. Evidence of this is the fact that on either side if you had no claim to land you were welcome. In Pakistan menial and artisan castes were urged to stay on for the simple reason that without them the ill-gotten acreage would be uncultivable. Landlords, on the other hand, were almost invariably threatened with extreme violence if they considered staying on but often were escorted safely from the village when they did decide to leave. Similarly on the "new" side of the border conflicts were mainly between members of landowning groups. Those with no claim to land were welcomed by the established non-refugees of the village in an attempt to fill the gap caused by the migration of Muslim agricultural labourers. Many members of these lower castes made a relatively easy transition to their new life but many remained loyal to their old landlords.

44. Robinson, *op. cit.*, p. 181.

45. This is consonant with the findings of the United States Strategic Bombing Survey which noted that civilian populations who had been bombed during World War II felt relatively little hostility towards the countries dropping the bombs as compared with the hostility they felt towards their own leaders for having not protected them.

46. Another root of the early hostility between refugees and local people is that in many cases the local people were viewed as having caused the troubles which struck the refugees. The reasoning goes that if the non-refugees had not attacked the Muslims or even had treated them better there would not have been a Pakistan or at least not the carnage which attended its birth. Since in many cases refugees were held hostage by Pakistani officials for the safe conduct of Muslim refugees, they actually did have to pay in blood for the atrocities of their co-religionists.

47. Wolfenstein, *op. cit.*, p. 153. Miss Wolfenstein believes that apprehensiveness about a recurrence of the disaster is a function of the lack of preparedness for the one which has just occurred.

48. Lifton, *op. cit.*, pp. 193 ff. This reluctance to accept relief and contempt for those who do was thought by Wolfenstein to be a uniquely American phenomenon (*op. cit.*, p. 194). Lifton however showed that Japanese *hibakusha* exhibited the same attitudes. The refugees in Punjab-Haryana likewise often bragged that they had not accepted aid. This makes me believe the anxiety over counterfeit nurturance is universal.

49. For an account of what life can be like in such circumstances one need only turn to the literature of the concentration camps. See Primo Levi, *Survival in Auschwitz*, New York : Collier Books, 1961. For a somewhat less literary approach but one pertinent to our study see Bright, *op. cit.*

50. See Randhawa, *op. cit.*, pp. 74-92, for the ideological problems of resettlement and the philosophical bases for the "quasi-permanent" allotment of evacuee land.

51. For a description of the arguments on graded land cuts and the concept of the standard acre see *ibid.*, pp. 93-107.

52. Cf. Wolfenstein, *op. cit.*, p. 194.

53. Prins, *op. cit.*, p. 30.

54. Lifton, *op. cit.*, p. 318.

55. Irving Janis, *Air War and Emotional Stress : Psychological Studies of Bombing and Civilian Defence*, New York : McGraw Hill, 1951.

56. Robinson, *op. cit.*, p. 191.

57. The *Statesman*, reporting on Dr. Sushila Nayar's testimony before the Gandhi Murder Conspiracy Commission (J. L. Kapur Commission), stated, "She said Gandhiji did his best to protect the minorities and this caused a certain amount of discontent among the refugees. When he undertook a fast in January 1948 some refugees began shouting 'Gandhiji Ko Marne Do (let Gandhiji die)'..." "Gandhiji Suspected Conspiracy Behind Bomb Explosion," *Statesman*, January 18, 1968.

58. For a discussion of the various explanations of this phenomenon see Roger Brown, "Models of Attitude Change," in Brown, *et al.*, *New Directions in Psychology*, New York : Holt Rinehart and Winston, 1962.

59. For an example of the disdain and contempt that Punjabis

felt for other Indians see Rudyard Kipling, "The Head of the District" and "The Enlightenment of Pagett, M. P.," *In Black and White*, New York: Scribners, 1897.

60. For reasons of the Congress' failure to capture the sympathies of the Punjabis see Baldev Raj Nayar, *Minority Politics in Punjab*, Princeton: Princeton University Press, 1966.

61. Wolfenstein, *op. cit.*, p. 213.

62. Gardner Murphy, *op. cit.*; Bakis, *op. cit.*

63. Others have observed that the victim identity is often cherished rather than disguised. Thus Nazi concentration camp inmates hold annual reunions, issue commemorative recordings, etc. ("1,000 Nazi Death Camp Survivors Meet Here," *New York Times*, November 25, 1965) and Armenian survivors of Turkish massacres take out large newspaper advertisements to commemorate the date ("April 24, 1915: The Day a Nation Was Sentenced to Death," *New York Times*, April 24, 1966)

64. See R. N. Saksena, *Refugees : A Study in Changing Attitudes*, Bombay: Asia, 1961, for a study of relationships between refugees and non-refugees in the market of Dehra Dun. Saksena places most of his emphasis on attitudes but does discuss the success of the refugees in taking over large sections of the bazaar. Also see Pars Ram, *A UNESCO Study of Social Tensions in Aligarh 1950-51*, Ahmedabad: New Order Book Company, 1955.

65. "Pulling Down of Refugee's Shop," *The Tribune* (Ambala), May 2, 1968.

66. Wolfenstein, *op. cit.*, p. 187.

67. Louise Pinsky in H. B. M. Murphy, *op. cit.*, p. 50.

68. Wolfenstein, *op. cit.*, p. 158.

69. *Ibid.*, p. 186.

70. This is one of the points made repeatedly in Gunnar Myrdal's *Asian Drama*, New York : Pantheon, 1968, but the argument is not a new one : Compare McKim Marriott, "Technological Change in Overdeveloped Rural Areas," *Economic Development and Cultural Change*, I, pp. 261-272. Marriott argued persuasively that the interrelationships of economic scarcity and individual attitudes prevented adoption of innovations in rural India. Going back to the same village in western Uttar Pradesh a decade later he found that the changes he had earlier thought unlikely had been in fact adopted. "Return to Kishengarhi," talk before the South Asia Seminar, University of Chicago, April 9, 1969. The implication is that in

the interim attitudes changed so that what was earlier seen as a very risky gamble was now regarded as a "sure thing." Obviously this is not what is being discussed here. For the types of "risks" which non-refugees are willing to incur see Richard G. Fox, *From Zamindar to Ballot Box*, Ithaca : Cornell University Press, 1969.

71. Robert J. Lifton, "Psychological Effects of the Atomic Bomb," in George H. Grosser, Henry Wechsler, and Milton Greenblatt, eds., *The Threat of Impending Disaster*, Cambridge, Mass. : M. I. T. Press, 1964.

72. Others too have found that traits related to earlier victimization endure over time. See William G. Niederland, "Psychiatric Disorders Among Persecution Victims," *Journal of Nervous and Mental Diseases*, CXXXIX, 1964, pp. 458-474. On a less pathological level we have already noted many victimized groups maintaining their identities. See also "Study Confirms Survivor Guilt," *New York Times*, May 7, 1965.

73. Lifton, *Death in Life : Survivors of Hiroshima*, *op. cit.*

74. Niederland, *op. cit.*

75. Prins, *op. cit.*, p. 29.

76. Pedersen, *op. cit.*

77. Robinson, *op. cit.*

78. "Study Confirms Survivor Guilt," *New York Times*, May 7, 1965.

79. Ross, *op. cit.*

80. A Punjabi folktale tells how Alexander the Great was forced to spare the life of King Porus whom he had just defeated because one of Porus's sisters or handmaidens had earlier played Rakhi (Raksha Bandhan) with Alexander but had deferred claiming her boon. When Porus had been defeated and was about to be executed she demanded that Alexander grant her the boon of saving Porus's life.

81. Ross, *op. cit.*

82. Although Sikhism started as a movement to reconcile Hinduism and Islam the intolerance and persecution of the Moghul emperors, especially Aurangzeb, forced Sikhism away from Islam and closer to Hinduism. Sikhism came to be looked upon by many Hindus as a branch of Hinduism and Sikhs, although they denied this, took Hindu brides and acted as self appointed protectors of the less military inclined Hindus. In gratitude until recently many Hindu families raised one of their sons as a Sikh.

83. On Baisakhi (a spring festival) day 1699, Guru Gobind Singh took the final step in turning what had started as a reform movement designed to bring Muslims and Hindus together into a distinct militaristic religion. After a psychological ordeal he selected five followers to form the *khalsa* or pure and enjoined all Sikhs to take up the emblems of the *khalsa*. These emblems known as the five K's (because the Punjabi word for each begins with a K sound) are uncut hair and beard (*kes*), a steel bangle (*kara*), a wooden comb (*kangha*), a dagger (*kirpan*), and special underwear suited for a warrior (*kaccha*). There have been many interpretations of the symbolism of these emblems in terms ranging from religious to military utility but the explanation most commonly put forward is that Guru Gobind Singh wanted his followers to be conspicuous. If they were visible, he reasoned, when challenged about their faith they could not shrink and claim to be something else but would be forced to renounce the faith or fight and only those who were prepared to fight for the faith were to wear the emblems of the *khalsa*. Nowadays a boy is confirmed into the religion at about the age of puberty by undergoing the Sikh form of baptism (drinking sugared water) and assuming the five K's.

84. The Sikhs, by fighting back not only for themselves but for the Hindus, had earned the enmity of the Muslims as long back as 1950. In the British suppression of the Mutiny, especially in the re-capture of Delhi, Sikhs played a prominent role. The outcome of that campaign, the exile of the last of the Moghuls, Mohammed Bahadur Shah had not been forgotten. But there was another more pragmatic reason for the fact that the Lahore branch of the Muslim League offered Rs. 250 for a Sikh head and only Rs. 100 for a Hindu head. With blood-lust running high in the city the leaders of the League wanted to be sure that Muslims didn't start bringing in each other's heads. Since it was almost impossible to palm off a Muslim head as a Sikh head they offered more for the latter. The more enterprising among the *goondas* (hooligans) often were able to circumvent this precaution by cutting off the heads of young women and turning them in as those of Sikhs too young to have beards.

85. Gangs of police were often roaming about committing atrocities in the disorganization of partition. Where British officers remained discipline was slightly better but with communications broken down even they had a difficult time in controlling the police. The respondent, along with 600 others, after fleeing from

a large massacre, was "arrested".

86. Guru Teg Bahadur, taken captive by the Moghuls, was brought to Delhi to face the Emperor Aurangzeb. When ordered to deny his faith or be killed he replied that his religion was so great that he could produce a charm that would save his life from the head-man. When asked to prove it he wrote on a piece of paper, tied it in a small pouch around his neck and put his head on the block. The head-man's axe severed his neck and the emperor was enraged at not having been able to torture the Guru. Curious at the charm, he ordered it brought to him. When the pouch was opened and the paper was found it had written on it, "I lose my head but not my faith."

The two young sons of Guru Gobind Singh were betrayed and taken to the Muslim governor of Sirhind. When they refused to renounce their father and their religion he ordered them walled up alive. Half way through the proceedings he offered them another chance which they turned down with the words, "Begone, miscreant; quench they (sic) thirst for blood, we are sons of the great Guru Gobind Singh. Fear approacheth us not. We would rather lose our lives at the hands of the Malechhas (the polluted)." (Bhagat Lakshman Singh, *Sikh Martyrs*, Ludhiana : Lahore Book Shop, 1923.)

87. There is one case of an eminent Sikh placing his life before his religious principles. Ram Rai, son of the seventh Guru, Har Rai, was summoned to Aurangzeb. Questioned on a passage in the Sikh sacred scriptures which was derogatory to Muslims, in recitation he changed the reference from "Mussalman" to *be-iman* (faithless). For this breach of faith he was excommunicated and although he was later established as a sort of puppet Guru by the Moghuls, his followers never were very numerous. These followers were later declared heretics by Guru Gobind Singh.

88. This is not the "identification with the aggressor" noted by Bruno Bettelheim in "Individual and Mass Behaviour in Extreme Situations," *Journal of Abnormal and Social Psychology*, XXXVIII, 1943, pp. 417-452, where one psychically embraces the identity of the oppressor and proceeds to persecute his fellows on the same grounds as does the original oppressor.

89. The only feature which distinguishes a Hindu (or a shaven Sikh) from a Muslim is his lack of circumcision. During partition checks were made on both the Indian and Pakistani sides to

ensure that no one was passing himself off falsely.

90. There is virtue in enduring hardship for *dharma* as in the case of Maharaja Hariscandra and the crow in the conclusion of the Tulsi Das *Ramayana*, but these trials are undergone as penance with a spirit of patient humility rather than the defiance of a martyr. One exception often raised by Indians is the Rani of Jhansi, heroine of the Indian Mutiny, but she is more of a martyr to feudalism or perhaps (as some would like to believe) to nationalism than to Hinduism.

91. Lifton, *op. cit.*, p. 497.

92. Leonard Berkowitz, *Aggression : A Social Psychological Analysis*, New York : McGraw-Hill Book Company, 1962, p. 32. The next chapter will discuss the various conceptions of "aggression" and attempts to measure aggressiveness.

93. Robinson, *op. cit.*, p. 83.

94. Berkowitz, *op. cit.*, p. 324.

95. See various routine articles in the Indian press, e.g. "153 Suicides in Delhi Last Year," *The Tribune* (Ambala), May 25, 1967.

96. *Ibid.* See Ross, *op. cit.*, p. 117 for the reasons for female suicide.

97. See Berkowitz, *op. cit.*, for an analysis which manages to integrate earlier views to fresh viewpoint.

98. Lifton, *op. cit.*, p. 514.

99. *Ibid.* p. 514.

100. *Ibid.*, p. 515.

101. Schechtman reports that of the 40,000-50,000 Muslims who flocked into Bahawalpur State in September 1947, 2,000 died within a few days. Schechtman, *op. cit.*, p. 109.

CHAPTER IV

Aggression and Invulnerability

At bottom no one believes in his own death...(and) in the unconscious every one of us is convinced of his own immortality.

—Freud

The previous chapter discussed certain psychological outgrowths of the refugee experience. Specifically, hypotheses were raised that the violence and trauma led to a sense of guilt and a feeling of invulnerability. The guilt in turn was transformed into paranoia and hostility or aggression. A sense of invulnerability also emerged which is manifested to others as what appears to be a willingness to take risks. Obviously, even aside from their etiology, all are intimately intertwined. For aggression to take place the aggressor must usually feel sufficiently invulnerable so that the fear of punishment does not immobilize him. The paranoia that stems from the guilt (which can be viewed as hostility turned inward) may be displaced as hostility to other groups. Then this hostility, combined with a sense of invulnerability, may lead to aggressive behaviour against the object of the displaced sentiments. In the next several chapters the methods utilized to measure the attitudes and behaviours associated with each of these characteristics will be discussed. Aggression, as we have discussed, is the most complex of these.

Psychologists differ on the definition of aggression. And, they disagree even more strongly (even aggressively) on how to operationalize the construct. Aggression is a very broad term ; consider how many different behaviours could be subsumed by one of the most widely cited definitions to be found in the psychological literature: "any action, thought, or impulse the presumed aim of which is physical or psychological injury, either real or symbolic, to an individual or surrogate"[1], compound these by the almost infinite number of possible targets (often unrecognizable as such), and some idea can be gained of the difficulties involved.[2]

The research project upon which this volume is based was predicated upon the assumption that aggressive acts may be of great consequence to political life.[3] After all, the political system is based on the legitimate use of force. When the monopoly of the state regarding the use of force is challenged by the acts of individuals or groups what results may be a transformation of all social life in a particular area. At one end of a continuum of illegitimate aggressive acts there is the sporadic rage of some groups of black American ghetto dwellers, unleashed without discrimination against the forces of a society that is seen as repressing them. On another level there is the act of the lone political assassin whose displacement of his personal conflicts to a specific target may upend empires. At a third level of analysis, the mass level, interpersonal aggression may be of momentous import for the political system even when not aimed at political structures or figures. This is especially so in the developing nations.

Any society having a high level of unchannelled aggression will find the agencies responsible for order maintenance severely taxed. Considering the nature of the developing societies with regard to economics, communications, the state of integration, etc., governments are likely to find that channelling these aggressive forces into constructive action for the improvement of society is difficult, if not impossible. The government that finds itself with a highly aggressive population is in the cruel dilemma of deciding whether to put sorely needed resources into bolstering the agencies of law and order and thereby slowing down economic development or using the resources in economically productive ways at the possible price of creating a society so strife-ridden that the routine business of government and the economy cannot proceed.[4] And, if economic development does not proceed at a rate acceptable to the public, anomic street demonstrations may not only destroy capital investment sources of wealth such as factories but may frighten off potential investors from other areas of the country or world. In such ways the tensions that exist within a society are released in acts that may be destructive of the orderly political process and that at the same time may exacerbate the frustrations that led to their release. Moreover, as the strains on the economic system in the form of unfulfilable demands force the regime to invest in repression a heretofore apathetic public may become politicized and in the process be transformed from an atomized mass with only individual, unfocussed aggressive drives into a mob both willing and able to vent its collective aggressiveness on its legitimate rulers.

Is there a way out of this rather discouraging spiral of underdevelopment and decay ? Is the existence of a high level of aggression likely to be dysfunctional in all cases in the developing areas ? Not necessarily. If we may be permitted the use of the terms of psychoanalysis to describe the collective psyche of a nation we can say that aggressive drives are subject to a number of transformations that may indeed be beneficial for a society. If policy makers can manipulate the psychological needs of their constituents, i.e., if policies are promulgated that enable the populace individually and collectively to redirect or modify their aggressive drives, enough time may be bought to stabilize the situation. Use of analogues of the defence mechanisms of projection and sublimation are likely to be the most productive although it is not difficult to see how even repression might serve to buy the time necessary for development to progress. Projection of hostile desires to an external enemy may be the quickest way to develop a sense of national identity in these areas and may also foster the spirit of integration with the society. Or, aggressive drives may be sublimated and placed in the service of economic development. This may be especially true when conditions favourable to synergistic activity can be created (see Chapter VI). If such conditions can be generated by judicious planning it is not unreasonable to predict that economic development might occur rapidly enough to sap remaining communal aggressive drives that have not been sublimated, perhaps through the creation of leisure time activities that would provide for further opportunities for sublimation.

What does all this mean at the individual level ? Psychologists tell us few individuals are uniformly aggressive in all spheres of life.[5] This research project hypothesized that aggressiveness was likely to result from the events of 1947. That is, Punjabi refugees, especially those who underwent extreme violence were expected to be more aggressive than Punjabi non-refugees, but the spheres in which they would be aggressive were unclear. Particularly we were interested in whether those attitudinal components of the aggressive personality that grant legitimacy to certain aggressive acts aimed at specific targets could be ascertained and in learning the independent variables that were related to these attitudinal components and to aggression.

It is immediately apparent that aside from theoretical problems involved in the measurement of aggression there are very substantial methodological problems that must be faced. especially in underdeveloped nations. Most people in any society are likely to be somewhat reticent about the aggressive acts in which they take part and this is apt to make interviewing a very frustrating job. Furthermore, questions that might be considered of a sensitive nature by the authorities must be eliminated from schedules or approached obliquely. In this project it also seemed desirable that emphasis be placed on the attitudinal components of aggression to see if new measures suitable for mass research projects could be developed. Nevertheless, despite the difficulty of getting direct measures and our bias toward attitudinal measures some indicators of actual aggressive behaviour were desired if only to validate some of the new measures of aggression (indices developed specifically for this project) and some of the more traditional measures not heretofore used in the Punjab-Haryana region, e.g. TATs.

Measurement

Because of these conditions and views and because previous work that had tired to get direct measures of personality aggression had proved so fruitless outside clinical and experimental situations it was felt that a new approach was called for. This new approach was a multi-pronged attack on the concept. First specific aggressive acts would be measured, then aggression was to be distilled into what were seen to be constituent parts in the hope that these might be easier to measure in a large population. The measurement was to be carried out using an interview schedule in addition to conventional TATs that had been modified for Indian use.[6]

From the interview schedule we wanted some indication of how aggressive the respondent was in "real life". Since aggression is generally conceived of as a behavioural concept manifested by an interpersonal act the obvious starting point in such a campaign to determine aggressiveness would be to discover whatever possible about the aggressive acts in which an individual may be involved.

Three separate series of questions on the interview schedule dealt with behavioural aggression at three levels: within the family, within the village or neighbourhood, and aggression that is punished by society. The first inquired directly of the subject whether he ever had to beat his children, how often this occurred and the reasons for the beatings. The second asked how often the respondent became involved in fights or arguments, with whom he fought and the causes and disposition of the conflict. The last series asked whether the subject had ever been arrested, how frequently and the alleged offences. It was recognized that a man may aggress against other targets than his children or family members and that aggression outside the family does not always lead to fights or arrests but the measures proposed were seen as useful for other reasons. Aggression against children by parents is almost entirely risk-free and the dyad symbolizes to a great extent the power relationships within a hierarchical traditional society. Fighting, to the average man, is much less risk-free and to a certain extent represents the degree to which a man may aggress against equals. Aggression contrary to societal norms is fraught with danger and exemplifies high risk activity. In addition to these theoretical considerations the direct approach using such questions was expected to not only overcome reticence on the part of the respondents but to allay any fears and suspicions the authorities might have had regarding the purpose of our presence.

Punishment of Children

The immediate task was to ascertain whether refugees were behaviourally more aggressive than non-refugees. The first of three series of questions aimed at getting accurate estimates of the behavioural aggressiveness of each group with regard to socially sanctioned aggression : punishment of children for misdeeds either actual or fancied. Considering only those respondents with children we found that among both groups physical punishment of children was fairly common. In response to the questions "Do you ever have to beat your children ?" "How often ?" and "For what offences ?" Four of every five refugees having children (77.2%) and more than half the non-refugees with children (55.0%) admitted beating their children at least once a year. (The word "beating" was used to eliminate the more casual connotations of "hit" or the possibly affectionate slap.) The fact that both groups see corporal punishment as an effective method of dealing with children should not be surprising: it has long been noted that family heads in traditional and transitional societies are more apt to use physical coercion than the more subtle pressures used in the modern West.[7] What is surprising however is the frequency with which the Punjabis and Haryanvis beat their children: 47.3 per cent of the refugees and 22.5 per cent of the non-refugees beat their children more than once a month, a figure certainly high by

TABLE 4.1

Frequency of Child Beating

	Per Cent Replying	
Frequency (only R's with children)	*Refugee*	*Non-Refugee*
Rarely (less than once a year)	22.8	45.0
Occasionally (once—several times a year)	29.9	32.5
Often (several times a month or week, or daily)	47.3	22.5
Total	100.0 %	100.0%
N	(57)	(40)
$x^2 = 6.85$	df = 2	p = .03

Western standards. These are rather large proportions even for India when we consider that a father involved in agriculture, or in trade to a lesser extent, is away from home and children from before dawn until after dark daily for the greater part of the year. Among refugees and non-refugees the most frequent reason given for beating children was disobedience: roughly half of each group, 46.6 per cent of the refugees and 49.1 per cent of the non-refugees, gave this response.

A Punjabi proverb advises fathers:

"Treat your son like a Rajah for the first five years,
like a slave for the next ten and then as a friend."

Clearly during the middle period a son is considered fair game for any sort of aggressive behaviour from his father. But since the period is only about one-half the time which a son spends at home before marriage and because the first five years and the period after fifteen are not part of the "open season" on him, the figures will be an underestimate to the extent that the sample contains respondents who are new husbands (their children will be young and hence "treated like Rajahs") or older men (their children will be treated "as friends"). For those in their prime years who produce a good many children it would be reasonable to expect that at least one son would be between five and fifteen.

The figures support the contention that there is a significant difference in the levels of aggression of refugees and non-refugees despite the finding that the non-refugees also punish their children severely and frequently. It is our belief that a certain baseline of aggressiveness exists in the population and that the difference between non-refugees and refugees is attributable to the experiences undergone in becoming a refugee. Before going on to discuss the factors creating the difference the concept of baseline aggressiveness must be discussed.

For many years observers have noted the contradictory traits of non-violence and violence in the Indian personality. Much of the nineteenth century British popular literature about the Empire had to do with the violent side of Indian life: *The Moonstone* told of a fanatical sect willing to go to any lengths to retrieve a precious jewel belonging to their deity, *Kim* and other works of Kipling dealt with the goings on of fierce warriors on the frontier. Accounts of *thugee* and the history of the mutiny also added to this literature (and perhaps told as much about the eager audiences these works found as about the Indians they represented). These descriptions and stereotypes were not entirely fanciful however. In recent years a number of social scientists have reached similar conclusions and have examined the roots of this basic aggressiveness. Joseph Elder believes that a good deal of the aggression against family members, animals and subordinates is universal in north India and perhaps the entire subcontinent. As Elder has put it:

> This hostility, if that is what it was, was exhibited on a number of occasions in what seemed to be needless cruelty expressed toward animals, children, and elderly persons. Children, especially, and even adults, would kick dogs and their puppies or hit them with sticks until they were thoroughly cowed. I often felt that the way adults teased children by pinching them or repeatedly withdrawing proffered goodies was a thinly-disguised form of aggression. Parents were occasionally carried away in their efforts to punish insufficiently humbled children. During the course of one year I treated three or four children's ears that had been torn along the base by the wrench of a furious parent...

> However, in view of the fact that the above behaviour violated the official standards for concern for living creatures, care for children and respect for the aged, it seemed to me that this behaviour could not be considered "normal." Instead it suggested that there was a reservoir of free-floating inner hostility in Rajpur—hostility with its roots perhaps in the inequities of the caste hierarchy.[8]

Elder goes on to show that where hierarchical rank is established the patterns of aggression are channelled, unidirectional (from superior to subordinate) and most important of all, regulated in intensity. When two individuals whose relative rankings are indeterminate confront one another unchannelled and unregulated aggression occurs according to Elder. Further, he states that because there are hierarchies of caste, age, and sex everyone has someone subordinate to him to aggress against and even the youngest untouchable children can aggress against animals.[9]

What Elder is saying is highly significant: that caste may contribute to, channel and regulate aggressiveness, (even if this is of limited use until one has some way of measuring and comparing "strength of caste" in different regions or even getting accurate statistics on crime and arrests with which to correlate "caste strength."[10]

That caste is weak in Punjab-Haryana does not invalidate the hypothesis because although weak, caste may still play the predicted role. But Elder's views—that a certain amount of aggression is learned (consciously and unconsciously) by individuals in their normal growing up period in a caste system—although persuasive, are not universally accepted.

Other explanations of the phenomenon we have called "base-line aggression" also exist. Lois Barclay Murphy finds the roots of the wild, chaotic aggression of Indian adults in a childhood free of frustration, an anger free childhood.[11] Later when frustrations impinge upon his life the individual, who has never learned to channel his aggression, lashes out without restraint and often without focus. G. Morris Carstairs traces much of the aggressiveness that he found in high caste Hindus in Rajasthan to an unsatisfactory resolution of the Oedipal conflict that results in many of the traits we have come to associate with authoritarianism, e.g. submission, domination, fatalism, etc.[12] Gitel Steed found that many factors other than those hypothesized by "pure" theories impinged on the subject of her study resulting in a somewhat deviant personality.[13] Miss Steed's work is especially illuminating in that it helps us to remember that many factors may be at work in creating the personality traits in which we are interested. Thus it may be that Elder's learning processes, Carstairs's Opedipal dilemmas, and Mrs. Murphy's frustration-free childhoods are all factors in creating "base-line aggression." In following sections, when a group is described as aggressive or non-aggressive we shall be speaking of the difference between them : that is in most cases the increment in aggressiveness exhibited by refugees. It should not be forgotten that the non-refugees and the non-aggressive refugees as well, are aggressive to a certain extent and that all the following statements should be taken as relative in nature rather than as absolutes.

Fighting and Arrests

Other behavioural manifestations of aggression mentioned earlier—fighting and committing acts punishable by arrest and imprisonment—are of interest since aggression takes place outside the family as well as within. Two series of questions, one on the frequency with which the respondent fought and the other on his arrest record were asked to gain a fuller picture of his aggressive behaviour in the past.[14] Unfortunately, these items were somewhat less productive than was expected because of a certain lack of candour on the part of the respondents which, if understandable, had not been foreseen. The subjects were clearly more open in their responses to the items regarding intrafamilial aggression. Even the frequency of responses testifies to a certain reserve on the extrafamilial indices that is not present on the intrafamilial ones: Of ninety-seven respondents having children, seventy-six admitted beating their children (some of these said they slapped them occasionally). Only twelve of the entire sample (9.5%) admitted that they had ever been arrested. The corresponding figure for fighting was forty-seven positive replies (37.3%). Of course fighting and getting arrested are less common in any society than is child-punishment because, as noted a little while back, the elements of risk are likely to be greater and sanctions imposed against offenders more severe when one vents his rage away from home but there is also reason to question the accuracy of the figures.

The paucity of data makes it difficult to make meaningful comparisons between refugees and non-refugees on these two points but a few rough indications of differences in their behaviours can be ascertained. In general the data help to bolster the contention that refugees are involved in aggression to a greater extent than non-refugees though the small number of respondents requires that the figures be viewed with some degree of caution. Of the 41.1 per cent of the refugees who admitted fighting, more than one-fourth (26.7%) admitted to having fought "many times." Of the non-refugees only 32.1 per cent said they had *ever* fought and only slightly more than one-sixth of these confessed to fighting many times (17.6%).

TABLE 4.2

Comparison of Refugee-Non-refugee Fighting

	Refugee	*Non-Refugee*
Respondents admitting fighting	41.0%	32.1%
Fighters who had fought many times	26.7	17.6
	N=30	N=16

Admissions of arrest were still less common. Only eight refugees (11.0%) and four non-refugees (7.6%) could recollect for the interviewer's benefit any time they had been arrested. While such small numbers of respondents don't allow firm statements the different pattern of offences for which they were *challaned* (arrested) is illuminating. One refugee each admitted arrests for murder, fighting, illegal distillation, breach of peace. Four had been arrested for having been involved in agitations against government. The non-refugee responses were typically less directly aggressive. Two had been taken in for "cheating" (short weighing), one for illegal distillation, and one for taking part in an agitation.

Despite the low response rate to these items, the Punjab-Haryana-Delhi area is clearly not one of brotherly love where the lion lies down with the lamb. The local press daily carries stories testifying to the aggressive behaviour of the inhabitants of the area. About once a week arrest statistics are published showing that violence is rampant in Punjab and Haryana.[15] On almost any given evening I could walk through the medium-sized town in which I lived and see at least one fistfight. Although these statements do not refer specifically to the sample that was interviewed, it is difficult to hold to the idyllic view of the Indian village after spending some time in Punjab or Haryana. Murders, assaults, and feuds did occur in the villages and towns in which I was working during the period in which I was there. (One member of the sample, a week before he was due to be interviewed, murdered his wife and three other persons. Since he had been jailed awaiting trial he was dropped from the sample and not interviewed.) Fights in the towns were, if not frequent, at least so routine that crowds would not even gather.

Since there is no reason to believe that the sample was biased (see Appendix I) this leaves us with the inevitable conclusion that the respondents were dissembling.

Most people in the sample claimed that they never fought and had never been arrested. Yet of those replying to questions concerning conflicts in their village or neighbourhood two-and-one half times as many of them (64.0%) thought there were more conflicts than there had been before Independence than those who thought they had decreased (26.7%). Although conflicts are not always fights they are aggressive confrontations. It might be argued that conflicts may be seen as more frequent because of the Hindu view of a declining universe. (According to Hindu belief the universe is in a constant state of decay. The fourth and final stage, *Kali Yuga*, the era in which the world now finds itself, is one of constant strife which is continually getting worse.[16] Social relations progressively decline and *dharma* is flouted until conditions become so unbearable that the era spontaneously ends and the cosmos begins the process of regeneration that leads to another cycle). This, however, does not seem to be the case. Most of the respondents were aware that this was *Kali Yuga* but at the same time they saw the material conditions of life improving, a view inconsistent with the existence of *Kali Yuga*. Generally, it seemed that while people can and did talk of them, the four *yugas* have very little effect on the life of the man in the world (as contrasted with priestly or mendicant individuals). Apparently a significant part of the view that conflict is on the rise is due to an objective consideration of the situation. It should be noted that forty per cent of the sample refused to answer this question either from fear of government action, reprisals from opponents, or because of a reluctance to present an outsider with a negative aspect of life in the area. No other question in the entire schedule was refused as often as this one.

Clearly for someone to say that there are more conflicts than there were twenty years earlier he must be aware of conflict occurring. While it is conceivable that members of the sample remained uninvolved in any of the conflict which they reported as burgeoning, given the tightly meshed social relationships of Indian village and town life, it is unlikely. Further, the low response to questions about previous fights and arrests cannot be construed to mean that Punjabis and Haryanvis seldom fight or get arrested. As noted such is far from the case. It would appear that the reasons for the underestimation of these forms of aggression is that the figures represent percentages *admitting* to various forms of aggressive behaviour. Punishment of children is a socially acceptable form of aggressive behaviour in north India while even in a province known for the aggressive nature of its inhabitants such behaviour in non-familial settings is something which occurs but is not spoken of, at least not to strangers. The invalidity of the figures on fighting and arrests was brought out sharply on several occasions. When I interviewed people whom I had observed involved in arguments and fights yet who insisted on denying that they had even been in a fight ("I wouldn't do such a thing. Such behaviour is only for *goondas*.") The arrest records of various members of the community were frequently referred to in the course of an interview with a respondent either mentioning in passing a false accusation which had been made against him that had led to some difficulties with the authorities or in telling (with only slightly suppressed glee) of the troubles of some particularly disliked rival. Doubt of the guilt of members of rival factions was never admitted and guilt of close allies or oneself never owned to. Naturally no one ever confessed to me, an outsider, of having gotten away with something illegal although a great many misdeeds which were common knowledge were brought to my attention.[17] Of course third person responses were not recorded in the interview schedule. Thus although the figures are certainly unreliable, it can only be hoped that their bias is uniformly an underestimate of the issues under investigation. There were too few data to run correlations or crosstabs on these indicators.

Indirect Measures

Before the project began it was clear that the problem of the reticent or untruthful respondent was likely to be encountered. Indeed there is a growing body of literature in the disciplines of sociology, social psychology, and anthropology which, although in many cases tends to be anecdotal in form, makes points that should be considered by any field researcher.[18] The most important of these points is the recognition that the shortest distance between two points, hypotheses and data, may not be a straight line but the path of least resistance. Often if a circuitous research design is not employed the researcher may find himself bogged down in a thicket of obfuscation due to a reluctance to let the interviewer know about sensitive personal matters which might be conveyed to neighbours or through a desire to show only attractive faces of individual, family, and community life to an outsider. But even if one could not discover enough information about aggressive behaviour by asking directly about it, other equally fruitful approaches might be made which might yield fringe benefits in other areas of research.

One way of overcoming the reticence of respondents with regard to acts of which they feel the interviewer might disapprove is to place the subject in a hypothetical situation in which he not only may aggress but is actually expected to. Nine types of people who were expected to be considered worthy of some sort of punishment were presented to the respondent individually. The respondent was asked what he thought should be done to each. The first two of these items had to do with another set of questions discussed earlier : aggression or punishment by parents against their children. One asked what was the best way to deal with a disobedient son. The second question asked what was the best way to deal with a son who insults or strikes his father. Other questions dealt with abandoning fathers, unruly neighbours, unfaithful spouses, irreligious persons, dishonest government officials, and lazy sons. The nine types of people are capable of being grouped in three larger categories. First of all there are those people who actively aggress against members of their own family and must be dealt with. Counter-aggression, i.e. punishment, against these people is culturally sanctioned. This category would subsume the disobedient son, the son who strikes his father, and the father who abandons his family.[19] In each case the act may be considered intergenerational aggression that if left unpunished might have serious consequences regarding the cohesion of the family. The offence is also likely to be common knowledge among family members and if unchecked could become common knowledge in the village or neighbourhood.

The second category involves acts which are not directly aggressive, i.e. not generally engaged in for the satisfaction to be gained from the aggressive potential of the act. Although it is true that this class of acts can do as much damage as those of the previous class the acts are much more likely to be engaged in surreptitiously and hence are less susceptible to detection. Where one of these acts is overt or should one of the acts come to light it is probable that family members, because of shame, would try to mitigate the censure of the community. Thus unfaithful husbands and wives try to keep their wanderings secret and lazy sons are likely to be explained to others in the community as being ill. Each of these acts is capable of undermining the solidarity of a family but they are non-specific in direction and not generally indulged in to bring pain to another person. The third class of offenders are those about whom everyone knows and whose actions may affect the larger community : the irreligious man, the unruly neighbour, and the crooked official. In a true traditional society an irreligious person's acts are seen as a threat to the entire community and its values, and steps must be taken to restrain him in his folly before a vengeful deity punishes the entire community. Actually Punjab-Haryana is relatively free of this view even though a number of political parties have as their goal the preservation or reinstatement of their particular view of *dharma* in the face of increasing secularization of the society. While such parties endeavour to reclaim backsliders the general reaction to people who do not follow the principles of their religion is restricted to a few disapproving clucking sounds from his immediate neighbours. The other two types, thieving officials and unruly neighbours, are considered very dangerous but also are of indeterminate power.

As often turns out some the items showed clear differences between the two groups while many did not. This was not a setback since the groups were never expected to be completely at variance with one another. An added bonus was the early recognition that such a method had uses far beyond the limited scope of the refugee project. If one can impute to respondents, and by extension to the universe from which they are drawn, the seriousness with which an offence is viewed from the severity with which they see fit to punish it—the case of letting the punishment fit the crime—one may gain a better insight into the values of a society than by solely studying folktales or proverbs.[19] And while pointing up the dominant values of a total society this type of approach may also, as in this case, be useful in pinpointing areas in which different groups place different values on certain cultural forms. Since it has often been noted that one of the major problems in the developing areas is lack of consensus regarding societal values,[20] the data gained from such methods could provide policy makers with tools with which to work that would lessen the danger of offending the sense of propriety of critical groups of the population. Obviously a great deal more work is called for, in this area both in the developed as well as the developing nations.

Intergenerational Intrafamilial Aggression

When an index of intergenerational aggression within the family is constructed of the three items mentioned above we find that refugees were a great deal more willing to aggress against offenders. That is, they showed themselves to be more willing to invoke more severe sanctions than did the non-refugees. Crosstabs showed the two groups to be significantly different (p=0.040).

TABLE 4.3

Index of Intrafamilial Aggression (Hypothetical)

1. What do you think should be done to a boy who disobeys his father ?
2. What do you think should be done to a boy who strikes or insults his father ?
3. What do you think should be done to a father who abandons his family ?

TABLE 4.4

Refugee Status versus Intrafamilial Aggression

		Per Cent Responding	
Intrafamilial Aggression Score		*Refugee*	*Non-Refugee*
Low		36.7%	58.7%
High		63.3	41.3
	Total=	100.0%	100.0%
	N=	(60)	(46)

Yates x^2 continuity corrected=4.236 p=0.040 gamma=−0.421

The main difference between the two groups are accounted for by the second and third items, i.e. the aggressive son and the abandoning father. Both groups are willing to bring down more severe reprisals for such an unfilial act, as a son striking his father but, refugees were considerably more punitive, feeling that the best way to handle the son was to beat him or hand him over to the authorities for a more severe beating than the father would be capable of. Four of every nine refugees (43.8%) prescribed such action. A large number of non-refugees felt the same way (32.1%) but an equally large number felt that if the son were properly instructed he would mend his ways. About one-seventh of each group (15.1% of the refugees and 13.2% of the non-refugees) advocated even more severe punishment than mere beating. Typical comments among this group were : "Turn him over to the police for a really good beating" or even in a few cases : "Kill him." Beating at home was recommended by 28.8 per cent of the refugees and 18.9 per cent of the non-refugees. In probing a smaller number of respondents as to their reasons for advocating a specific punishment (or none at all) another interesting difference was disclosed. Punishment (or reaction) was seen by refugees as an act of reprisal or counteraggression while the non-refugee responses were viewed as a teaching or socializing mechanism. When both groups were compared with regard to comparable punishments the rationale of the refugees was consistently more punitive than that of the non-refugees.

TABLE 4.5

Action to be taken against a son who actively aggresses against his Father

	Refugee	*Non-Refugee*
Do nothing	1.37%	13.21%
Find the cause and remove it, love him	4.11	3.77
Educate him, advise him	24.66	32.08
Scold him	8.22	5.66
Ostracise him, turn him out of home	15.07	11.32
Hit him	2.74	1.89
Beat him	28.77	18.87
Other, more severe	15.07	13.21
Total=	100.0%	100.0%
N=	(73)	(53)

The third type of intergenerational aggression had as its target the father who abandons his family for non-religious reasons.[21] More than one-half the non-refugees (50.9%) advocate no action against an abandoning father. About a third of the refugees (34.2%) feel the same. But with regard to those actions apt to be considered as real punishments in the sense that they are likely to hurt their object and be seen by all involved as counteraggression, i.e. ostracism, beating, official punishment, and very severe punishments, the refugees are considerably more punitive. One-fourth of the refugees (24.7%) advocated these aggressive acts but less than half that proportion (11.3%) could be found among the non-refugees.

Perhaps it is fanciful to characterize the refugees as a unitary group, but occasionally it may prove useful for an understanding of the complex mental processes that are going on. If one anthropomorphizes the refugee sample into a sort of giant refugee who holds all the attitudes of his community and characterize his mental state it would not be unreasonable to describe his sentiments toward the abandoning father as ambivalent: favourably disposed to excuse the old man's lapses on one hand and yet willing to impose rather extreme sanctions on the other. Although this hypothetical construct of an artificial refugee is open to many of the criticisms that have been levelled at the concept of national character[22] it does have some heuristic value. What really has to be explained is, assuming that refugees and non-refugees were alike before partition and assuming further that had that event not happened they would still share the same orientations, why the fairly easygoing ways of the past have been eroded (if such a gradual metaphor can be used for the cataclysmic social and psychological upheavals of partition), only to be replaced in whole or part by hostile sentiments.

The previous chapter discussed the role of parental figures in the trauma faced by the refugee. Individual governmental and political father figures urged their constituents to stay on at their old homes. Then, after such proposals had been discredited or overtaken by events and the victim had fled, the parental figures proved themselves incapable of providing the basic paternal function of protection. The government as *baap* had abandoned its wards. Many respondents, fathers themselves, who had become separated from their families in the collective flight, were ambivalent about protective roles. Especially where harm had befallen their wards a feeling of guilt at having allowed oneself to become separated germinated.

But they, like the rest of the refugees, had been let down by those figures that were supposed to protect them, and if this had not happened perhaps they themselves would not have become abandoning figures. In these people and in their children the apparent or real abandonment seems to have spawned or stimulated feelings of hostility and rage at father figures. In one sense this hostility and rage is manifested in some by a willingness to punish fathers in a way that they consider proper. At the same time however the outright display of hostility to fathers engenders intolerable guilt feelings as evidenced by the harsh punishment accorded the son who strikes or abuses his father. It should be noted that both groups, but refugees to an even greater degree, saved their harshest punishments for another malfeasant paternal figure: the government official who steals from the public. Although the two groups' scores do not differ significantly on this point I believe that this may be an artifact of the research design in that both groups were willing to endorse the most severe punishments that were scorable. Had an extended scale been devised the refinement might have led to different results. It is not accidental that someone in such an obviously fatherly position (once again the *baap* aspect of government) who, as the Punjabi saying goes, is "eating the food of his children," is especially singled out for hostility. Examining a series of questions on the degree of trust the respondent was willing to extend to various types of people bolsters this conclusion. The refugees' average trust in government turns out to be between "somewhat" and "very little." (Possible replies were "completely," "a great deal," "somewhat," "little," and "not at all."

TABLE 4.6

Trust of Various Groups

	Refugees	*Non-Refugees*	*P*
Family	1.38	1.69	0.092
Friends	2.32	2.53	0.354
Neighbours	2.77	3.20	0.085
Government Officials	3.29	2.90	0.135

They were scored 1, 2, 3, 4, and 5 respectively.) This is in contrast with the non-refugees' more trusting response. Interestingly, of the four types of people the other three groups—family members, friends, and neighbours—are trusted more fully by the refugees than the non-refugees yet for the clearly paternal roles, government officials, the pattern is reversed. Lest this finding be considered idiosyncratic or the result of specific recent events in which government officials proved themselves untrustworthy and in the process harmed the refugee we must examine other data to show that recent events and transitory factors played little or no part in refugee responses. When asked if the state and central governments had helped them the refugees answered with significantly more positive answers than did the non-refugees. (This difference between the two groups according to a test was significant at the 0.007 level for central government and at the 0.220 level for the state government.) This implies that the refugee sees the government as benefiting him to a greater extent than does him non-refugee neighbour (as indeed is the case) but that despite its beneficence—related to the expectations of the *ma* aspect of government—the *baap* aspect cannot be relied upon. Although there are other possible roots of this antagonism to paternal authority figures, the linkage between having been let down in 1947 and the mistrust and ambivalence exhibited toward the bearers of the mantle of government seems clear. Another possible interpretation, that refugees were reared differently as children, was checked by a series of questions. Refugees, in reporting on their own childhoods, did not report having been punished by different members of the family, than non-refugees, nor did they report different types of punishments. (Fathers were the most frequent punishers and the punishments were generally corporal in nature.)

The Acceptability of Aggression against Others

The remaining types of people north Indians were expected to consider worthy of punishment in varying degree were: a neighbour who repeatedly disturbs the public order; a man who is unfaithful to his wife; a son who is of working age but who refuses to work at all; a wife who is unfaithful to her husband; a government official who takes public property or cheats the common man; and a person who doesn't follow the principles of his religion. The possible pre-coded responses were: do nothing to him or her; advise him or her; scold him or her; community or *panchayat* action or ostracism; corporal punishment by the involved parties; official punishment; and other punishment, more severe than any listed. These were considered continuous and except for official punishment (which might have a variable position in the list according to the offence—i.e., government action against corrupt officials is not as severe as advocating a police beating for a noisy neighbour) have been listed in order of severity. Particularly bizarre punishments such as "he should be killed" or "he should be tortured" were recorded separately but coded under "other, more severe." Responses of the nature "God will punish him" were equated with advocacy of no action by temporal powers. The findings showed refugees and non-refugees to be fairly similar in their reactions to the acts of these malefactors. When grouped into the aforementioned categories of offences no differences could be seen between the two groups.

Survivor Guilt

In some cases refugees are more aggressive than non-refugees and that in recommending action against certain wrongdoers they are apt to be more severe than non-refugees. At the same time, however, on other indices comparable to these, no differences can be ascertained. Before returning to this issue in an attempt to explain the findings let us look at some of the hypotheses raised about the types of people who would be expected to be most aggressive. It is obvious that merely having been made a refugee is unlikely to have any lasting effect on personality in most cases. It is the events that surround flight and resettlement that affect a man's personality. In Chapter III, it was hypothesized that a good deal of the hostility and aggressiveness exhibited by refugees would stem from guilt over how various actors fulfilled their roles in 1947. There are many types of guilt deriving from many actions but the one of most concern here was guilt stemming from the individual's inability or failure to provide protection.

It is important in discussing protection to recognize relationships between threat and protection. Where there is no threat, protection is unnecessary. At low level of threat to himself and his family the individual is able to cope with danger and take whatever measures appropriate for his survival and that of those dependent upon him. As pressure mounts, however, the individual is less and less able to furnish protection to everyone and the slope of the curve levels off. Finally, as threat reaches disaster proportions he is forced to think only of survival. Now it is no longer a matter of "I can take care of it" or even of "women and children first," but rather "every man for himself." Figure 4.1 represents the relationships graphically.

Now, considering only the right hand part of the first curve, that is the section where ordinary threats of day-to-day life are superseded

FIG. 4.1

THREAT, PROTECTION AND GUILT

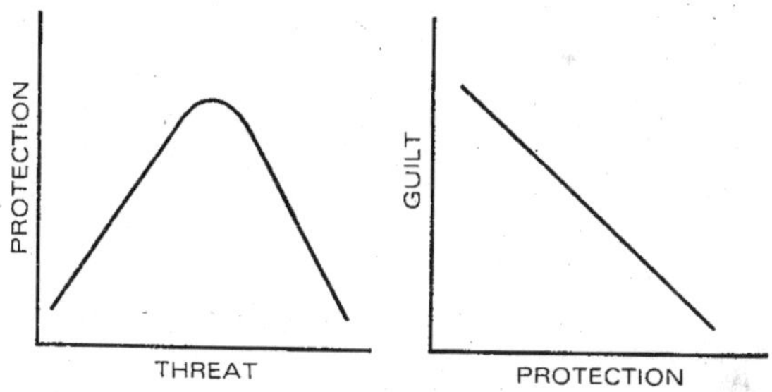

by horrors such as those that attended the partition of the sub-continent, a second curve can be derived of the relationship between the ability to provide protection and guilt over protection. This one clearly is monotonic and decreasing. That is to say, as the ability to provide protection decreases guilt increases (but only on those areas of the first curve that can be designated as "severe threat"). By combining these two curves into a third curve—guilt versus threat (again for only the extreme sections of the distribution)—we can see that guilt varies directly with threat. (Figure 4.2)

FIG. 4.2

THREAT AND GUILT

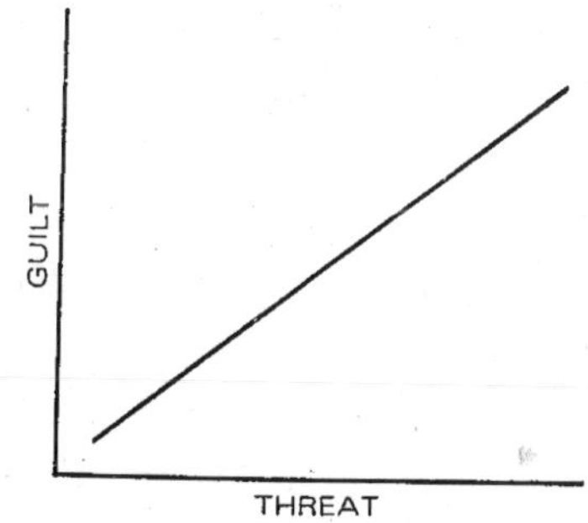

It is very difficult if not impossible in a mass survey situation to assess the degree of guilt felt by subjects. Even if this were possible could one, in a reasonable amount of time, separate out the various types of guilt and determine to what degree an individual suffered from "survivor guilt"? To get around this difficulty it was felt necessary to develop a proximate measure of guilt, preferably one that could be administered quickly in the context of a normal interview situation. Because of the relationships just described it was felt that the best measure of the guilt available to us would be the degree of violence encountered during that period. There are obvious shortcomings in such a method, especially when considering extreme cases, e.g., the complete coward and the great hero. The man who "ran scared" at the first hint of violence, abandoning his family and reaching safety unscathed, would be likely to suffer a great deal of guilt without having ever faced any violence directly, while the hero who expended all his energies fighting for others would be justified in feeling that he did all that was possible and as a result might not suffer from the predicted guilt. But from the stories gathered from the respondents few people fit the two special cases mentioned above. More common was the man who for personal reasons, the profit motive, or attachment to the land stayed on too long in Pakistan subjecting himself and his family to unnecessary risks and who, when these threats appeared, was at least in part unable to cope with them. As a result of the view that degree of violence encountered would be proportional to survivor guilt a degree of violence scale was constructed that would allow one to score each refugee on the basis of the account he gave of his escape from Pakistan. Possible scores ranged from one, representing no violence, to six, representing extreme violence.

TABLE 4.7

Degree of Violence Scale

1. None.
2. Slight: heard of violence but not directly involved.
3. Moderate: encountered violence but not affected directly.
4. Strong: personally involved in violence; loss of property through armed robbery or looting; coming into direct contact with corpses.
5. Severe: present in situation involving loss of life; loss of family member although R not present at the event; no direct threat to self.
6. Extreme: present in situation where there was direct threat to R's life; personally injured; present at loss of family member.

Since non-refugees did not undergo the open ended interviews about their experiences in 1947 there was no way to score them for the degree of violence which they encountered. Some of course did face trauma at that time but for most, any aggression in which they were involved saw them as subjects rather than objects of the violence. The guilt that develops from such actions is fundamentally different than survivor guilt in that it is guilt for what one did rather than guilt for what one was or what one failed to do. According to the doctrine of *karma* such a person who has done evil need not feel guilt—he is going to be punished anyway in this or the next life. Survivor guilt on the other hand can only be assuaged by paying the debt of life that one owes to those who did die. It is doubtful whether the sin of commission, for which expiation may be made, would be looked upon as seriously by Hindus and Sikhs as the sin of omission that left loved ones to die. Of course most non-refugees did not take part in violence and atrocities against Muslims. For the refugees degree of violence was strongly related to intrafamilial aggression (r=0.194, significant at the 0.05 level).

TABLE 4.8

Refugeeism versus Actual International Aggression : (Sikhs only)

Aggression Score		Refugee Status	
		Refugee	*Non-Refugee*
Low		31.6%	66.7%
High		68.4	33.3
	Total=	100.0%	100.0%
	N=	(38)	(18)

x^2=4.791 continuity corrected, df=1 p=0.029 gamma=−0.625

Guilt was also seen as associated with a failure to live up to the requirements of another role, one's religious identity. This was particularly so for many Sikhs who were forced to at least ostensibly renounce their faith. Sikhism with its high value on visible identity, bravery, martial self-image, and martyrdom would also then be expected to correlate with guilt and by extension with aggression. Of course it would have been more desirable to find out in the interview section whether an individual had "let down the side" but delving into such matters would certainly have impaired rapport in later parts of the interview. Hence it is only possible to show gross relationships between religion and on a single indicator of aggressive behaviour. Thus our hypotheses were at least weakly borne out: Sikh refugees proved to be significantly more aggressive within the family than Sikh non-refugees ($p=0.029$). Hindu refugees on the other hand did not differ from their co-religionists who were not refugees. Nowhere else did controlling for religion yield such differences between refugees and non-refugees. This is obviously an area for further research.

Age, Guilt, and Aggressiveness

Much of the psychological literature on stress, trauma, and violence places great emphasis on the age at which it is experienced. Supposedly, trauma encountered at certain points in the development of the personality can be especially damaging. Some of the views at first glance appear to be inconsistent. Bowlby claims that the events of the first months of life are critical in determining later personality.[23] Freud felt that the events of childhood, especially the resolution of the Oedipal conflict, were most significant in determining adult personality.[24] Erikson, on the other hand, in his earlier works, has emphasized the identity crisis of adolescence as a major turning point in the determination of personality.[25] Part of the apparent contradictoriness of the various approaches can be resolved if one considers that each of the authors is concerned with particular aspects of personality and that there is no reason to assume that any of them would subscribe to the view that all aspects of personality developed uniformly at a constant rate and as a result of the same moulding forces. This research project was also concerned with one particular aspect of personality: aggression. The notion of aggression is at best a hazy one and none of the various theories relating to it have proved comprehensive.[26] Thus it could be that Bowlby, Erikson, and Freud's earlier work may be of some help in explaining why certain Indian refugees behave more aggressively than others and also more aggressively than non-refugees who resemble them closely in other respects.

There is another tradition regarding the study of aggression and its relation to age in Indian society that could be called the "non-traumatist" school. Its members, mostly anthropologists and sociologists, do not deny that trauma can result in aggression. Rather they tend to emphasize the point that childhood training and trauma are fairly consistent across members of a society. Being more interested in societal handling of aggression they are able to see the forms it may take.[27] Students of Indian life have noted a correlation between sex, age, and aggression and dominance.[28] In the patri-oriented Indian family elder males can aggress against younger males and females. The patriarch of the family, be he the father or the grandfather, is the sole authority within the household on almost all affairs and as such can freely vent his aggressive sentiments on younger and more helpless members. Thus, the younger an individual the less scope he would have for aggression *within* the family. The same relationship between age and freedom to aggress also exists in the female wing of the household.[29] The intrafamilial relationships between members of opposite sexes where the woman is older than the man are more complex and often hinge upon degree of kinship.[30] Since no women were interviewed in this project this added complexity may be avoided.

There, of course, are other possible relationships between age and aggressiveness. We hypothesized that age would indeed be related to aggressiveness but in a more complex way, governed by the intervening variable of guilt. Specifically, those who were in parental roles in 1947 were expected to feel the greatest amount of guilt for not performing protective functions. This greater guilt was expected to contribute to greater hostility.

From the various possible explanations a number of hypotheses were tested. Regarding Erikson, Freud, and Bowlby we wanted to see whether refugees who were young and adolescent at the time of partition differed from non-refugees with regard to aggression. Their theories (in different contexts of course) would lead one to conclude that older refugees would presumably be more hardened to trauma and hence exhibit no difference from the non-refugees. Another test had to be run to see if age alone and not refugeeism could explain variations in behaviour. Finally, our own hypothesis, that the older refugees would be more aggressive than younger refugees and also more aggressive than similar non-refugees, had to be tested.

First, a simple correlation did not show any clear association between age and intrafamilial aggression ($r=0.079$, not significant). Following this crosstabs were run for the entire sample, refugees and non-refugees alike, to see whether any particular age group could be associated with intrafamilial aggression. None could. Finally tests were run to determine whether the factor of age had a differential effect on refugees and non-refugees. Three-way crosstabs showed that refugee and non-refugee respondents who had been children or adolescents at the time of partition were about equally aggressive. However, for those who had been mature at the time of partition there was a strong difference between refugees and non-refugees (p=0.033). Specifically it would seem that the events of the

TABLE 4.9

Refugeeism versus Intrafamilial Aggression : Mature at Time of Partition only

Intrafamilial Aggression		*Percentage Replying*	
		Refugee	*Non-Refugee*
Low		30.0%	63.6%
High		70.0%	36.4%
	N=	(30)	(22)
x^2=4.538 continuity corrected		p=0.033	gamma=−0.607

partition period had the greatest effect on older people. (Actually while these people are middle aged and old today it must be remembered that to qualify for this category they had only to be twenty-one years old at the time of partition.) That is, those who were old enough to hold paternal roles in 1947 are those exhibiting greater aggressive sentiments today, not directly because of their age then but because of the role that many of them held and the appropriate behaviour associated with that role. To recapitulate: Earlier we hypothesized that guilt was at the root of much of the aggressiveness of the Punjabi and Haryanvi. For certain types of people—those who bore paternal protective roles and were unable to fulfil them honourably and those who did all they could but still felt they had not done all they might have, guilt developed. Guilt was seen as anger directed inward (Freud called it moral masochism) which was capable of being transformed into aggressive sentiments directed at others.

We recognize of course that older refugees are not the only people who feel guilt and hostility. Younger refugees who lost their parents may also feel survivor guilt. Also, anyone may feel guilt or hostility for any number of reasons other than survival-protection considerations. We recognize that non-refugees also behave fairly aggressively within their families, perhaps as a result of the north Indian socialization process described by

Elder. Finally, of course age and its concomitant rank provides some freedom to aggress. The last point, however, can be overestimated. In Punjab when a son reaches a certain age he is too old to be aggressed against. Similarly, Elder has pointed out that age alone doesn't give licence to aggress. In fact he has shown that when a man is so old that he is economically unproductive he may be the target of the aggression of the children of the village.[31] While in Punjab I have never seen this form of cruelty it is the case that once a man can no longer work he relinquishes to his sons the power to enforce sanctions or else the eldest son merely assumes power.

All this should not be taken to mean that refugees are aggressive and non-refugees passive. A number of statements have been made all of which have been relative in nature. "Low" and "high" aggressive scores were obtained by dividing the scores of the entire sample at the median. In the seniormost group there was a difference between refugees and non-refugees that we feel is the result of different degrees of guilt. The refugees scored relatively higher than the non-refugees. While it cannot be demonstrated that guilt is actually the mechanism creating hostility the fact that it and closely related grief are still significant components of our respondent's psyches cannot be doubted. The events of 1947 are still fresh in their minds; they still weep when telling of those days. That their children, too young to remember the actual tragedy of those days, are able to recount the events of the flight indicates that that period has been considered worthy of inclusion in the folklore of the family and its socialization processes.

Other Measures of Aggression

The reader has by now recognized that the measures of aggression presented here are not the ones usually found in the literature of political science. Nor are the measures used here the ones found in most contemporary empirical research. We feel that perhaps political scientists have too often *directly* associated attitudes with a propensity for a particular behaviour. To be sure, the best works have clearly noted that such themes as "authoritarianism" or "cynicism" are not simple factors operating in isolation to create particular types of behaviour in individuals. Nevertheless the step to this conclusion for the reader has been an easy yet deceptive and unwarranted one: the association of single, discrete psychological traits with specific types of behaviours. As a result many sceptical political scientists and others have either shied away from the attempt to link psychology and politics or else decried this type of effort. In the past several years serious scholars have attempted to right the balance to show that although the relationships may be incredibly complex they do exist. Their point has been that merely to know a behaviour is not to know the psychological roots of it,[32] and conversely that we cannot predict behaviour from the presence of one or two psychological traits.[33]

When we get to the term aggression we get into still muddier waters for, aside from the two difficulties just described, there is a basic imprecision in the term. Adorno, *et al.* found that "authoritarian aggression" was one of the traits associated with potential fascism. Yet concrete examples of behavioural aggression are largely absent from their work.[34] Others have done extensive work on hostility to government manifested as cynicism without tying cynicism to actual anti-government activities. The problem with most of the studies is that the links between psychological states, attitudes (the things actually measured in most cases), and actual behaviours in real life are rarely stipulated. Thus, in poorer works we are asked to accept on faith the notion that attitudes and behaviours are perfectly congruent, a statement that is patently untrue, and in better works that there is a relationship that may not be clear but that must be assumed. Robert Lane in a recent book emphasizes this point.[35] Lane argues plausibly that personality formation in childhood and later activities are linked and through his discussion of the "politics of aggression" he persuasively shows, using Miller's and Berkowitz's work, why politics becomes the lightning rod for so many aggressive sentiments. Thus Lane is able to assert that certain respondents show their high level of aggressiveness in relatively non-aggressive ways (it could be said these drives have been sublimated to a degree or displaced): the son of a Democratic family votes Republican, a member of an outgroup leads a movement for "outgroup power" at Adams College. Nowhere however does Lane find a direct link between aggressive thoughts and aggressive actions. His respondents, some of whom are hostile to Negroes, Jews, and labour unions, do not get involved in pogroms or unionbusting, rather they rechannel their aggression into their work or social lives.[36] Lane seems to hold a view similar to ours, that highly aggressive opinions usually indicate an aggressive personality but that the aggressive personality will often not exhibit its aggressiveness behaviourally against the targets of the verbal aggression and perhaps not even aggress at all. However, it is expected that most people who regularly *act* aggressively will have aggressive personalities and will manifest these aggressive personalities in their verbal responses to questionnaire stimuli. Here again one must be cautious because recent work has indicated that to a certain extent attitudes and behaviours once thought to be indicative of personality are in actuality learned consciously.[37] Still it is probably not too far fetched to accept the idea that learned sentiments and behaviours spread much in the same way as in innovations and that until a certain critical mass is reached the conversion rate is rather low.

Personality cannot be measured directly but attitudes can be tapped and behaviours recorded. It is probable that many behaviours that are aggressive will be missed by questionnaire approaches, even more so when aggressive acts are limited to punishment in the family, fighting and being arrested. Also, as in other spheres of behaviour whole constellations of attitudes and personality traits are necessary to bring out certain effects. If all this is so, then behaviourally non-aggressive individuals may voice aggressive sentiments yet not hold another crucial element in the constellation and as a result be non-aggressive behaviourally. That is to say that the presence of aggressive attitudes is necessary but not sufficient evidence of actual aggressiveness but that for all the reasons cited above correlations between personality traits (had it been possible to measure these directly), attitudes and behaviours would be less than perfect but still positive.

With this in mind we set out to measure, in addition to behavioural aggression, hostility to certain objects (Muslims, outgroups, government, politicians) and in an effort to verify what we considered to be the elements of the constellation : concerns with power, without which aggression would be counter-productive; fantasy aggression or concern with violence; projection or a perception of the world as a dangerous place; personal efficacy; political efficacy. Between five and ten questions were formed into indices to measure each of these elements. Then a factor analysis was run and some of the items were regrouped. A few of the indices and factors, as we have seen, yielded results that showed that in some ways the refugees who had suffered great violence differed from those who had crossed peacefully and also from the non-refugees, but most of the indicators showed the sample to be relatively homogeneous. Although these indicators are probably also necessary but not sufficient causes of aggression discussion of these items, indices, and factors has been put off until a later chapter which describes the common political culture of the Punjab-Haryana region. The reason for this is that for ease in understanding the crucial elements of aggression it is more important at this point to discuss those elements that distinguish between aggressive and non-aggressive individuals.

Invulnerability

We have explained how guilt is associated with aggression. But guilt is not a necessary nor a sufficient explanation of aggressive behaviour. That is to say that the relationship between the two is over-determined : aggression can stem from a number of pre-existing emotional states of which guilt is merely one. On the other hand guilt can lead to any number of behaviours other than aggression. This section will be concerned with the latter issue: what is, for the refugees, the most important intervening variable between guilt and aggressive behaviour ?

Refugees and non-refugees differ with regard to intrafamilial aggression and the punishment they administer to their own children. On the other hand there is very little difference between the two groups in the attitudes that could be called a willingness to invoke aggressive sanctions against wrongdoers or in those traits felt to be components of aggression. Attitudes are supposedly related to behaviour. How is one to explain this seeming paradox?

The first question that must be answered is why the refugees and non-refugees share the same attitudes. It was hypothesized that distortions of personality occur in uprooting and resettlement and the guilt that ensues in some cases leads to aggressive attitudes and behaviours. Can it be that the findings of similar attitudes mean that personality has no effect on these specific attitudes regarding behaviour or can it be, as we hinted in the previous section, that the refugees have acted as opinion leaders and "taught" the non-refugees about what desirable attitudes to hold? We have already alluded to the fact that since the advent of the refugees many changes have taken place in the life of the non-refugees: the dress, diet, manners, and language of the westerners have to a large degree been assimilated by the easterners. All of these are highly visible outward forms however, perhaps unrelated to complex mental processes. While it is impossible to prove that refugee attitudes have been adopted by non-refugees there are ample indications that not only outward forms but sentiments about Muslims, certain political actions, and the utility of various agricultural practices have, over twenty-odd years, been incorporated by the non-refugees. (See the chapters on political culture and economic life.)

The second question—why attitudes are sometimes not congruent with behaviour—brings us to the crux of the discussion. As has been pointed out, the relationship between personality and behaviour is "overdetermined." Similarly attitudes and behaviour are not linked in an altogether consistent way. In part the difficulty stems from lack of knowledge of what factors are at work in stimulating or inhibiting any one form of behaviour. For example, long before psychology became a science parents came to realize that in many cases the best deterrent of aggression (or any other socially disapproved act) was punishment. Carried to its logical extreme the more severe the punishment the less likely the deed is to be repeated. Only recently however has the entire relationship between punishment and offence been re-examined. For example, the punishment of a child is likely to be frustrating to the child and the more frustrating it is the more likely it is to *stimulate* aggression, perhaps not against the punisher-frustrator but perhaps against someone else, not excluding the victim himself.[38] Out of these studies has come modification of the folk theory emphasizing the requirement that the child recognize the punishment as related to the offence. Empirical studies have gone still further in recognizing that severely punished children are more aggressive than permissively trained children.[39] Can it be then that refugees' children are more aggressive because their more aggressive parents punish them more severely and because they are more aggressive they have to be punished still more? The non-refugees' children being punished less may turn out less aggressive and require less punishment later. Similarly the perceptions of punishable behaviour (and punishment) of each group may be different from those of the other group. In an attempt to control for these problem areas the questionnaire, in addition to measuring the degree to which respondents punished their children for offences they saw as punishable, also presented them with the opportunity to aggress against hypothetical wrong-doers. It is likely that disobedient children, unfaithful spouses, and irreligious people, in the abstract are probably seen similarly by refugees and non-refugees.

Although attitudes may in some cases be unrelated to behaviour, we know personality creates constellations of attitudes and, at least in part, it is the combination of attitudes rather than a single one that is the intervening variable between personality and behaviour. This is merely to elaborate the notion of overdetermination which would say that any single behaviour can and in some cases must be the result of any number of personality variables or attitudes or that any single personality variable or attitude can be manifested through many types of behaviour. Attitudes about the appropriateness and utility of aggressive behaviour may exist as a result of personal trauma as in the case of the refugees or as a result of the learning of certain attitudes from the refugees by the non-refugees but unless the non-refugees come to share *all* the crucial attitudinal or personality variables it is unlikely that they will behave in ways similar to the refugees. That is attitudes and behaviour of two groups will only be definitely congruent if their *constellations* of attitudinal variables are congruent. Attitudes about the use of aggression may be necessary but not sufficient predeterminants of actual aggression. We believe that the crucial element of this constellation is a sense of decreased vulnerability. Considering the extreme case of this, complete invulnerability, it is not too difficult to hypothesize that this element acts catalytically. That is, many people who are highly aggressive attitudinally are more or less passive behaviourally if they lack this sense of invulnerability. Miller and others have observed that inhibitory tendencies lead to the deflection of aggression or its suppression.[40] Where a man feels invulnerable he will aggress against the frustrating agent. If his son disobeys he will punish him, if a neighbour disturbs the public order he will fight with him. It could be argued that aggression within the family, since it is done by male elders to a large extent, is relatively risk free for the aggressor. That is, the patriarch is invulnerable within the family and may act with impunity. Thus much of the aggression within the family represents the paradigm of "invulnerable aggression." There are of course countervailing pressures that reduce some of the force of such an argument: unreasonably harsh punishments and unbridled aggression within the family usually lead to splits in the joint family or the flight of the victim of the aggression. There is also the restraining influence of the *biradari*, which, afraid for the reputation of the entire caste, will try to tone down conflict. Other mechanisms exist for the protection of young brides from mothers-in-law (brothers come to visit).[41] Nevertheless it is true that aggression within the family involves less risk than that outside it since unless the conflict becomes very great no one will call in the authorities to halt it and neighbours will remain aloof. A sense of invulnerability among refugees then does not mean that refugees are completely untrammelled in their actions. Rather they feel relatively less vulnerable than non-refugees.

A number of items purporting to measure degrees of invulnerability had been included in the interview schedule. A factor analysis of all items grouped most of these together within one factor along with a few others that purported to measure "paranoia." The common thread running through the elements of the factor was an unease or fear of punishment or harm at the hands of human or supernatural forces. Because of the signs of the rotated factor loadings the factor was called Vulnerability.

When the two groups, refugees and non-refugees, were compared with regard to this factor the difference between the mean scores of the groups was significant at the 0.015 level! What is more, when a correlation matrix was generated, vulnerability correlated significantly with the degree of violence encountered (refugees only, $r=-.204$; significant at the 0.05 level) and also with intrafamilial aggression (entire sample, $r=.213$; significant at the 0.05 level). Controlling for age, religion, residence, caste status, education, income, and size of household did not produce any other significant relationships. Of course this is not the first time invulnerability has been noted among survivors. Almost every study of disaster has found that victims often come to think of themselves as having charmed lives. All of these earlier studies, however, were conducted relatively soon after the event giving the impression that many of the attitudes would be short-lived. Here in the Punjab-Haryana sample the same trait persists more than twenty years after the trauma.

The attitude of the survivors seems to be that they have been through the worst imaginable trials. Nothing that God or man can do could be worse so who is capable of punishing them for misdeeds? Part of this outlook is a residue of what was discussed

TABLE 4.10

Vulnerability Factor

	RFL
1. (a) Most people don't realize the extent to which their lives are controlled by accidental happenings OR (b) There is really no such thing as luck	—.505
2. We ought to worry about our own family and let the rest of the people take care of themselves.	—.491
3. Basically the world is a threatening and dangerous place and children must be protected from it.	—.481
4. Even though I am sure I am in the right in a discussion I usually give in because it is foolish to cause trouble.	—.433
5. (a) Many times I feel that I have very little influence over the things that happen to me OR (b) It is impossible for me to believe that chance or luck plays an important part in my life.	—.422
6. (a) Your own deeds will bring you salvation OR (b) What man wishes never happens; What God wishes always happens.	.417
7. There are so many evil people nowadays that it is dangerous to go out alone.	—.399
8. Nowadays, when so many people move around and mix together a person has to protect himself especially carefully against disease or infection from them.	—.372
9. One man says: "Our country needs a strong leader who will take over the government and make everybody obey him." Another man says: "Our country needs leaders who will act in accordance with the people's wishes." Which man do you think is more correct ?	—.361
10. An insult should always be punished.	—.338
11. One man says: "The most important thing for an eleven or twelve year old boy to learn is to always obey the wishes of his father." Another man says: "The most important thing a boy should learn is to think for himself." Which man do you think is more correct ?	—.336
12. Only wicked or foolish people would oppose a great political leader.	—.324
13. If a young boy, about ten years of age, disobeys his father, what do you think is the best way to deal with him ?	—.316

earlier as a recognition that higher powers had broken the rules of the game thereby freeing the victim from the constraints on his side. More than this however is a feeling that "It doesn't matter, whatever I do I can stand the consequences." In those survivors who felt no guilt and who therefore saw the earlier scourging as a pointless punishment the relationship between offence and punishment may become permanently blurred. These are merely variations on a theme however. The theme is : "Nothing that any one can do to us now could be as terrible as what was done to us in 1947. Not only did we survive that but we became prosperous as well; so, what can hurt us now ? We can do as we please."

TAT Measures of Aggression

When the research project began some of the hypotheses had not yet been formulated. Intuitively some relationship between the aggressive behaviour of refugees and the violence that they had encountered in coming to the Indian side was felt to exist but the linkages between attitudes, personality, and behaviour were unclear. It was felt that should the attitudinal questions not prove productive in our researches an alternate approach would be called for. In recent years the Thematic Apperception Test of Henry A. Murray has been one of the most extensively used projective techniques in the United States. The most active use of the technique has been in the measurement of achievement motivation (n-Ach) and in the last few years the approach has proven itself to be suitable for use in other cultures.[43] While most of the use of the TAT in other cultures has been with regard to n-Ach there is no reason to suppose that the TAT principles developed to measure aggression in the United States would not be equally applicable in other cultures.[44]

The literature on the use of the TAT in measuring aggression has had a slow painful development. A great many scoring techniques have been developed but with the passage of time each has given way to newer modes of analysis. The various techniques can be broken down into four approaches to the relationship between aggressive themes in TAT protocols and actual aggressive behaviour. First there is the notion that a high number of aggressive themes should correlate with aggressive behaviour.[45] When this notion proved too unsophisticated for some analysis it was modified and the types of aggressive themes were differentiated by type and according to the strength of the aggressive act.[46] A third approach was to distinguish between those acts in which the main character was the subject or the object of the aggression.[47] Lately, surprisingly, lately it would seem considering Miller's work on inhibition, came the view that in addition to aggressive themes and their direction analysts should consider the number of inhibitory themes, especially the presence and intensity of punishment themes.[48] As Berkowitz has pointed out, a number of experimental studies have shown that there appears to be a carry over of inhibition of aggressive behaviour from real life to fantasy. As he puts it: If a person has developed extremely strong inhibitions against expressing aggression, he is not likely to display hostility readily either in fantasy tasks or in 'real life'."[49] Following Berkowitz, and partly because as it worked out we were more concerned with the TAT as a validation technique, we decided that a rather simple modification of Jensen's aggression scoring method would serve.[50] Although Jensen's notions of directionality and punishment themes suffer from philosophical and methodological difficulties[51] these do not detract from his creation of a technique that provides a means of scoring both frequency and intensity of aggression themes.[52]

Our findings were that the refugees responded with approximately the same number of aggression themes but that themes were of much greater intensity than those of the non-refugees. The original value computed for each respondent, the levelled aggression score which was a total of the intensities of all responses to the entire set of TAT cards, showed the refugees' scores to be significantly higher than the non-refugees' (t=2.40; p=0.018). There was virtually no difference between the two groups with regard to the number of responses made (t=0.43; p=1,000). But here our main interest was in validation. How were TAT aggression scores related to other indicators that had been developed ? Total levelled aggression response correlated with intrafamilial aggression, (r=.269, p=0.01). TAT aggression scores correlated highly with the degree of violence encountered (r=.222; p=0.05). vulnerability (r=—.237; p=0.05), and fighting and arrests (r=.327, insignificant because of the small number of cases).

Most recent works on the TAT emphasize a quantitative approach rather than a qualitative approach, although some of the quantitative methods do manage to incorporate at least some qualitative nuances.[53] While we have concerned ourselves with a quantitative approach because of the need for comparability between a large number of respondents, we feel that to a large extent the obsession with measurement now running rampant through the various disciplines of the social sciences forces the researcher to examine his data at such a high level of abstraction that many very subtle distinctions are lost. For example, by looking at responses to certain TAT cards that had already been scored and which had yielded some interesting relationships between refugeeism or certain background information and the number and intensity of aggression themes we were able to recognize points which our initial model had not made as clearly as we would have liked. By studying the TAT responses certain personality elements were seen to be much more central to the Indian refugee than they had been to the World War II refugee. For example, entirely different types of responses were given by refugees and non-refugees to those pictures that in the United States most often elicit responses concerning intergenerational or familial relationships.[54] Among our respondents, only the refugees told stories of intergenerational relationships and these had mainly to do with conflictual situations. Card 6 portrays a white haired woman and a black haired man. The two are not facing each other and both have troubled, or at least puzzled looks on their faces. In the United States this picture commonly elicits responses having to do with misunderstanding or conflict between mother and son or a family problem that mother and son must face. Here are some typical refugee responses :

> There is a man. There is another man who is very old. No, she is a lady. Oh, she is definitely an old lady. The man who is wearing a coat is her son. They are looking at their work. They might be looking for someone. The mother is looking on one side and the son is looking on the other. They are waiting for someone. The person for whom they are waiting is their relative. He will come after a short while and they will greet him. Both sides will exchange greetings and move away.
>
> Is she his wife? No, she is his mother. Definitely she is his mother. He may have said something to his mother and the mother has got angry with him on this. She has turned her face aside. The boy is also angry. He might have demanded something from the mother and she has refused. Now he is thinking as to what to do. Something will be done. He will get her agreement

to his demand and will do his work carefully.

Here is a man and a woman, probably mother and son. Because of a family strife they have got some differences of opinion and have fought over it. Both are very sad and very serious. It seems that their family problem is very serious and complicated. They are trying to solve it but are unsuccessful, even after hard labour. Then they pick up a fight and now because of that they are sad and serious. After that someone, i.e. a relative or some near one will advise them and they will try to work upon his advice. Then they will try to solve that problem and will solve it with love.

Non-refugees saw the situation a little differently:

There is a man and a woman. The man has his face on this side and the woman has her face on the other side. They seem to be annoyed with each other. There might have been some trouble in the family. There may be a trouble over some edible thing. They are annoyed with each other. The wife might have done something wrong in the house. Either she has sold something without his knowledge or she has purchased something without his permission. Over this they might have trouble. After that they will again mix up. The wife will persuade him not to be annoyed over these things and both will be alright. But it seems that the wife is angry. They will be alright in the evening. The person at fault will admit his weakness. They are both educated persons.

A man and a woman are there. The woman is looking somewhere and the man is thinking. I think she wants to get promise of something from him but he is not agreeing. Perhaps she is asking something from him and he is showing his inability so she is annoyed because she is annoyed and he is helpless. So their home will become a bad house and they will remain quarrelling there. After some time it will be alright. Family trifles do not live long.

They are also husband and wife. They are annoyed. The wife is annoyed with her husband. Either he does not accept his demands or she does not like him. Both have their own ways. Both will suffer in this. In case they get along well both will be happy. Otherwise the life of both of them is spoiled. In this way both will remain troubled. The men may make amends because men are adaptable and intelligent but the ladies lack these things.

> Men think so many things but the women insist only on one point. They will have to leave each other.

In neither group is aggression a theme of major importance. There is, however, some reference to conflict and on this point the typical responses differ, refugees seeing more intergenerational conflict than non-refugees.

We postulated that one of the crucial points in the refugee experience was the breakdown of the paternal relationship. Is this borne out by responses to the TAT ? Card 7 shows an old man and a boy or young man. Only their heads are visible and these are close together as if some confidential advice is being passed between them. Typical refugee responses were :

> I think they are father and son and are making a plan of some business. They are discussing as to what they should do and how it will work. They are seriously thinking on his project. Let us see what happens. They will agree to the plan of the father which will be good.
>
> They are son and a father. The son wants to marry his beloved but his old father compels him not to do that. He advises him much but there is no effect on him. His mind is always on the remembrance of his beloved and he is always in a watch to see his beloved but his father never allows him to his beloved. That is why both have got differences of opinion and there comes a family strife. Now his father is getting angry with his son. But this son will not care for the wishes of his father and will run away from home by which he will meet his beloved and get solace and both will unite to make a family. His father is very traditional. The boy is an educated one. He wants to marry his class fellow. She belongs to a low status family or a poor family. That is why his father is not agreed to his marriage with that girl.

Non-refugee responses were typically less conflict oriented and often the characters on each side of the age gap were not seen as representing members of a single family.

> There is an old man. He has said something to his son and he is thinking what he should reply. The son has done something

which father does not approve of. He failed an exam. His father is giving him sympathy and teaching him courage. He will learn the advice of his father and will be successful.

Both the persons are sitting. They are sitting peacefully. They have eaten their food and now they are talking of their family matters. After this either they will do some family work. In case they are educated they will do some writing work otherwise they will do manual work. I think they are illiterate—they are doing manual work. They may be working according to their caste. In case they are *lohars* (iron smithers) they will do iron smithy and in case they are tailors, they will do tailoring.

It would seem then that in this one particular case where intensity of typical responses was approximately equal that ignoring the characteristics of the subjects and objects or the modes of aggression employed might lead to unwarranted conclusions that both groups are rather similar when in fact refugees see in pictures 6 and 7 more intergenerational tension than do non-refugees. As we have already noted these types of responses are very similar to those that the pictures elicit in an American audience. As we shall see in the chapter on economic attitudes the refugees are in some ways very "western".

Some pictures elicited responses of very different intensity from the two groups. Such cases are extremely interesting since we have already noted that refugee and non-refugee responses are at variance as much with regard to themes as with intensity. For example, Card 12 shows two men. One is reclining, apparently asleep. The second man is shown above him, partly leaning on the bed with one knee. He has one arm outstretched over the reclining figure. To this card the refugees responded with a greater number of and with stronger aggression themes than did non-refugees. Most frequently the refugee described the standing man as hypnotist who was mesmerizing the reclining man. In a good number of cases the reclining figure was described as a boy or young man although there is nothing to indicate any difference in age between the two figures. After being mesmerized the victim will be completely enslaved to this Svengali, forced to do his bidding without regard to his own will. The respondents seldom saw the master as requiring his slave to perform illegal or immoral acts; he was merely enslaved to another who had superior powers. The enslavement theme is related to the notion that the victim is seen as younger than the hypnotist and reminds us of the Punjabi proverb mentioned earlier that states that fathers should treat sons of certain age groups as slaves. In both cases the youth is enslaved to a senior figure against whom he is completely resourceless. Rebellion is both unthinkable and impossible as we know from people's views of what should be done to sons who insult fathers. Once again we find this darker side of the parent-child relationship. Here again is paternal authority that does not fulfil the nurturant or protective functions of a good *baap*. Like the Government in 1947 he does not recognize any *quid pro quo* where loyalty and fidelity and obedience are repaid by nurturance and the provision of safety. The difference between the two groups with regard to aggression themes in this picture was significant at the 0.007 level.

While it is possible to read too much into response styles on TATs it would appear that power relationships, especially those similar to those found within the family between father and son, are particularly significant to the refugees.

Frustration

The main attitudinal (and probably personality) difference between refugees and non-refugees that accounts for variations in aggressive behaviour is in their respective senses of invulnerability. The refugees, feeling less vulnerable and open to punishment, are able to transform their personality aggression into actual behaviour. To reassure ourselves on this matter we decided to examine the degree to which a respondent felt generally frustrated. Berkowitz sees aggression as a need, i.e. as a predisposition to be aroused to aggressive responses.[55] Dollard *et al* recognized that aggression grew out of frustration.[56] From these two viewpoints we can say that the aggressive individual is likely to have a heightened sense of frustration (not, of course, that frustration leads directly to aggression).

Although the particular frustration that leads to a particular act of aggression usually cannot be determined it is possible to see whether an individual feels frustrated in general. A number of questions were combined into a Frustration Index designed to measure the degree to which an individual feels frustrated in the economic situation in which he finds himself, in his personal life, and in his dealings with government. The items can be found in

Table 4.11.

The two groups proved to be about equally frustrated. Nor when any of the independent variables were controlled for could any

TABLE 4.11
Frustration Index

1. Can you tell me something that recently made you angry at home ?
2. Can you tell me something that recently made you angry in this village (neighbourhood) ?
3. Does it ever seem to you that everyone is working against you ?
4. Do you feel that you have often been punished without cause ?
5. There are times when I act like a coward.
6. I usually feel that life is worthwhile.
7. I would have been more successful if people had given me a fair chance.
8. I have had more than my share of things to worry about.
9. Thinking about the economic situation of your family—the money and possessions that your family has and its standard of living—are you, yourself, generally satisfied with the economic standard or not ?
10. How often do you feel that your problems are more than you can bear ?

difference be seen between refugees and non-refugees. The only independent variable that was related to the frustration felt by a subject was his caste status : low caste individuals felt a great deal more frustrated than members of higher castes. Refugeeism played no part. The questions in the Frustration Index attempted to measure the degree to which an individual recognized that he was being thwarted in achieving what he saw as justice and the rewards of the society in which he lives. In addition there is bias within the index toward a sense of being victimized by the system so the finding is not surprising. Since the member of a lower caste generally has less access to the values of Indian society his perception of himself as frustrated, unable to have his aspirations fulfilled, is an accurate one and congruent with that of an outside observer. Such a finding is interesting in that it contradicts an important school of sociologists and anthropologists and Indian apologists for the caste system.[57] These defenders of the *status quo* tend to see the security and well defined roles provided by caste as furnishing enough satisfactions to the individual so that he is contented with his lot. Recently another school has contended that caste is maintained not by the satisfactions it provides but rather by the economic sanctions that can be imposed on deviants by and through the *jajmani* system.[58] The data seem to substantiate this second view that, at least in Punjab-Haryana, having a secure, well defined niche does not necessarily make a man contented with his lot and that low castes regardless of their refugee status feel equally dissatisfied with their lot (caste status and frustration are highly correlated ; r= −.443).

Although the two groups are equally dissatisfied and frustrated in terms of index scores the items seem to touch different areas of frustration so that in fact there is great variability in the responses given to different items. Thus people see life in general as being worthwhile yet still feel that in part their present state of affairs is not only unsatisfactory but due to some unfair treatment in the past. Most people claim that they have not been angered at home or in their village or neighbourhood but a much higher percentage

INDEX 4.12

Frustration Index Responses

	Per cent Responding
1. Can you tell me something which recently made you angry at home ? (yes)	28.6
2. Can you tell me something which recently made you angry in this village (neighbourhood) ? (yes)	17.5
3. Does it ever seem to you that everyone is working against you ? (yes)	17.6
4. Do you feel that you have often been punished without cause? (yes)	29.6
5. Sometimes I act like a coward. (yes)	49.6
6. I usually feel that life is worthwhile. (yes)	92.0
7. I would have been more successful if people had given me a fair chance. (yes)	84.0
8. I have had more than my share of things to worry about. (yes)	60.8
9. Thinking about the economic situation of your family—the money and possessions that your family has and its standard of living—are you, yourself, generally satisfied with the economic standard or not ? (dissatisfied)	28.0
10. How often do you feel that your problems are more than you can bear ? (always and most times)	48.0

are in agreement with statements that assess dissatisfaction with the quality of their lives. ("I have had more than my share of things to worry about.")

Our earlier findings of greater aggressiveness among the refugees leads us to the conclusion that since both groups are approximately equal in their general level of frustration, non-refugees channel much of their aggressiveness through more acceptable mechanisms of defence while the refugees, feeling less vulnerable to the punishments of God and man, take fewer such unconscious precautions.

Conclusions

In the theoretical sections of the previous chapter it was hypothesized that two personality characteristics likely to emerge from the traumatic events surrounding partition would be a sense of guilt and a sense of invulnerability. Hypotheses were raised about the association between these two characteristics and a particular form of behaviour : interpersonal aggression. Specifically, guilt leads to hostility but for this hostility to be manifested as aggressive behaviour it must be accompanied by a sense that one's acts are not going to lead to disastrous consequences for the actor.

A major issue in the study of attitudes is the relationship between attitudes and behaviours. It has long been noted that verbal responses to an interview schedule are often unrepresentative of what a respondent would do if placed in an actual situation where he were faced with the behavioural equivalent of the questionnaire choice. Refugees and non-refugees harbour similarly aggressive sentiments toward various groups and individuals. Either the refugees have to a large extent inculcated these attitudes and views of the appropriateness of certain behaviours in members of the non-refugee community, or else refugees and non-refugees have always shared the same notions of propriety and punishment.

Despite the similarities in attitudes however the refugees exhibit greater aggressiveness in some spheres, than the non-refugees. We believe that the apparent paradox can be cleared up by the notion of constellations of attitudes, values, sentiments, and traits all of which must be present for "thoughts" to be translated into deeds. The crucial element in this particular case is invulnerability because all the other elements usually associated with aggressiveness, e.g. concerns with power, hostility, etc. are present in both groups. (See the following chapter on political culture for evidence of hostility towards Muslims, strangers, and deviants). Invulnerability is found in greatest strength among refugees and especially among those who faced extreme violence. In other words the refugees are the people who *do* aggress directly while the other members of the population only think about it. The refugees aggress because they feel that their actions cannot be punished in any way that they fear. Perhaps "feel" is a word having too many connotations of consciousness for all indications are that the sense of invulnerability is never or seldom verbalized. Rather it is manifested in responses to a number of attitudinal questions and, of course, in behaviour. In some ways then, aggression against children, in the guise of punishment, becomes the paradigm for all "invulnerable aggression."

Aggression against one's own children in the form of punishment is virtually risk free. And it is here where subjective risk disappears that the refugees and non-refugees differ most sharply. In other words, placed in a situation which to the outside observer appears to be one of relative freedom of action the refugee takes advantage of the situation and acts while the non-refugee remains bound by inhibition, either those commanded by *dharma*, custom, or merely humanity and commonsense. The refugee however is free of constraints not only in this one sphere but, in varying degrees, in many spheres of social interaction. As we shall see in a later chapter such a mental set has profound implications for the tone of economic life as well.

When one has reached the conclusion that the best measures of actual aggressiveness in individuals must take into consideration hostility, willingness to invoke aggressive sanctions, and invulnerability, and that only when this is done can meaningful statements be made about behavioural aggression, it becomes obvious that manifestations of behavioural aggression within the family probably result from different mechanisms. The refugees' aggression is likely to represent a different response : a lashing out at frustration experienced within the family while the non-refugee aggression could represent this or aggression stimulated by frustrations outside the family and displaced to handier, weaker targets. The refugee who encounters frustrations outside the family is relatively free of the most significant inhibitory tendency, the fear of punishment, for he is invulnerable. Thus his frustrations in the bazaar, the village, or in the fields are more likely to result in direct aggression right there rather than in displacement to the home front. Although a great deal more research would have to be done to substantiate these views the findings lead one to believe that for the refugee, intrafamilial aggression may be seen as an indicator of all aggressive behaviour.

We, of course, are not the first to notice the touchiness of the Punjabi. The concept of *izzat* (honour) has been widely noted all over north India, especially among those groups the British designated as the "martial races."[59] Under the codes of conduct of these groups one is to avenge all slights or insults to his *izzat* regardless of the costs. While these codes are still at work today, the aggressive behaviour of the refugees is somewhat different from aggression resulting from a slight to one's *izzat*. While affronts to a man's *izzat* invariably provoked retaliation from some groups (at any point in time not all Punjabis or Haryanvis felt constrained to follow these rules), the retaliation was often not spontaneous but rather was frequently undertaken after long intervals of premeditation. Furthermore, *izzat* forced one to act or pay the consequences in terms of losing status in the community and possibly even being outcasted *regardless of the fact that one often knew that he was committed to an act in which he was extremely vulnerable.* Indeed many of the senseless murders we read of in Kipling and others describing life on the Frontier and in Punjab lead to a clearly foreseen disastrous end for the perpetrator. Of course *izzat* is still a force to be reckoned with (albeit in somewhat vitiated form today), especially in rural areas, but the point being made here is that "*izzat*-aggression" can be distinguished from aggression that is both spontaneous and an outgrowth of a sense of invulnerability.

The idea of spontaneity in aggression is not ours alone. In part the commonly held Indian notion of the aggressive Punjabi and, since bifurcation, Haryanvi, is a stereotype based on certain elements of fact and perhaps the personal experience of its holder. The popular stereotype is given greater weight by the testimony of officials and the press. Virtually all the police and judicial officers contacted by the author saw a difference in the types of crimes committed by refugees and non-refugees. According to their expert eyes non-refugees were more likely than refugees to aggress via petty crime and sneak thievery against people who were often unknown to them personally, while refugees were responsible for more violent forms of crime in the areas over which they had jurisdiction. Much of this violent crime was spontaneous as when a refugee encountered some obstacle or irritant such as the much discussed "Five Naye Paise (slightly less than one American cent at the prevailing rate of exchange) Murder" in which a dry cleaning establishment proprietor shortcharged a Sikh refugee the aforementioned slight amount. After a brief argument the Sikh stabbed the shopkeeper to death. While this case is extreme in the small degree of provocation offered, it does exemplify the types of outbreaks of loss of control which some refugees are prone to.[60] In another story the provincial newspaper, *The Tribune*, which devotes a fair amount of its local news page to particularly ghastly crimes and chilling statistics about the lawlessness in the province, reported that in Punjab alone with a population of approximately twelve million, during the first seven months of 1967, 319 murders had been committed.[61] If the figures are adjusted proportionately to cover twelve months the figure would be approximately 550 murders *reported*—and thus would be an underestimate of the actual number because in India it is relatively easier for malefactors to conceal their crimes than it is in the West.[62] It is not very difficult, according to many people, to arrange an "accident" for one's enemies. If one is squeamish about such acts one can hire an outsider or arrange for a disappearance much in the way a Mafioso might let out a "contract".[63] Many missing persons are never discovered and those bodies which are found seldom provide enough evidence for the police to apprehend the criminal.[64] These first two factors that tend to deflate murder statistics are less likely to involve the "invulnerable-aggressive" individual than others for as we have said the invulnerable-aggressive is apt to kill in a fit of rage rather than by premeditation. Although the invulnerable-aggressives usually commit their crimes without thinking, they still manage to snarl the statistics by hiring false witnesses, suborning police officials, or intimidating survivors.[65] All in all then we can say that the figure of 550 murders per year or 4.56 per 100,000 population is likely to be an underestimate of the actual number of murders being committed in the province. Thus Punjab *reports* a slightly higher rate of homicides than did the United States during the same period.[66] And this in a predominantly rural area where a much larger percentage of the population is composed of children and where there is less access to efficient weaponry with which multiple murders might be committed. Measures of other types of aggression such as assaults or "rioting" are even less reliable.[67]

Invulnerability does not exist in all refugees. There appears to be a complex relationship between caste status and the degree of violence a person faced at the time of partition that contributes to the growth of this characteristic. Further research needs to be done in this area but at first glance it would appear that low status and low violence lead subjects to displace and project their unconscious aggressiveness while high status and great violence contribute to overt aggression. A larger number of cases should be examined to see whether any more exact relationship can be formulated.

REFERENCES

1. Urie Bronfenbrenner and Henry N. Ricciutti, "The Appraisal of Personality Characteristics," in *Handbook of Research Methods in Child Development*, ed. by Maul Mussen, New York: John Wiley and Company, 1960, p. 779.

2. For a detailed discussion of various approaches to the measurement of aggression and the difficulties encountered see Chapter V, "The Measurement of Aggression" of my unpublished Ph. D. thesis: Keller, Stephen L., *Uprooting and Social Change, The Role of Refugees in Development*, Massachusetts Institute of Technology, 1970.

3. Of course we are not the first to recognize the importance of aggression in political life. For a recent essay on the subject see Robert E. Lane, *Political Thinking and Consciousness*, Chicago : Markham Publishing Company, 1969, pp. 145-189. Also see H. L. Nieburg, *Political Violence*, New York : St. Martin's Press, 1969; the writings of Frantz Fanon, and Henry Bienens short book, *Violence and Social Change*, Chicago: University of Chicago Press, 1968.

4. Readers will recognize that in some ways these views parallel those of Samuel Huntington in *Political Order in Changing Societies*, New Haven: Yale University Press, 1968. One of Huntington's theses is that indicators of political development used by some scholars, e.g. equality, participation, etc., may be desirable as ends but are likely to prove destructive as means in the process of nation building. While many of Huntington's conclusions are open to question, for example the notion that increased participation leads to "political decay" (see Paul Brass, "Political Participation, Institutionalization and Stability in India," *Government and Opposition*, Winter 1969 for an empirical attempt at refuta-

tion), there can be no doubt that no system can function at near peak efficiency when all members of the populace begin to participate actively and constantly. If we consider that aggression may be indicative of "decay" as an initial state, then the notion of what government can do with aggression becomes an even more central issue.

5. Leonard Berkowitz, *Aggression : A Social Psychological Analysis*, New York: McGraw-Hill, 1962, Chapter V, "The Nature and Target of the Aggressive Response," pp. 104-131.

6. For a brief discussion of problems I encountered in using the TAT in north India see Appendix III.

7. For a psychological explanation of the high levels of aggression against children by parents in traditional societies see Everett E. Hagen, *On the Theory of Social Change*, Homewood, Ill. : Dorsey Press, 1962, pp. 143-148.

8. Joseph Elder, *Industrialism and Hinduism*, p. 211. (mimeographed).

9. For a brief illuminating illustration of the sort of step-wise displacement that may result in such a situation see Roger Brown's discussion of this phenomenon in Sheridan's *The Rivals* in Brown's *Social Psychology*, New York: Free Press, 1965, p. 750.

10. See David Bayley, *The Police and Political Development in India*, Princeton: Princeton University Press, 1969, pp. 97-106, for a discussion of the unreliability of crime statistics. Also see "Undetected Crime on the Increase," *The Statesman* (New Delhi), November 13, 1967.

11. Lois Barclay Murphy, "Roots of Tolerance and Tensions in Indian Child Development," in Gardner Murphy, *In the Minds of Men*, New York : Basic Books, 1953, pp. 46-58.

12. G. Morris Carstairs, *The Twice Born*, Bloomington: Indiana University Press, 1961.

13. Gitel P. Steed, "Notes on an Approach to a Study of Personality Formation in a Village in Gujarat," in *Village India: Studies in the Little Community*, ed. by McKim Marriott, Chicago : University of Chicago Press, 1955, pp. 102-144.

14. We recognize that fighting does not necessarily indicate aggression, since fighting may be either offensive or defensive in nature. Similarly a man may be officially punished for any number of offences of varying intensity of aggression and may even be innocent of the act for which he is punished. In India this may

come about through miscarriages of justice or through personal and factional feuds carried on through legal channels. However, since no better means of gauging a man's extrafamilial aggressive behaviour exists—attributional methods are out of the question in the factionally divided Indian village—we must continue to rely on proximate measures.

15. For example, "319 Murders in Punjab in Seven Months," *The Tribune* (Ambala), December 21, 1967; "Spate of Murders in Gurgaon Dist.," *The Tribune,* April 4, 1968; "64 Murders in 56 Days in Punjab," *The Tribune,* May 13, 1967; "The Capital Takes the Cake in Crime," *Times of India,* April 16, 1968; "A Murder Every Fourth Day" (in Ferozepur District), *The Tribune,* December 20, 1967; "Ferozepur Records a Murder a Week," *The Tribune,* September 14, 1967; "One Murder Every Four Days" (in Bhatinda District), *The Tribune,* November 8, 1967.

16. For lucid discussions of the *yuga* scheme see A. L. Basham, *The Wonder That Was India,* New York: Grove Press, 1959, pp. 320-322; and Heinrich Zimmer, *Myths and Symbols in Indian Art and Civilization,* New York: Harper Torchbooks, 1962, pp. 13-19.

17. The *Sarpanch* (headman) of one village often brought up the topic of his two arrests in social conversations with me. Despite the fact that all the evidence was that he had indeed on two occasions murdered some enemies, he constantly proclaimed his innocence and used the "unjust arrests" as evidence of sinister plotting by his rivals. Nevertheless, when he was interviewed he claimed that he never had fought (which I had observed to be untrue) or been arrested.

18. For a Theoretical approach to "image projection" see Erving Goffman, *The Presentation of Self in Everyday Life,* Garden City, N. Y.: Doubleday Anchor Books, 1959. More recently Goffman's theoretical framework has been utilized by Gerald D. Berreman in a monograph entitled *Behind Many Masks,* Ithaca, N. Y.: Society for Applied Anthropology, 1962, to show that "impression management" is a variable that must be taken into account by all field researchers. Also see Robert E. Ward, ed., *Studying Politics Abroad,* Boston : Little Brown and Company, 1964.

19. David McClelland, for example, believes that there is a definite correlation between achievement imagery in the popular imaginative literature of culture—the poems, drama, songs, and novels that are most widely accepted—and the achievement moti-

vation and economic growth of the society. "Achievement Drive and Economic Growth," *Harvard Business Review*, XL, No. 4, 1962, pp. 99-112.

20. The fact that values must be shared, at least to a certain degree, if any social system is to function at high levels of efficiency is almost a truism. Despite this however almost no research has been done on the value systems even in more developed societies where presumably such research is easier to conduct. Recently Milton Rokeach of Michigan State University has begun to labour in this vineyard which may eventually bear as much fruit as the already well developed study of attitudes. See his "The Role of Values in Public Opinion Research," *Public Opinion Quarterly*, XXXII, 1968-69, pp. 547-559.

21. The abandoning father, we felt, should not be interpreted as the *vanaprastha* (hermit) *ashrama* (stage of life) where a householder, having ensured the continuance of his family line, leaves the household for the life of a forest hermit. We were careful in the wording of the item to imply an irresponsible abandonment. As it turned out our respondents, when probed, said that they had understood the question to apply to a father who left the family for non-spiritual reasons.

22. See, for example, Alex Inkeles and Daniel J. Levinson, "National Character: The Study of Modal Personality and Sociocultural Systems," in *Handbook of Social Psychology*, ed. by Gardner Lindzey, Vol. II, Cambridge: Addison-Wesley, 1954. pp. 977-1020.

23. John Bowlby, *Attachment*, New York : Basic Books, 1969.

24. Sigmund Freud, *A General Introduction to Psychoanalysis*, New York : Washington Square Press, 1952 (first published 1924), pp. 333-346.

25. Erik H. Erikson, *Childhood and Society*, New York : Norton, 1950. Also see Erikson. *Young Man Luther*, New York : Norton, 1958, and *Identity and the Life Cycle*, New York : International Universities Press, 1959.

26. Keller, *op. cit.*

27. For an example of the societal approach to personality see John W. M. Whiting and Irvin L. Child, *Child Training and Personality*, New Haven: Yale University Press, 1953.

28. Elder, *op. cit.* See also Irawati Karve, *Kinship Organization in India*, Bombay : Asia Publishing House, 1965, p. 137, and Mrs. Karve's "On the Road : A Maharashtrian Pilgrimage," *Journal of*

Asian Studies, XXII, November 1962, pp. 13-29.

29. See Karve, "On the Road," *ibid.*, for accounts of this.

30. For a fascinating account of the relationships between the sexes and between different role holders see Lakshmibai Tilak, *I Follow After*, Madras : Oxford University Press, 1950.

31. Elder, *op. cit.*, p. 211.

32. See Gabriel A. Almond, *The Appeals of Communism*, Princeton: Princeton University Press, 1954.

33. M. Brewster Smith, Jerome Bruner, and Robert White, *Opinions and Personality*, New York : John Wiley, 1956. Recently Smith has refined the earlier approach and come up with a lucid and persuasive "Map for the Analysis of Personality and Politics," *Journal of Social Issues*, XXIV, 1968, p. 25, in which he is able to display graphically the complex interrelationships between the mind and political and social life.

34 Theodor W. Adorno, Else Frenkel-Brunswik, Daniel J. Levinson, and R. Nevitt Sanford, *The Authoritarian Personality*, New York: Harper & Brothers, 1950.

35. Robert Lane, *Political Thinking and Consciousness*, op, cit., pp. 145-189.

36. For an interesting report on the relationship between aggression and occupational performance see Ithiel de Sola Pool and Irwin Schulman, "Newsmen's Fantasies, Audiences and Newswriting," *Public Opinion Quarterly*, XXIII, 1959, pp. 145-158.

37. Herbert Hyman and Paul B. Sheatsley in *Studies in the Scope and Method of the Authoritarian Personality*, ed. by Richard F. Christie and Marie Jahoda, New York : Free Press, 1954, pp. 50-122.

38. Whiting and Child, *op. cit.*, found that severity of punishment of aggression in childhood is highly correlated with adult projection and displacement.

39. See Berkowitz, *op. cit.*, pp. 33 ff, 122 ff, for summaries of a number of these studies.

40. Neal E. Miller, "Theory and Experiment Relating Psychoanalytic Displacement to Stimulus-Response Generalization," *Journal of Abnormal and Social Psychology*, XLIII, 1948, pp. 155-178.

41. For an interesting discussion of some of these mechanisms, see David G. Mandelbaum, "Family, *Jati*, Village," in *Structure and Change in Indian Society*, ed. by Milton Singer and Bernard

Cohn, Chicago: Aldine Publishing Company, 1968, pp. 29-50.

42. For example see Martha Wolfenstein, *Disaster: A Psychological Essay*, Glencoe, Ill. : Free Press, 1957, pp. 158, 171.

43. For earlier uses of TATs cross culturally see David C. McClelland, *The Achieving Society*, Princeton : Van Nostrand, 1961, p. 261. Also see David C. McClelland and David G. Winter, *Motivating Economic Achievement*, New York : Free Press, 1969.

44. To get an idea of the scoring principles developed and the ingenious design of tests of hypotheses see John W. Atkinson, ed., *Motives in Fantasy, Action, and Society*, Princeton : Van Nostrand, 1958.

45. See Russell A. Clark and Minda Rae Sensibar, "The Relationship betwean Symbolic and Manifest Projections of Sexuality with Some Incidental Correlates," in Atkinson, *op. cit.*, pp. 117-129: or Paul H. Mussen and H. Kelly Naylor, "The Relationship between Overt and Fantasy Aggression," *Journal of Abnormal and Social Psychology*, IL, 1954, pp. 235-240.

46. See L. Bellak, *TAT Blank*, New York: Psychological Corporation, 1947, p. 3, for one type of scoring sheet that takes into account types of aggression and intensity. Also see Harold Stone, "The TAT Aggressive Content Scale," *Journal of Projective Techniques*, XX, 1956, p. 446. Also, Seymour Klebanoff, Chapter 12 in *Thematic Test Analysis*, ed. by Edwin S. Schneidman, New York : Grune and Stratton, 1951, pp. 127-128.

47. Jerome Kagan, "The Measurement of Overt Aggression from Fantasy," *Journal of Abnormal and Social Psychology*, LII, 1956, pp. 390-93.

48. Arthur R. Jensen, "Aggression in Fantasy and Overt Behaviour", *Psychological Monographs*, LXXI, 1957, No. 445.

49. Berkowitz, *op. cit.* p. 88.

50. This is not to say that we could not have used any of a number of other scoring techniques. Jensen's method appealed to us at first because it appeared to take into account many of the theoretical difficulties one encounters in the study of aggression while at the same time giving data that can be examined in terms of frequency as well as intensity. It was not until later that it became apparent that there are some serious shortcomings in Jensen's approach. At that point we decided to use only the point values Jensen devised for aggression, ignoring many other points made in the monograph. See below.

51. Jensen's scoring technique for punishment themes is based on a number of arbitrary considerations without any theoretical basis. Aside from the arbitrary scalar values associated with aggressive acts of various kinds Jensen tells us that punishments can only be scored if they are responses to aggressive acts of major proportions (*ibid.* p. 5.) In other words, if a respondent tells a story containing an aggression theme and a punishment theme, the former must be scored while the latter will only be scored as a punishment if the former has reached a certain value. There are two difficulties in this. The more important is the obvious fact that such a technique underestimates punishment themes. When one is comparing two groups giving aggressive responses of different intensity the group having given the weaker response will appear to be unconcerned about punishment relative to the more intense group even if they had responded with punishment themes with equal frequency and of equal intensity. Second, the method confuses scorers confronted with a low or moderate aggression score and an intense punishment score. Some score the punishment as the aggression because to do otherwise would mean that it would never appear in any form on the scoring sheet. Others score the aggression and ignore the punishment. These sorts of things can be worked out in the training period but the fundamental problem of determining when a punishment becomes harsh and unreasonable, and hence an independent aggressive act, still remains.

52. For this part of the scoring we used the same values as prescribed by Jensen, *op. cit.*, for scoring aggression themes. The only modification of Jensen's scale was our interpolation of some aggressive acts not specified in the original scoring guide. The scoring guide that was used for TAT aggression themes in this project can be found in Appendix V.

53. This is the object of Jensen's and many others' scoring procedures which try to distinguish between aggression instigated by the main character from that directed toward him. (Jensen also includes an indeterminate category). Most of these approaches also include a sample yes-no section for the scorer in which he notes other themes that might be related to aggression, e.g., natural death, suicide, illness, sex, etc.

54. The twenty card set used in this project was developed from the original set devised by Henry A. Murray. Costumes, appearances, and settings were modified so that the pictures could elicit

empathetic responses from a north Indian audience. For a discussion of the procedures used in developing this modified set of cards see Appendix IV.

55. Berkowitz, *op. cit.*, Chapter 10, "The Operation and Development of Aggressive Personalities", pp. 256-300.

56. Dollard, *et al.*, *op. cit.*

57. "Ideas of status were quietly accepted and did not prevent healthy co-operation and neighbourly feeling among the various caste groups represented in the various village communities of Southern India. In the case of Northern India we must remember that though, perhaps, village life did not lead to as much co-operation and fellow feeling, the system of castes was marked by a more lenient view and practice about food and social intercourse. The various castes, in so far as they contributed their respective services towards the common life of the village, were welded together and inter-dependent for the purposes of civic life. Inter-dependence of castes was such a deep-rooted principle that it prevented other exclusive aspects, inherent in the system, from getting the better of the idea of a common civic goal and human sympathy for co-residents and hardening into caste-spirit or caste-patriotism. If inter-dependence in civic and economic life of the village counteracted the centripetal forces of social restrictions of caste, certain special functions and occasions reminded some castes, ordinarily considered to be low, of their importance and even afforded them opportunities of enjoying temporary superiority." G. S. Ghurye, *Caste, Class and Occupation*, Bombay: Popular Book Depot, 1961, p. 25.

58. See T. O. Beidelman, *A Comparative Analysis of the Jajmani System,* Monograph of the Association of Asian Studies, VIII, Locust Valley, N. Y. : J. J. Augusten, 1959.

59. Virtually every fictional account of life on the frontier or in Punjab contains some reference to *izzat*. Thus we find Kipling's Pathans going on a rampage because of the affront to their *izzat* in having a Bengali as official in charge of their district. Rudyard Kipling, "The Head of the District," in *Black and White*, New York: Scribners, 1897. Joseph Elder presents us with an amusing account of the manifestations of *izzat* at a wedding ceremony, *op. cit.* pp. 219 ff.

60. For a good example of what we are discussing we herewith include the complete article, "Pattern of Murders in Karnal," *The Tribune* (Ambala), August 17, 1967:

"Karnal, Aug. 16.—A study of first information reports of

murders in Karnal district during the last seven months shows that the cause of murder in most cases has been either sudden loss of temper over a trivial matter or planned provocation to involve the other party in a fight.

Such murders were mostly committed by the refugees and the majority of them were Sikh Jats.

One Dalbir Singh of the Rajound area suddenly lost his temper when he found his elder brother had eaten away the entire boiled rice. Dalbir Singh in a fury gave a fatal blow with his kirpan to his brother who was asleep.

One Kulwant Singh of Bakal village was allegedly murdered by his brothers and another person after they became suspicious that Kulwant Singh was having illicit relations with the wife of a relative of one of his brothers.

One Sardara of Dabkheri village was allegedly assaulted by the accused who came to know that Sardara had shown disrespect to a woman relation of his. Hari Singh, who tried to intervene, was done to death by the accused.

Latkan Singh of Nalipur village was done to death with a sword by his son-in-law when the deceased refused to send his daughter with the accused.

Gurbachan Singh, Sedhu Singh and Lal Singh were murdered in Ramana village because of a dispute over the marriage of a girl.

Bakshish Singh of Pehowa was murdered in a land dispute."

61. "319 Murders in Punjab in Seven Months," *The Tribune* (Ambala), December 21, 1967.

62. *The New York Times* has summed up the reasons for this: "Criminologists consider homicide rates the most reliable of all crime statistics because over the years it appears that most homicides have become known to the police and because the legal definition—unlike some other crimes—has not undergone radical change." "City Study Shows Record Number of Homicides Last Year Almost Matched in 1931," *New York Times*, November 3, 1968. On the other hand *The Statesman* of November 13, 1967, reported "Undetected Crime on the Increase" in the Delhi, Haryana, Punjab region.

63. In another well publicized case, the "Phagwara Bomb Case," a factory owner hired a hooligan to mail a bomb to a labour leader who had been trying to organize the workers. Three workers were killed and nine others, including the labour leader, were wounded.

Through the testimony of an approver (state's evidence) both the hooligan and the factory owner were convicted but the factory owner received a life sentence while the hooligan was sentenced to death. See "Piara Singh to Hang; Life Term for Nand Lal Sehgal," *The Tribune* (Ambala), July 2, 1967.

64. In most cases this means simply throwing a body in a swiftly flowing canal or down an unused well but occasionally the killers take a leaf out of the annals of American crime (or simply strike on similar expedients by coincidence). In a case reminiscent of the exploits of Winnie Ruth Judd, a murderer killed a young woman, packed her in a trunk, and put her on the train from Pathankot in Punjab to Sealdah in West Bengal. As far as I know the killer was never apprehended for advertisements showing the partly decomposed body elicited no leads either to the identity of the victim or the culprit. See *The Tribune* (Ambala), July 5, 1967 for a copy of the advertisement.

65. In the course of my stay in the several villages and two towns I had direct knowledge of each of these types of procedures in two assault cases, a murder, and a sexual assault on a young Harijan boy. I believe that one reason for the ease with which facts are suppressed is that involvement with the police is a very threatening experience whether one is plaintiff or defendent. Although David Bayley in his book on *The Police and Political Development in India*, *op. cit.*, believes that police abuse of authority is not particularly great it must be remembered that most of his data come from police officials of fairly high rank and from public opinion polls. Bayley finds that twenty-five per cent of the *victims* of crimes do not report them; then how many other non-victims would report a crime? I suggest that if his information had come from lower level officers and from people who had the most direct contact with the police, i.e. members of the former criminal castes and tribes, the poorer elements of society who are frequently missed by the polls, e.g., rickshaw wallahs, day labourers, etc., he might revise his view. One close associate of mine happened to live next to a police substation and on the occasions when I went to visit with his family I was shocked by the sounds of beatings that emanated from the substation. There would be lulls, then a sound of a heavy leather belt cracking, presumably on the suspect's body judging by the groans and screams that followed. When I asked my associate about this and whether he knew that such acts were illegal and should be re-

ported he replied with the little man's age old response, something to the effect that it's better to let sleeping dogs lie and it was none of his business and involvement could only lead to trouble for him and his family. Since it is very difficult to live entirely within the complicated maze of municipal, state, and national laws in India (my associate, for example, had a brother who drove a scooter rickshaw which he rented from its owner despite the fact that he had been unable to get a licence, the family kept a cow tethered in front of their cottage which was contrary to municipal law) he was probably correct in his assessment of the possibility of trouble arising from any complaints that he might register. As we shall see in a later chapter, a Punjabi-Haryanvi's sense of efficacy varies with his social and economic power. One of the indicators of efficacy was the responses to a question having to do with what one would do if he were unjustly treated by the police. The lower a man's socio-economic status, the more likely he was to say something like "What can we do?"...and these are on questions about one's own ill-treatment, not possibly unjust or illegal acts against others.

66. Marvin E. Wolfgang and Franco Ferracuti, *The Subculture of Violence*, London: Tavistock Publications, 1967, p. 274, states that the homicide rate for the United States in 1960 was 4.5 per 100,000. More recent data indicate that by 1966 the rate had increased to 6.0 per 100,000. Task Force Report, *Crimes of Violence*, National Commission on the Causes and Prevention of Violence, excerpts reported in *The New York Times*, December 13, 1969.

67. For example, the article mentioned in reference 61 above ("319 Murders...") gives a few other statistics as well. For the same seven month period the police announced that there had been only one dacoity and thirteen robberies in the entire state.

CHAPTER V

The Political Culture of Punjab and Haryana

As in the bosom of the earth vestiges of all earlier life may still be found, so in the bosom of public opinion are to be found vestiges of the early dinosaurs of thought.
—Alvin Saunders Johnson

The last chapter dealt exclusively with one of the components of the refugees' personality: aggression. On this one parameter the refugees and non-refugees were significantly different and this difference was attributed to the events undergone in becoming a refugee. This chapter will discuss some other aspects of the political culture of the Punjab-Haryana region, emphasizing both points of similarity and dissimilarity between the refugees and non-refugees in an attempt to delineate significant components of the political culture of the area.

The concept of political culture emphasizes common themes running through the political life of a particular group of people.[1] It concerns itself more with the psychic realm of politics than with the institutional. To uncover that "ordered subjective realm of politics"[2] one must probe the sentiments and cognitions of a large number of people who are members of the group being examined. Although the sample drawn for this project is not very large there is no reason to suppose that their feelings and their awareness of political life are not representative of the inhabitants of the Punjab-Haryana region. Of course, particular facets of the political culture may also be representative of larger groupings, say the north Indian public, the entire subcontinent, and perhaps in some ways the entire developing world. But although the attitudes may not be unique my statements should be understood to apply to this limited region of India, if only because the political culture is in reality a constellation of elements which only in its entirety governs the individual's behaviour in the institutional political world.

A political culture is not a uniform constellation of these elements across all the members of the group. No large body of people share a common set of attitudes, cognitions, and affective valences. If they did then the political culture would be easily recognizable and not the elusive will-o-the-wisp that it has proven to be. Political culture, like its cousin national character, must be viewed as a statistical concept whereby the dominant values of the group under examination are those in the central areas of a bell shaped curve.[3] Recently it has been recognized that among societies in transition the distribution is apt to have a wider spread.[4] Further, in modernizing societies, especially the diverse models of the ideal life available, often create multimodal distributions.[5] As one moves out toward the tails of the curve one encounters the holders of deviant values and views. These deviants, who on one tail of the curve may be the Panglosses and on the other prophets, true believers, and malcontents, cannot be ignored. Often by their very deviance they can strike a responsive chord of recognition for unworldly virtue or self sacrificing idealism among the mass and rise to positions of charismatic leadership.[6] If their number is large the presence of such deviants may be indicative of an identity crisis among the citizens of the area or perhaps represent the vanguard of insurgency or chiliastic movements. Thus in starting this project we sampled the population, realizing that while a dominant profile would probably emerge, there would also be a great deal of confusing and contradictory information as well. A number of the more interesting dominant themes as well as a few fascinating variations on them will be discussed in this chapter. The concepts to be covered will be authoritarianism and concern with power, sense of efficacy, trust, hostility to outgroups, and concern with conflict.

Concern with Conflict

> Strife is a loss, friendship a gain...
>
> A North Indian proverb

A dominant theme in classical Indian political thought is an almost pathological fear of conflict. According to Manu, the law-giver, Kautilya, the most important political theorist of ancient

India, and many myths, kingship is essential to settle disputes quickly by consensus or by force if a state of anarchy is to be avoided.[7] In fact anarchy is seen as the justification for the creation of the institution of kingship. This much dreaded anarchy (which, while to be avoided at all costs in one's own kingdom is to be fomented in those of rivals) is known as *matsyanyaya* or the way of the fishes[8] (because in the sea the great fishes devour the smaller ones) and is a particular hazard during the current decadent era, the *Kali Yuga*.[9] As Zimmer notes: "Kali means the worst of anything; also, 'strife, quarrel, dissension, war, battle.' "[10] Any action of the state or individual that is capable of dissipating or stamping out conflict is considered praiseworthy, while any act promoting or leading to a "continuation of conflict was to be condemned." Basham tells us that "Even delay in justice was visited with dire penalties[11], for a legendary king called Nrga was reborn as a lizard, because he kept two litigants waiting in a dispute over a cow."[12] But in reducing the conflict, justice itself is not a consideration: "In this dark age the innocent must suffer with the guilty, in order that society may be protected, anarchy avoided, and men enabled to pursue the Sacred Law in peace."[13] More than justice, what is called for is discipline. As T. N. Ramaswamy points out, greater discipline is required in *Kali Yuga* to maintain the balance of the four elements of human existence necessary for continuation of the state which, as has already been noted, is vital to the prevention of anarchy.[14]. The *Canti Parva*, part of the *Mahabharata,* tells us that "If chastisement had not existed, all creatures would have grinded one another. Through fear of chastisement, O Yudhisthira, living creatures do not slay one another."[15]

Although very few Indians today are well acquainted with the writings of the early political thinkers the fear of the consequences of conflict and the dangers of not managing it have filtered down through the consciousness of generations into the attitudes and motivations of Indians at all levels of society. In fact, it is likely that the need for consensus to avoid disputes which could lead to ungovernable conflict and aggression is a core component of the Indian value system. Myron Weiner has observed that even in labour-management negotiations and in the modern political arena disputes are settled in the traditional way, by arbitration. The arbitration mechanism is felt to be a "safer" way of confining and regulating inherently conflictual situations.[16] Such a view can be seen at the root of the Rajasthan Government's policy of offering a bonus to villages that elect their *panchayats* unanimously.[17] In virtually all studies of village life and politics, regardless of the geographical area being discussed, one hears of high levels of anxiety over conflict and an overwhelming desire for complete consensus. Prakash Tandon, in *Punjabi Century*, has described how the mechanisms of conflict management worked when he was a boy. He has noted that the traditional dispute settlement machinery of the *biradari* was directed at obtaining consensus lest the close symbiotic relationships of village and caste be sundered.[18] G. Morris Carstairs discusses the fear of a loss of self control which would lead to unmanageable interpersonal conflict.[19] Richard Fox has shown how when traditional means of conflict management are removed or weakened by the impact of social change, a Hobbesian situation of "all against all" emerges to eliminate any chance for the cooperation necessary for development activities.[20] Adrian Mayer, in Madhya Pradesh, found that when villagers discovered that the new statutory panchayat system was incapable of handling conflict they created a new, partially overlapping institution, the "comprehensive committee"[21] that could use traditional consensual means to resolve conflict.

When the project started I believed that a concern with conflict although probably universally Indian would be associated in inten-

TABLE 5.1

Index of Concern with Conflict

1. Preserving harmony in the village (neighbourhood) should be considered more important than the achievement of its programmes.
2. Even though I am sure I am in the right in a discussion I usually give in because it is foolish to cause trouble.
3. Do the people around here usually get along well with each other or do they not get along well?
4. Are there more or less conflicts around here than there were before Independence?
5. One learned man says : "When people compete with each other they work harder and do their best and there is progress." Another learned man says : "When people compete with each other they become enemies and progress becomes impossible." Which man do you think is more correct?

sified form with aggressiveness. Before the project had begun I had expected that this association would be shown by a relationship between refugeeism and concern with conflict. The reasoning behind this was that aggressive personalities would be highly sensitized to aggressive cues, often perceiving them where they did not exist. This, it was supposed, would lead them to view many situations as conflictual relationships. When the questionnaire was made up it was decided to include five items that could be combined into an Index of Concern with Conflict. When the data had been gathered, the index score, however did not correlate with aggressive behaviour within the family ($r=-.020$; not significant) or in society in general ($r=-.657$; not significant). Examination showed that both groups, refugees and non-refugees, scored equally high on the index and did not differ significantly from one another. Nor could any significant differences between the two groups be determined by controlling for any of the other variables, e.g. residence, age at partition, caste, religion, education, degree of violence encountered in 1947, etc. Refugees and non-refugees shared their views about the incidence of conflict about them and the dangers inherent in conflict situations.

Many respondents refused to answer item 4 of the Index, perhaps a further indication of a reluctance to let conflict emerge into the open. This reduced the number of respondents who could be scored on the Index to 68, a figure too small to do very much with in terms of data analysis. The mean score of 68 was much higher than chance (22.2 and 17.5 respectively) but a high standard deviation robs the difference of any great significance. There are hints though, from the separate items, that a larger sample would have shown significance and that respondents are extremely fearful of the dangers of conflict. About three quarters of the total sample (73.8%) felt strongly that preserving harmony in the village or town was more important than the achievement of community or developmental programme goals. Another one-eighth agreed with this statement to some degree (moderately 9.5%, slightly 2.4%). Only an eighth (11.9%) disagreed at all. Almost four-fifths (78.6%) of the entire sample were reluctant to assert themselves, even when they were sure of the correctness of their position, for fear that such pushiness would lead to trouble. (Item 2) Another item not included in the Index asked about the relationship between participation and conflict. Three-fourths of the total sample (73.0%) felt strongly that widespread participation leads to conflict. Another fifth agreed moderately or slightly (19.0% and 1.6%).

When a factor analysis was run, a group of items obviously related to concepts of harmony and conflict was generated. (The factor was called "Harmony" because of the signs of the related factor loadings. Some feeling for the tone of life in the area can be gained from the responses. See Table 5.2.

TABLE 5.2
Responses to Attitudinal Components of Harmony Factor

Item	*Per cent Replying*
3. (a) Most people are honest in their dealings with others. OR (b) Most people will use unfair means in their dealings with others. ("b" responses)	64.8
4. Sometimes I feel like smashing things. (agree)	27.8
5. People pretend to care more about one another than they really do. (agree)	92.8
6. Human nature being what it is, there will always be war and conflict. (agree)	73.8
7. When one is involved in some business deal he should care little about the feelings of the other party. (agree)	68.8
8. I believe that most of my neighbours would not hesitate to do something harmful to me if they thought they could get away with it. (agree)	55.6
9. At time I feel like starting a fistfight with some-one. (agree)	25.4
10. An insult should always be punished. (agree)	96.0

Conflict is believed to be endemic in the world. At the local level one source of conflict is business deals but even in other relationships one can never be sure of the true sentiments and aims of other people, including one's neighbours. As long as the other party maintains his false front, conflict can be kept within acceptable bounds (using unfair means and caring little about others' feelings) but when conflict emerges through the showing of one's true colours through an insult, conflict is believed inevitable (and punishment just).

One logical outcome of the viewpoints highlighted by the data described in this section, where harmony is valued so highly that everything including wealth and personal comfort will be sacrificed to it, is that without profound attitude change among the population the Government of India, despite its cherished notion of participatory democracy through *Panchayati Raj* and the Community Development Programme will probably, in the near future at least, be unable to achieve its stated goals of enlisting the support of villagers in the development of the nation.[22] However, as we shall see in the next chapter the situation in terms of economic attitudes and values is not entirely hopeless.

Orientations to Power and Authority

> Even a sheep bites the man without a stick......
> Four *vedas*, the fifth a cudgel......
>
> A North Indian proverbs.

In ancient India the concept of *danda-niti* (literally "stick-policy," but better phrased "force in the service of the state") was an integral part of the concept of kingship and the state.[23] Kautilya, in the *Arthashastra* written about 2,000 years ago, instructs his king-pupils that one of the most effective ways to hold a kingdom is to be unstinting in the application of force.[24] In the *Mahabharata*, after the great battle has been fought, King Yudhisthira has qualms about using the *danda* in ruling over his newly secured domain.[25] He considers retiring from the world but is dissuaded by Bhishma and Arjuna who tell him of all the misfortunes that accrue to a state from the timidity of its ruler. It is *danda*, wielded by legitimate authority which prevents *matsyanyaya* (the way of the fishes, described in the previous section) and *danda* which keeps the world righteous in *Kali Yuga*.

The non-refugees and refugees both have strong feelings about the appropriateness of the use of power. The refugees' views however seem to represent an accentuation of the ancient Indian desire for a strong and righteous king who, if not by goodness then by force, will bring unity and suppress those elements that threaten the tranquility of the state. The wielding of *danda* is the proper occupation of the ruler who is also expected to be as a father to his subjects. Earlier we found equally strong feelings among both groups about the appropriateness of punishing wrongdoers. The higher rate of intrafamilial aggression among refugees is merely another facet of the concept of *danda*. To keep order in a family and to prevent all the dangers which threaten one must wield *danda* with authority and without fear of the consequences. Literally a man's home is his domain and who ever heard of a king who feared the consequences of his actions? However, when power begins to waver, or when it is not exercised with the certitude and swiftness that stem from strength, then its holders are allowing conflict and then anarchy to creep in and thus are not fit to wield power.

The respondents' replies on the virtues of punishment have already been described. We were also interested in their views of the reasons for troubles within the household. A question that asked whether children got in trouble because their parents were too lenient with them or because the parents punished them too much showed that five-eighths of the sample (61.6%) believed that children got into trouble because of the laxity of parents in administering the *danda.* (29.6% felt too much punishment led children astray.) Parents who don't rule with an iron fist are likely to find their sons in trouble. And the trouble most feared and most frequent in Punjab is fighting and drunken brawling, i.e., conflict, either controlled or uncontrolled (56.7% of those replying to a question on causes of conflict in their neighbourhood or village. n=74).

In an earlier chapter the harshest punishments were seen to be reserved for the son who challenges his father's power by striking him or insulting him. In such cases the *danda* is not to be spared unless the power holder is prepared to step down. In this age of *Kali Yuga* although *danda* is necessary for the maintenance of the world there are few who are seen as either worthy of wielding it or having enough character to wield it in the service of society. Another parental figure, the judicial system, was also seen as being too lenient. The statement, "Nowadays the courts don't give as severe punishment to law-breakers as they ought to" evoked agreement from almost three-fourths the entire sample (69.8%; N=126).

To some extent the view that power must be exerted and the ruler who proves himself unable to wield it either through vacillation or through his not actually having the strength others had thought he possessed may account for some of the unexpected reversals of political fortunes in the subcontinent. For some time now political pundits have been shocked at what they see as the hollowness of a great number of public figures. These public figures, once considered unbeatable and indeed unchallengeable, have as often as not proven themselves to be men of straw who were blown over by what many saw as the first strong breeze. The most dramatic example of this in the subcontinent was the overthrow of Field Marshal Mohammed Ayub Khan in Pakistan in 1969 but less spectacular instances are also abundant. Partap Singh Kairon, leader of Congress in Punjab and Chief Minister of the state for about ten years (1955-1964) was ruthless in the application of his power until a dispute with a police official (the Grewal case) showed him unable to cope with a rather minor problem. Within a short period the clmour for his removal rose to such a pitch that the Central Government was forced to remove him from office. A little later he was murdered in broad daylight on the main highway from Delhi to Chandigarh. The similar falls of Kamarswamy Kamaraj, Atulya Ghosh, and S. K. Patil (who has since made a comeback) are eloquent testimony that once the charisma that comes from strength falls into doubt, leadership positions are as good as lost.

But what about leaders whose power has not been called into question? To examine Punjabi-Haryanvi sentiments about power and the people who wield it an Index of Concern with Power was constructed from six items on the interview schedule. The Index can be found in Table 5.3. A high score on the Index was interpreted as indicating the desirability of strong superior-subordinate relationships and an unwillingness to challenge any holder of power (because of the danger involved).

TABLE 5.3

Index of Concern with Power

1. Only wicked or foolish peole would oppose a great political leader.
2. Disobedience to any government is never justified.
3. One man says : "The most important thing for an eleven or twelve year old boy to learn is to always obey the wishes of his father." Another man says : "The most important thing a boy should learn is to think for himself." Which man do you think is more correct ?
4. One man says : "Our country needs a strong leader who will take over the government and make everybody obey him." Another man says : 'Our country needs leaders who have been chosen by the people and who will act in accordance with the people's wishes". Which man do you think is more correct ?
5. (a) Facing an officer is equal to standing behind a horse

   OR

   (b) Officers are public servants and are helpful to common man.

At the outset of the project it was expected that aggressive and non-aggressive individuals would respond differently to these questions. Aggressive persons, we hypothesized, would be very concerned with power for without power aggression is inefficacious or even counter-productive. When it was discovered that the major difference between aggressive and non-aggressive individuals was a sense of invulnerability this hypothesis was called into question. A person lashing out against a frustration because of a sense of invulnerability will be unconcerned with whether or not he has the power to succeed for even if he fails and is punished "he can take it." Indeed, there was no discernible relationship between a concern with power and any of the measures of behavioural or attitudinal aggression. Instead, income seemed to be the crucial variable in determining the attitudes that together represent a concern with power. The relationships can be found in Table 5.4.

TABLE 5.4

Household Income vs. Concern with Power

Concern with Power		*Household Income* Low	Medium	High
Low		35.9%	45.5%	70.7%
High		64.1	54.5	29.3
	Total =	100.0%	100.0%	100.0%
	N =	(39)	(44)	(41)
$x^2=10.485$	$p=0.005$		gamma $=-0.442$	

(Because the respondents were split at the median to create "high" and "low" groups, 16.8 per cent of the subjects scored low and yet were above the midpoint of possible scores on the Index.)

Further analysis showed that a concern with power correlated very strongly with whether or not the individual in question actually had power. Scores on the Index of Concern with Power yielded high correlations with the customary Indian attributes of powerlessness: low caste status and low income. Not only were index scores correlated with the above characteristics, they were also linked to some western notions of the correlates of powerlessness, such as a low sense of personal efficacy, low media exposure, and a low level of political knowledge. (Descriptions of the indexes used to determine scores on the above indicators can be found in later sections of this chapter.) The correlation coefficients can be found in Table 5.5.

The rich know that they have local power today. Those having power do not want strong political leaders to tell them what to do. They prefer responsive and even pliable types. Whether officials

TABLE 5.5

Coefficients of Correlation between Concern with Power and Background Variables

	r	p
Caste rank	—.197	0.05
Household income	—.396	0.01
Political knowledge index	—.376	0.01
Media exposure	—.231	0.01
Personal efficacy	—.232	0.05
Political efficacy (practice)	—.275	0.01
Organizational membership	—.203	0.05

and politicians in this area of India are as malleable as these local strong men would like is beyond the scope of this study but the table shows that the people least desirous of externally imposed power are those who know most about the political personnel, political parties, and other organizations in the area, the men who are most likely to take action against what they consider the unjust acts of the police, the Deputy Commissioner and to a lesser degree even the Central Government (See the sections of this chapter dealing with efficacy and awareness). This can be shown another way. Table 5.5 shows that caste status is inversely related to concern with power. That is, members of the least powerful group, the low castes, are strongly in favour of externally imposed power, probably because they feel it would act as a constraint upon the members of the high castes who run things. For probably the same reasons the high castes are least in favour of this.

An interesting point emerges when caste rank is controlled for it then turns out that there are significant differences between refugees and non-refugees but only among the high caste members of both groups. (Cultivating, Merchant, and Brahmin castes were classified as "high"). The relationship can be seen in Table 5.6.

In each research location, as far as could be determined, it was these "high" refugees who held power in panchayats, cooperatives, town councils, etc. (This, I have been told, is a common pattern.

TABLE 5.6

Refugeeism vs. Concern with Power (High Castes only)

Concern with Power		*Per cent Replying*	
		Refugee	*Non-Refugee*
Low		68.9%	41.9%
High		31.1	58.1
	Total=	100.0%	100.0%
	N=	(45)	(31)
x^2 (Continuity corrected)=4.420	p=0.036		gamma=0.508

Where refugees settle in sizeable numbers they have frequently been successful in gaining control of power.) In addition, the refugees had closer ties with politicians. All respondents were asked how frequently they met with various types of people, e.g. priests, newspapermen, members of the military, factory workers, trade unionists, big businessmen, etc. The only difference between refugees and non-refugees with regard to contact with holders of these different roles had to do with frequency of contact with politicians. Answers were coded into eight categories of frequencies. Tests of the difference of group means showed the refugees to meet politicians more frequently (t—test, p=0.01) and the people responsible

TABLE 5.7

Frequency of Meetings with Politicians

Frequency		*Per cent Replying*	
		Refugees	*Non-Refugees*
Never		15.1%	37.3%
Once a year or less frequently		21.9	21.6
Several times a year		23.3	15.7
At least once a month		38.4	25.5
DK, NR		1.4	
	Total=	100.0%	100.0%
	N=	(73)	(51)

for this difference were the powerful, high caste refugees. (See the section on efficacy below.) Table 5.7 is a collapsed version of the frequency results.

It is not because these people are refugees that they seek out politicians or that politicians come to them. Rather it is because these people have the power to influence the politicians in the execution of their duties and are also the people whom the politician must please if he is to get the block of votes that they control.

Affect toward Government and Political Objects

> The uncle a thief and the nephew a judge....
> In a quarrel between bulls, it's the calf's leg
> that gets broken....
>
> A North Indian proverbs.

Concern with power then is mainly determined by the social and political realities of one's local, personal situation. The next question that must be answered is whether sentiments about more distant political objects also result from one's social position or from psychological characteristics. Certainly in some respects this notion of societal position is plausible and applicable to large numbers of Indians and some of their political orientations : one finds few industrialists supporting the CPI Naxalites and not very many landless labourers actively backing Swatantra. But what about broader issues of the political culture : loyalty and commitment, attitudes regarding political performance and relationships between competitors for power? This is politics in a more abstract sense (and most of politics above the local level was very abstract to members of our sample) which, although partly shaped by actual experience, also conditions the individual's vision and actions in the political arena.

Not everyone would agree however that sentiments about authority and politics are shaped purely by sociological factors. Out of the World War II bombing studies,[26] later work on disaster victims,[27] and survivors of atomic bombing[28] often blamed their own leaders for not providing adequate protection and had jaundiced views of politicians. Another possible relationship was proposed most clearly by officials in the Punjab-Haryana region during informal interviews I had with them. Their view was that the refugees have done so well with the help of the government that they have become the firmest supporters of the existing state of affairs.

Thus there are three major hypotheses about the derivation and direction of affective sentiments toward political objects. Two of these predict directly that being a refugee predisposes one to harbour favourable or unfavourable sentiments toward these objects. Each predicts opposite responses. The third claims that social realities are more significant determinants of affect toward government and politics than whether or not one is a refugee or not.

An Index of Affect toward governmental and political objects was constructed from the several items on the interview schedule. The Index can be found in Table 5.8. [29]

TABLE 5.8

Index of Hostility to Governmental and Political Objects

1. Most political leaders in this country are concerned only with their own good.
2. (a) Facing an officer is equal to standing behind a horse

   OR

   (b) Officers are public servants and helpful to the common man.
3. The present government is too weak in dealings with Pakistan.
4. Dishonesty seems to be more prevalent in the government services than in other professions.
5. People often say that politics is a fraud. To call it a form of "authorised crookedness" would be a pretty good description.
6. How much do you feel you can trust government officials ?
7. I don't think public officials care much what people like me think.
8. On the whole do you think that the Indian political system is working very well, fairly well, not too well, or badly ?
9. And the Community Development Programme, do you think it is working very well, fairly well, not too well, or badly ?
10. And what about the Five-Year Plans, are they working very well, fairly well, not too well, or badly ?

The most interesting finding was that refugees and non-refugees do not differ significantly in the affect they have for government (t-test, $p=0.66$). Nor from the moderateness of the responses does it appear that either extremely hostile or extremely favourable sentiments about authority are held by the refugees or the non-refugees. The mean scores of the two groups were very close and were also close to the centre of the range of possible scores, i.e., neutral in affect. Thus if Lifton's work and the psychological approaches that predict hostility to government after extreme events are applicable to refugees (and we have reason to believe that they are from the accounts of flight given by our respondents) the hostility among the refugees appears to have been dissipated by the passage of twenty years.

The Hostility to Governmental and Political Objects Index drew forth moderate mean responses from both groups but the sample was not homogeneous with everyone holding moderate views. When cross-tabs of place of residence by hostility to governmental and political objects were run it was clear that place of residence was an important determinant of one's affect toward government. Villagers were relatively satisfied with politicians and officials, towns people were less so, and city people were downright hostile. The difference was highly significant. (p=.03). See Table 5.9 for the cross tabulations of residence vs. hostility. The findings apparently represent at least a partial recognition of political realities

TABLE 5.9

Residence vs. Hostility to Governmental and Political Objects

		Per cent Replying		
Hostility Score		*Village*	*Town*	*City*
Low		57.5%	50.0%	18.7%
High		42.5	50.0	81.2
	Total=	100.0	100.0	100.0
	n=	(40)	(14)	(16)
x^2=6.944		p=0.031		gamma =0.485

in the area. It is no secret to anyone in either state that their state governments are the representatives of rural interests and especially rural Jats. Then, urban groups' dislike of governmental and political figures may reflect a recognition that these are not only their representatives but are representatives of interests that are often inimical to their own. If this is indeed the case, the significance might have been still greater had some people with interests in the urban sphere not preferred to live away from the bustle of the city and many rising landed squires not preferred to live in towns near their villages for the social amenities provided.

While indices can be very useful in some circumstances to illuminate gross relationships caution in their use is also advisable since only those respondents answering all the items receive scores. Here only about sixty per cent of the entire sample did so. Thus, the least informed respondents hadn't the slightest inkling of the Five-Year Plans, much less a view on whether they were good or bad. More were aware of what was meant by the Community Development Programme but a surprisingly large number (23.2%) were unclear as to its work, goals, personnel, and degree of success. As a result, the Index scores are biased in the direction of those members of the community who are best informed. Information level and participation will be discussed in a later section.

Table 5.10 displays the percentage of the entire sample giving specific responses to a number of questions dealing with politics and government. Some of the items are from the Index, others are not. At first the responses to individual items appear anomalous. For example, very few respondents felt that government policies were bad. Only twenty per cent felt the government was too weak in dealing with Pakistan; twenty-eight per cent thought it was too weak with China. Virtually everyone (96%) felt the government had his best interests at heart, that both central and state governments had aided his interests (72.0 and 63.2% of all respondents. Eliminating "don't knows", "no responses", and unclear answers the figures rise to 85% and 87.5% respectively.) Similarly high percentages felt that the Indian political system, the Community Development Programme, and the Five-Year Plan were working well. (All respondents : 74.4%, 58.4%, 52.8% respectively; clear answers only : 79.0%, 75.2%, 82.5%).

On the other hand political leaders and government officials are seen as selfish, dishonest, uncaring, and untrustworthy. That is, the respondents differentiate between the "Government" and the men who compose that structure. They seem to feel that the Government is beneficial or at least well-meaning and would help the people if there was not such dishonesty among its personnel. [This pattern exists also in the Index items discussed earlier. In Table 5.8 Items 1, 4, 6, and 7 measure attitudes towards holders of political roles: items 3, 5, 8, 9, and 10 toward government defined institutionally. Item 2 consists of two contradictory statements (or so we thought) that appear to tap both of these dimensions...it received the most ambiguous responses : an almost even split between sentiments of approach and avoidance.] The figures of table 5.10 show even more clearly that there is a high degree of political cynicism with regard to personnel but relative satisfaction with the system in general and even with specific programmes.

Hostility to present office holders is aimed at individuals and not at the roles themselves. Most respondents seem to think that they could do a better job (if not for the nation or community, then for themselves) than those now holding positions of authority.

In an earlier section we saw that the offices of the truly powerful were not to be challenged, probably because of the danger of unmanageable conflict. Yet people still want power for themselves. More than three-fourths (76.2%) said that they would approve of a

TABLE 5.10

Sentiments regarding Government and Politics

Item	*Per cent Responding*
1. Most political leaders in this country are concerned only with their own good. (agree)	79.4
2. (a) Facing an officer is equal to standing behind a horse	49.6
OR	
(b) Officers are public servants and helpful to the common man.	46.4
3. The present government is too weak in dealing with Pakistan. (agree)	20.0
4. Dishonesty seems to be more prevalent in the government services than in other professions. (agree)	73.6
5. People often say that politics is a fraud. To call it a form of "authorized crookedness" would be a pretty good description. (agree)	31.6
6. How much do you feel you can trust government officials ? (somewhat, little, and not at all responses)	62.4
7. I don't think public officials care much what people like me think. (agree)	72.0
8. On the whole do you think that the Indian political system is working very well, fairly well, not too well, or badly ? (very well and fairly well)	74.4
9. And the Community Development Programme, do you think it is working very well, fairly well, not too well, or badly ? (very well and fairly well)	58.4
10. And what about the Five-Year Plans, are they working very well, fairly well, not too well, or badly ? (very well and fairly well)	52.8
11. The present government is too weak in dealing with China (agree)	28.0
12. Do you think the central government has aided or hurt interests ? (aided)	72.0
13. Do you think the state government has aided or hurt your interests ? (aided)	63.2
14. Do you think the government has your best interests at heart ? (yes)	85.6

son's decision to go into politics. Almost no one (5.6%) said he would disapprove. The reasoning behind this decision was pragmatic. When asked *why* they would approve or disapprove of a son's decision to enter politics, almost half the respondents (45.9%) of all respondents, (60.2% of those approving) explained their view by saying that politicians had great opportunities for amassing wealth or helping their relatives. Only a third of those approving (35.7%) found public service or the good of the nation as sufficient reason for letting a son go into political life. Hostility towards government officials and politicians then is not so powerful that one doesn't want to become one of them. Only a handful (3.2%) disapproved of their sons becoming politicians for moral reasons ("It's a dishonest profession", "He will become corrupted"). Still fewer (0.8%) felt that a son should not go into politics because it was a dangerous profession. This last response was somewhat surprising in light of the then recent murders of Partap Singh Kairon, the former Chief Minister of Punjab and Harjinder Singh Behla, a member of the Punjab Legislative Assembly and participant in the coalition that was ruling Punjab with a very slim margin. Incidents were not infrequent where politicians, including Ministers, were beaten by *goondas* hired by their rivals. In North India, politics is seen as a high risk-high gain occupation but apparently the potential gain is considered worth the risks involved.

Authoritarianism

What seems to emerge from the discussion thus far is that the sample scores fairly high on items that appear related to some dimensions of the original F-scale, e.g. Power and "Toughness", Authoritarian Submission and Conventionalism. This is not surprising since descriptions we have of family and village life portray characteristics similar to what has been called authoritarianism in the west. The factor analysis substantiated this by generating a factor that seemed to include still more of the originally hypothesized components of authoritarianism. The main addition to the points already discussed was the inclusion of some items that could be characterized as Authoritarian Aggression and an intolerance of deviance. While the generation of a factor was consistent with our expectations, the public was not uniformly authoritarian. In fact very great differences exist between the refugees and non-refugees on this particular factor. A t-test of the means of the two groups with regard to this factor showed that there was only a minuscule chance ($p=0.004$, $N=126$) of the two groups actually belonging to the same universe.

The intolerance of deviance that is a core component of the factor is surprising in India, a country recognized for its people's

TABLE 5.11

Anti-Authoritarianism Factor

		RFL
1.	Most of our social problems would be solved if we could somehow get rid of the immoral, crooked, and feeble-minded people	.564
2.	People with unpopular opinions should not be allowed to speak in public	.507
3.	The main threat to Indian institutions in this century has come from the infiltration of foreign ideas, doctrines and agitators	.484
4.	What do you think is the best way to deal with a ten year old boy who strikes his father and insults him	–.381
5.	Are there more or less conflicts around here now than there were before Independence	–.332
6.	One man says : "Our country needs a strong leader who will take over the government and make everybody obey him." Another man says : "Our country needs leaders who have been chosen by the people and who will act in accordance with the people's wishes."	
7.	Muslims should give up their separate customs and become average citizens of this country	–.303

broadminded treatment of (or complete disregard for) even the most bizarre sects and practices. More than mere intolerance as thought of in the west, the intolerance of the factor is more political in nature, a willingness to suppress deviant or dissident elements of the population with legitimate force. Actions in this line are felt by the refugees to be in the service of the country and grow out of the refugees' views of themselves. Several respondents reported that refugees felt differently about some things: "We have sacrificed a lot for this country. Now we have become the best farmers and small industrialists. But now no one cares for us or for Hindustan. Everyone is selfish and there is no discipline. Evil elements cause troubles that no one does anything about. A strong government should straighten things out and punish the wrongdoers." The tolerance of deviance or anti-authoritarianism factor (sign changed) correlated highly with aggressive behaviour ($r=-.276$, $p=0.01$).

Fantasy Aggression

In a strong position even a coward is a lion. . . .

A North Indian proverb

Aside from an intolerance of deviance some aggressive personalities were expected to exhibit high levels of hostility to others. For those with no inhibitory tendencies or conflicting response tendencies the aggression takes place at the point of frustration, but for many people and in many situations inhibitory tendencies such as the fear of punishment make immediate aggression impossible. Instead of hitting the policeman who has been harassing you, the hostility and perhaps the aggression is displaced to weaker targets. For those who have strong inhibitory tendencies either through what was described as a higher sense of vulnerability or other mechanisms, the targets may be so safely distant that no aggression could ever take place. Then, only hostility or fantasy aggression towards these objects remains. Even in the case of those having a high sense of their own invulnerability there are likely to be some

TABLE 5.12

Fantasy Aggression Factor

Items	*Loadings*
1. There are some people whom I dislike so much that I am inwardly pleased when they are in trouble for something ney have done	—.610
2. It is no honour to attack a weak person OR Might make right	.548
3. If a young boy, about 10 years of age, disobeys his father, what do you think is the best way to deal with him ?	.437
4. Nowadays the courts don't give as severe punishment to law-breakers as they ought to	.405
5. Human nature being what it is, there will always be war and conflict	—.396
6. Children get into trouble because their parents punish them too much OR The trouble with most children nowadays is that their parents are too easy with them	.379
7. Too many people in high places are doing things that hurt the people	—.348
8. India is spending too much money on the pampering of its criminals and for the education of inherently incapable people	—.335
9. People pretend to care more about one another than they really do	.313

inhibitory tendencies, for even the most aggressive individual will only last so long if he aggresses against some targets. Psychological theory states that the displacement of hostility will always be in the direction of weaker targets who, in the case of this study, will sometimes be minority groups and/or types of people with whom the respondent either has never been in contact or would have a hard time finding even if he had the inclination to aggress against them. The factor analysis produced a factor containing many of the items having to do with fantasy aggression. The items of the factor and their loadings can be found in Table 5.12.

Not all the targets of hostility in the factor items are weak out-groups, but those targets that are stronger than the individual (people in high places, criminals) are distant enough to be safe objects of animosity (this is not to say that one would act against them); those closer to home are passively aggressed against ("There are some people I dislike so much that I am secretly pleased when they are in trouble for something they have done"), while those that are weak may actually be physically aggressed against. No differences between refugees and non-refugees could be ascertained even after a large number of crosstabs were run.

Hostility to Muslims

Another area of fantasy aggression, one with potentially great significance for both internal and external political affairs in India, has to do with public opinion regarding Muslims and their role in India's future. Recent communal rioting at Ahmedabad and elsewhere has shown how fragile the bonds between the Muslims and the rest of the population are. In the last few years the latent anti-Muslim sentiments of certain elements of the population have been both responded to as well as developed and shaped by rabble-rousers out to loot and pillage, opportunistic politicians looking for "easy" issues, and unscrupulous local labour leaders who can rally crowds by supposedly showing how Muslims take jobs away from Hindus. Naturally such actions lead to fear and defensiveness among Muslims that is often misinterpreted by Hindu neighbours. While the Congress Party is committed to the maintenance of a secular state with no bars to Muslim opportunities, some other parties have, on occasion, been willing to mobilize the sentiments of the various frustrated sections of the population and focus attention on the Muslims as a cause of frustration.

To people unable to find jobs to match their qualifications, or those being pushed off the soil by land reform and mechanization, or those suffering from a galloping inflation that keeps them poor despite hard work, the Muslims and a government that appears to favour them may be targets on which they can focus their rage. Anti-Muslim backlash is potentially so great in India that the *New York Times* recently devoted almost six full-page columns to a major report on the problem.[30]

While the provinces of Punjab and Haryana have few Muslims among their population, there is no shortage of problems and frustrations and Punjab does share a long border with the West Pakistani province known also as Punjab, a border that has been contested militarily several times in recent years. Also many Punjabis remember very vividly what happened to them and their relations at the time of partition. Various hypotheses were mooted : that high levels of frustration would contribute to uniformly high levels of hostility to Muslims; that refugees in particular, having been forced to leave their own homes for the creation of a Muslim state, might be expected to resent the presence of Muslims in India; that, as found in World War II and Hiroshima, the hostility is displaced from the actual aggressor (the Muslims of 1947 in this case) to more accessible targets, often protective figures who failed to protect.

TABLE 5.13
Hostility to Muslims Factor[31]

	RFL
1. Muslims are as valuable, honest, and public spirited citizens as any other group	.787
2. Muslims should not be employed in the government service	—.785
3. Hindus and Sikhs should treat Muslims as Indian citizens without any discrimination	.745
4. The Muslims are a menace to any nation and to any country in which they happen to live	—.711
5. The Muslims are a decent group of people on the whole	.668
6. The Muslims should give up their separate customs and become average citizens of this country	—.349
7. Human nature being what it is, there wlll always be war and conflict	.346
8. Widespread participation in decision making often leads to undesirable conflicts	.324

Although the various tests do not show that the refugees and non-refugees differ from one another with regard to hostility to Muslims, there are a number of possible interpretations of the findings. It could be that the refugees, like the earlier victims of oppression, have targeted their animosity away from the group that was the immediate cause of their trauma. Or, it could be that over a period of years they have readjusted themselves and no longer bear any ill-will to the Muslims. Another possible explanation is that they are still hostile to the Muslims but that here, as in other areas, they have inculcated in their non-refugee neighbours the same values that they themselves harbour.[32] That is to say their hostility has spread to the non-refugee community. A fourth possibility is that both groups are hostile to Muslims but for reasons not related to partition and perhaps independently arrived at.

There is no way to directly test these sub-hypotheses but some conclusions can be drawn by various rearrangements of the data. First, we know that if at one time the refugees displaced hostility from Muslims to government the government is no longer a primary target : t-tests and cross-tabs showed no difference between refugees and non-refugees with regard to this even when other variables were controlled for. One cross-tab, not having to do with refugeeism, did however find significant differences in affect toward Muslims within the sample. This was when residence was run against hostility to Muslims. The cross-tabulation can be found in Table 5.14.

TABLE 5.14

Residence vs. Hostility to Muslims

		Per cent Replying		
Hostility		*Village*	*Town*	*City*
Low		42.0	77.8	65.0
High		58.0	22.2	35.0
	Total=	100.0%	100.0%	100.0%
	N =	(88)	(18)	(20)
$x^2 = 9.553$		p = 0.009		gamma = —0.478

The highly significant findings were that villagers were more apt to feel hostile to Muslims than were their more urbanized fellows

($p=0.009$). One tentative conclusion is that the Muslims are a conveniently absent target for hostility that cannot be vented elsewhere. It will be remembered that there are virtually no Muslims left in rural Punjab and Haryana and that the villages in which interviews were conducted had *no* Muslims present (so that we could not be accused of fomenting communal hatred). In the towns and cities where the few remaining Muslims do live the people do not feel them to be a great menace. The possibility that in rural areas the refugees have taught the non-refugees to hate Muslims is unlikely because of the hostility between the two groups themselves.

Further support for the view that hostility to Muslims represents targeting and displacement of hostility for both more vulnerable refugees and non-refugees comes from the correlation matrix. The correlation between the Frustration Index and the Hostility to Muslims factor was $r=.332$. Because of the small number of cases in the cell (18) this turned out not to be significant. However, looking at other, more complete data the fact that hostility to Muslims is one case of displaced hostility becomes apparent. Examining those possible causes of frustration for which we have more complete data, we find that hostility to Muslims correlates negatively with caste rank ($r=-.200$; $p=0.05$), with household income ($r=-.239$; $p=0.01$) and with a wealth factor that included items on income, education, frequency of travel, media exposure, etc. ($r=-.305$; $p=0.01$). Hostility to Muslims also correlated highly with the combined items on hostility to out-groups ($r=.387$; $p=0.01$). From the findings it would appear that hostility to Muslims as evidenced by the responses of the sample represents displacement of aggressive sentiments to safer, more conveniently absent targets. More than incidentally, the factor correlates highly with behavioural aggression *but in a negative direction* ($r=-.551$) but only very weakly with intrafamilial aggression. It will be remembered that we saw interfamilial aggression to be displaced aggression for most non-refugees and invulnerable rage aggression for many refugees. These conflicting vectors would be expected to cancel one another out, thus explaining the low correlation.

This raises the important issue of "why the Muslims?" After all, there are a great many other conveniently absent targets to displace one's aggressions onto. A likely answer can be found in the public affairs and international events that preceded our work, events that affected both refugees and non-refugees, Sikhs and Hindus, and indeed the entire population of the area. It can be said that although refugees and non-refugees still disliked each other, and Hindus and Sikhs still distrusted each other's political goals, external events such as the Indo-Pakistani war and the frequent border skimirshes in the months that followed enabled each group to forget, at least for a time, the suspicion and enmity it felt toward the other and to focus hostility on the Muslims and Pakistan. Before going into these direct causes it is necessary to digress briefly.

Classical Indian political thought makes much a theory of inter-group and international relations known as "the doctrine of circles". This doctrine is in many ways very similar to modern social psychological theories of balance, congruity, psycho-logic, etc. What it says is that if you control some area, your immediate neighbour is automatically your enemy and you are his. But a third party whose property is contiguous to your neighbour's but not to your own is his enemy and automatically your friend. Psychological notation would represent this three party relationship as a triangle with the three parties as the apexes and the bonds between them as positive or negative charges on the sides. For a state of balance to exist the product of all the signs should be positive. According to both theories if there are three parties; each of whom hates the other two, some change will occur to restore balance and a positive product. There are many resolutions of the imbalance but the most common one in the case of an external threat to two internal enemies is not, as Kautilya, the author of the doctrine would suggest, for one party to make an alliance with the outside power, but for the two to bury the hatchet at least for the time being in order to present a united front. Both the Chinese and the Pakistanis found that aggression from outside, rather than exacerbating internal tensions, resulted in heightened unity within India. This was the outcome in the Punjab-Haryana region as well. (At that time there was no state of Haryana.)

In the Indo-Pakistani war of 1965 much of the fighting took place in the as yet unbifurcated Punjab. The Pakistani Air Force even dropped bombs on Ambala, a major city and at that time the only cantonment in the eastern part of the state. At this point in time Pakistan became the target of a great deal of psychological aggression among the people in the area. At the same time however much aggression was displaced to the domestic Muslim community. This hostility increased during the 1967 electoral campaigns in both states. (As a reward for Sikh contributions to the military effort and to meet a long standing demand of the Akali party erstwhile Punjab was split into the two states of Punjab and Haryana in 1966.) In both states (as well as nationally) the Jana Sangh emerged as a power to be reckoned with. The election propaganda of the Sangh made extensive use of appeals to Hindu voters based on a theme of the dangers to Hinduism and to Hindustan. To most Hindu inhabitants of Punjab this meant Sikh domination in the new state but the threat of possible Muslim subversion nationally had to be raided because of the distinct possibility that an Akali-Jana Sangh alliance would become necessary after the elections. At the same time the Akali Dal, already having had its demand for a Sikh state met and needing an election issue took up its old standby threat appeal having to do with the vulnerability of Sikhism.[33] A short time earlier the Akali leaders had been playing up the common themes of threats from Pakistan and Muslims in general and the need for a strong, happy, loyal first line of defence in their successful attempt to persuade and coerce the leaders of the national government into bifurcating Punjab to create two new states, one of which would have a slight majority of Sikhs plus most of the material resources of the erstwhile province. Now, deprived of an issue by their very success, they launched another set of demands, this time for Chandigarh, the capital city which had been declared a Union Territory to be shared by both new states following bifurcation.[34]

At any rate both the Akalis and the Jana Sangh did well in the 1967 and 1969 elections in Punjab and found themselves both times in coalition governments that proved that politics indeed does make strange bedfellows. Appeals to the Centre for increased investment or cession of Chandigarh were based on two issues which although seldom badly spoken were implied and understood by all : "Punjab produces more and better things than anywhere else" and "Keep us happy or we might not fight so hard against Pakistanis".

In Haryana the political picture was extremely muddled due to repeated floor crossings and a series of rapidly shifting alliances so that it becomes unclear as to who is saying what and with how much conviction at any particular point in time.

Of course talking of two minority political parties who only together are strong enough to capture a majority of seats in the Legislative Assembly is not the same as talking of the sentiments of the man in the street. As has been noted in study after study, people in India vote for candidates for a multitude of reasons, most of which have little to do with party rhetoric and here we must turn our attention to how the sample felt about Muslims.

Hostility to Muslims can take many forms ranging from subtle views to outright advocacy of repressive measures. Questionnaire items regarding sentiments towards Muslims tried to cover a good part of this range. The findings show that indeed there is not a population holding homogeneous views regarding Muslims. Table 5.15 shows extreme responses to items having to do with sentiments about Muslims.

TABLE 5.15

Intense Hostility To Muslims

Item	*Per Cent Responding*
1. The Muslims have too much power and influence in this country (strongly agreeing)	9.6
2. Hindus and Sikhs should treat Muslims as Indian citizens without any discrimination. (Strongly disagreeing)	24.0
3. Muslims are as valuable, honest and public spirited citizens as any other group. (Strongly disagreeing)	28.0
4. The Muslims are a decent group of people on the whole (Strongly disagreeing)	34.4
5. The Muslims are a menace to any nation and to any country in which they happen to live. (Strongly agreeing)	35.0
6. Muslims should not be employed in the government service. (Strongly agreeing)	44.8
7. The Muslims should give up their separate customs and become average citizens of this country. (Strongly agreeing)	66.4

It would appear from the data that there seems to be a hard-core of about one-fourth of the total sample, both refugees and non-refugees, who are extremely prejudiced against Muslims both in their personal attitudes and in their willingness to see Muslims aggressed against. The first item is an exception to this. It is patently obvious to all that Muslims do not have a great deal of influence in the country. (Despite the fact that the President of

India at the time of the fieldwork was a Muslim, Dr. Zakir Husain, Muslims were most conspicuous by their absence from public life.) Nevertheless, ten per cent of the sample strongly felt that Muslims had too much influence in the nation. A third of the respondents felt strongly that not only were Muslims not very nice people but that there was a positive danger to the nation from their presence. Two-thirds felt strongly that Muslims should give up Islamic ways. Such a high percentage of people holding extreme views is indeed alarming and the only comforting thought is that there are few Muslims in the area. Even more disturbing than the number of people who strongly agree or disagree with anti- or pro-Muslim statements is the very large number who agree and disagree with somewhat less intensity. The comparable figures can be found in Table 5.16.

TABLE 5.16
Hostility To Muslims

Item	*Per cent Responding*
1. The Muslims have too much power and influence in this country. (Agree)	36.8
2. Hindus and Sikhs should treat Muslims as Indian citizens without any discrimination. (Disagree)	34.4
3. Muslims are as valuable, honest and public spirited citizens as any other group. (Disagree)	48.8
4. The Muslims are a decent group of people on the whole. (Disagree)	71.2
5. The Muslims are a menace to any nation and to any country in which they happen to live. (Agree)	48.8
6. Muslims should not be employed in the government service. (Agree)	48.8
7. The Muslims should give up their separate customs and become average citizens of this country. (Agree)	76.8

All in all then it would seem that anti-Muslim sentiments are fairly strong among a large part of the population, especially in the rural areas. Although, and perhaps because, many of these individuals have not even seen a Muslim in the twenty years since partition, they hold very strong negative views of Muslims and displace much of the hostility and aggression that is generated by the frustration of their lives onto this conveniently absent target. The target is constantly reinstated and reinforced in their minds by political leaders and international events.

Trust

> Man's enemy is man. . . .
> He who trusts others is soon ruined,
> Would you keep meat on trust with a
> jackal ?
>
> North Indian proverbs

One facet of political culture that has received a great deal of attention in the past several years is the degree of trust that exists within a political system. Unfortunately there has been little agreement on use of the term "trust." For example, Gamson understands trust to pertain to the quality of the relationship between partisans at one level of the system and the authorities, usually at a higher level.[35] Specifically Gamson means the attitudes of the former toward the latter. As Gamson points out, his use of the words "trust" is very close to what others have called "allegiance",[36] "support",[37] "output affect",[38] "faith"[39] etc. In all these terms there is an implicit relationship: that of the ruled to his ruler. Very little of the tone of horizontal relationships between groups enters the discussion of these terms and since we have already discussed the phenomenon that our Indian respondents trusted the system in which they found themselves but distrusted the incumbents who man the system, we will not pursue this aspect of trust any further.

Some scholars have emphasized the importance of trust between actors who may be at the same level within a political system. Daniel Lerner's concept of empathy, for example, refers to the ability to understand the feelings of others.[40] While a number of the questions Lerner uses to measure empathy refer to an understanding of very different levels of the society[41], the concept can also be applied to other actors and roles at the same level within the system. Lucian Pye's work on Burma discusses the uncertainty of all relationships in the culture of that nation.[42] What is uncertainty in human relationships if not mistrust ?[43] In any pluralistic society, but especially so in a developing or transitional one, the feelings of the individuals of one group about other groups and actors may be extremely significant for a nation's resolution of the problems of integration. Gamson sees this too as a problem that exists between the ruled and his rulers. His citizens distrust rulers who favour other rival groups and this is a crucial dimension of the trust-mistrust relationship. Indeed many of the secessionist and linguistic separatism movements in the underdeveloped world represent a fear on the part of one group that another group is being favoured by those in power. But clearly this is not the only way in which trust relates to the political culture. For example, it is hard to see how a society can be run in an orderly way if certain groups—who may even believe that the system and incumbents are trustworthy—also feel that other groups will "cheat" to gain certain ends. In such situations there may be a rash of coups and countercoups, factional warfare, preemptive massacres, and assassinations. In many of the developing areas the public's knowledge of higher levels of the system may be very scanty. What an individual does know about is who are his traditional enemies. And since the governments of most developing nations have very real problems of communications and only limited ability to cope rapidly and effectively with communal disturbances this second dimension, horizontal trust, becomes of critical importance, if the new nations are to resolve the problems of national integration in peaceful ways.

Trust has been likened to the cement that holds society together. Our data however, suggest another analogy : Trust, in any pluralist society and perhaps to an even greater extent in a highly segmented one like India's, may be likened to the gravitational and electromagnetic forces holding atoms together. The further one moves from the nucleus, the weaker is the binding force between the nucleus and the orbiting electrons. Looking back at data presented earlier we could say that the family is the nucleus of the

TABLE 5.17
Willingness to Extend Trust

Items	*Per cent Responding*
Complete and a great deal of trust in family members	87.2
Complete and or a great deal of trust in friends	52.0
Complete or a great deal of trust in neighbours	34.4
Complete or a great deal of trust in government officials	37.6

atom where members are so inextricably bound together that complete trust is never even questioned. In successively more distant orbits can be found friends and neighbours and government officials. At very distant orbits are the Muslims and deviants expressing unpopular opinions and espousing "foreign ideas."

The data make this clear: Family members were highly trusted, friends only somewhat, and government officials and neighbours were lumped together as not very trustworthy. The figures on *complete* lack of trust showed the progression to be a four-step one; family, friends, neighbours, and government officials, with the last two classes now distinguishable.

To carry the physical analogy a little further it could be said that traditional man and his world correspond to one of the lighter elements in the periodic table, the individual being the nucleus and the orbiting electrons those objects to which he can extend trust. The lighter elements have few electrons, all of which are in orbits fairly close to the nucleus. Transitional man and his mental world would be analogous to the intermediate elements and modern man and his world to the heavier elements having a great many electrons in orbits at varying distances from the nucleus. Not only does the heavier nucleus exert forces on electrons at greater distances from it that would even be possible for the lighter elements, but the atom possessing such a nucleus also has room for more electrons in those orbits furthest from its nucleus. Modern man can include many items in his cognitive atom, some of which are almost incredibly remote in terms of physical, temporal and psychological distance.

This atomic model of trust is empirically testable by scaling methods. What is more, the model not only describes "trust" but also the closely related concept of empathy by introducing physical analogy comparable to the concept of social distance. The model has a number of other uses as well. It manages to incorporate some of Lerner's thinking that one's psychological reach is extended as he becomes modernized. More important, the notion of individual elements, atoms, and particles points up the need for political scientists to concentrate on how these atoms may be united with other atoms to become, in physical terms, molecules and compounds and in political terms nation states. The modernization process then can be likened to the efforts of the medieval alchemist who tried to transmute one element into a more valuable one. As our knowledge of the modernization process grows, perhaps the physicist with his particle accelerator can be substituted for the alchemist in the analogy, and perhaps later the chemist who can show us the ways in which elements combine.[44] We have posted that trust and empathy are closely related although one may be able to empathize with a particular object without extending the least amount of trust (the psychologist who treats a pickpocket would be a good example of this) and that one may blindly trust objects that are so distant psychologically that empathization is impossible (the description of the "subject" political culture comes immediately to mind).[45] In general, however, there will be a high positive correlation between the two traits. The questionnaire did not measure empathy *per se* but it did ask a number of questions regarding trust, all of which clustered together in a factor analysis. The items of the factor and their loadings can be found in Table 5.18.

TABLE 5.18

Mistrust Factor

Item	*Factor Loading*
1. How much do you feel you can trust your friends ?	.762
2. How much do you feel you can trust your neighbours ?	.654
3. How much do you feel you can trust the members of your family ?	.550
4. Trust in People and you will go a long way OR Never trust in anyone but yourself	.400
5. How much do you feel you can trust governmen tofficials?	.399
6. One learned man says : 'When people compete with each other they work harder and do their best and there is progress." Another learned man says : "When people compete with each other they become enemies and progress becomes impossible"	.382
7. Facing an officer is equal to standing behind a horse OR Officers are public servants and are helpful to the common man	—.367
8. Sometimes I feel like smashing things	.320

Lerner has hypothesized that a crucial step in modernization is the development among individuals of an ability to empathize. We have said that empathy and trust are likely to overlap. Although Lerner's hypothesis cannot be tested directly here, other items from the questionnaire enable us to see if those individuals who are more trusting are also more progressive and innovative. Factor analysis yielded two clusters closely related to the attributes of modernity. The items composing the first of these can be found in Table 5.19.

TABLE 5.19
Progressiveness Factor

Items	*Factor Loadings*
1. That which is already known is better than that which will come to be known OR If Society is to progress newer solutions to problems are essential	.646
2. We would be better off with less scientific development and more simple faith OR One cannot learn how to improve things by continually referring to the ways problems were solved in the past	.598
3. Modern problems require modern approaches OR The best way of life is to walk in the paths of our fathers	—.585
4. Today many young men are trying to make decisions that used to be made for them by their parents—say on marriage. In general, do you think it is a good thing or a bad thing if young men decide on their own marriage ?	—.519
5. (After having been asked about major changes in his area in the previous twenty-five years the respondent was asked:) Do you think these changes were good or bad ?	—.443
6. People who want to do things in new ways forget that this may bring about even worse conditions.	.439
7. If a new and useful way of working were made known to you, would you be willing to be the first person in this village (town, neighbourhood) to try the new way ?	—.432
8. Hindus and Sikhs should treat Muslims as Indian citizens without any discrimination	—.413
9. Muslims are as valuable, honest, and public spirited citizens as any other group	—.405
10. If you felt unjustly treated by the police what do you think you would do about it ?	.394
11. Facing an officer is equal to standing behind a horse OR Officers are public servants and are helpful to the common man	.385

12. If success is desired do not belong to any group OR Success comes to those who join together in pursuit of common goals	.385
13. Muslims should not be employed in the government service	.361
14. One man says : "Our country needs a strong leader who will take over the government and make everyone obey him." Another man says : "Our country needs leaders who have been chosen by the people and who will act in accordance with the people's wishes"	.360
15. Only through ambition and hard work can one be successful OR Only through God's will can success be achieved	—.358
16. One learned man says : "When people compete with each other they work harder and do their best and there is progress". Another learned man says : "When people compete with each other they become enemies and progress becomes impossible"	—.355
17. I believe that most of my neighbours would not hesitate to do something against me if they thought they could get away with it	.315

TABLE 5.20

Dimensions of Progressiveness Factor

Dimensions	*Items*
1. Positive attitudes towards change	1, 2, 3, 4, 5, 6, 7
2. Tolerance of minorities (Muslims)	8, 9, 13
3. Value of cooperation and conflict	12, 16
4. Democratic ideology	11, 14
5. Belief in efficacy of one's own deeds	4, 7, 10, 15

Because the factor contained all these dimensions that seemed to be characteristic of a modern, democratic society, the factor was entitled Progressiveness. According to Lerner those individuals who are more empathic (here more trusting) should hold the more modernized viewpoints. Correlations bear this out : [The coefficient of correlation (r) between Mistrust and Progressiveness was $r=-.322$, $p=0.01$.] Perhaps even more important than having a modern ideology—what the Progressiveness Factor measures—are the dimensions of action. Does the individual who verbally espouses the ideals of modernity "put his money where his mouth is" ? The next Chapter will deal with the relationships between modern behaviour, ideology, economic development, and a notion of invulnerability.

Efficacy

> Run as far and as fast as you wish;
> you will reach only that which is
> ordained...
>
> A Punjabi proverb

If interpersonal faith can be characterized as trust, then intra-personal faith, what Erikson refers to as the balance of autonomy and doubt, can be characterized by what the literature of political science calls self-confidence, competence, and efficacy.

Early works on political efficacy considered the concept undifferentiated.[46] By the 1960's there were some indications that political efficacy was part of a larger sense of personal efficacy,[47] and this led to the hope that one would soon be able to gauge political efficacy indirectly from an analysis of personality traits. The usefulness of the efficacy concept has gone far beyond its place of origin, studies of American voting behaviour, and has been of immense import to the literature of modernization. If modern society is a participant society[48] marked by equality and differentiation of roles,[49] then a sense that one's deeds can lead to predictable, desirable results becomes a prerequisite for modernization. With this realization, the need to break the concept into a number of components became apparent. Almond and Verba recognized that what an individual said he *could* do was not necessarily what he *would* do and broke down "competence," their term for efficacy, into a subjective dimension dealing with possible actions and "political competence" concerned with probable actions. Robert Hess carried the analysis of the concept in a slightly different direction by not dealing with actions so much as by describing three components of subjective political efficacy.[50] The first of these, trust in the political system and its representatives, has already been discussed. The second and third components deal with the confidence that one can work within the system to manipulate it and, when it cannot be manipulated, one can still coerce officials and political figures. At about the same time, Easton and Dennis argued that the term political efficacy had been used in the literature in many ways : as description of psychological dispositions or feelings, and as a behavioural concept and that if the concept was to be of real use more precision in its use was called for.[51]

In an attempt to differentiate between three types of efficacy, three indices were created. The first contained items designed to measure the subject's general opinions of what he was capable of. It was called the Index of Personal Efficacy. The second index consisted of items that measured what could be called an individual's cerebral political efficacy. This, very much like Almond and Verba's subjective competence, examines what the individual feels he is capable of and the degree to which he sees the political sphere of life as amenable to influence by the common people. This group of items will be referred to as the Index of Political Efficacy (Attitudes). The third measure corresponds to Almond's and Verba's concept of behavioural political competence. It aims at measuring whether an individual's hypothetical actions reflect a sense of efficacy and was called the Index of Behavioural Political Efficacy.[52] Some further indicators of a general sense of efficacy will be discussed in the next chapter, on economic development. They have not been included here because they have to do with only a few out of an infinite spectrum of deeds that might be representative of personal efficacy. On the other hand, the range of political behaviours is much more limited and amenable to survey research types of analysis. And, we were interested in whether an individual's sense of what he *could* do was related to what he felt he *would* do.

There is a certain element of fantasy in much of the democratic process but one must partake of this fantasy if the system is to operate. By measuring these three dimensions—dimensions that seem to be the obverse of cynicism—something may be learned about the viability of democracy in a given area. Finally, by asking two sets of questions about political efficacy relationships between sentiments and behaviours may become more clear.

Personal Efficacy

To make and to mar is in God's hands...

A North Indian proverb

The attitudes about general personal efficacy were obtained from five items' that combined into an index. The index can be found in Table 5.21.

TABLE 5.21

Personal Efficacy Index

1. Most people don't realize the extent to which their lives are controlled by accidental happenings

   OR

   There is really no such thing as luck.
2. Many times I feel I have very little influence over the things that happen to me.

   OR

   It is impossible for me to believe that chance or luck plays an important part in my life.
3. Your own deeds will bring you salvation.

   OR

   What man wishes never happens; what God wishes always happens.
4. It is impossible for an honest man to get ahead in the world.
5. Only through ambition and hard work can one be successful.

   OR

   Only through God's will can success be achieved.

Three of the items composing the Index were also found in the factor having to do with vulnerability. With the index however, perhaps because of the lack of factor loadings and the absence of the remaining items composing the factor, no difference was found to exist between refugees and non-refugees. Neither was the control of independent variables differentiated between the two groups. Only when these other independent variables' direct relationship to a sense of personal efficacy was examined did significant relationships emerge. The most important of these was the relationship between a sense of efficacy and level of education attained. Closer examination and controls did not dilute the significance of the finding. It would appear that education, any education, is significant in helping man to understand his universe and the forces that affect his life. The extent to which a man is "educated" is the extent to which he comes to understand that his own actions and not those of supernatural powers are those which shape his own life. A simple correlation between education and sense of personal efficacy yielded a coefficient equal to .499 (significant at the 0.01 level).

TABLE 5.22

Personal Efficacy Attitudes vs. Education

Efficacy Attitudes		*Per cent Responding* *Low*	*Medium*	*High*
Low		68.9	45.2	32.3
High		31.1	54.8	67.7
	Total=	100.0	100.0	100.0
	N =	(45)	(42)	(31)

$x^2 = 10.676$ Significant at the 0.005 level gamma = 0.470

Political Efficacy (Attitudes)

Put your hope in princes but never go near them...

A North Indian proverb

The Political Efficacy (Attitudes) Index dealt with more ostensibly political concepts than the General Efficacy Index but did not attempt to determine whether attitudes held by the respondent were related to any particular behaviours on his part. The items of the Index can be found in Table 5.23.

TABLE 5.23

Index of Political Efficacy (Attitudes)

1. The average citizen can have an influence on government decisions.
   OR
   The world is run by the few people in power, and there is not much the little man can do about it.
2. As far as world affairs are concerned, most of us are the victims of forces we can neither understand nor control.
   OR
   By taking an active part in political and social affairs the people can control world events.
3. How much do you feel you can trust government officials ?
4. I don't think public officials care much what people like me think.

The refugees did not score any higher on this index than non-refugees. When other variables were controlled for, refugee status could not be shown to have any marked effect of an individual's sense of political efficacy. Another test however, political efficacy (attitudes) vs. caste status, did yield interesting results : both low and high castes had a strong belief in the efficacy of individual action in the political arena, the lower castes feeling this even more strongly than the high castes. The medium rank castes however did not share this sense of their own relevance to the political process.

TABLE 5.24

Caste Status vs. Political Efficacy Attitudes

Political Efficacy		*Caste Status*		
		Low	*Medium*	*High*
Low		27.8%	64.3%	46.1%
High		72.2	35.7	53.9
	Total=	100.0%	100.0%	100.0%
$x^2 = 6.034$	p=0.049	gamma = 0.023		

The high castes' feeling of potency is easily explained. High castes are specifically those with money and political influence. (In the sample the correlation between caste status and income was strong; r=.401, p=0.01)[53] Since these are the people to whom the politicians must not only listen but to whom they must also cater if they are to hope for the votes of their dependents, the high caste individual's sense of political efficacy is well founded. In the terms of the questionnaire, "average" citizens like themselves can and do affect government policy and performance. People like themselves can afford to trust government officials and politicians because neither of these types would dare to cross these local notables. An officer who decided to buck a member of this aristocracy would, if he were lucky, find himself reprimanded by the Minister in charge of his department; if he were unlucky he might be transferred to one of the less choice centres of administration. The politician who breaks faith with the notables may find himself denied a ticket for the next election and should he manage to get a ticket from his party or run on another ticket or as an independent he will almost certainly lose many votes in the surrounding area.

The lower caste groups' perception of themselves as even more politically potent is difficult to explain. To any observer this perception is clearly not valid. One explanation for the misperception may be that the lower castes' political power has increased markedly since Independence and the introduction of Panchayati Raj. That their starting point was so low may lead them to overemphasize their importance in the system today, not realizing that they are still a long way behind other groups. The increase in their importance *is* a fact that cannot be denied. Twenty per cent of the population of pre-bifurcation Punjab was listed as "scheduled". This has led to the courtship of these groups by many individuals and groups having political aspirations and to some extent these lower caste and low status groups have been able to negotiate effectively with state and local politicians to their mutual advantage. Nevertheless the political 'clout' of the lower classes is still marginal since many of their members are still embedded in the *jajmani* system and hence are at the mercy of their *jajmans* for their livelihood and perceptions are not necessarily related to acts as we shall see below.

Political Efficacy (Practice)

> When the loincloth is burning, it is impossible to refrain from speaking out...
>
> Spit at the sun and your spittle will fall in your own face...
>
> North Indian proverbs

One indication of the lower castes' inflation of their actual efficacy is found in the different responses given by them to the items of the third index, which purports to measure behavioural political efficacy. When asked what were the actions upon which they would embark if confronted with political or governmental injustice the lower caste and lower income group individuals were found generally to lack the courage of their convictions. They may feel that the system is responsive to their wishes but when it turns out

TABLE 5.25

Index of Behavioural Political Efficacy

1. Supposing the central government were planning to do something you considered harmful or unjust. What do you think you would do to stop it ?
2. Now, suppose it was the district or *tahsil* level officers. What would you do ?
3. If you felt unjustly treated by the police, what do you think you would do about it ?

not to be, they remain quiescent. The index of Behavioural Political Efficacy is found in Table 5.25.

Of these items we discovered once again that those individuals possessing high education, high income, and high caste status were those most likely to act when faced with a situation not to their liking. The group that claims most strongly that all citizens can and do have an influence on government, i.e., the lower castes, who are also the poorer members of the population, in general do not dare speak up when confronted with a situation involving unjust acts by public officials. Rather, status and wealth once again appear to be the critical variables in determining whether one will act. Table 5.26 shows the relationship between Behavioural Political Efficacy and household income.

TABLE 5.26
Behavioural Political Efficacy vs. Income

Efficacy		*Income* *Low*	*Medium*	*High*
Low		80.6%	47.2%	24.2%
High		19.4	52.8	75.8
	Total=	100.0%	100.0%	100.0%
	N=	(36)	(36)	(33)
x^2=22.246		p=0.000		gamma=0.678

But statistical means, chi-square statistics, t-tests, and coefficients of correlation rob many of the findings of their original pungent flavour. Punjabis and Haryanvis have long been noted for their strongly held and outspoken views so it would be useful to look at responses to the individual items.

The index of efficacy we have been discussing could be considered a measure of how a man reacts to frustrating situations. With increasing proximity of the frustrating agent the members of the sample turned out to be less passive in their reactions. More than half (53.4%) felt that against an unjust act of the central government they are impotent and that there is no point in taking action. Against district administration about a third (31.5%) feel action is useless. However, more than one-third (34.3%) believe that they can retaliate either by invoking the power of politicians or higher authorities. When we reach that nearest of all branches of government, the greatly feared police, only slightly more than a fourth (27.4%) would put up with injustice passively. More than six out of ten (60.3%) would take direct action. This apparent contradiction of Miller's hypothesis that it is easier to aggress (at least verbally) against more distant targets can be understood more easily if one looks at the types of actions that respondents are likely to take in these frustrating situations. In almost every case the respondent allies himself with someone at a higher level than his frustrator and gets this person to take action. The problem is that the more distant the frustrator, the less likely the respondent will be to be able to find a more powerful individual whom he can approach personally to act as a surrogate.

Political Behaviour and Knowledge

The above measures of efficacy were chosen because more conventional participatory measures of the trait would be less sensitive indicators in the Indian setting than they have been in Western societies. Nevertheless voting frequency was requested, keeping in mind that some people would try to appear more public spirited than they actually were and that others vote because they are ordered to by their *jajman*. As something of a safeguard against such prevarication an index of political awareness was also constructed from a number of informational questions.

With regard to turnout both groups, refugees and non-refugees, scored extremely high (probably fictitiously so as we shall see). Four of every five (80.2%) respondents claimed to have voted in every national election for which they had been eligible. About the same proportion (79.4%) claimed perfect voting records for *panchayat* or local elections. Turnouts of this magnitude would be impressive in any democratic system but unfortunately the figures are less than adequate for an understanding of a sense of political efficacy in north India. While the figures could conceivably present a true picture of voting behaviour they appear to be too high to be true. Looking at other indices of efficacy and awareness it becomes apparent that even if people are voting this frequently (which is not altogether certain) they often vote knowing little or nothing about the candidates, issues, or dimensions of politics in the national and local arena.

A number of straight information questions were asked of each respondent to determine his level of political awareness. Included were items on the names of the present Chief Minister, the present Prime Minister, the major parties in the Province, etc. The items can be found in Table 5.27.

Refugees and non-refugees turned out to be approximately equally badly informed about politics and the affairs of the nation despite the fact that all our interviews were conducted

TABLE 5.27
Index of Political Awareness

1. How old does a person have to be in order to vote ?
2. Do you know who is our Prime Minister now ?
3. And who is Chief Minister of Punjab (Haryana) ?
4. To which party does the Chief Minister belong ?
5. Will you please name the main opposition party in the state legislature.

during a period of frantic political activity by all parties in both provinces. Although the first question turned out to be not quite as good as it looked in advance (because it turned out that many answers of "twelve" or "thirteen" were indeed accurate perceptions of reality), the other items do measure a man's involvement in the political life of the state and nation. The results, in terms of the development of a responsible and well informed electorate, could be considered disappointing. Items were scored either right or wrong and wherever possible the respondent was given the benefit of the doubt. Thus, during periods just after the Haryana or Punjab governments had fallen or when President's Rule was imposed or new governments had been formed, there was a grace period of two weeks during which "old" answers and the correct new ones were both considered correct. Even so, more than a quarter (27.0%) did not know who the Prime Minister was; about half (49.2%) could not identify the Chief Minister of their state; two-thirds (65.2%) were unclear on the Chief Minister's party identification; and three-fourths (73.0%) did not know the main opposition party. These responses could be considered indicative of a failure of the public and private communications networks in the area, for most individuals have some, if not great, exposure to the mass media. This will be discussed further.

More important than this however is our view that earlier studies that made efforts at measuring the level of political awareness in India and whose findings led their authors to be fairly sanguine about the prospects for the growth of democracy in that nation may have been over-optimistic. Our findings, of low awareness, are the opposite of the earlier studies, yielding two possible explanations. The first is the more gloomy, but also the less probable of the two. It is that the common Indian has gotten so disgusted with the shenanigans of politicians that he has become depoliticized. Although newspaper articles in the Indian press like to stress this view, there are obvious difficulties with this argument. The most important, of course is, if people are so fed up with politics why do they bother to vote in such great numbers and why do they claim such high interest. We have seen that almost everyone claims to vote at every opportunity. When asked about their interest in politics and the affairs of the nation more than half (52.4%) said they were "very interested".

Why then are people so very interested and yet so poorly informed ? One explanation can be derived from the data and the unique political configurations in both states at the time of our survey. During 1967 and 1968 most of north India was politically unstable following the 1967 General Elections. In these elections and during the months that followed non-Congress governments were formed in both states. Without going into the intricacies of state politics let it suffice to say that for the first time since Punjab absorbed the erstwhile PEPSU area in 1956 a non-Congress government was in the saddle. Nehru, Shastri, and Kairon had recently died. It would seem from the data that over the years response sets had developed within the public, and especially within the rural public, so that when one asked about the party in power, the answer "Congress" came back almost as a conditioned response. Similarly Nehru (and less often Shastri) was often named as Prime Minister and Kairon as Chief Minister. These answers are the same ones that other scholars have gotten *only at the time when they were working the responses were correct.* Now, for the first time perhaps, the inappropriate answers that heretofore had always been taken to indicate high levels of civic-mindedness betrayed a greater lack of involvement than had been guessed.

It may just be that all it will take will be the emergence of some new leaders with some degree of charisma and the old awareness will return, but it must be remembered that both Nehru, Kairon, and the Congress were bigger than life : Nehru and the Congress inextricably intertwined with the freedom movement and Kairon with refugee rescue and relief and later with strong stable rule. In light of these findings it would be profitable for other researchers to re-examine other areas of India to see whether what has been called political awareness is really that.

The point that Punjabis and Haryanvis were ill-informed about politics although they saw themselves as very interested (or at least tried to pass themselves off as such) has been stressed. In part this finding may be explained by the individual's frame of reference. The current generation sees itself as more interested than its predecessors. If this is in fact so, then we might expect the young to be more positive in their protestations of interest and claims of involvement than the old. But such is not the case. For the respondents age correlates positively with participation as measured by voting ($r=.226$; $p=0.05$). This is very similar to findings in the United States that the voting habit takes a little time to develop and that the young very often defer their first vote.[54] In a more traditional society the feeling that the young do not have the wisdom of age and should not exercise their franchise may be more widespread. The correlation between political awareness and age was weak. It was in the direction that would support the notion that the young are better informed about politics than their elders...and still vote less.

Asking about Prime Ministers, Chief Ministers, and voting habits is important when one is interested in the relationship between democratic citizenship and nation building. That awareness is low on these indicators is serious but it is not to say that political awareness is low or non-existent. At the local level, and in terms of wielding pressure, awareness, as indicated by behavioural political efficacy and the use of personal influence, is considerable—but this is the awareness of *sipharish* (personal relations or "pull") that has been passed down through the ages. Only the roles of the actors one approaches have changed. Earlier we said that for democracy to function as intended a certain amount of fantasy had to be indulged in by the participants. It would seem that fantasy is a luxury for the hardheaded pragmatists of the sample who, when something must be done, despite their protestations of civic-mindedness, get them done out of channels.

Communications Behaviour and Political Life

The sample of refugees and non-refugees feel strongly about politics and certain elements of political life. Yet we have seen that they are navigating blindly in the sea of supralocal politics, without a compass, unaware of the characteristics of the shoreline that might guide their course. This lack of awareness of the true forms and dimensions of supralocal political life is not new in discussions of traditional or transitional societies, indeed it is one of their defining elements.[55] Perhaps because of this, would-be nation builders in the developing areas feel the need to penetrate the fog of apathy, ignorance, and misinformation in order to mobilize a population for the efforts required for the various forms of development. Lacking many of the channels that could be used for mobilizations such as voluntary organizations or active political parties, many leaders, having an inflated view of the effectiveness of mass communications, have invested heavily in the electronic media, hoping that these could awaken and inform a lethargic public.

But national leaders are not the only ones who see the mass media as a tool for development. In the past fifteen years a large, if sometimes contradictory, body of literature has emerged on the relationships between the two. Much of this literature has to do with India. Despite this spate of reports, monographs, articles and books the leaders of the emerging nations appear to have been most strongly influenced by the views of the early observers of mass culture who assumed that the media had incredible powers to change men's attitudes and behaviours. Thus, in many of the new nations we find media policies that seem to rest on the assumption that once the message is delivered to the audience beneficial changes will occur without a great deal of further effort. The deep-seated optimism underlying such views seems to be able to withstand all sorts of contrary indications such as the findings of the voting studies[56] or the literature on the diffusion of innovations.[57] The Government of India is more fortunate than most new nations in having an unusually sophisticated group of men involved in the planning process and in the mass media. Much of their work regarding rural radio forums has been not only creative in concept but successful in practice[58], yet the data lead one to suspect that the mass media have not been used as fully as they might have been with regard to political awareness and mobilization. For our respondents at least, the media appear to mobilize without furnishing the information necessary for rational choice. According to common indicators of participation, i.e. voting frequency and claimed degree of interest in political affairs, they are highly participant and similar to citizens of countries having much longer traditions of participation. At the same time, however, they know very little about the men and institutions crucial to the political life of their region and nation. Interested in whether this indicated a failure of the media to reach the people (either physically or psychologically) an Index of Media Exposure was created (see Table 5.28) and scores on the index were tabulated and then analyzed in terms of their relationships to other variables.

TABLE 5.28
Index of Media Exposure

1. How frequently do you listen to the radio ?
2. How often have you been to the cinema in the past year ?
3. How often do you read a newspaper (or have it read to you) ?

The shortcomings of using this index as a measure of exposure to political communications are obvious. First, a high score on all items gives no assurance that the individual has been exposed to any political content. Most people in Punjab and Haryana say that the most interesting media channels are those which don't bother with political affairs and that those that do are quite dull. Foreign visitors to this region often note that the most popular newspapers feature pinups rather than politics and that at cinemas during the mandatory newsreel and documentary there is a great deal of talking, walking around, and a spirit of general disorder that makes it impossible for even the genuinely interested individual to gain anything from these short subjects. The disorder rarely carries over to the feature film, a general hushing of the audience accompanying the shift from educative to entertainment content.

The case of radio is slightly different. All-India Radio is a governmentally operated monopoly within the country is required to remain politically neutral. This requirement has contributed to something of a withdrawal from discussion of domestic politics rather than the desired aloofness and fairness. As a result, All-India Radio news appears to consist of tedious repetition of speeches made by public figures at the opening of public libraries, cooperatives, and the like. The only political news one hears is of major events, such as the fall of a state government.

One might say that because of this emphasis on public figures and their speeches that the respondents should do well on the index, at least on those questions asking about incumbents. Unfortunately, the response to AIR news that I saw as most common in the villages was either a drifting away from the *panchayat* radio receiver, the *sarpanch*'s turning it off, or someone (usually the *sarpanch*) tuning to Radio Ceylon or Pakistan to hear some recent Indian film music.

TABLE 5.29
Communications Exposure

	Per cent Responding
Daily radio listening	65.9
More than three movies in a year	30.2
More than twelve movies in a year	13.5
Daily newspaper exposure	27.0
One paper per week or more	39.7
One or more political discussion(s) per week	42.1
Radio as major source of political information	65.9
Newspaper as secondary source	42.1

At any rate, Table 5.29 shows that exposure to mass communications is by no means a rare occurrence among the sample. Two-thirds (65.9%) listen to the radio daily, two of five (39.7%) are exposed to a newspaper once a week, one-fourth (27.0%) are exposed to a newspaper daily, a third (30.2%) go to the cinema at least three times a year. These figures are impressive in a society making the leap from traditional subsistence agriculture to a broader world.

The most significant finding was not that all forms of communications activity were intercorrelated (a fact noted by Lerner over a decade ago and true here as well) or even that communications activity is related to political activity (also true here) *but that the mass media are the private preserve of one group.*

Earlier it was found that despite protestations of high interest and excellent voting records a good part of the sample knew next to nothing about politics at the state and national level. A correlation matrix was generated showing strong positive relationships between media exposure, political awareness, and behavioural political efficacy (See Table 5.30). The obvious conclusion seemed to be that the mass media perform an educative function, generating the knowledge and competence and self-confidence necessary for political action. But the case is not so simple. Earlier it was discovered that behavioural political efficacy was strongly related to income (cross-tabs showed the relationship to be significant at the 0.000 level !). Now correlations showed that the media exposure and political awareness were also strongly related to income.

TABLE 5.30

Correlations : Media Exposure, Awareness Efficacy and Participation

	r			
	1	*2*	*3*	*4*
1. Media Exposure	X	.417**	.510**	—.186
2. Political Efficacy (Practice)		X	.614**	—.102
3. Political Awareness			X	.119
4. Political Participation (Voting)				X

**=significant at the 0.01 level

The coefficient of correlation between media exposure and wealth is r=.471 (p=0.01), for political awareness r=.513 (p=0.01). (The correlation between wealth and behavioural efficacy was r=.510, p=0.01.)—a more conservative result than that obtained from the cross-tabulation. It is unlikely that media exposure or any of the other variables or indices leads to wealth. Rather, it is probable that those people having a surplus of income are able to partake of the media to a fuller extent than people living in relatively straitened circumstances. With extra income one can buy his own radio, subscribe to a newspaper and visit the cinema more frequently. More important, he can use his income either as a tool in the political life of the community or as a buffer against unfair treatment. What the figures mean is that the rich use the media, understand their system and are able to manipulate the system while the poor get fragmentary media messages and merely think they can manipulate the system. The rich know which levers to pull and those levers are not necessarily those connected to the electoral machinery. In this context the ballot box may to a large extent be irrelevant to the political process in the area. This is indicated by the negative, weak, and inconsistent correlations between voting participation and political knowledge, behavioural political efficacy, and wealth. (See Tables 5.30 and 5.31)

Low correlations between voting behaviour and other indicators of participation could be explained by the fact that many people lie about their record of voting, inflating the figures given to the inter-

TABLE 5.31

Correlations between Voting Behaviour and Other Indicators

Index	
1. Political knowledge	—.119
2. Personal efficacy (practice)	—.102
3. Household income	—.178*
4. Media exposure	—.186*

*=significant at the 0.05 level

viewer. But assuming that everyone does this would merely reduce the correlations, not change their signs. The only way for signs to be changed would be if those people who are most exposed to the media, most efficacious, most politically kowledgeable confess to voting less than do their less exposed, less efficacious, and less knowledgeable neighbours. Who are these people who vote less? The rich, higher caste, educated gentry. It could conceivably be that these people are more truthful in their accounts of their voting behaviour but it is more likely their recognition that the fulcrum where they can most effectively exert leverage to move government is located in the secretariat, district headquarters, and police station rather than at the polling place that accounts for the negative correlations.

What this means of course is that the Government of India's communications policies may be working imperfectly, with those groups who least require information getting a great deal of it while the masses whom the government is trying to inform and mobilize participate on the basis of incorrect stereotypes, incomplete information, and in terms of immediate goals, perhaps at the inappropriate level of political action. Indeed, media exposure was correlated with political knowledge ($r=.510$; $p=0.01$). To Lerner's observation that "If one danger to developed democracies comes from literate non-voters, the parallel danger in developing democracies comes from the reverse configuration, i.e. *non-literate voters*"[59] we must add "and educated elements working outside the electoral process."

Conclusions

This rather diffuse chapter has discussed a few of the cognitive, evaluative, and affective elements that contribute to the political culture of the Punjab-Haryana region. Particular emphasis has been placed on the ways in which some of these variables seem to be dependent on the personal characteristics of the individuals who make up the sample. The findings show how much of an oversimplification it is to speak of *the*, or even *a*, political culture within this area because so many different combinations of what appear to be independent variables exist and create a multitude of configurations. Nevertheless, a few points of commonality exist showing that certain cultural and economic-social factors contribute to the orientations of the sample.

Status and wealth are intimately intertwined with exposure to the media, political awareness, and an operational sense of political efficacy. The rich person not only has more sources of information at his disposal, he knows more and does more...*but his actions are generally through channels of* personal influence rather than through the electoral process. His less powerful neighbours may think they know how to effect change but their limited information and misunderstanding of where to apply pressure (as the system now works) combine with a lack of resources to keep their influence marginal at best. Although they may feel that their acts have consequences, even if they are able to elect a representative their efforts to establish a network of control are soon short-circuited by the more direct approach of the powerful. It could be said that the constricted lives of the poor e.g. their lack of media exposure, infrequency of travel, etc. combines with their material poverty to keep them politically torpid.

Although many of the behavioural characteristics found in the sample derived from economic and social factors, others showed deep cultural roots. A concern with conflict, manifested as a dread of disharmony (seen in part as stemming from widespread participation), was found to be so great that most of the sample preferred the preservation of harmony to the accomplishment of community economic or social goals. A great majority also said that they themselves withdrew from discussions in which they were sure that they were right in order to avoid trouble. In traditional Indian thought the view that conflict was inherent in all situations and that it was to be avoided at all costs was tempered by the acceptance of the notion that power exists to prevent conflict and anarchy from tearing society apart. This traditional view, that strong authorities are to be desired, is no longer as widely subscribed to as perhaps it once was. Participation through direct approach and the universal franchise has led many to see government as a tool to be manipulated for their own interests. To be manipulable government officials and politicians should not be too powerful. For the same reasons those elements who are least powerful desire a strong administrative and political hierarchy that will be able to protect them not only from conflict but which also will be strong enough to withstand the demands of powerful local figures, e.g. big landlords, who are their *jajmans* or moneylenders.

Most respondents expressed satisfaction with the present political system and governmental structures (although the level of knowledge of these was limited) but were generally hostile to the individuals who man the system on the grounds that they were insensitive and corrupt. Out of this rather jaundiced view of politicians and administrators came the pragmatism of the old adage "if you can't like 'em, join 'em": most of the respondents felt that politics would be a good thing for a son of theirs to go into because it was likely to be a lucrative profesion.

Refugees more than non-refugees favoured authoritarian solutions to social and political problems and frequently justified these in terms of the fear of unmanageable conflict that we have already discussed. One other dimension of conventional authoritarianism: fantasy aggression, was also examined when it emerged as an important facet of the personalities of the entire sample. It could not be traced to any sociological or psychological variables. Many authors have claimed that the nuclear conflicts of a common childhood socialization process result in much of the aggressiveness found in Indian society. We have no data to support or refute this contention. The questions measuring fantasy aggression were vague and general. More specific questions were asked about sentiments to India's most important minority, the Muslims, because they are not only of great psychological significance to the refugees but are also nationally politically visible yet weak, very different and yet conveniently absent from Punjab and Haryana. We found that indeed Muslims had become targets of the diffuse rage of the entire sample perhaps as the result of political campaigns and international events that had focussed attention on them. This general psychological aggression creates a baseline for hostility. From this baseline frustrations, and a number of possible contributors to a sense of frustration, e.g., poverty, low caste status, low sense of personal efficacy, all act intensify this hostility to Muslims.

Punjab and Haryana are not typical of the rest of India, but in a multitude of ways where Punjab and Haryana lead many people hope that India will follow. This is especially true in terms of agriculture and the development of small industries. The data described in this chapter may indicate that the pattern of political development in the two states may not be as worthy of emulation as the economic. In other spheres the Punjabi-Haryanvi attitudes may also be inappropriate for what is thought of as well ordered political development. For example, although many westerners make allowances for corruption as appropriate and perhaps even as a democratizing force in the new nations it is difficult to see how the cynicism inevitably bred of widespread corruption can aid in the creation of an orderly democratic process based on the universal franchise. In Punjab and Haryana some people vote and other people influence the administration in the exercise of its duties. Other provinces having greater inequalities between rich and poor and little or no development in prospect may not be able to keep the system going as well as have the Punjabis and Haryanvis who feel that the system (if not its personnel) is basically workable and good.

In conclusion we are compelled once again to recognize that a political culture is indeed a many splendoured thing and that we have touched only upon a number of those themes that we see as significant. A great deal more work will be required in this field and in this geographical area before one can state with any degree of assurance what the dimensions of the subjective realm of politics are.

REFERENCES

1. For general discussions of the concept of political culture see Gabriel A. Almond and Sidney Verba, *The Civic Culture*, Princeton: Princeton University Press, 1963, pp. 1-44; Lucian W. Pye, Chapter I : "Introduction : Political Culture and Political Development," in Lucian W. Pye and Sidney Verba, *Political Culture and*

Political Development, Princeton : Princeton University Press, 1965, pp. 3-26; and Sidney Verba, Chapter 12, "Comparative Political Culture," in *ibid.*, pp. 512-560.

2. Lucian W. Pye, *ibid.*, p.7.

3. The recognition of the distributional character of these concepts has led to a shift in terms used by anthropologists and psychologists from national character to model personality type. See Anthony F. C. Wallace, "The Cultural Distribution of Personality Characteristics," in *Culture and Personality*, New York: 1961, pp. 84-119.

4. *Ibid.*, p. 117-119.

5. See Myron Weiner, "India : Two Political Cultures," in Pye and Verba, *op. cit.*, pp. 199-244 and W. H. Morris-Jones, "India's Political Idioms," in C.H. Phillips, ed., *Politics and Society in India*, New York : Frederick A. Praeger, 1962, pp. 133-154.

6. See Lloyd I. Rudolph and Susanne Hoeber Rudolph, "The Traditional Roots of Charisma : Gandhi," in *The Modernity of Tradition*, Chicago: University of Chicago Press, 1969, pp. 155-249. For the pioneering work in this area see Erik H. Erikson, *Young Man Luther*, New York : W.W. Norton and Company, 1958.

7. A.L. Basham, "Some Fundamental Political Ideas of Ancient India," in Phillips, *op. cit.*, pp. 14-15.

8. For a brief discussion of *matsyanyaya* and the origins of the concept as well as some verses from the *Ramayana* illustrative of the shape of things in such a period see A.L. Basham, *The Wonder That Was India*, New York : Grove Press, 1954, pp. 85-86.

9. For a description of the four yugas and the Hindu world cycle see Heinrich Zimmer, *Myths and Symbols in Indian Art and Civilization*, ed. by Joseph Campbell, New York : Harper Torchbooks, 1962, pp. 13-19.

10. *Ibid.*, p. 15.

11. Basham, *Wonder*, p. 114.

12. *Ibid.*, p. 114.

13. *Ibid.*, p. 119.

14. T.N. Ramaswamy, *Essentials of Indian Statecraft : Kautilya's Arthasastra for Contemporary Readers*, Bombay : Asia Publishing House, p. 31.

15. From the *Classical Indian Civilization Syllabus* (*CLIC, 1968*), Chicago : College Syllabus Division, The University of Chicago, 1968, p. 141.

16. Weiner, *op. cit.*, pp. 214-215.

17. *Ibid.*, p. 236.

18. Prakash Tandon, *Punjabi Century, 1857-1947*, London: Chatto and Windus, 1961, pp. 82-87.

19. G. Morris Carstairs, *The Twice Born : A Study of a Community of High Caste Hindus*, Bloomington : Indiana University Press, 1961.

20. Richard G. Fox, *From Zamindar to Ballot Box*, Ithaca : Cornell University Press, 1969.

21. Adrian C. Mayer, *Caste and Kinship in Central India : A Village and its Region*, Berkeley: University of California Press, 1966.

22. The Panchayati Raj system of three-tiered local government was either set up or under consideration in all the states of India by the early 1960's. It was created at least partly to remedy the lack of local participation in the Community Development Programme which had been created ten years earlier, in 1952. For good descriptions of the organization and history of both Community Development and Panchayati Raj as they are referred to see W.H. Morris-Jones, *The Government and Politics of India*, Garden City : Anchor, 1967, and David C. Potter, *Government in Rural India*, London : London School of Economics and Political Science, 1964. For the workings of these local governmental bodies see Adrian Mayer, *op. cit.*, Ralph Retzlaff, *Village Government in India*, New York : Asia Publishing House, 1962.

23. Basham, *Wonder*, p. 114.

24. Kautilya, ever the pragmatist bent on maintaining and expanding an empire, rules out passionate, harsh and unreasonable punishment because they may generate rebellion. As he puts it, such behaviour "incites even hermits, let alone householders" (Ramaswamy, *op. cit.*, p. 49). But he says in the same paragraph that "he who gives mild punishment becomes contemptible" and urges "punishment justly deserved" because "when authority is neutralised, anarchy, as in the parable of the fishes, reigns." (*Ibid.*)

25. "Selections from the Canti Parva," in *Classical Indian Civilization Syllabus* (CLIC, 1968), Chicago: College Syllabus Division, University of Chicago, 1968, pp. 118-143.

26. Irving L. Janis, *Air War and Emotional Stress : Psychological Studies of Bombing and Civilian Defence*, New York : McGraw-Hill, 1951.

27. Donald B. Robinson, *The Face of Disaster*, New York :

Doubleday, 1959, p. 191.

28. Robert J. Lifton, *Death in Life : Survivors of Hiroshima*, New York : Random House, 1967, pp. 193 ff.

29. All questions in this particular index were general in nature for two reasons: First, to determine general sentiments that could be expected to be operational in the political life of the respondent regardless of the actors involved. (To some extent this is impossible of course, but the broad dynamics of Punjab-Haryana politics was of greater interest than the specific and specialized relationship of the subjects with particular actors.) Second, to gauge sentiments about particular actors would be to invite misunderstanding and misinterpretation by local authorities. For these reasons no questions having to do even with specific roles other than the common "what would you do if you were...?" type were included.

30. Joseph Lelyveld, "India's 55 Million Moslems Living in Rejection and Isolation," *New York Times,* October 28, 1968. The above is a general article. For the sentiments of Hindus and Muslims immediately following a communal riot, see Sidney H. Schanberg, "After Communal Riots in Ahmedabad, Venom and Fear." *New York Times,* December 19, 1969.

31. The items on hostility to Muslims are modifications of those used by H.J. Eysenck to determine hostility to Jews. The original items used by Eysenck can be found in his *The Psychology of Politics*, London : Routledge and Kegan Paul, 1963, pp. 89-91.

32. In the years following partition several studies found that refugee hatred of Muslims was spreading to non-refugees. For descriptions of some of these studies see R.N. Saksena, *Refugees : A Study in Changing Patterns*, Bombay : Asia Publishing House, 1961 and Gardner Murphy's summation of several research projects in his *In the Minds of Men*, New York : Basic Books, 1953. Although all these various efforts have been fairly well publicized there are serious methodological grounds on which their conclusions can be questioned.

33. It was this great fear among orthodox Sikhs that Hinduism would engulf, absorb, and digest the entire community of the Khalsa, that had led to the growth of the Akali Dal into an important political party in the previous fifty years. See Baldev Raj Nayar, *Minority Politics in the Punjab*, Princeton : Princeton University Press, 1966, for a detailed discussion.

34. Chandigarh was awarded to Punjab in January 1970 to ward

off the Akali leader, Sant Fateh Singh's threat of self-immolation. Haryana was granted some fertile agricultural land from Punjab, a $13 million grant and an additional $13 million loan, both amounts to be used for construction of a new capital.

35. William A. Gamson, *Power and Discontent*, Homewood, Ili. : The Dorsey Press, 1968, pp. 39-58, 154-183.

36. Robert E. Lane, *Political Ideology*, New York : The Free Press, 1962, p. 161; Robert A. Dahl, *Political Opposition in Western Democracies*, New Haven : Yale University Press, 1966, p. 351.

37. David Easton, *A Systems Analysis of Political Life*, New York : John Wiley, 1965.

38. Gabriel A. Almond and Sidney Verba, *The Civic Culture*, Boston : Little, Brown and Company, 1965, p. 63.

39. Hadley Cantril, *The Politics of Despair*, New York : Collier Books, 1962, p. 81 ff.

40. Daniel Lerner, *The Passing of Traditional Society*, Glencoe : The Free Press, 1958, pp. 47-52.

41. *Ibid.*, pp. 69-70.

42. Lucian W. Pye, *Politics, Personality and Nation Building*, New Haven : Yale University Press, 1962.

43. In recent years the unpredictability of actions and the mistrust between different ethnic groups in the new states has proven to be a fertile ground for a number of serious and humorous novelists. See for example the works of Anthony Burgess, especially his Malayan trilogy *The Long Day Wanes*, New York : W.W. Norton and Company, 1964 and *Devil of a State*, New York : W.W. Norton and Company, 1962.

44. For a more thorough discussion of the problems of integration of diverse groups see Clifford Geertz, "The Integrative Revolution," in Geertz, ed., *Old Societies and New States*, Glencoe : The Free Press, 1963, pp. 105-157.

45. Almond and Verba, *op. cit.*, p. 17.

46. Most of the work of political efficacy is a direct outgrowth of the work presented by Angus Campbell and his colleagues at the Michigan Survey Research Centre first reported in *The Voter Decides*, Evanston, Ill. : Row Peterson and Co., 1954.

47. See Angus Campbell, *et al.*, *The American Voter*, New York : John Wiley and Sons, 1960, pp. 517 ff.

48. Lerner, *op. cit.*, p. 50.

49. Lucian W. Pye in Pye and Verba, *op. cit.*, p. 13.

50. Robert D. Hess, "The Acquisition of Feelings of Political Efficacy in Pre-Adults," paper presented at the 1968-69 Lecture Series, Department of Government, Florida State University (mimeographed).

51. David Easton and Jack Dennis, "The Child's Acquisition of Regime Norms : Political Efficacy," *American Political Science Review*, LXI, 1967, pp. 25-38.

52. A Personal Efficacy (Practice) Index was not included because measuring personal efficacy in practice would involve a large number of hypothetical situations that would necessarily be of varying degrees of salience to different individuals. The questionnaire (in two languages), was already one hundred pages long, not counting the lengthy and time consuming TAT section.

53. For particularly interesting accounts of specific cases of what happens when inconsistencies exist between income, power and caste status, see Lloyd Rudolph and Susane Hoeber Rudolph, "Horizontal Mobilization," in *The Modernity of Tradition*, Chicago: University of Chicago Press, 1967, pp. 36-64 and F.G. Bailey, *Caste and the Economic Frontier*, Manchester : Manchester University Press, 1957.

54. For the relationship between age and turnout see Campbell *et al.*, *American Voter*, pp. 493-498.

55. Daniel Lerner, for example, says: "Traditional society is non-participant...people's horizons are limited by locale and their decisions involve only *known* people in *known* situations." Daniel Lerner, *The Passing of Traditional Society*, Glencoe, Illinois : The Free Press, 1968, p. 50. Everett Rogers, in listing ten characteristics of peasant societies, finds one of them to be a limited view of the world : "Localiteness is the degree to which individuals are oriented within, rather than external to, their social system." Everett Rogers, *Modernization among Peasants*, New York : Holt, Rinehart and Winston, 1969, p. 37. Almond and Verba claim that an important part of the political culture is the cognitions of the members of that culture and find that lack of awareness of political objects correlates with other indicators of a lack of political development. Gabriel A. Almond and Sidney Verba, *The Civic Culture*, Princeton, New Jersey : Princeton University Press, 1963.

56. Paul F. Lazarsfeld, Bernard R. Berelson, and Hazel Gaudet, *The People's Choice*, New York : Columbia University Press, 1944 and Bernard R. Berelson, Paul F. Lazarsfeld, and William N.

McPhee, *Voting*, Chicago : University of Chicago Press, 1954.

57. Elihu Katz and Paul F. Lazarsfeld, *Personal Influence*, Glencoe, Illinois: The Free Press, 1955. Everett Rogers, *The Diffusion of Innovations*, New York : The Free Press, 1962, and Rogers, *Modernization among Peasants*.

58. B.P. Bhatt and P.V. Krishnamoorthy, "Radio Rural Forums Spread throughout India", *Radio Broadcasting Serves Rural Development*, Paris : UNESCO, 1965. Selden Menefee and Audrey Menefee, "An Experiment in Communications in Four Indian Villages", *Indian Journal of Social Research*, VI (1965), pp. 148-58. S.C. Dube comments briefly on the topic in his article "Communication, Innovation, and Planned Change in India", in Daniel Lerner and Wilbur Schramm, eds., *Communication and Change in the Developing Countries*, Honolulu : East-West Centre Press, 1967, pp. 129-67.

59. Daniel Lerner, "Toward a Communication Theory of Modernization, A Set of Considerations", in Lucian W. Pye, ed., *Communications and Political Development*, Princeton, New Jersey : Princeton University Press, 1963, p. 343.

CHAPTER VI

The Refugees and Economic Development

To maintain prosperity of the state, troubles should be removed, causes eliminated, impediments removed and financial distress eliminated.

—Kautilya, **The Arthasastra**

In the quarter century since India gained independence many changes have taken place in the economy of the nation. First came the massive changes that resulted from the dislocations of partitioning a subcontinent. These involved reorganizing the jute industry, the shipping enterprises, banking and commerce, railroads, and the like. Then came other changes that were more conscious in their origin, the result of government planning for economic development. These included the construction of new steel mills, irrigation, and hydroelectric projects, and other large scale projects. With a series of Five Year Plans government now took on a more active aspect. Other, less dramatic changes also came about as a result of the nation's attainment of freedom. Communications were developed, agriculture aided and the creation of small, medium, and large scale industry encouraged. With the exception of large scale industry, nowhere in India was economic change as diverse and spectacular as in the Punjab-Haryana region.[1] This statement applies to the growth of all sorts of industries where none existed previously, the expansion of agricultural production and cultivation of new crops, the development of ancillary enterprises such as transportation companies, electroplating workshops, mechanical and electrical repair industries, and trade. This chapter, without going into great detail on the larger issues of economic development, will attempt to explain why the Punjab-Haryana region has been such a fertile ground for all sorts of diverse activities when other, ostensibly more promising areas have developed more slowly and in some cases even stagnated.

Economic Development in Post-Partition Punjab-Haryana

It is fashionable these days to describe the partition of India as a dismemberment. In many ways the simile is apt for the state lost its head, its control centre, the state capital at Lahore ; its arms, the productive lands of the West ; and even its lifeblood, the canal system. When all the migrations were completed the new state of Punjab had not only absorbed a large number of refugees (7 million by most estimates) but found itself the net loser in the land-man exchange of partition.[2] Not only did the government find that it had less land for the refugees than they had possessed on the other side of the new frontier but that the refugees' land on the Indian side was poorer in quality than that which they had left. The new state was by no means a desert but it had never produced as much food as it had consumed. In contemporary terms it was a food deficit area.[3] Within twenty years the state had recaptured the title of pre-partition Punjab : "the granary of India." During the first two Plans (from 1950-51 to 1960-61) gross agricultural production rose 76.5 per cent (as opposed to All-India increase of 46.4 per cent).[4] The increases in production came partly as the result of increasing the acreage under crops, but even more important was the fact that agricultural productivity steadily increased during that period at a rate of 2½ per cent per annum *even before the much hearlded "green revolution" !*[5] The introduction of new seeds, fertilizers, methods of irrigation and implements, etc. that have led to the recent sharp jump in yields have, of course, met with their greatest success in the same area (now constituting the states of Punjab and Haryana).[6]

Although agricultural development was what India most needed during and immediately following two successive failures of the monsoon in other areas of north India, the Punjab-Haryana region was in the forefront of development in other spheres as well. Especially encouraging to planners hopeful of an eventual industrial revolution in India was the development of a myriad of small scale industries in towns that hitherto had been railroad junctions and district headquarters. Wherever transport, power, and raw materials could be combined—and in many places where they could not[7]—small and medium scale industries sprang up. To gain some idea of the growth of these one must look at statistics. In 1951 there were 1,486 registered factories in Punjab.[8] By 1961 there were 4,089.[9] In 1967, after bifurcation of the state had resulted in much of the medium and virtually all large scale industry going to Haryana, Punjab still could boast of 15,000 small scale industry enterprises.[10] (Although the basis for classifying "factories" and "small scale industries" may not be the same the figures do give some idea of the industrialization of the area that only a brief time before was almost entirely agricultural and rural-based.)

Almost every other indicator shows equally dramatic increases. In the fifteen years following 1951 the number of schools increased six times (from 6,917 to about 40,000).[11] Paved road mileage increased during the same period from slightly over 3,300 miles to almost 8,500;[12] hospital beds increased from 9,138 to 15,095.[13] While it is very difficult to break these figures down in order to compare the two new states, it seems that both are continuing to undergo rapid development.

Our task in this chapter is to try and explain why the Punjab and Haryana region has succeeded (or at least embarked) on the road to success where so many other provinces have failed. Many different explanations have been put forward to explain the remarkable progress of this area. Most contain at least some elements of truth. We will describe these briefly and then add another factor which we believe is also important if one is to understand the way individuals interact with the dynamics of economic growth.

Some Explanations

There are undoubtedly some very persuasive economic reasons why Punjab-Haryana has succeeded where other states have failed. While heavily populated, the area does not have the tremendous disparities in the size of landholdings that one finds in other areas of India. This appears to have been true of the province for at least the last century,[14] and as we shall see is even more true today. What this means in economic terms is that improvements in agricultural methods that require investment, such as introduction of a tubewell or use of fertilizer, can be afforded not only by a small number of large landlords but also by the much greater number of smallholders. Although absentee landlords did exist, their holdings were and are much smaller than those of their counterparts in other areas of the country. In many cases this required them to introduce improvements if they wish to maintain their standard of living in the towns.[15] In addition, the soil, when watered, is rich; the climate, while extreme in terms of human comfort, is almost perfect for growing wheat and a number of other crops; a canal system started by the British has been expanded since Independence so that today Haryana has more than a third and Punjab more than sixty per cent its acreage in irrigated land[16] : and an ever increasing road network[17] and bus system[18] gives the farmer easy access to markets and government headquarters.

On the industrial front the factory owner is benefited by cheap electric power from the Bhakra-Nangal hydroelectric complex, good rail and road transport facilities, and a reliable, hardworking and cheap labour force. There are also excellent banking and credit facilities.[19]

The above economic advantages possessed by the two states are both natural and man-made. Much of the literature on economic development deals with the actions of government and it is here, with the man-made advantages, that we will start. A policy of expanding economic opportunity was started by the British a century ago with their road building, canal construction, and colonization projects and followed up at the turn of the century in the passage of the Punjab Land Alienation Act.[20] The work has been carried on admirably by state governments since partition.[21] With the flight of virtually all the Muslims from the eastern part of the state, the government found itself in the position of having to resettle seven million Hindu and Sikh refugees. Although today the government's actions at that time may seem tame and even slow, they undoubtedly were courageous and even daring in the years immediately following partition.[22] Government policy with regard to land was two-fold; having less land to distribute than had been possessed by the refugees in what was now Pakistan, the Government instituted "graduated land cuts" based on the artificial unit of the standard acre.[23] What this really amounted to was introduction of a method of land reform (through progressive redistribution) long before that term became politically fashionable. The necessity for swift action and the setting obviously helped government in its work. Still, allocations progressed by fits and starts over more than a three year period. Fortunately, there were no large estates owned by Hindu and Sikh non-refugees in the areas where the refugees settled so that feelings of relative deprivation among the refugees were minimized. Of course almost all refugees in those early years could look back on pre-partition days with a sense of economic loss (to say nothing of personal loss) but the scramble to earn a living and start over didn't allow for a great deal of rumination. The second prong of the government policy was to consolidate plots into economic holdings. This was not a new development in Punjab[24] but here once again the government found itself with a freer hand than most governments have had when confronting this matter.

Government policies certainly aided in setting the refugee back on his feet but even after this restoration he found himself much worse off than he had been before. In most cases he had less land, poorer land, and less irrigated land. In the years that followed the government of Punjab, and later Punjab and Haryana, with the help of the Central Government expanded the canal irrigation system,[25] electrified most villages, promoted the use of tubewells,[26] and often aided the farmer in the purchase of a pumping set[27] and tractors.[28] These actions of course have not been directed exclusively to the refugees.

The urban classes have been no less fortunate in receiving help from the government. Although trading classes whose major source of income came from moneylending have been hurt by the expansion of credit facilities and the general prosperity of the area, trade itself has expanded to make up some of their loss. Those who were rentiers obtained urban evacuee property. Some of the urban classes as well as some previously rural types have provided a great deal of the impetus to the development of small industry, something that Punjab and Haryana can be especially proud of. In recent years the growing importance of these small industries has led to great solicitousness of the part of government. Here too, however, aid to industries in the form of concessions, government constructed industrial estates, and quotas are not restricted to refugees.

Thus, it would be no exaggeration to say that the Punjab-Haryana region has benefited not only from natural factors but also from man-made and situational factors. The most important of these would appear to be the evenness in the size of land holdings, the richness of soil and a history of progressive governments. But other explanations exist and even if we feel that the above factors are important they may not be sufficient nor even necessary causes.

At this point we shift from broader economic explanations to more individual explanations. The shift will be a gradual one for the first of these theories that will be examined says that refugees, because of the material aid they received from government, are at the root of the economic development of the area. Superficially the argument (which most frequently comes from less successful non-refugees) is persuasive, for it is in those areas where refugees have settled that growth has been most dramatic. One has only to compare those districts of erstwhile Punjab that have absorbed the largest numbers of refugees with those that received the fewest refugees and then compare each with economic development indicators to note strong correlations.[29] Excluding PEPSU (for which comparable figures could not be obtained) and Kangra and Simla districts (because of the ethnic difference of the population) the districts of Punjab and Haryana that absorbed the greatest number of refugees are Ferozepur and Karnal, two districts that are relatively advanced in terms of agriculture. The two lowest are Gurgaon and Rohtak, both known as "backward areas" agriculturally. Although there does seem to be some relationship between refugees and development, can it be attributed to favoured treatment by government ? The argument does not stand up, at least in terms of gross measures. What the refugees received as compensation was, for most, much less than what they had lost, both quantitatively and qualitatively. When one points this out to proponents of this argument the reply usually comes back : "Ah yes, but those refugees all lied about their losses and they were able to get back more than they had lost." It is hard to see how a system of graded cuts, based on poor land whose total acreage was less than two-thirds the total amount of land left behind,[30] could be worked so that many people wound up better than before.[31] In terms of *taccavi* loans the refugees did receive some preferential treatment but, as M. S. Randhawa points out, the figures on the cash loaned out (Rs. 30 million) may be impressive "but when we remember that the number of families settled on land was 2½ lakhs, and each one of them needed financial assistance very badly, the amounts advanced were hardly adequate."[32] More important, it must be remembered that refugees were settled where Muslims had left so that any correlation between development may be unrelated to the presence of refugees and more due to the fact that these areas may have been more developed in the first place. For example, since the introduction of canals around the end of the 19th century the Ferozepur area has always been highly productive. Karnal was less so, but once canal and drainage systems had dried up the marshy soil and public health measures had eliminated the dangers of plague, malaria, and small pox notable progress was made. By the same token Gurgaon district has always been the most backward despite its proximity to Delhi.[33] These disclaimers notwithstanding the refugees do seem to be associated with economic development in the two states although *not as the direct result of rehabilitation* projects. Some of the data substantiate this view. Before going on to those data however let us just briefly describe several other explanations popular among many Punjabis and Haryanvis.

Although these days it is very difficult for scholars to take racial or climatological explanations seriously such views are still widespread even among educated people in India. Thus one hears that the fierce extremes of weather in Punjab and Haryana breed a hardy people with (naturally) all the virtues that the Punjabi and Haryanvi possesses. Such arguments are hard to refute since the climate is obviously there and so are the character traits. (It is interesting to note that every proponent of a climatological theory finds that his own particular climate possesses the optimum mix necessary for the creation of strong character, firm will, perseverance, and industriousness—the virtues that lead to development and progress.) The fact that other areas may have the same climate and different traits or a different climate with the same traits does not deter them. Nor do they approach the question of why development is so recent while climate has changed virtually not at all within the last 500 years at least.

Still other people claim that much of the hardiness, etc. of the Punjab peasant comes as the result of repeated invasions that either left only the strongest alive or resulted in inbreeding. As one very prominent Punjabi (a Jat Sikh) puts it :

> ..., the terms Jat and cultivator have become, more or less, synonymous in the Punjab. They are a sturdy, self reliant, industrious, and a manly race. Apart from the influence of climate and diet, their distinctive qualities are possibly due to racial factors. It is said that they are the descendants of Scythians and Huns. The Scythians were a Central Asian tribe, who entered the plains of the Punjab in the second century B.C. driven by a drought and

> a more powerful tribe, Yuch-chi. The Huns invaded India about 450 A.D. in the reign of Skand Gupta and after suffering a preliminary defeat, they ultimately overwhelmed the Gupta empire in 510 A.D., and established their own kingdom. The Jats are a mixed race and are possibly the descendants of the soldiers of these Central Asian tribes who married Indian women. Miscegenation has usually resulted in racial vigour; whenever distantly related communities have inter-married the progeny has usually been stronger than the parents. This phenomenon has also been seen in the U.S.A where individuals from different European countries have settled, inter-married, and produced a vigorous race. The Soviet Union on account of its liberal racial policy has also encouraged miscegenation.[34]

That the alleged miscegenation took place a millennium and a half ago and that from all we know of recent times the Jats have been as endogamous as many other castes is irrelevant to these people. Similar types of explanations are put forth by other subgroups, with Sikhs claiming that their religion calls for hard work and thrift and that these two virtues have built the new economy of north India. Hindus may make disparaging remarks about their stereotype of the Sikh—vain and stupid—and claim that their own financial acumen is responsible for development, to which the Sikh peasant objects, calling them cheats, leeches, and sharpers. All in all, racial, religious, and climatological explanations appear simplistic at best and potentially dangerous at worst. Both religious groups can be found today in trade and industry although higher caste Hindus have shied away from cultivation. (Many however have seen the economic opportunities presented by agriculture and now are "gentlemen farmers"[35].)

Hidus and Sikhs each claim to be the seed from which economic development has blossomed. In earlier years, long before partition when the distinction between Hindu and Sikh was less clear in the province (because of adoption of children and the widespread practice among Hindus of voluntarily rearing one child as a Sikh) the trait was generalized to a larger population (and not only by Punjabis themselves):

> Here the true Punjabi, so simple in his habits and dignified in his bearing, is seen at his best—vigorous, shrewd, and immensely

> laborious. It would be difficult in India to find either a better cultivator or a better co-operator.[36]

Today the picture is less clear and no one would claim that Punjabis are uniformly different than residents of other provinces. Even at the time the above quotation was written the author had to single out the "true" Punjabi to make the stereotype fit.

Earlier we referred to the fact that non-refugee malcontents feel refugee resettlement and agricultural development are linked through favouritism to and "chiselling" by the newcomers. The refugees, while denying this, also like to consider themselves responsible for development, but for different reasons. Their explanations centre around the hardships they had to face when they arrived on the Indian side. Refugees, so the argument goes, were so destitute that they had to work so terribly hard that they naturally succeeded where their lazy non-refugee neighbours had heretofore failed. As A. S. Kahlon and his associates at Punjab Agricultural University have described it:

> However when the lands were allotted, these farmers changed the whole complex of Punjab agriculture. With their traditions of hard work (sic), diligence, and labour they shared their rich experience of raising high yield of crops with the local farming population. They worked hard because they were facing a challenge and were engaged very desperately in a struggle for survival.[37]

The argument is interesting not only for its similarity to the American pioneer ethic of "Root, hog, or die" as for its implicit declaration that they had to work very hard, much harder than they had been accustomed to in the western parts of the state. At the mass level this struggle against tremendous odds meant that a great number of people were mobilized by sheer desire for survival to work for the very goals that governments and foreign aid advisors would in the coming decades set as targets for other states. The refugees certainly did have to struggle in those first years. Due to the structure of caste in Punjab, the population transfer that evacuated entire Muslim castes, and the smallness of temporary allotments the refugees had to do work that heretofore was done for them by their *kamins*. In the earliest days of resettlement things were indeed very bad with some refugees forced to beg or become peddlers. This period however was brief and affected only those who had no relatives they could call upon and who were unable to reach a government camp. One reason the period was so short was that a scheme of temporary allotments of land was started in September 1947, only a few weeks after partition and these enabled, and indeed forced, the evacuees to start working very hard on extremely little land (each family got about ten acres regardless of its holding in Pakistan).[38]

This argument, although probably the most widely espoused "explanation", leaves a number of questions unanswered. First of all, while there seems to be implicit agreement that refugees have started and fostered development, no one considers the fact that non-refugees in most areas also lost most of their *kamins* and were forced to do things they would never have considered before. Second, one does not have to look far in India to find people who have experienced some sort of disaster—locusts, drought, floods, etc.—who do not exhibit the resilience of the Punjabi refugee despite well organized rehabilitation efforts. The clearest examples of this would be the slow pace of agricultural development in Bihar following the drought years of 1966 and 1967, and the failure of Bengali refugees, transplanted to Madhya Pradesh, to adapt and settle down.

Some people say that the Punjabi refugees had become used to a high standard of living in the central and western districts and wanted to restore this in their new surroundings. This is of course partially true (partially, because in the western districts of pre-partition Punjab the standard of living and the level of agriculture were both quite poor)[39] but the questions must be answered : (a) why didn't the refugees stop when this restoration had been accomplished; and (b) why haven't other dispossessed, handicapped, and poverty stricken groups been able to do likewise elsewhere ? The second part is easier to answer than the first. The pattern throughout Indian history is for dispossessed groups or groups losing their traditional occupations because of technological change to be forced into low status, fringe occupations. Refugees were able to avoid this because their numbers gave them political power, because Muslim evacuee property was available for distribution to them, and because the government and the public really wanted to do something for them. The first question is more difficult, for refugees not only restored their previous standard of living very rapidly but surpassed it. More interesting than mere figures about income, diet, and the like is the fact that refugees in a great many cases didn't bother to restore their previous lives *in toto*—they branched out into new enterprises, grew new crops, used new implements, built differently styled houses. In other words they didn't merely reconstruct their previous lives but, without any blueprints, built a new society based on individual accomplishment. We will discuss this at greater length in the sections that follow.

Another Explanation

That none of the traditional explanations is entirely satisfactory does not mean that they are all entirely unsatisfactory. It may well be that several of these explanations postulate necessary but not sufficient conditions for development under certain circumstances. For example it could be that Punjabis, with a traditionally more nutritious diet than people in other areas, are stronger and more suited to the hard work necessary for successful farming but that hard work alone is not functional unless one has a large enough holding of sufficiently rich soil so that he can produce a surplus that can be invested in improvements in agricultural practices or in better housing or a better diet. So it may be that situational, governmental, and natural conditions have acted in concert to develop the Punjab. We believe that there is one more dimension to development without which the amazing progress of the Punjab-Haryana region would have been very difficult and perhaps non-existent. This is the more personal dimension : the individual's perception of change and the psychological determinants of individual and social success in a developing society. That is, development progresses most satisfactorily when a number of institutional and structural factors interact with a number of other factors including individual predispositions. We have touched on some of the material and situational factors that have probably contributed to development and have indicated which of them seem plausible and which do not. Because there is such a rich literature on the relationship between institutions, structures, and processes on the one hand and various forms of development on the other, we will not concern ourselves further with this and will devote the remainder of this chapter to three traits that we believe must be fairly widely shared if a society is to develop : a belief that change is desirable or at least not threatening; a willingness to take risks; and what has come to be called a synergistic outlook and the behaviours associated with it.

Desire for Change

As social scientists we know very little about social, economic and political change, and still less about "development" in these three realms. One way in which change can be looked at is according to who proposes the impetus for it. We know that change can sometimes be imposed by fiat and enforced by power from above but we also know that change often comes about as the result of pressures from below. The extreme examples of these two patterns in the political realm are totalitarianism and violent revolution. (That we can describe these as extremes does not mean they are unconnected. The more or less spontaneous uprising of the February revolution against the centralized power of the Czar succeeded in deposing him only to lead to another revolution in which the Russian citizen found him replaced by a more complete centralization.) The policy makers of most of the developing nations intensely desire social, economic, political, and educational change. These leaders however must face the prickly problem of whether change should come from decisions taken at the highest level of government and then be implemented by a bureaucracy or whether the government should confine itself to responding to the felt needs of its people. If the decision makers see their public as ignorant, apathetic, unpatriotic, and tied to obsolete practices, the changes are they will opt for more dictatorial means. On the other hand if the leaders realize that there is often great wisdom in traditional practices and have a faith in the processes of democracy they may feel that *laissez-faire* is the best course of action for the government. India stands somewhere between these two poles. She is the world's largest democratic state and yet has a planned economy. Committed to socialism, she finds herself criticized from within for having almost completely unregulated industry and domestic trade. One of the reasons for these paradoxes is that India's specific problems are not only unique but are so great that she cannot afford to adopt either pure socialist or pure market economic solutions.[40] The combination of planning at the top and democratic decision making at the local level is the best indicator of this. The Government of India realizes that most Indians in rural areas have led lives too circumscribed to make meaningful choices on such typically western community issues as bond issues or the curricula of schools but that in those areas where the villager has experience he can and should have some control over what changes are to take place around him.

Central to this approach is the notion that villagers want some changes and that through a democratically elected village council decisions can be taken to meet these "felt needs." Where this is the case and the changes are within the jurisdiction of the *panchayat* roads are built, ponds dug or cleaned or drained, and schoolhouses built. Where the public does not have any felt needs, decisions to change things are either not taken or taken by individuals with economic interests in the change. Recently it has become modish in some circles to say that a desire for change is not enough: that a will to change must exist if development is to occur.[41] This, while probably true, ignores the distinction between those who have the will to work for change, those who merely desire it, and those who do not desire it for various reasons including apathy or vested interests. Without a desire for change there is no ground on which to build a will to work for change. Hence the first step in democratic development seems indeed to be the creation of a desire for change.

On the individual level the changes are usually not very extreme. A desire for a cheaper marriage ceremony, the feeling that education for one's children will be beneficial, a notion that given the proper resources one can earn more—all are manifestations of a sometimes acute but more often vague dissatisfaction.[42] It is this dissatisfaction combined with a willingness to change one's practices that, if widely shared, can lead to larger scale development. In a sense this is what was called the "revolution of rising expectations" in the 1950's. By the 1960's it was recognized that popular desires and even a willingness to change would have no effect without the commitment of leadership, natural resources, etc. It was during this period that Lerner was able to say that the revolution had been transformed from one of rising expectations into one of rising frustrations.[43] We agree with Lerner that dissatisfaction, even on a large scale, is not sufficient cause for development...but we believe strongly that it is a necessary cause.

For a man to be dissatisfied he must be aware that better things and ways of doing things exist and must feel that these new objects and practices are desirable. It is from this knowledge and these favourable sentiments that a will to work for change will germinate; without both, change will be sporadic and uncoordinated at best and non-existent at worst. With these views in mind the respondents were asked a number of questions about actual and potential changes in their lives. Farmers and agricultural tenants were specifically asked about the use of new seeds, fertilizer, implements, and methods of sowing. Town dwellers, landless labourers and artisans were left to specify their own changes because most of the changes in their practices have come about by order of the government, e.g., the introduction of metric units or observance of regular shop hours. Then, regardless of whether a respondent had adopted the innovation or not he was asked to specify whether it was good or bad. (He was also allowed to say "both," "neither," or "don't know.") Then all respondents were asked if any changes had occurred in their village or neighbourhood in the previous twenty-five years and asked to assess whether these had been beneficial or harmful. A summary of their responses can be found in Table 6.1.

TABLE 6.1
Value of Change

Item	*Per cent Responding "good"*
Improved seeds (N=73)	82.2
Chemical fertilizer (N=73)	98.6
Improved implements (N=73)	97.3
New methods of sowing (N=73)	93.2
Non-agricultural change (N=53)	89.5
Village or neighbourhood change 1 (N=126)	82.5
Village or neighbourhood change 2 (N=126)	89.0

The items regarding specific changes showed no differences between the refugees and non-refugees but when left to select their own changes, the refugees more frequently saw the changes as beneficial (see below). The data of Table 6.1 show that the overwhelming majority of the entire sample looks upon change in their own areas of experience as beneficial. That they also look at more abstract change as beneficial can be seen from their responses to certain attitudinal questions that can be found in Table 6.2.

It would seem from the data that the Punjabi-Haryanvi's attitudes have changed a good deal over the past forty years. Malcolm Lyall Darling, despite his personal feeling that a hint of change

TABLE 6.2
Attitudes towards Change

Item	*Per cent Replying*
1. People who want to do things in new ways forget that this may bring about even worse conditions (disagree)	65.6
2. (a) That which is already known is better than that which will come to be known OR (b) If society is to progress newer solutions to problems are essential ("b" responses)	84.0
3. (a) Modern problems require modern approaches OR (b) The best way of life is to walk in the paths of our fathers ("a" responses)	65.2
4. (a) We would be better off with less scientific development and more simple faith OR (b) One cannot learn how to improve things by continually referring to the ways problems were solved in the past ("b" responses)	71.9 N=125

was in the air, was honest enough to recognize that it was still embryonic in form and that without a great deal of care it might be aborted. He reported a typical farmer as saying :

> God gives me two meals a day in my own village and amongst my own children. That man (a rich returned emigrant) can also (only) eat this much, and I do not want any more.[44]

Darling then goes on to add a personal aside : "Probably the majority of those who live in the 34,000 villages of the Punjab would say the same."[45] Later in the book he tells us that the typical farmer looks askance at improved implements because of their cost and because "experience tells him that the smallholder should depend more on his (own) labour than on other people's machines."[46] Like the Missourian who says : "Show me," the Punjabis and Haryanvis, having been shown that change need not be threatening are now more receptive to change and this could explain discrepancies between sentiments about actual changes and sentiments about change in general—that the respondents require a little more "showing." Whatever the genesis of this new spirit, we believe it to be one of the fundamental components of economic development and the refugees seem to possess it more than the non-refugees. Evidence for this can be found in the responses to various items. For favourable views of a single change in village or neighbourhood (the change selected by the individual) the difference between the two groups was significant at the 0.06 level, refugees more favourable. For the second change the difference was less dramatic but it did persist in the same direction. But the refugees and non-refugees differ not only in their view of past changes but in their attitudes to change in general. For example, the differences between the two groups on the first two items in Table 6.2 ("People who want to do things...", "That which is already known...") are significant at the 0.02 and 0.18 level respectively. (All these statistics are derived from t-tests.) We believe that the reason item 3 does not yield significant differences is that this is the crux of the ambivalence of man in transition : torn between tradition and modernity most people see both options as desirable. Item 4, on the other hand, is too one-sided, it being very difficult for respondents to choose "a" responses (only a fourth did so). On another item : "Nowadays more and more people are prying into matters that are the province of the gods and goddesses and the effects will probably be disastrous," the refugees also proved more amenable to change. Although significance is high for only two items, three others are consistent in the same direction, and no item finds the non-refugees more favourably disposed to change.

Risk Taking

It takes time to prosper, but no time to be ruined.

—A North Indian proverb.

A good deal of the literature on personal economic achievement is classified by librarians as fiction. Despite this it is perhaps this genre that displays most clearly that financial success can grow out of a combination of a number of factors. In addition to external factors there are three more personal variables that singly or in concert can contribute to success. The first of these, the one which most of mankind dreams of most frequently might best be called the opportunity factor, i.e., being in the right place at the right time, "dumb luck" leading to success, the finding of oil or uranium in one's backyard. The second variable might be entitled the Horatio Alger factor, where an individual starts modestly, but through hard work, perseverance, honesty, and frugality makes it to the top. A third variable, which can be associated with success had to do with a willingness to take risks, not in the sense of purchasing a lottery ticket or betting on the numbers (low risk–high gain situations) but with more realistic expectations and within, or closely related to, one's area of competence and experience.

Given certain external circumstances, e.g., a mix of certain economic factors, the presence or absence of governmental controls, etc., all three variables in combination can lead to fabulous pay-offs to the individual. In fact these are the success stories that in the past most enthralled western readers : the rags to riches stories of men of immense energy (if not probity) who, taking large risks, reaped huge fortunes. Because of limitations of space, but more important because of the focus of our interest, we are not concerned with individual success except insofar as it is representative of similar success by a large number of other individuals. Since we are trying to discuss economic growth as the summation of a large number of cases of perhaps less dramatic individual progress, we are less concerned with the Punjabi and Haryanvi equivalents of Henry Ford or Howard Hughes, such as the Behal Family of Ludhiana or the by now almost legendary Shri Ram, than we are with the countless number of small success stories that in concert have helped propel the Punjab-Haryana region to the forefront of Indian agriculture and small industry. In these success stories "dumb luck" plays an insignificant part relative to the two other individual characteristics : a capacity for hard work and perseverance plus a willingness to take risks. We believe that given certain initial resources these two characteristics can lead to the individual success that in the mass constitutes economic growth and change. We have already spoken about the region's fortunate position with regard to distribution of land holdings, one of the prime situational factors that can catalyze diligence at work and a favourable attitude towards risk taking into productive agricultural and industrial development.

There is no doubt that for at least the last hundred years the Punjab peasant has worked hard to increase the yield of his plot of land.[47] Over the last three generations his struggle against the elements and a harsh environment was made a little more equal through consolidation of land holdings (often at the instigation of the peasants themselves)[48] and the introduction of large scale irrigation projects and rural electrification by government.[49] Darling was able to describe the true Punjabi peasant as "simple...vigorous, shrewd, and immensely laborious".[50] More recent observers have seen this willingness to work hard as even having increased since 1947. A. S. Kahlon and his associates at Punjab Agricultural University believe the refugees from the central and western districts that became part of Pakistan have brought their own traditions of hard work with them and have been forced by circumstances to work even harder in their small, unirrigated holdings in the east.[51] As we saw earlier Kahlon *et al* believe these behaviours and the values underlying them were acquired by the non-refugee populace. These views are shared by others :

> Authority did invest a great deal on rehabilitation. But the rich dividends this investment has yielded has been due largely to the refugees' indomitable spirit, the business acumen and the determination to make good. If the West Pakistan refugee has been assimilated into the life of the capital, he has also become an integral, indeed dominant, part of Delhi's composite new society. Reborn himself, the refugee has given the ancient city a new life, and lately indeed a new swing.

Whether the ability and inclination to work hard has increased or remained constant does not concern us. The point is that no one has recently characterized the Punjabi or Haryanvi peasant as lazy.

Hard work alone can aid one in earning a livelihood but for the rapid growth necessary to feed an Indian population growing at the rate of fifteen million people per year or for the surplus production necessary to promote industrial development, new techniques, occupations, and entire ways of life must be adopted. How willing is the typical Punjabi, either refugee or non-refugee, to undertake changes that will lead him and the rest of India beyond self sufficiency to self-sustaining growth ?

In the past it has been customary to look upon peasant societies as tradition-bound, stagnant, unwilling to change. Such characteristics troubled colonial administrators but aside from desultory efforts to "stir the natives" or, as Mr. Brayne so colourfully put it:

> ...to jerk the villager out of his old groove, convince him that improvement is possible, and kill his fatalism by demonstrating that both climate, disease, and pest can be successfully fought; (to laugh him) out of his uneconomic and unhealthy customs...[53]

more energy was expended at keeping the natives passive in the political sphere than in activating them in the economic or social spheres. It was not until Independence that social and economic development became central concerns of government. With the increased need for change (because of burgeoning populations and rapid urbanization) social scientists began to search for the roots of the problem. Most succinctly this problem could be put as "why don't these people adopt these changes in ways of doing things that are clearly to their advantage." McKim Marriott pointed out that simplistic solutions were certain to fail because of the intimate relationships between various practices and the entire fabric of social life.[54] Changes in any one sphere that might indeed be beneficial *in that sphere* would lead to possibly disastrous consequences in other areas.[55] The typical villager was no longer a dunce; now he was recognized as entirely rational. Unfortunately such rationality, in the form of nay-saying, could not be expected to contribute to development.[56] What was called for were changes that would either give benefits in other areas of life or ones that might act independent of other spheres.[57] If such changes could be found, the supremely rational villagers would immediately adopt them and social, economic, and political life would be transformed. Unhappily such was not the case in most areas of India. It was soon found that liberalization of credit often led to more elaborate marriages, that improved seed varieties were being used for food, and that holders of raw material quotas for the production of agricultural implements were selling the quotas on the black market to producers of non-essential goods.[58] It seemed that the average Indian preferred to use these new inputs in tried and true ways rather than gamble on the new and unknown. In western terms there was a reluctance to take risks.

There are some indications that parts of India have by now passed this stage, although one cannot be sure that the transformations are irreversible.[59] What has come to be known as the "green revolution" is spreading rapidly in certain areas—new varieties of seed, the use of fertilizers, tubewells, and improved implements—transforming not only agriculture but social and political relationships as well.[60] Small industries are being started in many towns and "modern" consumer goods are in great demand from people who now produce more than they themselves can consume. In a word it appears that modernization has begun. The process, while certainly very dramatic, has, however, not been uniform in all areas of the country. First, the "green revolution" has so far been most successful in expanding production of wheat.[61] There is some indication that rice output can also be improved drastically[62] but work on the development of new varieties of sorghum, maize, millets, soybeans, and fodder crops has not yet reached the stage where output has been greatly affected.[63] Second, even in wheat growing areas certain farmers have been better able to avail themselves of the new crops because of their possession of tubewells and other related items. With a shortage of tubewells at the beginning of the "revolution" (1966-1967) many farmers who desired them and who, if they had had them, would have tried the improved seeds, were unable to do so. The same is true for the availability of the large amounts of fertilizer and special sowing implements needed for the new crops.[64] But even considering only those people who have equal opportunities to avail themselves of the new technology, certain people who adopt new methods and ways of life in advance of their peers can be identified.[65] Everett Rogers, one of the pioneers of diffusion research, has examined the phases of individual and group acceptance of innovations and postulated a five step process. According to Rogers, the dominant types of individuals who have adopted the innovation at each stage of the process can be characterized as innovators, early adopters, early majority, late majority, and laggards.[66] More recent work by Rogers has shown this progression of types, each superseding and incorporating the previous ones, to exist in societies other than the American.[67] Unfortunately in looking at the "green revolution", changes in occupational patterns, and new approaches to various forms of enterprise in Punjab-Haryana we, as observers at a particular instant in time, cannot examine all the steps of the process. Nevertheless some hypotheses about the diffusion process can be raised which, it is hoped, will be tested in the future.

Although in many areas of life optimum return from an innovation requires several new techniques to be adopted at once, there is much evidence that the actual adoption patterns occur differentially. Assuming that the pattern is regular (an assumption that is perhaps unwarranted but necessary for this analysis) we can see from Table 6.3 that adoption of innovations even when they are part of a "package," does not occur uniformly.

TABLE 6.3
Adoption of Innovations

Item	*Per cent Responding*
Improved varieties of seeds	54.8
Chemical fertilizers	82.2
Improved implements	85.1
New methods of sowing	60.3

The pattern can be explained in terms of two mechanisms. First, a villager may realize the utility of a particular innovation, say the use of new varieties of wheat, without realizing that the single innovation, without other new inputs, may have little effect. For example, if he plants his new wheat seeds and neglects to plant at the proper depth, fails to irrigate properly, or apply the correct amount of fertilizer he may actually find that he has suffered as a result of his innovativeness. Second, the villager, even if he realizes that there is an optimum mix or "package," often has only limited access to these inputs. This appears to be what has happened in Punjab-Haryana. New seeds showed the lowest adoption rate of the four innovations we questioned people about, yet one read in local newspapers of the period that farmers queued up for days for even a small amount of seed and that there was a thriving black market in Mexican varieties of seed. The effect of shortages of inputs is also evident from the disparities between those who see the innovation as helpful and those who adopt it. In Table 6.4 the agricultural items in Table 6.1 are compared with those of Table 6.3.

Another explanation of the gap is that some farmers realize that a "package" is required for optimum results but because one part of the package is unavailable they will not adopt the others.

TABLE 6.4
Utility and Adoption of Agricultural Innovations

Item	*Per cent Responding* *Utility*	*Adoption*
Improved seeds	82.2	54.8
Chemical fertilizers	98.6	82.2
Improved implements	97.3	85.1
New methods of sowing	93.2	60.3

Refugees and non-refugees follow a common pattern of change with the former exhibiting a slightly higher rate of innovation, especially with regard to the two innovations most readily available to the farmer, those items that exist in a more or less free market situation : improved implements and new methods of sowing. Approximately six per cent more of the favourably disposed refugees had acted on the basis of this disposition than had favourably disposed non-refugees. These figures probably represent earlier adoption. (Although they may in fact mean that the non-refugees have tried and given up the innovations, this is unlikely because of the high degree of residual adopters.) Differences between the two groups were not significant ($p=0.4$) because of two factors: the first was that meaningful overall comparisons were possible only for agriculturists, cutting deeply into the size of the sample. More important though is the fact that we are looking at a late stage of the diffusion process (when more than one-half the sample has adopted even the least available item and more than four-fifths have seen its utility). In Rogers' terms, we are looking at a late majority,[68] and it seems likely that significance would be greater immediately after the introduction of an innovation.

Most of the literature on the diffusion of innovations has yielded the conclusion that innovators can be distinguished from influentials in terms not only of when they adopt the method and the number of people they influence to follow suit, but also in terms of personal characteristics. In these studies innovators have had a broader range of contacts and were less likely to be viewed as solid citizens, while influentials turned out to be similar to the people they influenced, only "more so," and are usually seen as stable members of the community. One of the interesting questions that can be asked in a setting of rapid change, where adoption of new methods can lead to great success, is whether or not the entire diffusion process is compressed, with innovators and influentials tending to be the same people. Without more detailed analysis this question cannot be answered with regard to Punjab-Haryana but it seems likely that the innovator will be closely watched by his neighbours, at least partly because of his "foolishness," and in the event he is successful, emulated.

Why are some people more receptive to change than others? Why do they grow new crops, use fertilizer and go into new industries when others around them are content at least for the time being, to do the same old things in the same old ways until the innovators have shown them change is beneficial? David McClelland has theorized that an individual need for achievement (n=Ach), widely shared by members of a population, contributes the psychological "raw materials" for economic growth.[69] One of the characteristics that McClelland believes is associated with n-Ach is a willingness to take moderate calculated risks.[70] While McClelland's arguments—that extreme risk-taking behaviours are in fact inappropriate and often counterproductive—are persuasive when discussing situations in which economic development has already begun, it is not very difficult to conceptualize situations in which contrary strategies would yield greater individual and societal payoffs, e.g. in a relatively underdeveloped society where rapid growth has just begun or is on the horizon, either through the initiative of government, foreign investment, or through the efforts of pioneering domestic entrepreneurs and agriculturists. In such a high risk–high gain situation what may be called for is a class of speculators similar to the robber-barons of western trade, commerce, and industry. In developing their fiefdoms they not only pump new lifeblood into an economy but they provide models for the future. With such people n-Ach is probably a less significant motive than a need for power (n-Power). Hence we would expect that their engagement in risk-taking would not resemble McClelland's optimum too closely. If the western experience is any indicator, the most successful of this group are the people who realize that moderate risks yield only moderate payoffs while high risks often yield great payoffs, that the really "way-out" speculator wins most in an economy of scarcity. In the long run, of course, the behaviour of the speculator may be modified into conservatism but even if this occurs his earlier behaviour has still provided a model and shown more careful individuals that risk-taking behaviour is not to be shunned entirely. This type of speculator looks at his existence in terms of the boom atmosphere of his society. "If you take a chance and lose a fortune you can always make it back tomorrow" could be his motto. Lacking such gamblers, it could be argued, big things don't happen. What Tocqueville said about the young United States is true today for the Punjab. Hopefully it will be true for all India soon.

> It is not the ruin of a few individuals, which may be soon repaired, but the inactivity and sloth of the community at large that would be fatal to such a people. Boldness of enterprise is the foremost cause of its rapid progress, its strength, and its greatness. Commercial business is there like a vast lottery, by which a small number of men continually lose, but the state is always a gainer; such a people ought therefore to encourage and do honour to boldness in commercial speculations. But any bold speculation risks the fortune of the speculator and of all those who put their trust in him. The Americans, who make a virtue of commercial temerity, have no right in any case to brand with disgrace those who practise it. Hence arises the strange indulgence that is shown to bankrupts in the United States; their honour does not suffer by such an accident. In this respect the Americans differ, not only from the nations of Europe, but from all the commercial nations of our time; and, accordingly, they resemble none of them in their position of their wants.[71]

Without going into further detail we suggest that in transitional societies persons with high levels of n-Power go into business, commerce, and large scale agriculture because the doors to what we see as conventional careers for people high in n-Power, e.g., the military, the government, and, to a lesser extent political life, are blocked off by groups that have already staked out these vocations.

In life the refugee feels less vulnerable than the non-refugee (see Chapter IV): In risk-involved situations this means that refugees are more likely to take gambles than non-refugees. In addition to the questions on vulnerability discussed earlier another question was asked that measures directly how one feels about risk taking in the context of the adoption of an innovation. The question was: "If a new and useful way of working were made known to you, would you be willing to be the first person in this village (town, neighbourhood) to try the new ways?" The refugees overwhelmingly said they would be willing while the non-refugees were markedly more cautious. The difference between the two groups was highly significant ($p=0.004$). While none of the specific innovations that the respondents were questioned about represents very great risk today, all did at one time involve situations in which threat was inherent and it would appear that in such situations the refugees were the people who adopted first. Refugees in every case were more willing to do things in new ways: accept a son's advice, democratically decide on marriage partners, democratically decide on a son's choice of work. Although these differences were not always significant they are consistently in the predicted direction.

In Chapter III the occupational mobility of the refugees was discussed. To reiterate, even with a classificatory system that would minimize the figures, it was found that more than a fourth of the refugees of the sample (26.0%) "moonlight"; that more than half (50.7%) have done at least one other type of work in the past; that one-third of these (17.8%) have done at least two other types of work in the past. And this is still to say nothing of those refugees who went far afield—to Bengal, Bombay, and the Terai in search of opportunity and regardless of risk. In fact, occupational categories mean little in the world of the refugee. A man's occupation today may not be the one he held at the time of enumeration...in fact it may not be the job he has tonight should something that looks better to him come along between now and then. The Punjabi proverb: "Teeth, hair, nails, and men become worthless once removed from their proper place. A wise man sticks to his own station," has been forgotten.

It should be kept in mind that when we say that some attitudes and behaviours are indicative of a mental set ("invulnerability") that permits and perhaps even promotes a gambling instinct, we are saying this as outside observers. But one central element of risk is that it is a subjective phenomenon. Thus, what we see as risk-taking attitudes and behaviour may be felt by the individuals involved to be cautious and even prudent. For people like the refugees having a strong sense of invulnerability, the dangers of a course of action may be misperceived or even ignored just as the speculator says he can win back anything he loses. Thus the introduction of risk into the calculus of decision making will probably be very different for individuals who feel invulnerable and those who don't.

Synergy

The pre-partition Punjabi was not totally devoid of the gambling instinct. If accounts of earlier days are accurate, large numbers of Punjabis did take some chances. The most common varieties of risk-taking behaviour were emigration, military service, and litigation. The first two were most often motivated by economic adversity. The emigrant (either to a foreign land or to another part of India) never planned to give up his plot at home. In almost all cases he returned, either with what he had earned abroad or penniless.[72] Retired military men likewise returned when they had completed their service. Coming almost entirely from agricultural stock these people once again took up farming in the old ways. In some senses there was social and psychological risk involved in their emigration but since it was economic necessity that had forced them to serve or to drive a taxi in Calcutta the financial risk was minimal.[73] The third type of risk-associated behaviour, litigation, was much more common, not confined to the poor, and fraught with all sorts of danger.[74] The Punjabi has for many years been as litigious as most other Indians and has used the courts as instruments of his aggressive attitudes towards his neighbours. The cases in which he became involved were often long drawn-out affairs in which the outcome was either total victory or defeat. As such, great risk was involved. But, as Bernard Cohn has pointed out concerning Uttar Pradesh, litigation was used as much as a weapon which, although costly, was often as effective in ruining an opponent as it was for economic self-aggrandizement.[75] In other words, litigation was a form of economic aggression. In light of the original hypothesis that refugees were more aggressive than non-refugees we at first felt that examination of economic aggressiveness was in order but realizing that a great deal of time would be required to check out the roots and dispositions of law suits a different strategy was adopted.

Punjab-Haryana's rapid economic growth, especially in areas where refugees had settled in large numbers might, it was thought, be the result of aggressive economic policies and practices by refugees. Other observers had recorded the success of refugees in widely scattered sections of India and had noted that this success was most often at the expense of the local population.[76] They also described conflicts between refugees and locals that they believed had stemmed from economic rivalry, hinting that the aggressive business practices of the refugees were responsible for social tensions.[77] More recent newspaper items recording conflicts between refugees and non-refugees appeared to bolster their view.[78] Conflicts were certainly there, both in the political, social, and economic realms, but once fieldwork had begun and news stories checked into the earlier explanations were seen to be too pat. The refugees did engage in business successfully but not especially aggressively. Far more usual than a refugee trying to ruin a competitor was the case of the refugee taking chances, doing things in unorthodox ways (taking risks), and then being the target of aggression from envious non-refugees. The refugees responded either by fighting back or by shrugging off the intrigues and actual attacks of their rivals. Both behaviours are explainable in terms of the heightened sense of invulnerability which the refugees possess and that this newly created group, the refugees, for some still unclear reason saw nothing wrong with competition in economic life. Although in Chapter V a fear of social conflict was found to be widespread, it seems that many refugees do not see competition in economic life as necessarily leading to such conflict. The non-refugees, however, do.[79] As a result, the refugees' actions are misunderstood by many non-refugees who see these non-aggressive yet competitive actions as aggressive and aimed at them and they, naturally, respond to them aggressively. What typically occurs in this type of situation can be gathered from the following news item :

PULLING DOWN OF REFUGEE's SHOP

Gohana Situation Tensc

GOHANA, May 1—Following refugee shopkeeper Har Gobind's attempt to reconstruct his shop, the situation again became tense in the town yesterday.

(The shop had been allegedly pulled down and looted by members of another community of businessmen a few days ago.)

The police have registered a case of alleged rioting and looting against eight leading businessmen. Four of the arrested persons have been released on bail, while the remaining four have not yet been arrested.

The Gohana mandi remained closed as a mark of protest for two days.

Tension eased following the intervention by the Superintendent of Police, Rohtak, who succeeded in constituting a conciliation committee of elders. But before it could start functioning today's incident sparked off tension afresh.[80]

These speculations are supported by data. Factor analysis grouped a number of attitudinal items into a factor, the common thread of which is whether competition is beneficial (or neutral) or whether it is harmful to the individual and society. The factor was called the Synergistic Outlook Factor, and the items and their related rotated factor loadings can be found in Table 6.5.

The concept of synergy, first postulated by Ruth Benedict[81] and later expanded by Abraham Maslow[82] refers to a socially-shared world view that sees competition as legitimate. Each individual in a synergistic situation, in maximizing his personal goals, benefits society. In games theory terms this is a variable sum game; in common parlance it refers to the view that the size of the pie is not fixed and that it may be advantageous for an actor to settle for a smaller share of a larger pie than to try and maximize his share of a constant pie.[83] To a certain extent this is the basis of a free enterprise system: each person working for his own good helps expand an economy. (By the same token, in times of contraction working for one's own good can precipitate panic and recession.)

A synergistic outlook would not be expected to be the dominant one in an environment where economic scarcity has been the rule

TABLE 6.5

Synergistic Outlook Factor

		RFL
1.	Which of the following two statements do you believe is more correct : (a) If you want to get anywhere pay little attention to feelings of others. (b) A person should adapt his ideas and behaviour to the group which happens to be with him at the time.	.699
2.	In business deals one party always loses.	.566
3.	In business transactions the best policy is to never trust anybody.	.556
4.	In this world one person's gain is someone else's loss.	.458
5.	Sex crimes, such as rape and attacks on children, deserve more than mere imprisonment; such criminals ought to be publicly whipped or worse.	.451
6.	(a) Trust in people and you will go a long way. (b) Never trust in anyone but yourself.	—.448
7.	In business transactions it's up to the other fellow to be careful. Anything you can get away with against him is all right.	.443
8.	When one engages in a business transaction he cannot be too careful.	.442
9.	Anyone who trusts others is foolish. Sooner or later they will take advantage of him.	.385
10.	What do you think should be done to a son who refuses to work.	—.360
11.	How much do you feel you can trust your neighbours?	—.312

for centuries. It would be nice to be able to say that the Punjab-Haryana region is bubbling over with synergy but unfortunately this is not the case. However, some individuals, and they are disproportionately refugees, score high on the synergy factor. Specifically it is the wealthy refugees who were most synergistic. It is likely that synergy and wealth interact, with a synergistic outlook helping an individual to gain wealth. Once he has gained wealth he then can afford to be even still more good-natured towards competition. Thus one would expect that the general rise in living standards and incomes in the Punjab-Haryana area will lead to increasingly synergistic outlooks that in turn will contribute to "synergy." These values, as others, have been and are being transplanted from refugees to non-refugees and differences that now exist between the two groups will be narrowed as time goes on.

In terms of synergy this will occur because the synergistic individual, by declining to take part in zero-sum games and refusing to get involved in much of the petty conflict of economic life contributed the capital, goodwill, and stimulation that is necessary for an economy to move beyond narrow subsistence pursuits. His belief that parties to a business agreement should each leave the bargaining table satisfied means that few participants will be knocked out of the economic ring. The overall result is that more people participate in future transactions and that the values of a society do not become concentrated in the hands of a few magnates or *zamindars*. (It is interesting to note that the more synergistic refugees approach their dealings in the same way that the traditional Indian villager approached his *panchayat*, with a belief that what promotes harmony is beneficial. In the past such a viewpoint appears to have been restricted to social life, for with economic scarcity he who maximized his own payoffs was, by definition, minimizing someone else's. At the group level of Indian life even some social situations were viewed as zero-sum games with the gains of one caste in terms of status and purity being balanced by the relative decline of another.[84])

This is not to say that a synergistic outlook will be beneficial in all situations or in all developing societies. Such views can contribute to price-fixing collusion between producers or to variations on "What's good for General Motors is good for the country." A synergistic model can lead to the rationalization that whatever selfish pursuit one engages in is justified and, by extension, that ends justify means. Synergy and rapid economic growth do not make this the best of all possible worlds. Although a synergistic collective mind is certainly to be preferred to a zero-sum outlook and the economic and social aggression fundamental to it, some governmental regulation may be necessary if the needs of the disadvantaged groups are not to be forgotten in a mad quest for maximization by producers.

Conclusions

This leads us to a brief consideration of what is going on in north India today and what is likely to occur in the future. It will be recollected that invulnerability was strongest among refugees who had undergone extreme trauma in their flight. These people engage in behaviour that others see as risky but either minimize the risk or feel that even if they lose all, it doesn't matter since they have started from scratch before and succeeded. As the years pass, however, their proportion of the population will inevitably decrease (since it is unlikely that they are in actuality invulnerable). This does not necessarily mean that with their passing economic growth and social change in Punjab and Haryana will cease. Indeed there are reasons for the opposite view. First and most important, the "invulnerable" refugees have taken great risks and have to a large extent met with great success. Success has meant increased wealth. With greater wealth has come a more tolerant attitude toward competition : what has been called a synergistic outlook. (Synergy grows from wealth and also contributes to it as a sort of continuous interaction between mind and matter during conditions of economic expansion.) Then wealth is used not only for material things and investment but also for education for one's children. This education, in the next generation, can help to develop modern attitudes and the sense of efficacy that can be transmitted to future generations in place of the refugee's sense of invulnerability. As Kahlon *et al* have put it :

> In high growth areas of Punjab, the farmers are striving hard to improve their lot. In order to secure a decent level of living they are adopting such means as saving of money, investment of the savings in economic pursuits and enterprises such as agriculture and agro-industries, *risk taking, acceptance of innovation,* the ability to wait for returns on investments, selling one's labour, hiring the labour on the basis of ability rather than for considerations of caste and kin and some of the changes which are taking place in the attitudes and behaviours of the rural people (Italics mine).[85]

We believe that such changes take place first among the refugee community, especially the "invulnerable" refugees. (On all indicators of "Progressiveness" i.e. willingness to be first adopter, willingness to accept a son's advice, deciding about marriages democratically, and deciding about son's occupation democratically, the refugees scored higher than non-refugees.) When this has occurred the vulnerable refugees and the non-refugees have had to sit up and take notice. For many of these people the refugees have become a reference group with regard to innovation and, in some cases, other areas as well. They have seen the refugees achieve success through unorthodox behaviour and this has led them to discount the risks involved and to try some of the changes, the fruits of which are now seen as desirable. In Rogers' terms they have become a "late majority" who in turn will help to convert the remaining "laggards."[86] At this point we have described what many hope will be the route of development. Whether it will be so depends on chance and the skill of Indian planners and politicians. If they succeed growth and change will become the established terms in referring to Punjab and Haryana where once stagnation and apathy were considered appropriate. Already the new agricultural methods have swept the two provinces and there is every indication that people in other areas of India are gaining the self confidence necessary to repeat the process in their own provinces.

The growth of small industry appears to be a similar development although the movement has not yet measurably spread to other states. Increased agricultural prices combined with rising outputs have created surplus wealth that in turn has led to a greater demand for consumer goods that then has promoted higher factory wages. Simultaneously, mechanization of agriculture has pushed landless agricultural labourers into the expanding urban work force. While some of the social consequences of further mechanization at this time can be questioned, if continued economic growth can proceed, some of the undesirable effects can be minimized. While this is going on it is not unlikely that in urban centres at least, achievement criteria will become paramount. With increased financial independence lower status groups will be able to challenge "the establishment's" monopoly on the values of society. One result of this will be higher levels of education among lower status groups. With greater egalitarianism and independence from a *jajmani* system more and more people will be willing to assert themselves. Where once one was docile and did as one was told, he now may have the freedom necessary to follow his own inclinations to make economic decisions on (personally) rational grounds—and these decisions may involve risk-taking. This rough outline is but one possible scenario and that any number of factors could impinge upon it to change the outcome. One needn't catalogue all the troubles that could befall the country or the region—some new wheat blight, floods, a revolutionary movement among dispossessed tenants and labourers, continued rapid population growth are but a few—to realize how tenuous is man's control over the whole process of development. Nevertheless it would appear that Punjab and Haryana may have reached the "take-off" position. If they can avoid the many pitfalls that exist in their path their progress may be sufficiently encouraging to the rest of India to prompt all the peoples of the subcontinent to share their view that :

> Inferior men do not begin undertakings for fear of difficulties.
> Average men begin, but desist once difficulties appear.
> Men of superior nature never give up until they achieve their ends, however many the difficulties that appear.[87]

REFERENCES

1. Erstwhile Punjab did have some large scale industry in a number of centres. Amritsar had its textile industry long before partition. After partition the towns of Gurgaon district : Faridabad and Ballabhgarh like Ghaziabad in U.P. developed as satellites of Delhi but the overall tone of industry was set by the small and medium size units.

2. Public Relations Department, Punjab Government. *The Sword-Arm Rises*, Chandigarh : Public Relations Department, Punjab, 1963, p. 12. Both this and *Punjab on the March* are journalistic expositions of selected information from the State *Statistical Abstracts* but received much wider dissemination and present their information in more readable form than the Abstracts.

3. *Punjab on the March*, Chandigarh : Finance Department, Punjab, 1967, p. 1.

4. *Ibid.*

5. *Ibid.*

6. See Joseph Lelyveld, "Green Revolution Transforming Indian Farming but It Has a Long Way to Go," *The New York Times*, May 28, 1969 for some early statistics. For a more comprehensive account of the agricultural and economic dimensions of the "green revolution" see Carroll P. Streeter, *A Partnership to Improve Food Production in India*, New York : The Rockefeller Foundation, 1969.

7. The best example of poor planning in setting up what was hoped to be an industrial area was Nilokheri, the much publicized converted refugee camp about 85 miles north of Delhi. A few

industries continue there but the lack of adequate rail and market facilities and its proximity to a much more likely town, Karnal, prevents Nilokheri from reaching its hoped-for potential.

8. *Sword-Arm Rises*, p. 10.

9. *Ibid.*

10. *Punjab on the March*, p. 95.

11. *Sword-Arm Rises*, p. 10.

12. *Ibid.*

13. *Ibid.*

14. M. S. Randhawa, *Out of the Ashes*, Bombay : C. N. Raman, 1954, p. 204.

15. Forty years ago Malcolm Lyall Darling, in his *Rusticus Loquitur or the Old Light and the New in the Punjab Village*, London : Oxford University Press, 1930 noted that progressive landlords were becoming more common (pp 306, 332). Randhawa writing a quarter-century later agrees that landlords have always been a progressive force in Punjab. *Out of the Ashes*, p. 63.

16. S. C. Sarkar, ed., *Hindustan Yearbook and Who's Who*, Calcutta : M. C. Sarkar & Sons, Part II, pp. 13, 37.

17. The Punjab Government announced that one of its prime targets was to have a paved road within two miles of every village in the state : Ashok Thapar, "After the Harvest : Need for a New Methodology", *The Times of India*, March 8, 1968.

18. At the time of bifurcation the erstwhile state had a Punjab Roadways Fleet of 1,200 buses. In addition, the government-owned PEPSU Road Transport Company had 250 vehicles and there were numerous private bus companies. *Punjab on the March*, p. 90.

19. For a summary of the advantages of locating an industry in Punjab see Paramjit Singh, "Punjab Has Firm Base for Industrialization", in a special supplement devoted to industrial development in Punjab published January 18, 1968 as part of *The Times of India*, p. 10.

20. For a good description of the early large-scale development schemes see James Douie, *The Punjab, Northwest Frontier Province and Kashmir*, Cambridge : University Press 1916.

21. See the annual series, *Punjab on the March*, published by the Finance Department, Punjab.

22. Randhawa, in praising P. N. Thapar, mentions : "During the difficult days of 1950-51 when the Secretariat at Jullundur protected

by barbed wire was almost besieged by large crowds of discontented and angry refugee farmers he maintained his sense of humour and serenity of mind, and by his personal example inspired his staff to an almost superhuman effort and they worked over a long spell of time till late hours without enjoying a holiday." *Out of the Ashes*, p. xii.

23. *Ibid*, pp. 93-108. For a more detailed discussion of the principles guiding land redistribution see Tarlok Singh, *Land Resettlement Manual*, Simla : Punjab Government, 1952.

24. Darling, *op. cit.*, p. 353 and elsewhere, describes earlier., voluntary efforts at consolidation of holdings.

25. See Satya M. Rai, *Partition of the Punjab*, London : Asia Publishing House, 1965, pp. 166-171 and *Punjab on the March*, pp. 10-27.

26. *Ibid.*, p. 35.

27. *Ibid.*, p. 4.

28. *Ibid.*, p. 8.

29. For our analysis we have used the original place of resettlement as listed in *Out of the Ashes* (pp. 111-112) although we believe his figures under estimate the numbers of refugees (he lists only 2.46 million displaced persons in East Punjab, i.e. Punjab and Haryana). The reason for the low number is probably due to the fact that the basis for the figures are resettlement records. Hence those making no claims, e.g., some landless people, widows, orphans, and the very wealthy who already had property, would not be listed. Still, Randhawa's figures are the only ones listed by district and we use them on the assumption that the bias is uniform across districts.

30. *The Land Resettlement Manual*, pp. 16-20, reports that 6.73 million acres was left behind in the west and 4.74 assumed in the east. When converted to standard acres the land in the west was equivalent to 3.94 million standard acres and that in the east, 2.45 million standard acres.

31. Randhawa, *Out of the Ashes*, pp. 75 estimates that the original claims were inflated 25 per cent. To deter false claims the resettlement authorities instituted a system of verification by a *panchayat* of land holders from the original village. Punishments for false claims were severe (up to five years' imprisonment and/or Rs. 5,000 fine plus disqualification of the claim). By July 1948 an agreement had been worked out for East and West Punjab to

exchange land revenue records and these records helped to further reduce dishonesty.

32. *Ibid.*, p. 69.

33. Recently Gurgaon has been developing rapidly both agriculturally and industrially as Delhi-based magnates invest in the area. Most of those moving into the area are Punjabi refugees and not Gurgaonis, however.

34. *Out of the Ashes*, p. 40.

35. Some press surveys have made certain vitally relevant remarks in this connection.

36. Darling, op. cit., p. 160.

37. A. S. Kahlon *et. al.*, *Dynamics of Punjab Agriculture*, Ludhiana, Punjab: Department of Economics and Sociology, Punjab Agricultural University, 1966, p. 1

38. See Randhawa, *op. cit.*, p. 67-73 for a discussion of the temporary allotments scheme.

39. Darling, *op. cit. passim*, is extremely critical of the standard of living in the western districts of Multan, Jhang and Muzaffargarh. At one point he generalizes that all progress has been in the east while in the west the peasant is ill-fed, ill-housed, and ill-clothed. (p. 345).

40. For a discussion of the complexities facing those who advocate "pure" solutions see Raj Krishna, "Agrarian Reform in India : The Debate on Ceilings". *Economic Development and Cultural Change*, VII, 1959, pp. 302-317, and John Kenneth Galbraith, "Rival Economic Theories in India", *Foreign Affairs*, XXXVI, 1958, pp. 587-596.

41. See the recent report of Ambassador Edward Korry ("Report to Rogers Terms Aid Policy Self-Defeating", *The New York Times*, March 8, 1970), that of the task force headed by Rudolph Peterson ("Report to Nixon Urges Overhaul of Aid Programme", *The New York Times*, March 1, 1970) and some of the focuses of the task force headed by David L. Osborn ("New Aid Approach Sought for Asia", *The New York Times*, March 2, 1970).

42. Most people who have worked in the developing nations have at least one memory of someone who really hated his life thoroughly and dreamt of a world and life he would probably never see. Just as Lerner had his grocer, I, in my first visit to India, had met a Sikh who complained about everything in India—the weather, his colleagues, politicians—while idealizing everything

western. Unable to leave India he could only dream of the day he would escape and in preparation for that day he had laid aside a safety razor and fedora hat with which he was confident, he would shed his Indian identity and become part of modernity.

43. Daniel Lerner, "Toward a Communication Theory of Development," in *Communications and Political Development* ed. by Lucian Pye, Princeton : Princeton University Press 1963, p. 349.

44. Darling, *op. cit.*, p. 37.

45. *Ibid.*

46. *Ibid.*, p. 354.

47. For a discussion of social and economic change in pre-partition Punjab see "The Punjab and Social Change", Chapter IV of my unpublished Ph. D. dissertation (*Uprooting and Social Change : The Role of Refugees in Development*; Massachusetts Institute of Technology, 1970). My argument there is that the static view of life in Punjab held by most visitors from outside was not warranted but that while aggression and change were constantly going on such activities were tightly circumscribed and limited to spheres where the social life of the village would not be upset.

48. Darling, *op. cit., passim.*

49. Douie, *op. cit.*

50. Darling, *op. cit.*, p. 160.

51. Kahlon, *op. cit.*, p. 1.

52. "Delhi since Independence", *The Statesman*, August 17, 1967.

53. Quoted in Darling, *op. cit.*, p. 121.

54. McKim Marriott, "Technological Change in Overdeveloped Rural Areas", *Economic Development and Cultural Change*, 1, 1953, pp. 261-272.

55. Although Brayne had recognized that changes were called for in several areas of life and did develop what could be called the first 'package programme' he was hampered by a staff that thought development could be effected by fiat and that the villagers' opinions (which as Darling showed were quite sound) didn't matter. Thus Brayne, had he gotten some feedback, might have given up his ideas about bulls had he learned that they ate a lot and were too heavy for the cows to support in breeding. But he probably never learned the true reasons for the resistance he met.

56. On occasion the nay-saying can be quite creative. A refugee friend of mine who was not in the sample told the story of how his non-refugee neighbours had scoffed at him when he decided to install a tubewell on his farm. Their arguments went as follows : "How can you expect to get as much water out of that tiny five inch pipe as we get out of a sixteen foot (diametre) well ?" When they were shown, they countered with : "The water will be hot". Later this was changed to "the electricity takes the energy out of the water". It was not until his second year of operation that he was able to sell his surplus water. In the first year he even had difficulty selling some of his produce because people feared it had *bijli* (electricity) in it.

57. For a description of types of social change and a discussion of systemic relationships see Everett M. Rogers, *Modernization among Peasants : The Impact of Communications*, New York : Holt, Rinehart and Winston, Inc., 1969.

58. Stephen L. Keller, *Government and the Agricultural Implements Industry*, Chandigarh : Department of Industries, Punjab Government, 1962.

59. Darling, *op. cit.*, tells us of the growing pressure for land consolidation and cheaper marriages in the late 1920's yet we know that these movements were short-lived and that the public lapsed into its old ways.

60. For the agricultural consequences see Streeter, *op. cit.*; for some social effects see Lelyveld, *op. cit.*, and Francine Frankel, *Annex P : Employment and Income Distribution.* Washington : Agency for International Development, 1969.

61. Lelyveld, *op. cit.*

62. Streeter, *op. cit.*, p. 24-35.

63. *Ibid.*, pp. 36-85.

64. For optimum results the seeds must be planted shallower than ordinary seeds, must be heavily watered and treated to large dosages of chemical fertilizers. These four practices are the basic "package" that the extension services try to sell to the farmer.

65. Diffusion studies are quite numerous these days but in some ways the pioneering works remain the most satisfying. See Everett Rogers, *The Diffusion of Innovations*, New York : Free Press, 1962; Elihu Katz and Paul F. Lazarsfeld, *Personal Influence*, New York : Free Press, 1955; Herbert Menzel and Elihu Katz

"Social Relations and Innovation in the Medical Profession", *Public Opinion Quarterly*, XIX, 1955, pp. 337-352. Rogers's recent *Modernization among Peasants* shows how research in this field can have important policy implications in modernizing societies.

66. Rogers, *Diffusion of Innovations*, p. 19 and *passim.*

67. Rogers, *Modernization among Peasants*, p. 295, defines these types statistically.

68. *Ibid.*

69. David C. McClelland, *The Achieving Society*, Princeton : Van Nostrand, 1961 and "National Character and Economic Growth in Turkey and Iran" in Lucian W. Pye, *Communications and Political Development*, Princeton : Princeton University Press, pp. 52-181.

70. McClelland, *Achieving Society,* pp. 210.

71. Alexis de Tocqueville, *Democracy in America,* New York : Vintage Books, 1945, Volume 1, pp. 248-49.

72. Darling, *op. cit.*, p. 178.

73. Darling asked returned military men and the families of soldiers whether it was *bhuk* (hunger) or *shauq* (keenness for soldiering) that had drawn them to the army. The overwhelming response was hunger. Darling, *op. cit.*, pp. 28, 298.

74. Darling reports that over a three year period for which he had figures there was an average of 2,50,000 law suits per year. Of these more than half involved sums of less than Rs. 100 and 70,000 involved sums of less than Rs. 50. Darling, *op. cit.*, p. 113.

75. Bernard S. Cohn, "Some Notes on Law and Change in North India", *Economic Development and Cultural Change*, VIII October 1959, pp. 79-93.

76. See Gardner Murphy, *In the Minds of Men*, New York : Basic Books, 1953, pp. 194, 173; and R. N. Saksena, *Refugees—A Study in Changing Patterns*, Bombay: Asia Publishing House, 1961, pp. 23-27.

77. Murphy, *op. cit.*, Saksena, *op. cit.*

78. For example, "Kutch Observes Hartal," *The Times of India*, March 31, 1968; "Hindus and Sikhs Clash in Calcutta," *The New York Times*, March 30, 1967; "Pulling down of Refugee's Shop," *The Tribune* (Ambala), May 2, 1968; "Punjabi Businessman Shot to Death in Calcutta," *The Statesman*, March 4, 1968.

79. Murphy, *op. cit.*, pp. 171, 173.

80. *The Tribune* (Ambala), May 2, 1968.

81. Ruth Benedict, *Patterns of Culture*, Boston : Houghton Mifflen, 1934.

82. Abraham H. Maslow, "Synergy in the Society and the Individual, *Journal of Humanistic Psychology*, IV, 1964, pp. 45-58.

83. Rogers and others see this "perception of limited good" as a basic component of peasant societies. See his discussion in *Modernization among Peasants*, pp. 28 and *passim*.

84. For an interesting discussion of "the social anthropology of politics" see F. G. Bailey, *Stratagems and Spoils*, Toronto : Copp.-Clark, 1969.

85. Kahlon, *op. cit.* p. 7.

86. Rogers, *Modernization among Peasants*, p. 295.

87. A north Indian proverb.

CHAPTER VII

Conclusions

Misfortune is the touchstone by which
a man discovers the character of his wife, relations,
and servants; and of his own strength and skill.
—A North Indian Proverb

The Punjab-Haryana region, north of Delhi, is the fastest developing area in India. Like many modernizing societies in the past, social and economic change has not occurred without some strain and what some people have seen as a moderately high level of violence. Although in many parts of the world development and violence may be causally linked (in either direction), I have attempted in the preceding pages to show that both traits grow out of a historical event that had deep and long-lasting psychological effects. The partition of India in 1947 caused perhaps the largest population transfer of all time and created more refugees in a shorter period of time than any other political decision in history. Attending the population transfer (a term which has perhaps too many connotations of an orderly, organized inter-governmental arrangement) there was atavistic brutality on a scale that appalled even the most hardened war correspondents. More than one million died and no one knows how many were physically injured. The extent of psychic damage cannot even be guessed at.

In examining the refugee experience, either second hand or by directly interviewing survivors, the social scientist is immediately struck by how familiar it all sounds. What the refugees underwent, what they thought about and felt, and how they acted in situations of extreme stress directly parallels the accounts we have from inmates of concentration camps, the survivors of Hiroshima and Nagasaki, and those people who have lived through large scale disasters such as explosions, floods, and tornadoes. The Punjabi refugee, along with other survivors of extreme events, passes through a number of easily recognizeable stages and in the process is hurt in many of the same ways.

In the past two decades in addition to a great deal of press coverage there have been a fairly large number of clinical psychological, social psychological, and sociological studies of the survivors of these events. Despite the great amount of literature however, there have been only cursory attempts to link the events in question to ensuing economic and political developments through an examination of the psychological states generated by the events. In this study we have attempted to delineate some of the short-run and some of the more enduring consequences of trauma in an attempt to see how individual traits, taken in the mass, have consequences on the economic, political and social systems.

Specifically the problem was approached by examining how refugees saw their own experiences and then trying to integrate their views with more analytical work by psychologists who have studied survivors. Of the wide range of consequent traits found by some of these studies one, aggression, for a number of reasons, seemed to be of particular importance : First, in my own previous experience in dealing with members of this particular group of refugees I had noticed that they often acted in ways that most people would consider aggressive. Second, aggression is an extremely important concept to a political scientist, especially to one interested in the developing areas. Third, it was thought that perhaps some of the tremendous economic development that has occurred in the Punjab-Haryana region might be due to an aggressive entrepreneurial spirit among the people.

After a survey of the psychological literature on aggression showed the concept to be diffused new measures were developed. Behavioural aggression was measured by self-reports of child-beating, fighting, and arrests; attitudinal aggression by advocacy of hostile acts against Muslims, deviants, and family members. Several other traits felt to be components of aggression—a concern with power, a concern with violence, a sense of efficacy—were also examined and Thematic Apperception Tests were administered and scored. The various approaches did not create any clear cut answers. Rather it seems that behavioural aggression, at least in Punjab and Haryana, is the result of a gestalt. Both groups exhibited highly aggressive attitudes and both scored high on most of what were seen as the components of aggression. It also appears that some of the related traits that are significant elements of the political culture are more affected by economic or social factors than by whether a person is a refugee or not. The data, however, show that indeed refugees are more behaviourally aggressive than non-refugees. For that particular realm of affairs for which the data is most complete (intergenerational and interfamilial aggression) the relationship is highly significant. The crucial element of the gestalt, the one that determines in this case whether or not an individual will be behaviourally aggressive is the degree to which he feels invulnerable. Without recapitulating in detail let us say that vulnerability is somewhat analogous to the concept of inhibition. The issue then becomes why the refugees feel more invulnerable than the non-refugees.

Many observers have commented on the fearfulness of the traditional peasant. He dares not act in ways that will be to his advantage because these may be contrary to the spiritual norms of his society. Even the rare man in traditional or transitional society who is sceptical about the probability of supernatural punishment must consider what sanctions are available to his fellowman should he decide to break custom. The punishments may be ritual, symbolic, social, physical, or economic, depending on the culture and value system of the community. In India, depending on one's age and status, the individual may be aggressed against for transgressing the rules of the community. Should he be a *Harijan* he may be beaten or killed by enraged neighbours who believe *Harijans* should not use the village well. Even if he is of higher status he may be beaten by a father who dreads the crumbling of old ways, he may be ostracised or fined by a caste *panchayat*, he may be forced to partake of *panchgavya*[1] to purify himself and atone for his presumptuousness.

Why are refugees less susceptible to the threat of these sanctions than non-refugees ? One reason is their heightened sense of invulnerability. Beatings, loss of wealth, ostracism, *panchgavya* hold little dread for the person who went through the fire of partition.[2]

Even where he himself was not directly affected by the violence of that period he knows of many who were. He also knows of people who were forced to pollute themselves in order to survive and who had to undergo all the rituals of purification. Finally, he has seen that even complete economic disaster need not be a terminal state ; no matter how much a man has lost he can always stage a comeback. Having undergone some of the most extreme events conceivable, the refugee who faced violence is left with two somewhat conflicting sentiments. First, there is the fear of recurrence that has so often been noted in the literature on other types of survivors. But the second point is that one need not be fearful of one's fellow men or even of the powers of the universe. After what he has been through what can they do to him that could possibly be as bad? This sense that one need not worry too much about the consequences of one's acts means that these people act more freely and one of the realms in which they act more freely has to do with aggression.

In Punjab the official punishment for murder is very light. The death penalty, while still on the books, is rarely invoked and life imprisonment, deducting good behaviour time and commutations on visits of public figures, is equivalent to twelve years' imprisonment and there is even some talk of reducing it to ten years.[3] Other crimes against person are correspondingly leniently treated. Further vitiating the deterrent capacity of punishment in Punjab is the uncertainty of the apprehension of the actual malefactor. Thus we would expect that the main worry of Punjabis and Haryanvis would be less a fear of being punished for what they actually have done than a fear of being apprehended for something they have not done. Where a sense of vulnerability arises for the refugee who has not undergone violence or for the typical non-refugee is in his fear of the social consequences. Even if the victim of an assault survives, he and his entire family can be expected to seek vengeance. To the invulnerable person this doesn't matter : he can handle anything they try to do to him and if he can't, he can always flee and start his life over—he has already done this. To the vulnerable individual, however, such considerations are crucial and he ponders his aggressive acts much more thoroughly than the invulnerable. This accounts for the different types of crimes engaged in by refugees and non-refugees : rage assaults and killings by the former, vendettas and premeditated crimes by the latter. Invulnerability seemed to grow out of two separate characteristics : first, among refugees it was correlated with the degree of violence one had faced in 1947 ($r=.204$; $p=0.05$). Among all subjects, refugees and non-refugees alike, invulnerability (and efficacy) was also correlated with wealth and status. (Thematic Apperception Test scores of aggression also correlated with behavioural aggression indices but were extremely time consuming. Since they also correlated highly with invulnerability we believe that in this particular context examination of the constellation of attitudes about power, conflict, fantasy aggression and invulnerability is a more economical approach to the measurement of aggression.)

From the beginning I was also interested in why the Punjab-Haryana region which had been a food deficit area at the time of partition and almost entirely non-industrial had, within a mere twenty years, leaped to the forefront of the developmental revolution. Many authors had recognized the refugees as being in the vanguard of the modernization process and a few had conducted empirical studies that suggested that it was the economic aggressiveness of the refugees that accounted for their rapid recovery, at least in the areas of trade and commerce. I wanted to examine refugee and non-refugee attitudes about the appropriateness of economic aggression and to see whether any of the other measures of aggression were related to the way one engaged in economic life. If it had turned out to be true that the refugees' aggressive behaviour had sparked economic development, certain consequences would be expected to follow, e.g., with the passing of the refugees economic growth might cease, economic aggression might, under certain conditions of government control, become impossible, leading the aggressive individual to vent his hostility elsewhere. Then retaliation from other groups might result bringing the economy to a standstill, etc. The data gathered did not show any clear relationship between the aspects of social and economic aggression and indicators of individual economic development, e.g., adoption of innovations, progressive attitudes, etc. Yet the refugees were more in tune with the goals of development and modernization than the non-refugees. Closer examination of aggressive encounters between refugees and non-refugees over economic matters showed that refugees were more likely to be the victims of the aggressive encounter than they were to be the aggressor. If such was the case, how does one account for the rapid economic development that is occurring in Punjab-Haryana but that has barely begun elsewhere ? One way has been that of Kusum Nair in *Blossoms in the Dust.*

It is significant, however, that from all accounts it is the immigrant peasant who is today generally more progressive and ersupior in

> husbandry and in techniques of cultivation to the native farmer of east Punjab—even in the case of the refugee who belongs to the same stock as the latter, and is only the first generation descendant of the pioneers who had earlier migrated from these very districts to people the canal colonies in the West. It would seem, therefore, that even within a historically "uprooted" people it is the "more uprooted" element that is comparatively more receptive to new ideas, more ambitious and hard working.[4]

Mrs. Nair is not far off the mark when she sees the events of 1947 as contributing to the venturesomeness of the refugees but her concept of "more uprooted" and "less uprooted"[5] does not help to understand why some refugees are more progressive than others. Nevertheless her recognition that social and psychological factors interact to determine whether a community will modernize or not is significant. (In an aside she mentions that this accounts for the very different post-partition behaviour of the Bengali refugees.[6]) What then accounts for refugee progressiveness ? As with aggressiveness "progressiveness" is a diffused term embodying a number of possible configurations of attitudes, sentiments, and values. Three particular constellations appeared significant in the Punjab-Haryana case. First was the view that change, far from being threatening, was likely to be a beneficial thing for the individual and society. This is a far cry from the fearfulness of man in traditional society or the apathy exhibited by many traditional and transitional peoples. Second, and this is most important for industrial and commercial groups, there were a number of attitudes which we called a synergistic outlook. The tone of these was that competition was a good thing, that one could trust others in business dealings, and that conflict was not inherent in economic transactions but rather that each party to an agreement has a shared interest in a favourable outcome for both parties. This too is very different from the traditional view of life as a fixed-sum game where whenever one person gains, another loses. The third and most important difference between the refugees and non-refugees was in the way they approached situations in which risk was involved. Probably because of the sense of invulnerability discussed earlier the refugees are more willing to do new things or do old things in new ways. They are more geographically mobile, more occupationally mobile, and more likely to adopt innovations sooner than non-refugees.

Prakash Tandon, discussing his own experiences and the effects of partition gives us a more personal insight into what went on :

> Partition changed all this. For us there was no more Punjab. Many refugees settled in East Punjab, but to us and many others, it was all over when the West Punjab went, and home was now where we earned our living. Those amongst the refugees who did not find an immediate footing in the East Punjab went all over India. One could not help admiring their courage and enterprise. Simple people, who had probably never been further than fifty miles away from their homes, set off in all directions and landed up in places they had never heard of. An old Sikh, who was our company's wholesaler in Peshawar, came to my office in Bombay because he had heard that we had offered to help settle our uprooted wholesalers and staff on both sides of the border. He walked into my office, worn out and bent, and said that he was going to forget the past and settle anywhere he could. I offered him our wholesalership in Cuttack, a town four hundred miles south of Calcutta and over two thousand miles from Peshawar. He thought that was wonderful, just the place he would like to settle because he was sure that its air and water and business prospects were excellent. He thanked me profusely and said that he and his son would take the first train to Cuttack. But as he was going he turned to ask, 'Tandon Sahib, where is Cuttack, is it on the upper side of Hindustan or the lower? we haven't quite heard of it before in Peshawar.' He hoped I would forgive their ignorance, and it would make no difference to their accepting the offer. It did not matter how far it was but he thought he would just ask where it was.[7]

The recognition of these three factors : a favourable attitude toward change, a synergistic outlook, and a willingness to take risks presents a possible explanation for the aggression growing out of economic interaction that was noted by earlier observers. It is probable that the heightened sense of invulnerability and the willingness to take risks coupled with a view that change is good leads the refugee to seek the main chance. He doesn't care much about what he does as long as it will benefit him and his family. Having a synergistic outlook, he feels that his actions are perfectly legitimate, often forgetting that his non-refugee neighbours harbouring a zero-sum mentality may see his actions as pushy and aggressive. Indeed the bigger the risk that the refugee takes, the more threatening it is to the non-synergistic individual. Such unorthodox behaviour is seen as an attempt to capture the entire pie and as such it must be dealt with severely. The next step is for the non-refugee to aggress against the refugee but only through careful plots and perhaps vigilant action in which personal vulnerability need not be considered. This happens both in urban areas where refugees are successful in trade and in rural areas where refugees are successful in gaining influence on panchayats or cooperative societies. The refugees with their sense of invulnerability then respond to the challenge and the arena of conflict expands. The picture, although not pleasant, is not entirely dark for it seems that after the risk taking of the refugees has paid off, the non-refugees join them, becoming in Rogers's terms part of an early and late majority. They too reap financial rewards which then probably leads them to gain a more synergistic view of life. Thus it might be expected that conflict would be dampened out as per capita income increases.

An important question for policy makers in India to face is whether or not the tremendous energy of the refugees can be transmitted to other areas of India that are experiencing developmental troubles. Of course psychological energy is more difficult to transmit than hydro-electric energy but I feel that India can profit from her refugees and benefit the refugees at the same time. Given the refugees' enterprise and mobility the government might consider setting up colonies of refugees as examplars in other areas of India. This has already taken place without government help in the Terai area of Uttar Pradesh with outstanding results in productivity[8]. Nevertheless such colonization would have to be placed under the aegis of government to minimize political strains such as those that did develop in the Terai. In a sense such colonization, with small numbers of progressive refugees being settled in a given area, would confer many of the benefits of both the extension service and the Peace Corps without some of the shortcomings of these other approaches. Unlike workers in these two programmes a refugee would be entirely dependent on his own ability to produce. He would live full time in the area and would be there long enough to develop facility in the local vernacular. Aside from benefits in transmitting new techniques to backward groups one can easily see the benefits that would accrue to goals of national integration. The key to such a programme would have to be that the number of refugees in any area remains small. Such a policy would force the settlers to mix with the local people rather than sticking within their own colonies. Colonization of this type could disarm and debilitate any nascent Shiv Sena type organizations in the area.

In summing up, the experience of uprooting and resettlement has had tremendous consequences for the individual and for society. That, of course, is not to say that because some of the outcomes of partition have been beneficial that partition was a good thing. The cost in human misery and psychological damage can never be estimated. The creation of two impoverished nations each of whose single largest foreign expenditure is for arms to protect it from the other is tragic. The division of industries such as jute growing and processing means that each country is poorer than both together. The constant disputes over rights to water flowing between the two nations causes further friction. And over all hangs the spectre of Kashmir and the prospect of future wars that could involve the great powers and lead to a nuclear holocaust. Partition clearly was not to anyone's advantage.

Still, partition occurred, partly by chance, partly by miscalculation and partly through the unscrupulousness of certain individuals, and all, Indians and westerners alike, must live with the fact and try to salvage what we can from the tragedy that accompanied independence.

Perhaps what we know about refugees can be useful in other settings to rehabilitation officials and, specifically in India, to authorities whose responsibility includes developmental planning.

In closing, I find myself having difficulty in summing up my major finding more eloquently than did Alexis de Tocqueville a century and a half ago. Tocqueville in this passage was trying to explain the relationship between national character and individual economic and social development. By substituting the words "Punjabi refugee" for "American" in the passage the reader perhaps will come away from this dissertation more sanguine about the prospects for India's development :

> The Americans therefore change their means of gaining a livelihood very readily, and they suit their occupations to the exigen-

> cies of the moment. Men are to be met with who have successively been lawyers, farmers, merchants, ministers of the Gospel, and physicians. If the American is less perfect in each craft than the European, at least there is scarcely any trade with which he is utterly unacquainted. His capacity is more general, and the circle of his intelligence is greater.
>
> The inhabitants of the United States are never fettered by the axioms of their profession; they escape from all the prejudices of their present station; they are not more attached to one line of operation than to another; they are not more prone to employ an old method than a new one : they have no rooted habits, and they easily shake off the influence that the habits of other nations might exercise upon them, from a conviction that their nation is unlike any other and that its situation is without a precedent in the world. America is a land of wonders, in which everything is in constant motion and every change seems an improvement. The idea of novelty is there indissolubly connected with the idea of amelioration. No natural boundary seems to be set to the efforts of man; and in his eyes what is not yet done is only what he has not yet attempted to do...The whole life of an American is passed like a game of chance, a revolutionary crisis, or a battle. As the same causes are continually in operation throughout the country, they ultimately impart an irresistible impulse to the national character.[9]

Tocqueville in essence is saying the same thing as Nair[10], Tandon[11] and Kahlon[12] have said that people who take risks reap payoffs and societies having a sufficient number of such people can expect a brighter future than countries whose people do not exhibit this trait. As one of the respondents put it :

> We've been through so much; what more can happen to us ? No one can do anything to us that can be more terrible than has already occurred. Why should we be afraid ? Once everything was taken from us (in partition)—and we have come back from our pennilessness to prosperity. If we lose it all again we could do it once more.

REFERENCES

1. *Panchgavya* is a mixture of the five products of the cow (milk, curds, *ghi*, urine, and feces) taken in expiation for an offence involving pollution. Ingesting the mixture and performing a suitable Brahmin supervised ritual purifies the wrongdoer.

2. Although social scientists have to a large extent ignored the effects of violence, polemicists, especially revolutionaries have consistently recognised the power of violence to remake man and society. Frantz Fanon saw the need for colonial people to re-channel their internally directed violence in order to achieve these goals. And Mao has said that violence is useful to root out older, less acceptable patterns of behaviour.

3. *The Tribune* (Ambala), July 9, 1968.

4. Kusum Nair, *Blossoms in the Dust*, New York : Praeger, 1961, pp. 114-15.

5. Mrs. Nair sees all Punjabis (and Haryanvis) as less rooted than other regional groups because of the area's unique history. *Ibid*, p. 112.

6. *Ibid*, p. 115.

7. Prakash Tandon, *Punjabi Century*, London : Chatto and Windus, 1963, pp. 254-55.

8. The process seems to be occurring naturally at the moment. Joseph E. Schwartzberg has written : "There is currently, however, probably a considerable net emigration of Sikh Jats to other parts of India in search of a wide variety of jobs." (Joseph E. Schwartzberg, "Caste Regions of the North Indian Plains", in *Structure and Change in Indian Society*, ed. by Milton Singer and Bernard S. Cohn, Chicago : Aldine Publishing Company, 1968, p. 100.) We believe that a preponderance of these emigrants are refugees.

9. Alexis de Tocqueville, *Democracy in America*, New York : Vintage Books, 1945, Vol. I, p. 243.

10. Nair, *op. cit*., pp. 114-15.

11. Tandon, *op. cit*., pp. 254-55.

12. A. S. Kahlon *et al*., *Dynamics of Punjab Agriculture*, Ludhiana : Punjab Agricultural University, 1966.

APPENDIX I

The Population of Punjab and the Sample

The difficulty of an Indian Census springs mainly from two sources : the infinite diversity of the material to be dealt with, and our own infinite ignorance of that material.
—Sir Denzil Ibbetson

Let no man ask about caste.
Who worships Hari, he is Hari's.
—Ramanuja

Aside from the basic problems which every field researcher meets, such as selection of the members of the research team, translation of the questionnaire pre-testing, and so on, Punjab and Haryana and their refugee citizens offer a number of unusual difficulties. One of these is of sufficient magnitude and presents such additional complexities that it should be discussed in some detail.

The most glaring problem one is faced with in studies of this type in underdeveloped countries is how to sample. In India the problem is somewhat less difficult than elsewhere since the Indian census has a long and honourable tradition not matched in any other country of Asia, the Middle East or Latin America. While the Indian census is an admirable effort at classifying people according to various pre-determined categories and enumerating them within these categories in such a way as to make stratification relatively easy for most purposes, in this case the census proved inadequate, both masking the social changes which have occurred in Punjab since 1940 and, when one wants to examine refugees, actually distorting the picture. As an example of the first shortcoming, the masking of changes, just looking at the state atlas volumes of the census shows us there have been significant geographical transformations in what has been called Punjab in the period since the 1931 census. For example, if one considers the state as delimited at that time and use the census of that year as the last complete one before partition (the 1941 census due to the war was both incomplete and of less than perfect accuracy) he immediately finds himself in difficulty. First, by the time the 1951 census was taken, the state and the country had been partitioned. There were virtually no Muslims left in East Punjab.[1] The districts of Sialkot, Lahore, Gujrat, Montgomery, Lyallpur, Gujranwala, Jhang, Jhelum, Rawalpindi, Attock, Mianwali, Muzaffargarh, Multan, Dera Ghazi Khan, Shahpur, and a number of Muslim princely states, the most important of which was Bahawalpur, were no longer part of India or Punjab. The Hindus and Sikhs who had lived in those districts were now on the eastern side of the Radcliffe line, in many cases still living in the resettlement camps set up to provide immediate shelter for refugees. By the time the 1961 census was taken, further changes had taken place, including the 1956 absorption of the former princely areas of the state which had been linked since independence as the Patiala and East Punjab States' Union (PEPSU).[2] In 1966 the state was once again divided or, as the Punjabis like to say, "bifurcated," to distinguish this division from that of 1947.)[3] In this case, except for a few district level government officials who opted to work in the other state, no population transfer occurred. Despite the fact that the split was mainly an exercise in boundary drawing and had little effect on the day-to-day lives of the people, it did remove about one-half the districts of erstwhile Punjab from the jurisdiction of the new state and transferred them to the new state of Haryana.[4] At the same time both Lahaul and Spiti, and Kangra and Simla districts were turned over to Himachal Pradesh. While in most cases the division was made along district boundaries, a few exceptions were made to this rule. The most notable of these were the cases of Ambala district and the capital, Chandigarh, itself. Ambala district, according to the 1961 census, has what many suppose to be a refugee population equal to almost 12 per cent of its total population. As we shall see below this is a serious under-estimation of the figure, which would probably be closer to 35 or 40 per cent. In the bifurcation of 1966, the line splitting the state was drawn east-west. It passed through the former Ambala district and cut the district in two between Ambala City and Chandigarh. The northern part went to Punjab and the southern to Haryana. But the nerve centre of the state, the capital city Chandigarh, which had been part of Ambala district, was exempted from the division and made into a Union Territory which was to be the capital of both new states. Since Ambala City and the southern parts were now in Haryana, another district headquarters had to be set up for the area north of the dividing line which was not part of the Union Territory. The only town of any size, Rupar (1961 population : approximately 20,000), was made into a district headquarters. All these changes in the definition of the state have militated to make historical comparisons very difficult.

There is a further difficulty which is even more important than that caused by shifting state boundaries. The Indian census, as one way of enumerating people, records the place where they were born. At first glance this looks all right—there are categories for those born within the district of enumeration, in other districts of the state, in other states, in Pakistan, and in other countries. To an outsider, the natural assumption, looking at this data, is that birthplace is a significant category and that those people listing themselves as having been born in Pakistan are the refugees in whom we are interested. But one would be greatly misled by such an assumption for in some areas of north India the place of birth has, in many cases, only an indirect relationship with the respondent's native place or ancestral home. The reason for this is that in the past in Punjab a middle or upper class joint family would send its daughters-in-law back to their (the girls') native places to bear at least their first few children.[5] The children were then brought up not at their natal place but at their mothers' conjugal home. In a society in which village exogamy is practised then, all figures purporting to tell where people are from or which claim to make judgements about geographical mobility from such data would, to some degree, be inaccurate. A person unfamiliar with north Indian history and social customs might raise the objection that the error would not be very great since the smallest unit of classification is the district rather than the village and peasants in most societies are not very mobile over long distances. And it is true that in India most marriages are contracted between families living in the same or adjacent districts. Mathematically it could be said that in general in India there is an inverse correlation between the number of marriages arranged between two places and the distance between them.[6] But as we shall see, in the case of Punjab certain historical factors have complicated the picture and have, to a degree, invalidated such an assumption. The supposition that because only a small percentage of people in India marry outside their district the error would even out over all, i.e. that the 10 per cent of the population of, say, Jullundur district who report that they were born in Ferozepur district but who actually spent virtually their entire lives in Jullundur district would be evened out by their counterparts (actual Ferozepuris reporting Jullundur as place of birth), is based on an equilibrium model which, although persuasive, is not really applicable to many areas of India for one reason or to Punjab in particular for another, often overlooked, reason.

First, some castes in north India practise a sort of geographical hypergamy within their endogamous *jati.* That is to say that certain castes, the Rajputs among them, will take brides within their caste from their own areas or from areas to the east of the groom's native place but will not give brides to families from that area.[7] Thus for these people, should the bride go home to bear her children, the place of birth of the entire group if averaged out would be to the east of the place of enumeration. While such patterns have existed in Punjab they have never been very important numerically and therefore need not concern us further here. Second, and much more important in terms of the attempt to use census figures to locate refugees, is an historical factor. In the last decades of the nineteenth and the early twentieth century canal colonies were opened by the British in the west-central districts of Punjab.[8] The land irrigated by the new canals had previously been arid and unproductive. As a result the land had been sparsely settled. The few people who were natives of this area were not seen by the British as being the most progressive agriculturists.[9] To remedy this state of affairs, to siphon off surplus population from the crowded central districts of the state, and to fully utilize (and justify) the massive public works projects, the government invited colonizers from the agriculturally progressive castes to the east, mainly Jats, to settle and farm the new tracts. The Jats and other agricultural castes and the service castes upon whom they depended flocked to the colonies.[10] But the agricultural castes did not move *en masse*. In fact, individual families rarely moved *in toto* because the medium size farmer could not afford the risk of leaving his important holdings in the eastern part of the state. There is a Punjabi proverb that goes :

> The wise man keeps one foot firm, and moves the other. Without making sure of your next move, do not give up your present place.

A father would send his younger sons west to claim the land in the name of the joint family while he and his elder sons looked after the family's interests at home. These young men who had been sent out and the retired military men who received land grants free or on concessional rates formed the backbone of the population of the canal colonies. When the time came for these young men to be married they almost invariably went eastward, back to their native places in Jullundur or Amritsar district. There were several reasons for this. First, since fathers and elder brothers took care of arranging marriages it was only logical that they would look for prospective brides for their sons close to their homes. Second, and more important, few families had made the shift in the first wave and fewer families of the leading agricultural *jatis* were native to the place. As a result there were few eligible females of the proper marriageable castes in the new districts. So the younger son returned to his natal district or thereabouts to meet his bride and be married. After the marriage he returned to his plot of land in the canal colonies. When the new bride returned with her husband to her new home, the somewhat frontier-like atmosphere of the *chak* (settlement) often made her very unhappy. At every possible opportunity she went back to her natal home. The annual festivals and life cycle rituals helped to ensure that the ties between her and her family which might have been weakened by the strains of distance were maintained. For the birth of her first child (and often for subsequent ones also) she returned to her natal family. Thus the first generation to have grown up and spent its entire life in the canal colonies was unlikely to have been born there. In succeeding generations this pattern was maintained albeit in less pronounced form because of the wider choice of prospective brides from any particular *jati* available in West Punjab.

By now the direction of the argument has become clear. The category "born in Pakistan," while technically correct, seriously underestimates the number of refugees from that country now living in India. The error is even more complex than this however because it is not consistent. We have shown that among older refugees the error is likely to be greater since they had to return to the east to seek brides to a much greater extent than did succeeding generations. And there was a difference between castes as well. Rich, agricultural families did not move *in toto* while poor menial or untouchable castes, having little to lose, often did. These castes having less money for travel were likely to see their family ties to relatives in the east attenuated very rapidly.[11]

Given an awareness of these difficulties, how does one decide in which areas to work? Since the statistics of the Rehabilitation Ministries and the various relief organizations are not generally available to outside observers one is forced to use the census and yet must constantly keep in mind the problems discussed above. But the state census volumes only break figures down into district sized chunks and a district may contain a million and a half people and be spread over hundreds of square miles. *Tehsil* level figures from which the district figures have been tabulated are available from the State Census Office but even these are likely to be too gross to be of much use for most projects since *tehsils* in Punjab average about 300,000 people. Obviously, the best way out of this bind in trying to stratify a community of refugees is to accept the Census figures of the number of people born in Pakistan as proportional to the actual number of refugees in a given area. While this is not strictly true and varies with caste and age as we noted earlier, it appears to be the easiest way out of the difficulty.

The figure of 10.4 per cent born in Pakistan was recognised as an underestimate and was manipulated in such a way as to give a weighting factor which would be more closely related to reality. Estimates vary as to how many Hindu and Sikh refugees managed to reach India in 1947 and early 1948. Generally they centre around the figure of seven million. If we consider that the canal colonies contributed as much to the population boom of the second and quarter of this century as did other areas, we could assume that an uneven age distribution existed at the time of partition with the young heavily outnumbering the old.[12] As a result, a comparatively smaller number would be expected to have died of natural causes during the period between partition and the 1951 census than if there had been a perfectly uniform distribution of age. So, making extravagant allowance for three-quarters of a million refugees settling in Delhi and other states, we still find ouerselves with at least five and a quarter million refugees still alive in Punjab in 1951. Out of a total population of approximately 16 million this represents about a third of the population. Yet the figure for "born in Pakistan" is only slightly more than ten per cent. For this reason the statistics for districts and *tehsils* was multiplied by three to get a more accurate estimate of the refugee population of a *tehsil* or district.

Of course, the proportion of refugees in the population must decrease with time and eventually disappear. Thus the percentage for 1967 must be smaller than that for 1961. However, the survey was only to be of adult males—those over twenty-one years old and hence old enough to be actual refugees. Thus the 1951 percentage for the entire population would be approximately the same for the universe of this project (barring a differential mortality rate for refugees and non-refugees). In some ways this self-imposed limitation made work a lot easier. Aside from the difficulties of interviewing children or adolescents in India,[13] the cut-off age of twenty-one proved somewhat felicitous because twenty-one is also the legal voting age. Since a general election was held in February 1967 and a state election in Haryana in 1968, the voting lists were up to date and available for drawing samples. Rural areas (villages) were selected in Rupar *tehsil*, Karnal *tehsil*, and a few miles south of Chandigarh, within the Union Territory area. The towns were a small market centre in Rajpura *tehsil* and a town which had been a refugee camp but which has been encroached upon by the growing sprawl of Karnal city. The few actual city dwellers of our sample were drawn from the industrialist-capitalists and factory workers of Ludhiana, a booming centre of small industry. A number of urban dwelling yet rural oriented absentee landlords from Karnal and white collar workers from Chandigarh were also chosen. The village sites were chosen on the basis of typicality : they had to resemble an average village in terms of size, numbers of castes, distance from urban centres, distance from metalled roads, etc. but had, in addition, to possess several other important characteristics. The refugee population of the villages to be examined had to be between twenty and forty per cent to reflect something of the general refugee composition of the state and to capture some of the tone of refugee–non-refugee relationships. Also, since among the questions to be asked were some about minority groups in general and Muslims in particular, there could not be any Muslims resident in the village lest we be accused of fomenting communal hatred. Last and most important the acceptance and approval of village leaders had to be assured. The last was accomplished by countless visits to *sarpanches*, leaders of rival factions, *lambardars*, *vaids*, and other influential people.

Fortunately, through the marvellous hospitality of the Punjabi villagers I was able to select and work in a number of villages where I was extended the complete cooperation of the public. From the voting lists a sampling frame consisting of the names of all male refugees in the village was constructed. A refugee sample was drawn and then individual non-refugees were matched with the refugees of the sample with regard to what were felt to be possibly relevant variables, e.g. age, caste, income, education, religion, occupation, etc. From this it was hoped that it would be possible to see whether or not there were any differences between refugees and non-refugees.

For the industrialists and workers of Ludhiana we were fortunate enough to discover that the Economics Department of Punjab University had already drawn a small sample for a UNESCO-sponsored study. They very graciously allowed us access to their sample. The few absentee landlords and white collar workers were selected less systematically and more arbitrarily. While there is no justification for this other than expediency, the few subjects interviewed were not a typical in any way that might affect our results.

The sample appears to be typical of the population of the undivided (pre-1966) state of Punjab. Although one cannot be sure of whether the sample is as representative of the refugee population as it is of the general public we can only hope that such is the case. To give some idea of the type of people who were interviewed we will present some statistics.

The average age of the entire sample was 42.2 years. For the refugees the figure was 43.5, for the non-refugees 40.5. As emphasized earlier, this is one area in which we do not purport to estimate for the entire population of the state. To be placed on our list of prospective respondents a person had to be a male of at least twenty-one years age. Thus the sample includes men from twenty-one to ninety-four years of age. Seventy-three men are refugees, fifty-three non-refugees. Of the 73 refugees, 50 are from rural areas, 10 from towns of population less than 10,000 and 13 from cities larger than this. Of the 53 non-refugees the respective figures are 40, 8, and 5.

The sample then is predominantly rural as is the state of Punjab as enumerated in the 1961 census. That document found 79 per cent

TABLE I.1

Composition of the Sample

	Village	*Town*	*City*
Refugee	50	10	13
Non-refugee	40	8	5
Total	90	18	18
Per Cent	72%	14%	14%

of the total population living in villages and 21 per cent in towns and cities (there is no distinction made between town and city with regard to population). By 1967 the rural population had declined

TABLE I.2

Population of Pre-bifurcation Punjab (1961)

	Total	*Males*	*Females*
Total	20,306,812	10,891,576	9,415,236
Rural	16,218,217	8,637,284	7,580,933
Urban	4,088,595	2,254,292	1,834,303

to 77 per cent of the total.[14] These figures must however be treated with caution if one is interested in making judgements about styles of life and sources of wealth for in Punjab the dividing line between town and village is at times unclear. For example, the market town in which interviews were conducted has throughout time been one or the other depending on whether the cutoff level has been 5,000 or 10,000 at the time of the census. But this town, like others in Punjab unlike many towns in other areas in North India, does not exist solely through trade. Many more shopkeepers here take an active interest in agriculture and cultivate lands directly. Others in the town are full-time farmers who find the attractions of town life worth the slightly extra distance they may have to travel to their fields. This type of person, both refugee and non-refugee, arrived in town in the period after 1946 when many abandoned Muslim properties were up for grabs. They are both Hindu and Sikh. This, however, is not the only type of town; the suburban town near Karnal is an entirely different sort of unit. Originally built in 1947 to house refugees, it boasts amenities that few towns of comparable size present—wide *pakka* streets, a number of hand pumps, a few *pakka* latrines (unused), and new housing. On the other hand almost none of the inhabitants subsist on the basis of agriculture because the land in the area is poor and the settlement is hemmed in by the city on one side, the National Dairy Research Institute on another and the Western Jumna Canal on a third. Those inhabitants who received compensation for land lost in Pakistan have preferred to take land from government at a distance of 50 to 100 miles in some cases and then lease it out to someone else for cultivation. Neither does trade flourish here. Being so close to Karnal city (about three miles to the central bazaar) the shopkeepers specialize in services, necessities, and snack foods. Any resident who is making a sizeable purchase of any item will find it to his advantage to go to Karnal city. In the morning its men pedal their cycles with friends perched on the carrier and/or crossbar into the bazaar to earn a few rupees as labourers, carpenters, weavers, hawkers, or rickshaw-wallahs. A few of the more prosperous have a handloom or two at home which they either operate themselves or rent out to a friend on a daily basis. With Karnal growing rapidly in westward direction, the refugee town's days of distinctiveness are numbered. Already some Karnal-wallahs dissatisfied with the quality of urban life ("It's so noisy and dirty in the *mohallahs*") have built large bungalows on the fringes of the town. Soon the settlement will be part of the city, no longer 100 per cent refugee, another layer of accretion on "the pearl of Karnal."

The reason for emphasizing the different character of these two towns is to try to dispel the notion that all north Indian towns are alike in their emphasis on trade.[15] I suspect that Punjab may be unique in having mixed towns partly because of the ease of transport and communications. Looking at the distance to metalled roads and distances to urban centres shows that almost the entire state is no more than five miles from the former and ten miles from the latter.[16] Thus village, town, and city are more tightly intertwined in Punjab with towns and cities appearing to a much lesser extent as "oases" than in other areas of the country. This was not always the case however. While the British-built road system was extensive in Punjab, it was only under the Kairon administration (1956-1964) that virtually every village was provided with some means of contact with the outside world. Furthermore, the burgeoning of many townsites can be seen from our date to be a result of both an influx of refugees and a desire among many rural people to live better in the towns. Thus as mentioned above, the total sample of 126 finds 90 or 71.4 per cent living in villages, 18 or 14.3 per cent living in towns and 18 or 14.3 per cent living in cities. Yet the same people report overwhelmingly that they were born in villages. This is partly due to the birth place category difficulty mentioned above, but the figures are still impressive. Of 126 respondents, 111 reported having been born in a village and only 15 in towns. None reported having been born in a city. The data are reported in tabular form below. Part of the disparity between the tabulation of birth place and that of residence can be accounted for by natural growth of villages into towns when the refugees arrived on the scene twenty years ago. Douie reports that in 1916 there were only 174 towns in the undivided state. At the same time there were 44,400 villages that sheltered 90 per cent of the population. The only city in the area was Lahore with a population of 228,687.[17] (Delhi in the 1911 census was listed as having a population of 232,837 but work on the new capital had not yet been begun.) The mean age for the sample is 42; hence an "average resident" was born in 1925. The

TABLE I.3

Parents' Residence at Respondent's Birth

	Village	*Town*	*City*	*Total*
Refugee	66	7	0	73
Non-refugee	45	8	0	53
Total	111	15	0	126

census tells us that 10.3 per cent of the population lived in towns in 1921,[18] and 12.4 per cent in 1931.[19] There were few towns to speak of in East Punjab in those years. The 1921 census lists 106 and the 1931 census 118 while today there are 189.[20] But besides the advent of the refugees much of the increase can be attributed to peaceful migration in search of greater opportunities. The refugees in the sample, when asked to report all villages, towns, or cities in which they had lived more than three months, listed an average of 4.6 places. Part of this is due of course to difficulty in being resettled but even non-refugees listed an average 3.1 places of residence. Lest this be considered a too localized measure—villagers may move to outlying hamlets and consider this a different locale—we enquired also about the number of districts in which respondents had lived. The refugee mean was 3.3 districts (two would be the necessary minimum for refugees : one on each side of the border) and the non-refugee mean was 2.3, indicating that geographical mobility in Punjab and Haryana has not entirely been due to uprooting. The total population is to a certain extent residentially mobile. The poor move from village to town as their economic interests dictate and when it is harvest time they may return to their own or another village to help bring in the crop. The rich may want a luxurious *kothi* in town with electricity and other amenities which are in short supply or unavailable in the village. All this reinforces the cautionary note about the dangers of trichotomizing a population on the basis of the size of the place of residence or the type of work currently being done and while at least on the surface the sample drawn for this project closely resembles the overall profile of the state given in the census, it must be remembered that the very definitions of the classifications of the census introduce a certain element of unreality to any analysis.

Caste, one of the most important facts of Indian religious, social and political life is singularly weak in many of its manifestations in Punjab-Haryana as compared with other regions of India. There are several theories to account for this, all of which tend to emphasize the *relative* lack of importance of caste as an operational fact of life. However, while it is true that many of the elaborate precautions against pollution by a lower caste are not to be found in Punjab, it is not true to say that caste is insignificant in the life of the Punjabi-Haryanvi. Caste and its sub-unit *gotra* not only determine who a man may marry[21] but also very often whom he will vote for and in many cases his economic status and power.[22] The sample of refugees includes nineteen different castes. One of the factors in determining who would be a suitable non-refugee to match with an individual was caste. Wherever possible a non-refugee of the same caste, age, education, and occupation was found but within a single village this sometimes proved impossible. Rather than go to another village where different environmental factors would be at work, in these few cases members of castes of similar status were selected for comparison with the refugees. As a result we have twenty-four different castes for the entire group, refugees are represented by nineteen and non-refugees by fifteen.[23] The number of respondents from each caste is listed below in Table I.4

TABLE I.4

Castes (by Frequency)

	Refugee	*Non-Refugee*	*Total*
Jat Sikh	16	5	21
Arora Hindu	7	9	16
Saini Sikh	4	10	14
Ramdasia-Chamar	8	3	11
Rai Sikh	9		9
Ramgarhia-Lohar	4	3	7
Banjara		7	7
Khatri	5	1	6
Jain	1	4	5
Arora-Sikh	5		5
Balmiki Harijan		5	5
Brahmin	2	1	3
Rajput	3		3
Baniya-Vaish	1	1	2
Maid Sunakh (Sonar)	1	1	2
Nai	2		2
Jheewar	2		2
Bajigar	2		2
Kamboj	1		1
Gadria		1	1
Chhimba		1	1
Harijan Weaver		1	1
Total 22 castes : refugees in 17, non-refugees in 15			

For the past thirty years caste has not (with the exception of scheduled castes) been a unit of enumeration in the Census. As a result we must look to earlier sources for figures on the presence and significance of castes within the population, to see if indeed the sample at least reflects these social divisions. The standard work on caste in Punjab is Ibbetson.[24] But his figures are from the Census of 1881 and hence are somewhat dated. Their most serious shortcoming however is that they are percentages of the entire population of the state at the time, i.e. including Muslims. Hence to adjust them to reflect the exodus of Muslims from the state the figures must be multiplied by a factor of 2.25 as well as including the princely states. Figures for Jats and Rajputs, groups which were Muslim as well as Hindu and Sikh were not adjusted. The orders of magnitude are comparable although for a number of reasons, the most important of which is the social changes that have occurred since Ibbetson's time, perfect correspondence was not found (or even expected).

TABLE I.5

Caste as per cent of Population

	Ibbetson (I)	*I Adjusted*	*Sample*
Jat	19.5		16.6
Rajput	7.4		2.4
Brahmin	4.8[25]	10.8	2.4
Chamar	4.7	10.6	8.7
Arain	3.6	8.1	7.1
Arora	2.6	5.9	12.6
Baniya	1.9[26]	4.3	5.5
Jheewar	1.9	4.3	1.6
Khatri	1.8	4.1	4.8
Nai	1.5	3.3	1.6
Lohar	1.4	3.2	8.5

For example, Jheewars or water bearers have had their function made obsolete first by the canals and Persian wheels and now by tubewells and pumping sets. In the early days many Jheewars probably had to take up work as menials, a change which may have led to their having been outcasted by caste *panchayats*. Such a step down the ladder in the hierarchy of caste is not unusual. Most frequently it occurs during hard times when a group or individual is forced either by natural causes (famine, drought, etc.) to break caste rules, usually those pertaining to diet or with whom they may be in contact. However, with a new factor, technological obsolescence, many castes find themselves in the position where their earlier occupation is no longer in demand. Without education or skills other than their traditional ones they became, in Marxian language, part of the lumpenproletariat. Prominent castes which have had their function rendered obsolete over the past one hundred and fifty years include the once thriving Lombardis who were grain transporters before the building of the railroads and the Mirasis and Bajigars who were village entertainers before the advent of the transistor and the movies.

Education

Because education was expected to be so important in determining some of the constellations of attitudes in which we were interested the respondents were asked in some detail about their own and their father's educational attainments. Table I.6 presents the level of education *claimed* by sample members. About half way through the interviewing it became apparent, to our dismay, that the definition of literacy used by the Government of India (and the one intended in the questionnaire, i.e., the ability to read and write a letter, was not the one used by the respondents : being able to sign their names—a standard of literacy used during the British raj. It being too late to reconduct all interviews completed up to that time we plunged on. From the time of the discovery onward, however, all respondents answering "literate" were double checked. This procedure showed that roughly half of these people were not actually so and belonged to the illiterate category. If these people are typical of the entire sample a rough correction factor that would shift half of category two into category one would give a more realistic picture of the refugees' and non-refugees' actual achievements. The new figures obtained from such a correction would be 47.3 per cent and 55.7 per cent illiterate respectively. The overall Punjab and Haryana figure from Government sources is 57 per cent.[27] The original figures have been retained in their given form in the table so that a common baseline might be used in making comparisons between the respondent's view of his own educational level and that which he perceived as his father's level of attainment.

TABLE I.6
Educational Level claimed by Respondents

	Refugee	*Non-Refugee*
Illiterate	34.3%	45.3%
Literate or some primary	26.0	20.8
Primary completed or some middle	9.6	11.3
Middle completed or some high	9.6	11.3
High school completed	6.9	5.7
Some college but no degree	9.6	
Degree and above	4.1	5.7
	100.0% (N=73)	100.0% (N=53)

The refugees and non-refugees are very similar with regard to educational attainment. According to their own estimates they both have an average educational level somewhere between "some primary" and primary completion with the refugees' being slightly higher. Other indices substantiate the similarities in educational achievement. About two-thirds of the refugees (65.8%) claim to be literate in at least one language. The corresponding figure for non-refugees is 54.7%. One half of each group claims to be able to speak another language although this is almost always Punjabi for those claiming Hindi as a mother tongue and *vice-versa*.[28]

Refugees reporting about their fathers' level of education claimed that almost half (48.0%) had had some education. The mean was about the level of some primary education. For non-refugees' fathers the figures were well below this. Only a third (32.1%) had had any education and the mean was between illiterate and some

TABLE I.7

Educational Level claimed for Respondent's Father

	Refugee	*Non-Refugee*
Illiterate	52.1%	67.9%
Literate or some primary	24.7	18.9
Primary completed or some middle	4.1	7.6
Middle completed or some high	8.2	3.8
High School completed	6.9	1.9
Some college but no degree	1.4	
Degree and above	1.4	
DK	1.4	
	100.0% (N=73)	100.0% (N=53)

primary. If the figures of Table I.6 are compared with those of table I.7 it is clear that while both groups have improved on their fathers' educational standard, the non-refugees' improvement has been greater and the overall age distribution shows the improvement to be almost entirely among those educated after the refugees arrived in East Punjab. An interesting hypothesis to test would be whether the refugees are indeed acting as role models or opinion leaders for the non-refugees in this sphere as well. Can it be that they have been so successful in other ventures that a halo effect has developed whereby they teach new values, such as the importance of education as well as new methods ?

Income

It was found that after controlling for all the other variables, it was impossible to equate refugees and non-refugees on the dimension of income. That is, in a village if the sampling procedure selected a forty-three year old literate farmer of the Arora caste who had six members in his household and who earned Rs. 3,700 per year, a similar non-refugee, similar in all respects could not be found. One could select a non-refugee who met all the qualifications with the exception of income (which would be lower) or opt for income and forget about caste, occupation, age, and the like. The former course was chosen since one indication of the refugees' greater progressiveness (one of the factors we are interested in measuring) would be higher income as a result of higher achievement motivation. The mean income of refugees in the sample was found to be Rs. 3,800 and that of non-refugees Rs. 3,100. However, here again a note of caution is necessary : for a nummber of reasons figures on income are very often unreliable. First of all the notion of family or individual income is hazy and never really calculated by most rural families. Following Mr. Micawber's attitude toward finances "Annual income twenty pounds, annual expenditure nineteen six, result happiness. Annual income twenty pounds, annual expenditure twenty pounds ought and six, result misery"—the average Indian peasant and shopkeeper tries to keep expenditure below a certain point beyond which he cannot earn or borrow.[29] Even where it is made the calculation of personal income is clouded by the issue of the joint family and the way different castes define it. In seeking comparability should one divide total income by the number of adult males (of any age) as some castes do ? Complicating the issue still further is the fact that many groups will lie about their earnings—and they all do not lie in the same way. Fox has noted that shopkeepers who were members of Baniya castes consistently undervalued themselves while members of other castes overestimated their earnings and his inquiry in Uttar Pradesh shows how unreliable the calculations of town-dwelling trading classes may be.[30] I too feel that figures for town-dwellers must be viewed only as a sort of "order of magnitude" and not as a reliable or even consistent estimate. But in the rural part of the project also there were obvious discrepancies : bragging tendencies in members of some of the former "martial castes" which leads them to overevaluate their income for strangers. One method in which such problems can be dealt with with cultivating groups is to inquire of the respondent how much land his family owns—a question about which he knows the investigator can get accurate data. This however involves the investigator in having to make a sort of crude settlement report in his head—e.g., "Jagjit Singh has twelve acres of tubewell irrigated land and five of rain irrigated land. That amount of land is capable of producing, under favourable conditions, a certain number of bushels of wheat which are worth a certain amount of rupees if sold." The assumptions made in this kind of analysis: that all of a certain type of tubewell irrigated land is equal in productivity, that Jagjit Singh plants only wheat, that he sells it all at the current market price, and that he is debt free, i.e., he receives payment for his produce, are obviously risky. Despite the shortcomings, there doesn't appear to be a more reasonable way of gaining even roughly comparable figures on wealth or income of agricultural classes.

Obviously because of this differential bias, comparisons between urban and rural dwellers can only be made with extreme caution. Even if such comparisons could be made the costs of the styles of life expected of various groups in different settings would be very unequal. That is, a shopkeeper earning Rs. 3,000 per year has to, aside from stocking his shop, dress well, decorate the shop, offer credit and frequently act as one of a number of co-sponsors of religious-cultural events. His income may be equal to that of a certain farmer but the farmer has a great deal more freedom in disposing of his income.

Conclusions

This appendix has attempted to show that even where large amounts of data exist as they do in the Indian Census and various ethnographic reports, the data (or the population) may not be amenable to analysis for a variety of reasons. If the field researcher is not to be completely immobilized he must come to grips with the problem somehow. Where I thought I could assume certain characteristics I have; where the footing was less secure I have noted the difficulties and tried to work out some sort of *modus vivendi* with the demographic characteristics of the inhabitants of Punjab-Haryana. In a study with the limited scope that this one has, one must sacrifice some fastidiousness in order to get the job done in a reasonable length of time. While these sacrifices were made (though not without pangs of conscience) I still feel that the sample drawn in this study is representative of the refugees of the

TABLE I.8
Demographic Variables

	Refugee	*Non-Refugee*	*Total*
Number in household (mean)	6.6	6.6	6.6
Married	76.0%	83.0%	79.0%
Single (never married)	11.0%	6.0%	9.0%
Number of children (mean)	3.9	3.5	3.7
Household income (mean)	Rs. 3,820	Rs. 3,100	Rs. 3,580
Age (mean)	43.5	40.5	42.1

area and only to a slightly lesser degree of the entire population. The following table summarizes the findings.

REFERENCES

1. Muslims in Punjab in 1961 comprised only 1.94 per cent of the population. (R. L. Anand, *Census of India, 1961*, Vol. XIII: Punjab, Part II-C(i), p. 351.) Before partition they had made up 57 per cent of the population of the state. (Penderel Moon, *Divide and Quit*, London : Chatto & Windus, 1964, p. 29.) The table below shows the Muslim population by district for 1951 and 1961. Only two districts have more than a sprinkling of Muslims. They are Gurgaon which could almost be considered part of Delhi and Ambala which has far less but still a considerable number. The reasons for this are that the boom town of Yamunanagar is adjacent to Saharanpur district of Uttar Pradesh and also contains several important Muslim religious shrines. The large number of Muslims in Sangrur district is partly due to the integration of the former state of Malerkotla. Malerkotla's Muslims were virtually untouched by the pre-partition violence in recognition of the kindness shown to the Sikh gurus by the Muslims of the area more than two centuries earlier.

TABLE I.9
Muslim Population of Punjab by Districts (1961)

	1951	*1961*
Punjab	284,993	393,314
Simla	1,535	1,214
Ferozepur	4,257	3,369
Amritsar	4,237	2,401
Gurdaspur	9,370	5,566
Kangra	6,417	6,701
Kapurthala	854	856
Mahendragarh	1,450	1,456
Hissar	3,312	6,203
Rohtak	2,562	7,349
Gurgaon	163,663	216,767
Karnal	3,646	14,159
Ambala	24,424	40,351
Lahaul and Spiti	2	1,210
Sangrur		24,953
Hoshiarpur	1,360	7,050
Ludhiana	3,357	4,686
Bhatinda	1,677	3,340
Patiala	5,597	11,714

From A.L. Anand, *Census of India, 1961*, Vol. XIII : Punjab Part II-C(i) p. 351.

2. For a more detailed account of these changes as well as a listing of other less significant changes see Anand, *op. cit.*, Part II-A, pp. 9-14.

3. In the recent literature on Punjab (including Indian newspaper reports) there appear a number of terms to describe the state in its various forms. The most common usages are :

United Punjab......................Pre-partition Punjab
Divided Punjab....................The state between 1947 and 1965
Partitioned Punjab
Erstwhile Punjab
Bifurcated Punjab................Post-1965 Punjab
Reorganized Punjab

4. Reorganized Punjab received the districts of Ferozepur, Amritsar, Gurdaspur, Kapurthala, Hoshiarpur, Sangrur, Ludhiana, Patiala, Bhatinda, and part of Ambala. Haryana received Mahendragarh, Hissar, Rohtak, Gurgaon, Karnal and the remainder of Ambala district. Himachal Pradesh got Simla, Lahaul and Spiti, and Kangra districts.

5. A possible explanation of this seemingly anomalous method of classification is that this sort of arrangement may be uniquely Punjabi, so much so that many astute observers have failed to note the fact that girls return to their natal home to bear at least their first children. Thus we find Mrs. Karve, in her *Kinship Organization in India* (Bombay : Asia Publishing House, 1965) not mentioning it and saying (about the brides of the northern zone) : "When she goes with her husband after *gauna* (the ceremony in which the groom takes the bride to his home), she comes back but rarely on some ceremonial occasions." (p. 127) The *Karnal District Gazetteer* of 1918, an otherwise outstanding work, goes so far as saying : "When once the ceremonial goings and comings are over...she may never return to her father's house except with his special leave; and if he sends for her he has to give her a fresh dower." (Punjab Government, *Karnal District Gazetteer,* Lahore, Superintendent, Government Printing, 1918, p. 59).

6. See Karve, *op. cit.*, pp. 13 and 125 for geographical considerations in marriage.

7. *Ibid.*, p. 125. Also see Adrian Mayer, *Caste and Kinship in Central India*, Berkeley : University of California Press, 1965, p. 210 ff. for a clear account of the same phenomenon in the Malwa region of Madhya Pradesh.

8. For a good description of the development of the canal system see Sir James Douie, *The Punjab, North-West Frontier Province and Kashmir*, Cambridge : The University Press, 1916, pp. 132-141. See M. S. Randhawa, *Out of the Ashes*, Bombay : C. N. Raman, 1954, pp. 35-36 for the mechanism by which colonists were selected.

9. As Douie put it : "When the Lower Chenab Canal was started the population of the vast Bar tract which it commands consisted of a few nomad cattle owners and cattle thieves. It was a point of honour to combine the two professions." Douie, *op. cit.*, p. 139.

10. In the canal districts the population grew enormously. During the decade 1901-1911 while the overall population of the state declined due to plague and malaria epidemics the canal colonies grew. Jhang district increased its population 21 per cent, Shahpur 30 per cent, and Lyallpur 45 per cent. *Ibid*, p. 99.

11. Irawati Karve has noted the inverse relationship between caste status and the distance which one travels to find a bride. (Karve, *op. cit.*) Thus it is likely that these depressed groups travelled back to their home districts to a lesser extent than their

jajmans.

12. In the period between 1891 and 1911 the population of the state increased by less than 4 per cent (Douie, *op. cit*., p. 96) while in the period 1921-1941 it jumped almost 30 per cent. (Anand, *op. cit*., p. 27.)

13. Joseph Elder in a lecture to the Indian Civilization course on January 20, 1969 at the University of Chicago discussed his extensive work in interviewing adolescents in India and the problems he faced.

14. *Punjab on the March*, Chandigarh Finance Department, Punjab Government, 1967, p. 1.

15. See Richard G. Fox, *From Zamindar to Ballot Box*, Ithaca : Cornell University Press, 1969 for a discussion of a very different type of town. Fox, working in eastern Uttar Pradesh, believes his town, "Tezibazar," to be typical of towns throughout the entire underdeveloped world but his example is certainly at variance with the Punjabi pattern.

16. The Atlas volume of the 1961 census shows virtually the entire state having easy access to both metalled roads and urban centres. The use of the word "virtually" is to exclude the sparsely populated areas along the Rajasthan border and in the hills. (Anand, *op. cit*., Part IX, pp. 58-59, 292-93.) The road network is still expanding at the rate of about 150 miles per year. By the end of 1967 it was estimated that the new, bifurcated Punjab would have almost 2,100 miles of metalled roads. (*Punjab on the March, op. cit*., p. 82.)

17. Douie, *op. cit*., p. 97.

18. L. Middleton and S.M. Jacob, *Census of India, 1921*, Volume XV : Punjab and Delhi, Part I, p. 107.

19. Khan Ahmad Hasan Khan, *Census of India, 1931*, Volume XVII : Punjab, Part I, p. 89.

20. The 1951 census reported 1954 towns (Anand, *op. cit*., Part II-A, p. 14). The decline in number (to 189) does not seem to be the result of changes in the units defined as towns but rather to the demise of a number of ill-conceived refugee towns that managed to continue while government support was forthcoming but collapsed after it was withdrawn. The best known of these towns, Nilokheri, still limps along unable to attract any real industry, surviving mainly on the infusions of cash to support a training centre for extension officers and a school for the state's armed police. For a more flattering view of Nilokheri, its formation and

early existence see the account written by its "father" : S. K. Dey, *Nilokheri,* Bombay : Asia, 1962.

21. Although Ibbetson misunderstood much about caste (he believed occupation was the primary basis of caste, Sir Denzil Ibbetson, *Punjab Castes,* Lahore : Superintendent, Government Printing, Punjab, 1916, p. 3) he offers a valuable catalogue of any unique marriage (and other) practices a caste might have. Also see Karve, *op. cit.*, Chapter III : Kinship Organization of the Northern Zone, pp. 104-162. Another description of the significance of marriage rules in intra- and inter-caste relations can be found in J. H. Hutton, *Caste in India,* Bombay : Oxford University Press, 1963, pp. 46-64 *et passim.*

22. Yadava in his analysis of factions in Haryana notes the correlation that still exists between ritual status and income. J. S. Yadava, "Factionalism in a Haryana Village," *American Anthropologist,* LXX, No. 5, October, 1968, pp. 898-910.

23. The biggest problem in matching was among low castes. An oversupply of menial or serving castes cannot be supported by an Indian Village and often there will be only a single family of a given caste. This is especially so as the caste's traditional occupation becomes technologically obsolescent.

24. Ibbetson, *op. cit.*

25. The figure on Brahmins in the entire old Punjab is misleading, especially if one is interested in refugees from the West. Brahmins in the western part of the state were a very small group, only about 10 per cent of the total Brahmin population of the entire province.

26. Ibbetson does not mention Jains as a separate caste. Since most of them are occupied as small traders he probably classified them as Baniyas For comparability in this Table I have done likewise.

27. Anand, *op. cit,* Part II-C(i), pp. 80-129.

28. As spoken languages Hindi and Punjabi are very similar, especially in the central districts of the erstwhile Punjab where the spoken language is to all intents a patois. However, for political reasons (the state was partitioned on the basis of language and the issue of Chandigarh has still not been settled) or from ignorance, a man may answer that he speaks one language when in fact he is speaking the other. Further complicating the issue is the matter of script : that Punjabi, until very recently, had little

literature aside from the Sikh sacred texts. During the century or two preceding partition, the *scripta franca* of the province was Urdu which was used to write an entire spectrum of dialectical and linguistic variation from almost pure Hindi in the south-east to Punjabi in the central districts to more Persianised forms in the west and to Pushtu on the frontier. Thus when any respondent (even one claiming to be a Hindi speaker) reports that his father was literate he is most likely to be referring to literacy in Urdu script. In a fair number of young men this is also the case with self-reports and it is almost always the case if the respondent is over forty and knows how to write only one language. Clouding the entire discussion still further is *Landey,* a shorthand type of language which has a written but no separate spoken form. It is used by shopkeepers to hide business data from the eyes of the curious.

Although the two languages are very similar in terms of vocabulary, syntax, etc., pronunciation did vary somewhat from district to district before partition. Thus, when respondents were asked about what they considered to be the biggest difference between refugees and non-refugees, the most frequent response among both groups was "language" although in fact except for pronunciation the main difference is in the articles and post-positions used and both groups understand all the spoken variations.

29. Fox has recently described the book-keeping methods, mainly mental, carried out for small traders in a U.P. town. He found that *baniyas* there, having what he characterizes as a "sub-sistence" profit and investment ideology were unable or unwilling to calculate beyond Mr. Micawber's dictum. Fox, *op. cit.*, pp. 142-181.

30. *Ibid.*, p. 147.

APPENDIX II

Questionnaire

PUNJAB-HARYANA REFUGEE PROJECT, 1967-68
QUESTIONNAIRE

1. Name
2. Village/Town
3. Tahsil
4. District
5. State
6. Age
7. Place of birth
8. Father's place of birth
9. Father's occupation
10. Caste
11. Mother tongue
12. How much education do you have ?
13. What languages can you speak ?
14. In which of these languages are you literate ?
15. How much education does your father have ?
16. Please tell me about all the members of your household. (relationship, age, education, occupation, sex).
17. Who is the head of the household ?
18. Are you married ?
19. How many children do you have ?
20. What is your main occupation ?
21. (a) Do you have another job ?
    (b) (if yes) What is this other job ?
22. What other jobs have you had in the past ?
23. Are you currently doing anything to get a better job—perhaps looking for other work or taking some training that would help you find better work ?
24. Have you ever worked in the armed forces ?

25. (a) Have you been outside India ?
    (b) Where ? When ?
26. How often do you go to..............................? (Name nearest city of more than 100,000 population).
27. Please tell me all the places you have lived in for more than three months. (Record village or town, district, and state). Please tell them to me in the order in which you lived in each place. That is, the first place first and so on.

Ask those in Agricultural Occupations

28. Are most of the crops grown on your land sold to others or consumed by those who grow them ?
29. (a) Here are a few items that some farmers use and some don't. We would like to know if you think their use is good or bad. How about improved seeds ? Do you think it is good or bad to use them ?
    (b) And chemical fertilizers ?
    (c) What about using an improved plough or some new agricultural implements ? Do you think it is good or bad to use them ?
    (d) And how about new methods of sowing crops ?
30. (a) And now we would like to know which of these four items you use. Do you use improved seeds ?
    (b) And chemical fertilizers ?
    (c) And an improved plough or some new agricultural implement ; do you use any of them ?
    (d) Do you employ any new methods of sowing crops ?

Ask those in Non-agricultural Occupations

31. (a) Are there any new methods or techniques or machines and implements being used where you work ? (OR 'in your work').
    (b) (if yes) What are they ?
    (c) Do you think it is good or bad to use them ?
32. If a new and useful way of working were made known to you, would you be willing to be the first person in the village (town, neighbourhood) to try the new way ?
33. Suppose that a new practice were learned by a son of yours. Do you think it would be good to accept his recommendation of this new practice, even though you

are his parent ?

34 (a) When you think about this village (town), what do you think have been the two or three most important changes that have taken place in recent years—say, in the last twenty-five years ? (IF R doesn't understand, ask : Since World War II ?)

(b) On the whole, has this first change (Repeat first chance) been good or bad ?

(c) On the whole, has the second change you mentioned (Repeat second chance) been good or bad ?

35. Would you tell me whether you strongly agree, moderately agree, slightly agree, slightly disagree, moderately disagree, or strongly disagree with the following statements : (Take out multi-coloured ruler and explain it to R). Sometimes I feel like smashing things.

36. Only wicked or foolish people would oppose a great political leader.

37. At times I feel like starting a fist fight with someone.

38. Nowadays the courts don't give as severe punishment to lawbreakers as they ought to.

39. Sex crimes, such as rape and attacks on children, deserve more than mere imprisonment; such criminals ought to be publicly whipped or worse.

40. Too many people in high places are doing things that hurt the people.

41. Human nature being what it is, there will always be war and conflict.

42. I believe that most of my neighbours would not hesitate to do something against me if they thought they could get away with it.

43. Nowadays when so many people move around and mix together a person has to protect himself especially carefully against disease or infection from them.

44. Most political leaders in this country are concerned only with their own good.

45. What do you think is the most notable characteristic of Punjabis ?

46. What do you think is the most notable characteristic of refugees ?

47. Would you tell me if you strongly, moderately, or slightly agree or disagree with the following statements :
Preserving harmony in the village (neighbourhood) should be considered more important than the achievement of its programmes.
48. There are some people whom I dislike so much that I am inwardly pleased when they are in trouble for something that they have done.
49. Widespread participation in decision making often leads to undesirable conflicts.
50. An insult should always be punished.
51. Most people are secretly pleased when someone else gets into trouble.
52. Even though I am sure, I am in the right in a discussion, I usually give in because it is foolish to cause trouble.
53. There are so many evil people nowadays that it is dangerous to go out alone.
54. Disobedience to any government is never justified.
55. How do you get most of your information about politics and the affairs of the nation ? (IF R mentions only one source) Is there any other way ?
56. (a) In general, how often do you discuss politics and the affairs of the nation ?
(b) With whom do you discuss these matters ? (Get more than one answer and record order of mention).
57. How interested are you in politics and the affairs of the nation ?
58. (a) How frequently do you listen to the radio ?
(b) Where do you listen ?
59. How often have you been to the cinema in the past year ?
60. How often do you read a newspaper ? (OR have one read to you).
61. Do you own a radio ?
62. Among your friends, in your leisure time, what specific topics do you actually talk about most often ?
63. If a young boy, about ten years of age, disobeys his father, what do you think is the best way to deal with him ?
64. What do you think is the best way to deal with a ten year old boy who strikes his father and insults him ?

65. (a) Do you ever beat your children ?
    (b) About how often do you have to do this ?
    (c) For what reasons ?

66. Which two people in all the world, living or dead, do you admire most, and why ?

67. As a parent, what two lessons for living will you try hardest to teach your children ?

68. (a) Has anything unpleasant happened to you today ?
    (b) Was this any more unpleasant than what happened to you yesterday or what happens generally ?

69. (a) When you were a small boy and had done something you shouldn't have done, who in your family were you most afraid of ?
    (b) What would this person do to you if you were discovered ?

70. (a) What do you think should be done to a father who abandons his family ?
    (b) What do you think should be done to a neighbour who repeatedly disturbs the public order ?
    (c) What do you think should be done to a man who is unfaithful to his wife ?
    (d) What do you think should be done to a son who is of working age but who refuses to work at all ?
    (e) What do you think should be done to a wife who is unfaithful to her husband ?
    (f) What do you think should be done to a government official caught taking public property or cheating the common man ?
    (g) What do you think should be done to people who don't follow the principles of their religion ?

71. (a) Can you tell me something that recently made you angry at home ?
    (b) What did you do ?

72. (a) Can you tell me something that recently made you angry in this village (town, neighbourhood) ?
    (b) What did you do ?

73. (a) Have you ever been in a fight ?
    (b) When was the last time ?
    (c) How often have you come to blows with others in the past ?
    (d) With whom ?

(e) What were the reasons ?

74. (a) Were you ever arrested ?
(b) How many times ?
(c) What were the reasons ?

75. Which of the following two statements do you believe is more correct :
(1) The average citizen can have an influence on government decisions.
(2) The world is run by the few people in power, and there is not much the little man can do about it.

76. (1) As far as world affairs are concerned, most of us are the victims of forces we can neither understand nor control.
(2) By taking an active part in political and social affairs the people can control world events.

77. (1) Most people don't realize the extent to which their lives are controlled by accidental happenings.
(2) There is really no such thing as luck.

78. (1) With enough effort we can wipe out political corruption.
(2) It is difficult for people to have much control over the things politicians do in office.

79. One man says : "The most important thing for an eleven or twelve year old boy to learn is to always obey the wishes of his father." Another man says : "The most important thing a boy should learn is to think for himself." Which man do you think is more correct ?

80. (1) Many times I feel that I have very little influence over the things that happen to me.
(2) It is impossible for me to believe that chance or luck plays an important part in my life.

81. One man says : "Our country needs a strong leader who will take over the government and make everybody obey him." Another man says : "Our country needs leaders who have been chosen by the people and who will act in accordance with the people's wishes." Which of the two men do you think is more correct.

82. (1) Your own deeds will bring you salvation.
(2) What man wishes never happens; what God wishes always happens.

83. How old does a person have to be in order to vote ?

84. (a) If you had a son who was thinking of going into politics,

would you encourage him, discourage him, or say nothing ?

(b) Why do you feel that way ?

85. (a) Do you know who is our Prime Minister now ?

(b) And who is the Chief Minister of Punjab (Haryana) ?

(c) To which party does the Chief Minister belong ?

(d) Would you please tell me the name of the main opposition party in the state legislature ?

86. Which of these two statements do you think is more correct ?

(1) He who climbs falls.

(2) Your own deeds will bring you salvation.

87. (a) How often have you voted in National Elections—have you voted every time, most of the time, or rarely ?

(b) How often have you voted in Panchayat/Municipal elections—have you voted every time, most of the time, or rarely ?

(c) Did you vote in the recent election ?

(d) Whom did you vote for (which party) ?

(e) Why did you vote for this party ?

88. For what end would you be willing to make the greatest sacrifice of your personal comfort, time, and money ?

89. What two events in your past life have had the greatest effect on your present life ?

90. What two things could you conceivably accomplish in your lifetime of which you would be most proud ?

91. (a) Do the people around here usually get along well with each other or do they not get along well with each other ?

(b) What are some major conflicts around here ? Name one or two.

(c) Are there more or less conflicts now than there were before Independence ?

92. One learned man says: "When people compete with each other they work harder and do their best and there is progress." Another learned man says : "When people compete with each other they become enemies and progress becomes impossible." Which man do you think is more correct ?

93. (a) If we wait for all groups in the community to accept a programme it would not be possible to get anything done.

(b) Even if it takes twice as long to reach a decision it is still important that everyone has his say.

94. (1) Children get in trouble because their parents punish them too much.
(2) The trouble with most children nowadays is that their parents are too easy with them.

95. (1) It is not an honour to attack a weak person.
(2) Might makes right.

96. (1) One who does wrong to you should be repaid in the same coin.
(2) To forgive is better than to punish.

97. (1) Facing an officer is equal to standing behind a horse.
(2) Officers are public servants and are helpful to the common man.

98 Two men are watching some children tying a rope to a puppy and otherwise teasing it. The first man says, "The poor puppy. It must be feeling unhappy from all this teasing." The second man says, "It's just an animal. It does not matter what it feels." Which man do you think is correct ?

99. Basically the world is a threatening and dangerous place and children must be protected from it.

100. Most of our social problems would be solved if we could somehow get rid of the immoral, crooked and feeble-minded people.

101. The main threat to Indian institutions in this century has come from the infiltration of foreign ideas, doctrines, and agitators.

102. India is spending too much money on the pampering of its criminals and for the education of inherently incapable people.

103. I tend to be on my guard when things go too well for a stretch of time.

104. Minority groups, when they are given too much money and freedom, just misuse the privileges and create disturbances.

105. The present government is too weak in dealing with Pakistan.

106. The present government is too weak in dealing with China.

107. People with unpopular opinions should not be allowed to speak in public.
108. Dishonesty seems to be more prevalent in the government services than in other professions.
109. Muslims should not be employed in the government service.
110. Hindus and Sikhs should treat Muslims as Indian citizens without any discrimination.
111. They say all men are equal before the law but in practice it's not so.
112. The Muslims have too much power and influence in this country.
113. You can be elected to almost any public office if you have the money.
114. People often say that politics is a fraud. To call it a form of 'authorized crookedness' would be a pretty good description.
115. Muslims are as valuable, honest, and public spirited citizens as any other group.
116. The Muslims are a menace to any nation and to any country in which they happen to live.
117. Lawbreakers are almost always caught and punished.
118. The Muslims should give up their separate customs and become average citizens of this country.
119. It is impossible for an honest man to get ahead in the world.
120. People pretend to care more about one another than they really do.
121. The Muslims are a decent group of people on the whole.
122. Anyone who trusts others is foolish. Sooner or later they will take advantage of him.
123. (1) Most people are honest in their dealings with others.
(2) Most people will use unfair means in their dealings with others.
124. (1) No belief without proof.
(2) A good man's word is enough to convince anyone.
125. (1) Trust in people and you will go a long way.
(2) Never trust in anyone but yourself.
126. When somebody does something nice for you, do you commonly think that he has some reason of his own for

doing this ?

127. (a) How much do you feel you can trust the members of your family ?
(b) And your friends and acquaintances ?
(c) Your neighbours ?
(d) Government officials ?

128. Does it ever seem to you that everyone is working against you ?

129. Do you feel that you have often been punished without cause ?

130. There are times when I act like a coward.

131. I usually feel that life is worthwhile.

132. I feel that almost no obstacle can hinder me from achieving my final goal.

133. I would have been more successful if people had given me a fair chance.

134. I have had more than my share of things to worry about.

135. Thinking now about the economic situation of your family—the money and possessions that your family has and its standard of living—are you, yourself, generally satisfied with the economic standard or not ?

136. How often do you feel that your problems are more than you can bear ?

137. (a) Is there anything that you or your family needs but don't expect to obtain, let's say within the next five years ?
(b) What is this ?
(c) What is the principal reason you don't think you will be able to obtain it ?
(d) In your opinion, in such a situation what should a person do ?

138. (a) Has anything the government done, or failed to do, irritated you in the past year ?
(b) Has this occurred frequently, a few times, or a very few times ?
(c) Can you give me an example of the types of things that most irritated you ?
(d) What did you do ?

139. (a) What is the biggest problem people in the same circumstances of life as yourself face in life ?
(b) Is there anything you as an individual can do to solve

the problem ?
(c) What ?

140. Supposing that the central government were planning to do something you considered harmful or unjust what do you think you would do ?

141. Now, suppose it was the district or *tahsil* level officers. What would you do ?

142. If you felt unjustly treated by the police, what do you think you would do about it ?

143. (a) What do you think is the most important problem facing India today ?
(b) What do you think can be done about this problem ?

144. I don't think public officials care much what people like me think.

145. On the whole do you think that life will be better for you or worse in the next few years than it is now ?

146. Do you believe the chances are good that your children will have as good or higher position and be better off than you are now ?

147. (1) If you want to get anywhere pay little attention to the feelings of others.
(2) A person should adapt his ideas and behaviour to the group which happens to be with him at the time.

148. (1) If success is desired do not belong to any group.
(2) Success comes to those who join together in pursuit of common goals.

149. We ought to worry about our own family and let the rest of the people take care of themselves.

150. When the people make a decision, it is up to a person to help carry it out even if he had been against it.

151. In this world one person's gain is someone else's loss.

152. In business deals one party always loses out.

153. In business transactions it's up to the other fellow to be careful. Anything you can get away with against him is all right.

154. When one engages in a business transaction he cannot be too careful.

155. In business transactions the best policy is never to trust anybody.

156. When one is involved in some business deal he should

care little about the feelings of the other party.

157. In business deals it is best to try to get the upper hand early and keep it.

158. When you are cheated, do you tend to get angry, somewhat angry, or not at all angry ? Describe.

159. People should not have to pay taxes for the schools or other government services if they do not use them or benefit from them.

160. (a) Suppose that your community decided to build something for the common good of all in the area and each person had to contribute some of his labour to the project. Would you be willing to participate in such a project ?

(b) Has this ever happened ?

161. Have you ever taken part in forming a new group or a new organization to try to solve some village (town, neighbourhood) problems or meet some village (town, neighbourhood) need ?

162. (a) We are interested in the groups and organizations to which an individual belongs. Do you belong to any group or organization that deals with social, economic, work, or recreational affairs ?

(b) Do you belong to any caste association or religious organizations ?

(c) Are you a member of any other organizations ?

163. A person should not be expected to do anything for his community unless he is paid for it.

164. The trouble with the world today is that it is changing faster than it should.

165. People who want to do things in new ways forget that this may bring about even worse conditions.

166. (1) That which is already known is better than that which will come to be known.

(2) If society is to progress, newer solutions to problems are essential.

167. (1) Only through ambition and hard work can one be successful.

(2) Only through God's will can success be achieved.

168. (1) Modern problems require modern approaches.

(2) The best way of life is to walk in the paths of our fathers.

169. (1) We would be better off with less scientific development

and more simple faith.

(2) One cannot learn how to improve things by continually referring to the way problems were solved in the past.

170. Nowadays more and more people are prying into matters that are the province of the gods and goddesses and the effects will probably be disastrous.

171. (a) Today many young men are trying to make decisions that used to be made for them by their parents—say, on marriage. In general, do you think it is a good thing or a bad thing if young men decide on their own marriage ?

(b) If such a decision were to be made in your family, how would it be made ?

172. (a) What do you think about decisions about an occupation or what kind of work to do ? In general, do you think it is a good thing if young men make these decisions themselves, or is it better if their parents make these decisions ?

(b) If such decisions were to be made in your family, how would they be made ?

173. Do you ever get as worked up about some things that occur in politics or public affairs as you do about problems in your personal life.

174. (a) First, about how much effect do you think the activities of the central government have on your present day-to-day life ?

(b) Next, about how much effect do you think the activities of the state government have on your present day-to-day life ?

(c) Last, about how much effect do you think the activities of local government have on your present day-to-day life ?

175. (a) On the whole, do you think the Indian political system is working very well, fairly well, not too well, or badly ?

(b) And the Community Development Programme, do you think it is working very well, fairly well, not too well, or badly ?

(c) And what about the Five-Year Plans, are they working very well, fairly well, not too well, or badly ?

176. (a) Do you think the central government has aided or hurt your interests ?

(b) Do you think the state government has aided or hurt

your interests ?

177. Do you think the government has your best interests at heart ?

178. (a) Now I am going to read a list of groups. Would you please tell me how frequently you have a chance to talk to each of the following types of people ?
Military men.
Big businessmen.
Farmers.
Workers.
School teachers.
Union leaders
Those men who inform the country through press and/or radio.
Government officials.
Priests.
Police.
Politicians.

(b) Now I am going to re-read the list of groups. I would like you to tell me if you think what each of these groups is doing for the country is positive, negative, or neither of the two.

(c) Do you think what each of these groups is doing for you in particular is positive, negative or neither of the two ? (re-read the list).

179. Often I feel I get angry too quickly.

180. I must admit that I feel sort of scared when I move to a strange place.

181. The things my family has done have frightened me.

182. What were the reasons for India's greatness in the past ?

183. What do you think would be a good motto for India ?

184. What do you think would be a good motto for Punjab (Haryana) ?

185. Suppose you were Prime Minister of India. What are some of the things you would do ?

186. And if you were Chief Minister of the state ?

187. In what circumstances do you feel a *satyagraha* or *hartal* against the government to be justified ?

188. What two things would you like most to know about the next fifty years ?

189. (a) Are there any spirits around here ?
(b) What are their attributes ? What do they do and what is their history ?

190. (a) How much do you dream ?
(b) What do you dream about ?
(c) Please describe two recent dreams in detail.
(d) Have you ever killed in your dreams ?

191. If a man such as yourself were to receive a lot of money, what do you think would be the best thing to do with it ?

192. (a) What is the total monthly income of the household from all sources ?
(b) What is your personal monthly income from all sources ?

The following questions are to be asked only of refugees

1. Are you a refugee ?

2. (a) When you first came to India from Pakistan, where did you go ?
(b) Was that a camp made up of refugees only ?
(c) Can you describe what that place was like in those days ?
(d) How long did you stay there ?

3. (a) Please tell me everything that happened to you just before, during, and after you left West Punjab and came to India.
(b) Did any members of your family, or you yourself, encounter any physical violence at that time ?
(c) Would you please tell me ?
(d) At the time of partition, did you suffer any losses ?

4. (a) Was the government helpful and sympathetic to refugees such as yourself when you first came to the Indian side ?
(b) In what ways ?
(c) Did they remain this way ?
(d) What was your reaction to government actions then ?

5. (a) Were the local people helpful and sympathetic when you first came to the Indian side ?
(b) In what ways ?
(c) How did you feel about them at first ?
(d) After the initial period did your relations with the local people change ?
(e) Can you describe any incidents that illustrate this change ?

6. How long was it before you became self-sufficient and permanently settled ?

7. Can you tell me of any changes that took place in your

life after coming to East Punjab ?

8. How far is it from your old home (in Pakistan now) to your present home ?

9. Do you think there are any differences between refugees and non-refugees ?

10. What do you think caused the partition of India ?

11. What do you think caused you to become a refugee ?

12. (a) Are you and your family better off today than you used to be before you became a refugee ?

(b) What do you think should be done to make things better for yourself ?

13. (a) Do you think you will ever be able to return to the land of your ancestors ?

(b) (if yes) What events do you think will precede this return ?

APPENDIX III

Glossary

Text Version	*Gloss*
abat	cooperative labour.
ashrama	one of the four stages of life.
bania (or baniya)	a member of a number of trading castes. The term is often used to describe anyone involved in trade.
biradari	literally brotherhood. Frequently used in Punjab and Haryana as a synonym for *jati*.
chak	settlement.
challan	charged with some crime. The term has come into Indian-English as a passive verb as in "Three people were challaned today for illegal distillation.
daftar	office.
dharna	a form of individual sitdown strike designed to shame the opposition into capitulation.
dhingli	a beam and dipper arrangement for drawing water.
ghi	clarified butter.
goonda	hooligan, ruffian.
gotra (or got)	an exogamous clan. a subcomponent of the jati.
gurudwara	a Sikh temple.
harijan	a member of the scheduled castes.
hibakusha (Japanese)	literally explosion-affected persons. A survivor of the Hiroshima or Nagasaki atomic blasts.
hooka pani	literally smoking and water. "Stopping *hooka pani*" means ostracism or outcasting.

Text Version	*Gloss*
Id	a Muslim festival.
izzat	honour, "face."
jagir	a grant of land, usually tax free.
jajman	the patron in the patron-client relationship known as the *jajmani* system.
jajmani system	a patron-client relationship in which the jajman pays a fixed amount annually, usually in grain, to his servitors in return for which they do all the work that he requires (within certain limits).
jatha	caravan.
jathedar	leader of a *jatha.*
jati	caste.
kacca	impermanent, inferior, raw. Other uses also include the lack of ritual purity inherent in certain foods, unpaved (when used with "road"), built of mud and straw (when used with "house"), etc.
kamin	servitor. The serving half of the *jajman-kamin* dyad of the *jajmani* system.
khalsa	literally the pure. Used to donote the Sikh community.
kharif	the winter crop.
lakh	100,000
lambardar	a village official whose duties include revenue collection.
ma-baap	literally mother-father. Used to refer to a benevolent government. Extreme dependency or what Almond and Verba have called the subject political culture is referred to as *ma-baapism.*

Text Version	*Gloss*
mohalla	a small block of houses opening on a square.
nawab	a Muslim nobleman.
pakka	permanent, superior, cooked. (The opposite of *kaccha.*)
panchgavya	a mixture of the five products of the cow (milk, curds, *ghi,* urine, and feces) taken as part of a purification ritual.
patwari	the village accountant. A minor revenue official.
rabi	the summer crop.
sarpanch	chairman of the village committee.
vaid	a practitioner of ayurvedic medicine.
vanaprastha	the third *ashrama* of life in which the householder leaves his family to become a forest hermit.
yuga	one of the cosmic ages.
zamindar	In Punjab the term is used synonymously with landholder without the connotations of absenteeism and huge tracts that the term evokes in other areas of India.

APPENDIX IV

Some Notes on Methodology

I do not wish to go into problems of questionnaire wording, translation of instruments into the local vernacular, sampling, or the effects of one's assistant on his data at this point, for they have been admirably discussed at greater length than is possible here.[1] What I do wish to discuss are some of the problems one faces in using the Thematic Apperception Test cross-culturally. Some of the difficulties of using TATs cross-culturally, notably the way in which one records responses, also apply to open-ended depth interviewing techniques.

The rationale behind the TAT is that when a subject is presented with an ambiguous stimulus he will interpret it in terms of his own personality "needs." Since the stimulus is presented as a picture about which the subject is supposed to tell a story it is expected that he will be less defensive than if asked for direct confirmation of sentiments and needs.

One of the problems of the TAT that one must face in cross-cultural research is obvious : Murray's pictures, culled from magazine illustrations, abstract art and other sources, are designed for and have been validated for an American audience. If we are to work in India we must have a set of cards designed for the clientele with which we are working. The issue is far more complex than merely changing costumes and hair styles,[2] for as we know from experience and the work of some anthropologists, what is perfectly clear to us is often ambiguous to members of another culture and *vice versa.*[3] But how are we, members of an alien culture to design an ambiguous stimulus ? One way, the way that we chose, was to ask a number of Punjabis of varying degrees of westernization to look at the Murray set of pictures and list all possible themes that they could.[4] The results were tabulated. No picture proved to be unambiguous, but it was clear that westernized Punjabis were getting different cues from the pictures than their less westernized countrymen. At this point I decided that the pictures should be modified so as to present each respondent with an "Indian" stimulus

To do this I searched for an Indian artist. Not just any Indian artist, but one, so to speak, with a foot in each camp. To my mind he had to be a Punjabi who was totally familiar with village life as well as somewhat attuned to the west so that he could translate the Murray pictures into a Punjabi equivalent. After some searching I found such a man and he was instructed to modify the pictures in such a way as to capture the moods and emotions of the original. That is, he was given a list of a number of possible themes for each picture and asked to draw his pictures so that people might disagree on the dominant theme. He was asked not to modify the pictures that were considered to be non-culturally based (the blank card, the abstract cards, the man in the window frame, and the man climbing the rope). He achieved this very difficult task and the results were pre-tested on another group of Punjabis of varying backgrounds and, as we had hoped, there was disagreement over what was being portrayed. We had succeeded in producing what most social scientists abhor : ambiguity !

This accomplished, we had to face another issue. Since Murray developed the Thematic Apperception Test there has been a recognition that for many specific purposes use of the entire set is either uneconomical or inappropriate. Since certain pictures are better than others at eliciting certain types of responses, researchers have often used abbreviated sets of cards or else modified the Murray pictures, and in many cases devised entirely new pictures. That is to say, if one is interested in measuring need-Achievement one will use cards high in n-Ach "pulling power," i.e., capable of eliciting a large number of responses involving achievement imagery. The reason for the procedure, at the individual level, is because the other TAT pictures that are stronger in, say, aggressive pulling power might mask an individual's achievement motivation. In dealing with groups this consideration is less important because a group high in one trait would still show up with higher scores than another group that did not possess the trait, but the difficulty in group projects is that it is uneconomical to subject a large number of respondents to a twenty picture set, fifteen of which might be most productive for use on traits in which the researcher is not interested. The problem however in using an original set of pictures for the first time is that they have not been validated with regard to pulling power. Thus I had no idea whether the Indian analognes of cards useful for measuring aggressiveness in the

West would actually be the ones best suited for similar work in the Punjab-Haryana area. As a result I was forced to subject each respondent to the full twenty card set (in two sessions of ten cards each).

As it turned out the artist had been skilful in recapturing the mood of the original pictures. With only a few exceptions the cards elicited similar responses from our sample of Punjabis as the original set does from Americans.[5]

Some of the deviations were interesting and at least one should be mentioned briefly at this point to give the reader some idea of the difficulties involved. The most outstanding deviation had to do with the picture that portrays a semi-nude woman lying on a bed with a young man standing nearby, turned away from her with one arm flung across his face. This picture frequently evokes stories of sex or aggression in the United States : a young man has just raped or killed the woman and is suffering feelings of remorse, or a young wife has just died, usually in childbirth. Among my respondents, the people in the picture were most commonly felt to be mother and son. The son is feeling badly because his mother has refused to grant some wish of his. At first, we thought these responses were merely aberrations but as we progressed and their number mounted it became apparent that something we had not thought about sufficiently was at work. It did not take too much careful consideration to reach the conclusion that different cues were being presented to Punjabis. Why was this ? Specifically there were four points. First, breasts (the part of the woman that was bare) are not erotic symbols in India as they are in the United States. The sight of nursing mothers is common in the Punjab-Haryana region. If we were to stimulate sexual imagery we would have been better off displaying the woman's legs (which in the picture were covered by a sheet). Second, because of the large number of people around in the joint family household, a rape is almost impossible to conceive of at home. Third, even if they were husband and wife, if they were as young as they appear in the picture, it is unlikely that they would be left alone together in the house. Young couples in the rural area are often forced to have sexual intercourse outside the home, usually among the standing crops in the fields. Fourth, the scene could not be considered a death in childbirth because childbirth is polluting and men (and other family members) will stay away and leave the work to the midwife. If the woman is dead the entire family would be mourning and the body would be clothed. I think that some of the difficulties of cross-cultural research using the TAT can be gathered from this one example.

Once the project had begun the TAT stories told by the respondents were tape recorded. The reasons for this were several. Taping responses to the TAT not only allows for the uninterrupted flow of a story and the assurance that significant details are not left out in the interviewer's frantic attempt to keep up with the respondent, but also emphasizes our acceptance of Theodor Reik's principle that often *how* something is said is more important than *what* is said. By having responses on tape not only is the interviewer freed to probe (he is not constantly scribbling) but the transcriber and translater are also enabled to note unusual turns of phrase that are frequently extremely revealing. A side benefit gained by taping the interview has to do with the use of time in field research. By using a tape recorder we were done sooner than if we had directly written what we were being told, thus freeing the respondents sooner and lightening the burden on them. Equally important, the transcription and translation of the TAT and open-ended sections of the interview allowed us to spread our work out to include those days when visits to the village were likely to be fruitless, e.g., during *melas* (fairs), during the ploughing season, when authorities were due to visit the area, etc. A further advantage to be gained from the use of a tape recorder, one that did not concern me because of the reliability of my chief assistant who did all the TAT interviewing, is that having a *pakka* recording that can be referred to by the project head later ensures a conscientious approach to interviewing and translation.

It is problems like the ones discussed that present one of the biggest challenges to the political scientist. Indeed, if the discipline is to escape from some of the criticisms that have been levelled against it ("mere description," "triviality," etc.) we, as members of a scholarly tradition, must not only define things and raise interesting hypotheses but also make sure that we can operationalize our definitions and empirically test hypotheses.

REFERENCES

1. For a readable introduction to problems of questionnaire wording see Stanley L. Payne, *The Art of Asking Questions*, Princeton : Princeton University Press, 1951. Problems of translation are well covered in Eugene A. Nida, *Toward a Science of Translating*, Leiden : E. J. Brill, 1964. The issue of sampling in Punjab has been discussed in Chapter VI, and Gerald D. Berreman, using the concepts of Erving Goffman, has admirably and briefly discussed the effect a research assistant may have on the perceptions of his foreign employer in his monograph *Behind Many Masks* (Ithaca : Society for Applied Anthropology, 1962).

2. This issue is discussed by Robert C. Birney in his article "Thematic Content and Cue Characteristics of Pictures", *Motives in Fantasy, Action and Society*, ed. by John W. Atkinson, Princeton : Van Nostrand, 1958, pp. 630-43.

3. See Edward Hall *The Silent Language*, Garden City : Doubleday, 1959; and *The Hidden Dimension*, Garden City : Doubleday, 1966.

4. This is similar to the approach taken by Berne Jacobs, Jr. in his article "A Method for Investigating the Cue Characteristics of Pictures" which appears in Atkinson, ed., *op. cit.*, pp. 617-29, except that our approach was more open-ended.

5. Naturally many of the details were different. Thus while both audiences might see intergenerational conflict in a picture the Indian might see a conflict over an arranged marriage where an American might see conflict over the use of the family car.

APPENDIX V

TAT Aggression Scoring Instructions

Scoring Instructions (after Jensen[1])

1. Inert, no action, mere contemplation; neutral or non-aggressive action; no indication of aggression in any form.
2. A character in the story dominates or controls another, takes self-initiated action, seems to do things with a purpose of his own.
3. Octracism, scolding, deception.
4. Character in the story is actively working, struggling, striving, wilfully overcoming obstacles, resisting pleas of others, performing daring exploits, being actively brave, etc.
5. Arguing, being disputatious.
6. Verbal aggression, swearing at another, "telling off" another, threatening another; verbal coercion.
7. Forcing, compelling unwilling compliance.
8. Physical aggression not resulting in death and which usually is not expected to cause death : fighting, struggling with another, hitting, causing injury, physically subduing, rape, robbery, and deliberate destruction of property.
9. Physical aggression not resulting in death but which usually results in death, such as shooting another person, choking someone, knifing, inflicting any kind of injury which seems severe enough to result in death. (This score differs from 10 in that killing or death, or the intent to kill or cause death, are not explicit).
10. Physical aggression resulting in death : murder, killing. (Killing or intent to kill must be explicit).

Scores of 3, 5, and 7 do not appear in Jensen's schema but were added to smooth out the scoring into a more continuous arrangement and to allow for classification of some behaviour not included in the original scoring instructions.

REFERENCES

1. Arthur R. Jensen, "Aggression in Fantasy and Overt Behaviour," *Psychological Monographs*, LXXI, No. 445, 1957.

Select Bibliography

INDIA

Ahmad, Aziz. *Studies in Islamic Culture in the Indian Environment.* London : Oxford University Press, 1964.

Anand, R. L. Census of India, 1961, Vol. XIII : Punjab.

Bailey, F. G. *Caste and the Economic Frontier.* Manchester: University of Manchester Press, 1957.

Basham, A. L. "Some Fundamental Political Ideas of Ancient India." *Politics and Society in India.* Edited by C. H. Phillips, New York : Frederick A. Praeger, 1962.

———. *The Wonder that was India.* New York : Grove Press, 1959.

Bayley, David. *The Police and Political Development in India.* Princeton : Princeton University Press, 1969.

Bedi, Kishan Singh. *Agricultural Proverbs of the Punjab.* Chandigarh: Public Relations Department, Punjab Government, 1962.

Beidleman, Thomas O. *A Comparative Analysis of the Jajmani System.* Monograph of the Association of Asian Studies. Locust Valley, New York : J. J. Augustin, 1959.

Berreman, Gerald D. *Behind Many Masks.* Ithaca, New York : Society for Applied Anthropology, 1962.

Beteille, Andre. "The Future of the Backward Classes : The Competing Demands of Status and Power." *India and Ceylon : Unity and Diversity.* Edited by Philip Mason. London : Oxford University Press, 1967.

Bhalla, Ram Lall. *An Economic Survey of Bairampur in the Hoshiarpur District.* Lahore : Superintendent, Government Printing, 1922.

Brass, Paul. "Political Participation, Institutionalization and Stability in India." *Government and Opposition,* IV (1969), pp. 23-53.

Brown, D. Mackenzie. "Traditional Concepts of Indian Leadership." *Leadership and Political Institutions in India.* Edited by Richard L. Park and Irene Tinker. Princeton : Princeton University Press, 1959.

Brown, W. Norman. *The United States and India and Pakistan.* Cambridge: Harvard University Press, 1953.

Caird, Sir James. *India : The Land and the People.* London : Cassell, 1883.

Carstairs, G. Morris. *The Twice-Born.* Bloomington : Indiana University Press, 1961.

Chaudhuri, Nirad C. *The Continent of Circe.* Bombay : Jaico Publishing House, 1965.

———. "The Martial Races in India", *Modern Review,* XLVIII. No. 1. pp. 41-51, No. 2, pp. 295-307; XLIX, No. 1, pp. 67-79; No. 2 pp. 215-228.

Cohn, Bernard S. "The Changing Status of a Depressed Caste." *Village Indi.a* Edited by McKim Marriott. Chicago : University of Chicago Press, 1955.

———. "The Changing Traditions of a Low Caste", *Traditional India : Structure and Change.* Edited by Milton Singer. Philadelphia : American Folklore Society, 1959.

———. "The Initial British Impact on India" *Journal of Asian Studies.* Vol. XIX, 1960, pp. 418-431.

———. "Some Notes on Law and Change in North India." *Economic Development and Cultural Change* VIII (1959), pp. 79-93.

College Syllabus Division, The University of Chicago. *Classical Indian Civilization Syllabus.* College Syllabus Division, The University of Chicago, 1968.

Cotton, Henry. *New India.* London : Kegan Paul, 1907.

Darling, Malcolm Lyall. *Rusticus Loquitur or The Old Light and the New in the Punjab Village.* London : Oxford University Press, 1929.

———. *Wisdom and Waste in the Punjab Village.* London : Oxford University Press, 1934.

Datta, K. K. "Changes in the Structure of Indian Society in the XX Century". *Journal of World History.* VI (1960), pp. 403-29.

Douie, James. *The Punjab, Northwest Frontier Province and Kashmir.* Cambridge : The University Press, 1916.

Eastwick, Edward B. *A Handbook of the Panjab.* London : John Murray, 1883.

Ebright, Donald F. *Free India : The First Five Years.* Nashville, Tenn : Parthenon Press, 1954.

Elder, Joseph. *Industrialism and Hinduism.* (Mimeographed)

Fallon, S. W. *A Dictionary of Hindustani Proverbs.* Benares : E. J. Lazarus & Co., 1886.

Finance Department, Punjab Government, *Punjab on the March : 1967*. Chandigarh : Finance Department, Punjab Government, 1967.

Fox, Richard G. *From Zamindar to Ballot Box*. Ithaca : Cornell University Press, 1969.

Gandhi, Mohandas K. *An Autobiography : The Story of My Experiments with Truth*. Boston : Beacon Press, 1957.

Gangulee, N. *The Indian Peasant and his Environment*, London : Oxford University Press, 1935.

Ghurye, G. S. *Caste, Class and Occupation*. Bombay: Popular Book Depot., 1961.

Gopal, Ram. *British Rule in India*. Bombay: Asia Publishing House, 1963.

Gorrie, R. Maciagan. *Land Management in the Punjab Foothills*. Lahore: Superintendent, Government Printing, Punjab, 1946.

Gupta, Hari Ram. *Panjab on the Eve of the First Sikh War*. Hoshiarpur, Punjab: Department of History, Punjab University, 1956.

Gupta, Sulekh Chand. *Agrarian Relations and Early British Rule in India*. Asia, 1963.

Harrison, Selig S. *India : The Most Dangerous Decades*. Princeton : Princeton University Press, 1960.

Hitchcock, John T. "The Idea of the Martial Rajput." *Traditional India: Structure and Change*. Edited by Milton Singer. Philadelphia: American Folklore Society, 1959.

———. "Leadership in a North Indian Village: Two Case Studies" *Leadership and Political Institutions in India*. Edited by Richard L. Park and Irene Tinker. Princeton: Princeton University Press, 1959.

Hutton, J. H. *Caste in India*. Bombay: Oxford University Press, 1963.

Ibbetson, Sir Denzil. *Panjab Castes*. Lahore: Superintendent, Government Printing, Punjab, 1916.

Karve, Irawati. *Kinship Organization in India*. Bombay: Asia Publishing House, 1965.

———. "On the Road ; A Maharashtrian Pilgrimage." *Journal of Asian Studies*. XXII (November 1962), pp. 13-29.

Keller, Stephen L. Review of "From Zamindar to Ballot Box." By Richard G. Fox. *The Annals of the American Academy of Political and Social Science*. CCCLXXXVI (1969).

Kessinger, Thomas. "The Problem of the 'Martial Races' in the Writing of Indian History" (Mimeographed) n.d.

Khan, Khan Ahmad Hasan. *Census of India, 1931.* Volume XVII. Punjab.

Khilnani, N. N. *The Punjab Under the Lawrences.* Simla: Punjab Government Record Office, 1951.

Kipling, Rudyard. "The Enlightenment of Pagett, M. P." *In Black and White.* New York: Scribners, 1897.

———. "The Head of the District" *In Black and White,* New York: Scribners. 1897.

Kolenda, Pauline Mahar. "Toward a Model of the Hindu Jajmani System." *Human Organization.* XX (Spring 1963), pp. 11-31.

Latif, Syad Mohammed. *History of the Punjab.* New Delhi: Eurasia Publishing House, 1964.

Leigh, M. S. *The Punjab and the War.* Lahore: Punjab Government, 1922.

Lewis, Oscar. *Village Life in Northern India.* Urbana,Ill : University of Illinois Press, 1958.

Loehlin, C. H. *The Sikhs and their Scriptures.* Lucknow : Lucknow Publishing House, 1958.

Lucas, E. D. *The Economic Life of a Punjab Village.* Lahore: The Civil and Military Press.

Lynch, Owen M. "Rural Cities in India: Continuities and Discontinuities." *India and Ceylon : Unity and Diversity.* Edited by Philip Mason. London: Oxford University Press, 1967.

Majumdar, R. C.; Raychaudhuri, H. C.; and Datta, Kalikinkar. *An Advanced History of India.* London: Macmillan, 1965.

Mandelbaum, David G. "Family, Jati, Village." *Structure and Change in Indian Society.* Edited by Milton Singer and Bernard Cohn, Chicago: Aldine Publishing Company, 1968.

Marriott, McKim. "Little Communities in an Indigenous Civilization." *Village India : Studies in the Little Community.* Edited by McKim Marriott. Chicago: University of Chicago Press, 1955.

Mayer, Adrian C. "Caste and Local Politics in India." *India and Ceylon : Unity and Diversity.* Edited by Philip Mason. London: Oxford University Press, 1967.

———. *Caste and Kinship in Central India.* Berkeley: University of California Press, 1965.

Middleton, L. and Jacob, S. M. *Census of India, 1921.* Volume XV: Punjab and Delhi.

Morris-Jones, W. H. *The Government and Politics of India.* Garden City, New York: Doubleday Anchor Books, 1967.

———. "India's Political Idioms." *Politics and Society in India.* Edited by C. H. Phillips, New York: Frederick A. Praeger, 1962.

Mukherjee, Radhakamal. *The Rural Economy of India.* London : Longmans Green, 1926.

Mukherjee, Ramakrishna. *The Dynamics of a Rural Society.* Berlin: Akademie Verlag, 1957.

Nayar, Baldev Raj. *Contemporary Political Leadership in the Punjab,* unpublished Ph. D. thesis, University of Chicago.

———. *Minority Politics in the Punjab.* Princeton : Princeton University Press, 1966.

———. "Punjab." *State Politics in India.* Edited by Myron Weiner, Princeton: Princeton University Press, 1968.

Nehru, Jawaharlal. *The Discovery of India.* Garden City : Doubleday Anchor Books, 1959.

Newcombe, A. C. *Village, Town and Jungle Life in India.* Edinburgh: William Blackwood, 1905.

Nicholas, Ralph. "Structures of Politics in the Villages of Southern Asia." *Structure and Change in Indian Society.* Edited by Milton Singer and Bernard S. Cohn. Chicago: Aldine Publishing Company, 1968.

Ojha, P. N. *Some Aspects of North Indian Social Life, 1556-1707 A.D.* Patna: Nagari Prakashan, 1961.

Opler, Morris Edward. "Factors of Tradition and Change in a Local Election in Rural India." *Leadership and Political Institutions in India.* Edited by Richard L. Park and Irene Tinker, Princeton: Princeton University Press, 1959.

Orans, Martin. "Maximizing in Jajmaniland." *American Anthropologist.* LXX (1968), pp. 875-897.

Pandian, T. B. *Indian Village Folk : Their Works and Ways.* London : Elliot Stock, 1898.

Potter, David C. *Government in Rural India.* London: London School of Economics and Political Science, 1964.

Punjab Government. *Karnal District Gazetteer.* Lahore : Superintendent, Government Printing, 1918.

Prior, L. F. Loveday. *Punjab Prelude*. London: John Murray, 1952.

Public Relations Department, Punjab Government. *The Sword-Arm Rises*. Chandigarh : Public Relations Department, Punjab Government, 1963.

Rahman, Fazlur. *Islam*. New York: Holt, Rinehart and Winston, 1966.

Ramaswamy, T. N. *Essentials of Indian Statecraft : Kautilya's Arthasastra for Contemporary Readers*. Bombay, Asia Publishing House, 1962.

Ramusack, Barbara N. "Incident at Nabha"; Interaction between Indian States and British Indian Politics." *Journal of Asian Studies*. XXVIII (May 1969), pp. 563-77.

Rataul, Sardar Singh. *The Khalsa*. Amritsar: Shiromani Gurdwara Parbandhak Committee, 1964.

Research and Reference Division, Ministry of Information and Broadcasting, Government of India. *India : 1964*. Delhi : Publications Division, Ministry of Information and Broadcasting, 1964.

Retzlaff, Ralph. *Village Government in India*. New York: Asia Publishing Co., 1962.

Rosen, George. *Democracy and Economic Change in India*. Berkeley : University of California Press, 1966.

Ross, Ailine. *The Hindu Family in its Urban Setting*. Toronto: University of Toronto Press, 1961.

Rudolph, Lloyd I., and Rudolph, Susanne Hoeber. *The Modernity of Tradition*. Chicago: The University of Chicago Press, 1967.

S. C. Sarkar, ed. *Hindustan Yearbook and Who's Who: 1968*. Calcutta: M. C. Sarkar and Sons, 1968.

Schwartzberg, Joseph E. "Caste Regions of the North Indian Plains". *Structure and Change in Indian Society*. Edited by Milton Singer and Bernard S. Cohn, Chicago: Aldine Publishing Company, 1968.

Seal, Anil. *The Emergence of Indian Nationalism*. Cambridge: Cambridge University Press, 1968.

Segal, Ronald. *The Anguish of India*. New York: Stein and Day, 1965.

Sethi, Narendra K., ed. *Hindu Proverbs and Wisdom*, Mount Vernon, N. Y. : Peter Pauper Press, 1962.

Sethi, R. R. *The Lahore Durbar*. Simla: Punjab Government

Record Office, 1950.

Singer, Milton and Cohn, Bernard S., eds. *Structure and Change in Indian Society.* Chicago: Aldine Publishing Company, 1968.

Singer, Milton, ed. *Traditional India : Structure and Change.* Philadelphia : American Folklore Society, 1959.

Singh, Bhagat Lakshman. *Sikh Martyrs.* Ludhiana: Lahore Book Shop, 1923.

Singh, Indera P. "A Sikh Village." *Traditional India : Structure and Change.* Edited by Milton Singer. Philadelphia : American Folklore Society, 1959.

Singh, Kapur. *The Sikh Situation After the Death of Master Tara Singh.* Report to the convention of the Sikh Intelligentsia, Chandigarh, December 23, 1967. Chandigarh : Nirbhai Singh Dhillon, 1968.

Singh, Khushwant and Singh, Suneet Vir. *Homage to Guru Gobind Singh.* Bombay: Jaico Publishing House, 1966.

Singh, Khushwant. *A History of the Sikhs.* 2 vols. Princeton : Princeton University Press, 1963-1966.

———. *The Sikhs,* London : Allen and Unwin, 1953.

Singh, Mukhtar. *Rural India.* Allahabad : Leader Press.

Singh, Teja. *The Religion of the Sikh Gurus.* Amritsar : Shiromani Gurdwara Parbandhak Committee, 1963.

———. *The Sikh Prayer.* Amritsar : Shiromani Gurdwara Parbandhak Committee, 1963.

Smith, Wilfred Cantwell. *Modern Islam in India.* London: Victor Gollancz, 1946.

Sovani, N. V. "British Impact on India." *The New Asia.* Edited by Guy S. Metraux and Francois Crouzet. New York: New American Library, 1965.

Spear, Percival. *India : A Modern History.* Ann Arbor: University of Michigan Press, 1961.

Spellman, John W. *Political Theory of Ancient India.* London : Oxford University Press, 1964.

Srinivas, M. N. "The Cohesive Role of Sanskritization" *India and Ceylon: Unity and Diversity.* Edited by Philip Mason. London : Oxford University Press, 1967.

———. "Mobility in the Caste System." *Structure and Change in Indian Society.* Edited by Milton Singer and Bernard S. Cohn, Chicago : Aldine Publishing Company, 1968.

———. *Social Change in Modern India.* Berkeley: University of

California Press, 1966.

Tandon, Prakash. *Punjabi Century.* London : Chatto and Windus, 1961.

Thomas, P. *Indian Women through the Ages.* London : Asia, 1964.

Thompson, S. J. *The Real Indian People.* Edinburgh : Blackwood, 1914.

Tinker, Hugh. *India and Pakistan : A Political Analysis.* New York : Frederick A. Praeger, 1962.

Titus, Murray, T. *Islam in India and Pakistan.* Calcutta : Y.M.C.A. Publishing House, 1959.

Toynbee, Arnold J. *Between Oxus and Jumna.* New York : Oxford University Press, 1961.

Weiner, Myron. *Party Building in a New Nation.* Chicago : University of Chicago Press, 1967.

———. "India : Two Political Cultures." *Political Culture and Political Development.* Edited by Lucian Pye and Sidney Verba, Princeton: Princeton University Press, 1965.

———. *Political Change in South Asia.* Calcutta: Mukhopadhyay, 1963.

———. *The Politics of Scarcity.* Chicago: University of Chicago Press, 1962.

———. "Urbanization and Political Extremism: An Hypothesis Tested." *Civilizations.* XVII, No. 7 (1964), pp. 1-7.

Wilcox, Wayne. "The Economic Consequences of Partition." *Journal of International Affairs,* XVIII, 1964.

Wiser, William H., and Wiser, Charlotte V. *Behind Mud Walls.* New York: Agricultural Missions Inc., 1951.

Woodruff, Philip. *The Men Who Ruled India.* Vol. 1: *The Founders.* London: Jonathan Cape, 1963.

Yadava, J. S. "Factionalism in a Haryana Village." *American Anthropologist.* LXX (October 1968), pp. 898-910.

Young, Miriam. *Seen and Heard in a Punjab Village.* London: Student Christian Movement Press, 1931.

Zimmer, Heinrich. *Myths and Symbols in Indian Art and Civilization.* New York : Harper Torchbooks, 1962.

———. *Philosophies of India.* Princeton : Princeton University Press, 1951.

PARTITION

Ali, Chaudhri Muhammad. *The Emergence of Pakistan.* New York:

Columbia University Press, 1967.

Ambedkar, B. R. *Pakistan or the Partition of India*, Bombay : Thacker, 1946.

Anand, Balwant Singh. *Cruel Interlude*. Bombay: Asia Publishing House, 1961.

Azad, Abul Kalam. *India Wins Freedom*. Bombay: Orient Longmans, 1960.

Brecher, Michael. *Nehru : A Political Biography*. Boston : Beacon Press, 1962.

Brown, W. Norman. "Hindu-Muslim Differences." *The Partition of India*. Edited by T. Walter Wallbank. Boston: D. C. Heath and Company. 1966.

Campbell-Johnson, Alan. *Mission with Mountbatten*. Bombay: Jaico Publishing House, 1951.

Coupland, Reginald. "The Congress Ministries and the League." *The Partition of India*. Edited by T. Walter Wallbank. Boston : D. C. Heath and Company, 1966.

Garratt, G. T. "Economic Realities." *The Partition of India*. Edited by T. Walter Wallbank. Boston: D. C. Heath and Company, 1966.

Gopal, Ram. *Indian Muslims, a Political History*, London: Asia Publishing House, 1959.

Jones, Kenneth. "Communalism in the Punjab: The Arya Samaj Contribution." *Journal of Asian Studies*. XXVIII (1968), pp. 39-54.

Khan, Abdul Waheed. *India Wins Freedom : the Other Side*. Karachi : Educational Publishers, 1961.

Khosla, Gopal Das. *Stern Reckoning*. New Delhi : Bhawnani & Sons, n.d.

MacPherson, Hugh. "The Long Record of Communal Antagonism." *The Partition of India*. Edited by T. Walter Wallbank. Boston : D. C. Heath and Company, 1966.

Majumdar, R. C. "Gandhi's Role." *The Partition of India*. Edited by T. Walter Wallbank. Boston : D. C. Heath and Company, 1966.

Menon, V. P. "Summing Up : An Indian Viewpoint." *The Partition of India*. Edited by T. Walter Wallbank. Boston : D. C. Heath and Company, 1966.

Moon, Penderel. *Divide and Quit*. London : Chatto & Windus, 1961.

Morrison, Theodore. "The Muslim Revival." *The Partition of*

India. Edited by T. Walter Wallbank. Boston: D. C. Heath and Company, 1966.

Mosley, Leonard. *The Last Days of the British Raj,* London : Weidenfeld and Nicolson, 1961.

Nanda. B. R. *Mahatma Gandhi : A Biography.* Woodbury, New York: Barron's Educational Series, 1958.

Nehru, Jawaharlal. "Hindu-Muslim Relations : The Congress View." *The Partition of India.* Edited by T. Walter Wallbank. Boston: D. C. Heath and Company, 1966.

———. "A Single Indian Nation." *The Partition of India.* Edited by T. Walter Wallbank. Boston : D. C. Heath and Company, 1966.

Pandey, B. N. *The Break-up of British India.* London : Macmillan, 1969.

Parton, Margaret. "India's Great Migration." *New York-Herald Tribune,* December 13, 1947.

Prakasa, Sri. *Pakistan : Birth and Early Days.* Meerut, U.P. : Meenakshi Prakashan, 1965.

Puckle, Sir Frederick. "The Pakistan Doctrine: Its Origins and Power" *Foreign Affairs.* XXIV, (April, 1946), pp. 526-38.

Qureshi, I. H. "The Development of Pakistan." *The New Asia.* Edited by Guy S. Metraux and Francois Crouzet. New York : New American Library, 1965.

Rai, Satya M. *Partition of the Punjab.* London : Asia Publishing House, 1965.

Russell, Wilfrid. *Indian Summer.* Bombay: Thacker, 1951.

Shiromani Gurdwara Parbandhak Committee. *Muslim League Attacks on Sikhs and Hindus in the Punjab.* Amritsar: Shiromani Gurdwara Parbandhak Committee, 1950.

Singh, Khushwant. *Train to Pakistan.* New York: Grove Press, 1956.

Singh, Tarlok. *Land Resettlement Manual (for Displaced Persons in Punjab and Pepsu).* Simla: Government of Punjab, 1952.

———. "Rural Resettlement in Punjab" Delhi, 1950. (Mimeographed).

Smith, Robert A. *Divided India.* New York : McGraw-Hill, 1947.

Spear, Percival. "The Muslim Way of Life." *The Partition of India.* Edited by T. Walter Wallbank, Boston : D. C. Heath and Company, 1966.

———. "The Position of the Muslims Before and After Partition"

India and Ceylon: Unity and Diversity. Edited by Philip Mason. London : Oxford University Press, 1967.

Sunderland, Jabez T. "Hindu-Muslim Antagonism : A British Creation." *The Partition of India*. Edited by T. Walter Wallbank. Boston: D. C. Heath and Company, 1966.

Vakil, C. N. *Economic Consequences of Divided India*. Bombay : Vora, 1950.

———. *Economic Consequences of the Partition,* Bombay: National Information and Publications, 1948.

Wallbank, T. Walter, ed. *The Partition of India*. Boston : D. C. Heath and Company, 1966.

Refugees and Disaster

Antar, Elias. "A Day in the Life of Ibrahim Badran." *Aramco World*. XX, No. 3 (May-June 1969), pp. 34-41.

Bakis, Eduard. "D.P. Apathy." *Flight and Resettlement*. Edited by H.B.M. Murphy. Paris: UNESCO, 1955.

Barton, Allen H. *Communities in Disaster*. Garden City, N.Y. : Doubleday & Company, Inc., 1969.

Bentwich, Norman. "Human Rights and the Reduction of Statelessness." *Contemporary Review*, CCI, 1962.

Blackstock, Charity. *The Children*. Boston: Little, Brown and Company, 1966.

Borrie, W. D. *The Cultural Integration of Immigrants*. Paris : UNESCO, 1959.

Bright, J. S. *Scandals of a Refugee Camp*. New Delhi : Tagore Memorial Publications, 1948.

Brockington, Leonard W. *Journey Among the Homeless*. Beirut : United Nations Relief and Works Agency for Palestine Refugees in the Near East, 1963.

Brown, Francis J., ed. *Refugees*. Philadelphia: American Academy of Political and Social Science, 1939.

Chinnock, Frank W. *Nagasaki : The Forgotten Bomb*. New York : World Publishing Company, 1969.

Cirtautas, K. C. *The Refugee*. New York : Citadel Press, 1963.

———. *The Refugee : A Psychological Study*. Boston : Meador Publishing Company, 1957.

Dey, S. K. *Nilokheri*. Bombay : Asia Publishing House, 1962.

Form, William H. and Nosow, Sigmund. *Community in Disaster*. New York : Harpers, 1958.

Gaertner, Miriam L. "A Comparison of Refugee and Non-Refugee Immigrants to New York City." *Flight and Resettlement,* Edited by H.B.M. Murphy. Paris : UNESCO, 1955.

Grodka, Sonya and Hennes, Gerhard. *Homeless No More.* National Council of Churches, 1960.

Handlin, Oscar. *The Uprooted.* Boston : Little, Brown and Company, 1951.

Henderson, William, "The Refugees in India and Pakistan." *Journal of International Affairs.* VII (1953).

Hoff, Hans. "The Young Refugee." *Growing Up in a Changing World.* London : World Federation for Mental Health, 1958.

Hoke, Donald E.; Peterson, Paul B.; and Donaldson, L. LaVerne. *Refugee.* Chicago : Moody Press, 1962.

Ingles, Jose D. *Study of Discrimination in Respect of the Right of Everyone to Leave any Country, Including His Own, and to Return to His Country.* New York : United Nations, 1963.

International Labour Office. *International Migration : 1945-1957.* Geneva: International Labour Office, 1959.

Janis, Irving. *Air War and Emotional Stress : Psychological Studies of Bombing and Civilian Defence.* New York: McGraw-Hill, 1951.

Kee, Robert. *Refugee World.* London: Oxford University Press, 1961.

Lackanpal, Kul Bhushan. *Social Organization of a Refugee Community.* Unpublished Masters Thesis, Punjab University, 1964.

Levi, Primo. *Survival in Auschwitz.* New York: Collier Books, 1961.

Lifton, Robert J. "Psychological Effects of the Atomic Bomb." *The Threat of Impending Disaster.* Edited by George H. Grosser, Henry Wechsler, and Milton Greenberg. Cambridge : M.I.T. Press, 1964.

———. *Death in Life : Survivors of Hiroshima.* New York: Random House, 1967.

Mahajan, Amarjit. *Change in Punjabi Marriage : A Study of a Displaced Community.* Chandigarh, undated. (Mimeographed).

Ministry of Rehabilitation, Government of India. *Displaced Persons in Delhi.* Delhi : Ministry of Rehabilitation, 1962.

Muller, K. V. *et. al. Weggis Report 1960.* Vaduz, Nansen Institute, 1961.

Murphy, H. B. M., ed. *Flight and Resettlement.* Paris : UNESCO, 1955.

Niederland, William G. "Psychiatric Disorders among Persecution Victims". *Journal of Nervous and Mental Diseases.* CXXXIX,

1964, pp. 458-474.

North American Civic League for Immigrants. *Messages for Newcomers.* Boston : North American Civic League for Immigrants, 1916.

Pedersen, S. "Reaching Safety" *Flight and Resettlement.* Edited by H.B.M. Murphy. Paris : UNESCO, 1955.

Poslavsky, A. "The Refugee in His New Country." *Growing Up in a Changing World.* London: World Federation for Mental Health, 1958.

Prins, S. A. "The Individual in Flight". *Flight and Resettlement.* Edited by H.B.M. Murphy. Paris : UNESCO, 1955.

Ram, Pars. *A UNESCO Study of Social Tensions in Aligarh, 1950-1951.* Ahmedabad : New Order Book Company, 1955.

Randhawa, M. S. *Out of the Ashes.* Bombay : C. N. Raman, 1954.

Rees, Elfan. *We Strangers and Afraid.* New York : Carnegie Endowment for World Peace, 1959.

Robbins, Richard. "The Refugee Status: Challenge and Response." *Law and Contemporary Problems.* XXI (1956), pp. 311-33.

Robinson, Donald B. *The Face of Disaster.* Garden City, N.Y. : Doubleday & Company, 1959.

Saksena, R. N. *Refugees: A Study in Changing Attitudes.* Bombay : Asia Publishing House, 1961.

Schechtman, Joseph B. *On Wings of Eagles.* New York: Thomas Yoseloff, 1961.

———. *Population Transfers in Asia*, New York: Hallsby Press, 1949.

———. *The Refugee in the World : Displacement and Integration.* New York : A. S. Barnes, 1963.

Smolen, Kazimierz. *Auschwitz : 1940-1945*, Oswiecim, Poland : Panstwowe Muzeum W. Oswiecimiu, 1961.

Stern, Henri. "The Aftermath of Belsen." *Flight and Resettlement.* Edited by H.B.M. Murphy. Paris: UNESCO, 1955.

Stewart, Wentworth. *The Making of a Nation.* Boston : The Stratford Company, 1919.

Stoessinger, John George. *The Refugee and the World Community.* Minneapolis : University of Minnesota Press, 1956.

Sutton, Jacqueline Young. "The Psychological Adjustment of Displaced Persons." *Social and Psychological Factors in the Resettlement of Refugees.* Cambridge, Centre for International Studies, M.I.T., 1952.

Thomas, Brinley. *International Migration and Economic Development.* Paris : UNESCO, 1961.

UNESCO. *The Positive Contribution by Immigrants.* Paris: UNESCO, 1955.

United Nations. *Report of the United Nations High Commissioner for Refugees.* New York : United Nations, 1965.

United Nations Commission on Human Rights. *Definition and Classification of Minorities.* Lake Success, New York : United Nations Commission on Human Rights, 1949.

———. *The Main Types and Causes of Discrimination.* Lake Success, New York: United Nations Commission on Human Rights, 1949.

United Nations High Commission for Refugees. *Meeting A Challenge.* Geneva : United Nations High Commissioner for Refugees, undated.

Vermani, Ravi. *Partition and its Social Problems in East Punjab.* Unpublished M.A. thesis, Madras School of Social Work, 1957.

Webb, Kaye and Searle, Ronald. *Refugees 1960.* Harmondsworth, Middlesex : Penguin Books, 1960.

Wolfenstein, Martha. *Disaster : A Psychological Essay.* Glencoe, Illinois : Free Press, 1957.

World Federation for Mental Health. *Uprooting and Resettlement.* London: World Federation for Mental Health, 1960.

Yeld, R. "Implications of Experience with Refugee Settlement." Undated. (Mimeographed).

Psychology and Sociology

Adorno, Theodor W. Frenkel-Brunswik, Else; Levinson, Daniel J., and Sanford, R. Nevitt. *The Authoritarian Personality.* New York : Harper and Co., 1950.

Allport, Gordon W. "Attitudes." *Handbook of Social Psychology.* Edited by C. Murchison, New York: Oxford University Press, 1935.

———. *The Nature of Prejudice.* Cambridge: Addison-Wesley, 1954.

Almond, Gabriel A. *The Appeals of Communism.* Princeton: Princeton University Press, 1954.

Ardrey, Robert. *African Genesis.* New York : Atheneum, 1961.

———. *The Territorial Imperative.* New York : Atheneum, 1966.

Ashley, Montagu, M. F. "The New Litany of 'Innate Depravity' or

Original Sin Revisited." *Man and Aggression*. Edited by M. F. Ashley Montagu. New York : Oxford University Press, 1968.

Atkinson, John W., ed. *Motives in Fantasy, Action and Society*. New York: Van Nostrand, 1958.

Bakan, David. "The Test of Significance in Psychological Research." *Psychological Bulletin*. LXVI, No. 6 (1966), pp, 423-37.

Bellak, L. *TAT Blank*. New York: Psychological Corporation, 1947.

Berkowitz, Leonard. *Aggression : A Social Psychological Analysis*. New York : McGraw Hill, 1962.

Bettelheim, Bruno. "Individual and Mass Behaviour in Extreme Situations." *Journal of Abnormal and Social Psychology*. XXXVIII (1943), pp. 417-452.

Bloom, Benjamin S. *Stability and Change in Human Characteristics*, New York : Wiley, 1964.

Blumer, Herbert. "Social Disorganization and Individual Disorganization." *American Journal of Sociology*. XLII (1937), pp. 871-77.

Bowlby, John. *Attachment*. New York: Basic Books, 1969.

Bronfenbrenner, Urie and Ricciutti, Henry N. "The Appraisal of Personality Characteristics in Children." *Handbook of Research Methods in Child Development*. Edited by Paul H. Mussen. New York : John Wiley and Sons, 1960.

Brown, Roger. "Models of Attitude Change" *New Directions in Psychology*, New York: Holt, Rinehart and Winston, 1962.

Buss, Arnold. *The Psychology of Aggression*, New York : John Wiley and Sons, 1961.

Clarke, Helen Jane. "The Rosenzweig Picture-Frustration Study." *An Introduction to Projective Techniques*. Edited by H. H. Anderson and G. L. Anderson. New York : Prentice-Hall, 1951.

———. Rosenzweig, Saul; and Fleming, Edith E. "The Reliability of Scoring of the Rosenzweig, Picture-Frustration Study." *Journal of Clinical Psychology*, III. (1947), pp. 364-370.

Clarke, Russel A. and Sensibar, Minda Rae. "The Relationship between Symbolic and Manifest Projections of Sexuality with Some Incidental Correlates." *Motives in Fantasy, Action and Society*. Edited by John W. Atkinson. Princeton: Van Nostrand, 1958.

Dollard, John; Doob, Leonard; Miller, Neal E; Mowrer, O. H.; and Sears, Robert R. *Frustration and Aggression*. New Haven : Yale University Press, 1939.

Dunham, H. Warren. "War and Personality Disorganization."

American Journal of Sociology. XLVIII (1942), pp. 387-97.

Durkheim, Emile. *Suicide*, Glencoe, Illinois : Free Press, 1951.

Erikson, Erik H. *Childhood and Society*. New York: W. W. Norton, 1950.

———. *Identity and the Life Cycle*, New York : International Universities Press, 1959.

———. *Young Man Luther*, New York, W. W. Norton, 1958.

Eysenck, H. J. *The Psychology of Politics*. London : Routledge and Kegan Paul, 1963.

Freud, Sigmund. *A General Introduction to Psychoanalysis*, New York : Washington Square Press, 1952.

Fruchter, Benjamin. *Introduction to Factor Analysis*. Princeton : Van Nostrand, 1954.

Goffman, Erving. *The Presentation of Self in Everyday Life*. Garden City, New York : Doubleday Anchor Books, 1959.

Haner, Charles F. and Brown, Patricia A. "Clarification of the Instigation to Action Concept in the Frustration-Aggression Hypothesis." *Frustration and Conflict*. Edited by A. J. Yates, Princeton : Van Nostrand, 1965.

Hoedemaker, Edward D. "Distrust and Aggression : An Interpersonal-International Analogy." *Journal of Conflict Resolution*. XII (1968), pp. 69-81.

Horobin, G. W. "Adjustment and Assimilation : The Displaced Person". *Sociological Review*. V (1957), pp. 239-54.

Hyman, Herbert and Sheatsley, Paul B. "The Authoritarian Personality — a Methodological Critique." *Studies in the Scope and Method of "The Authoritarian Personality*." Edited by Richard Christie and Marie Jahoda. Glencoe : Free Press, 1954.

Inkeles, Alex and Levinson, Daniel J. "National Character : The Study of Modal Personality and Sociocultural Systems." *Handbook of Social Psychology*. Edited by Gardner Lindzey, Vol. II, Cambridge: Addison-Wesley, 1954.

Jensen, Arthur R. "Aggression in Fantasy and Overt Behaviour." *Psychological Monographs*. LXXI (1957), No. 445.

Kagan, Jerome. "The Measurement of Overt Aggression from Fantasy." *Journal of Abnormal and Social Psychology*, LII. (1956), pp. 390-93.

———. "Thematic Apperception Techniques with Children," *Projective Techniques with Children*, Edited by Albert I. Rabin and Mary R. Haworth, New York: Grune and Stratton, 1960.

Klebanoff, Seymour. "Chapter 12" *Thematic Test Analysis*. Edited by Edwin S. Schneidman. New York: Grune and Stratton, 1951.

Kramer Ralph. "The Conceptual Status of Social Disorganization." *American Journal of Sociology*. XLVIII (1943) pp. 466-74.

Leach, Edmund. "Don't Say Boo to a Goose." *Man and Aggression*. Edited by M. F. Ashley Montagu. New York : Oxford University Press, 1968.

Lorenz, Konrad. *On Aggression*, New York : Harcourt, Brace and World, 1966.

McClosky, Herbert and Schaar, John H. "Psychological Dimensions of Anomy." *American Sociological Review*. XXX (1965), pp. 14-40.

Malzberg, Benjamin. "Social Disorganization." *Journal of the American Statistical Association*. XXXI (1936).

Mandelbaum, David G. "The Family in India." *Southwestern Journal of Anthropology*. IV (1948).

Maslow, Abraham H. "Further Notes on the Psychology of Being." *Journal of Humanistic Psychology*. IV (1964), pp. 45-58.

———. *Motivation and Personality*. New York: Harper and Row, 1954.

———. "Synergy in the Society and in the Individual," *Journal of Individual Psychology*. XX (1964), pp. 153-64.

Mercer, Margaret and Kyriazis, Christ. "Results of the Rosenzweig Picture-Frustration Study for Physically Assaultive Prisoner Mental Patients." *Journal of Consulting Psychologists*. XXVI, No. 5, 1962, p. 490.

Miller, Daniel R. and Swanson, Guy E. *Inner Conflict and Defence*. New York : Holt, Rinehart and Winston, 1960.

Miller, Neil E. "Theory and Experiment Relating Psychoanalytic Displacement to Stimulus-Response Generalization." *Journal of Abnormal and Social Psychology*. XLIII (1948), pp. 155-178.

Murphy, Gardner. *In the Minds of Men*. New York: Basic Books, 1953.

Murphy, Lois Barclay. "Roots of Tolerance and Tensions in Indian Child Development." *In the Minds of Men* by Gardner Murphy. New York : Basic Books, 1953.

Murray, Henry A. *Thematic Apperception Test: Manual*. Cambridge: Harvard University Press, 1943.

Mussen, Paul H. and Naylor, H. Kelly. "The Relationships between Overt and Fantasy Aggression." *Journal of Abnormal and*

Social Psychology. IL (1954), pp. 235-40.

Pool, Ithiel de Sola and Schulman, Irwin. "Newsmen's Fantasies, Audiences and Newswriting." *Public Opinion Quarterly*. XXIII (1959), pp. 145-58.

Rokeach, Milton. "The Role of Values in Public Opinion Research." *Public Opinion Quarterly*, XXXII (1968-69), pp. 547-59.

Rosenberg, Morris. "Misanthropy and Political Ideology." *American Sociological Review*. XXI (1956), pp. 690-95.

Rotter, Julian B. "Generalized Expectancies for Internal vs. External Control of Reinforcement." *Psychological Monographs*. LXXX, No. 609 (1960).

———. "Word Association and Sentence Completion Methods." *An Introduction to Projective Techniques*. Edited by Harold H. Anderson and G. L. Anderson. New York : Prentice-Hall, 1951.

Scott, John Paul. *Aggression*. Chicago: The University of Chicago Press, 1958.

Sears, Pauline S. "Doll Play Aggression in Normal Young Children : Influence of Sex, Age, Sibling Status, Father's Absence." *Psychological Monographs*. LXV (1951), No. 6.

Sears, Robert R. "A Theoretical Framework for Personality and Social Behaviour." *American Psychologist*. VI (1951), pp. 476-483.

———. Maccoby, Eleanor ; and Levin, Harry. *Patterns of Child Rearing*. Evanston: Row Peterson and Company, 1957.

Siegel, Alberta E. "Aggressive Behaviour of Young Children in the Absence of an Adult." *Child Development*. XXVIII, pp. 371-378.

Siegel, Saul M. "The Relationship of Hostility to Authoritarianism." *Journal of Abnormal and Social Psychology*. LII (1956), pp. 368-72.

Smith, M. Brewster; Bruner, Jerome; and White, Robert. *Opinions and Personality*, New York : John Wiley and Sons, 1956.

———. "Map for the Analysis of Personality and Politics." *Journal of Social Issues*. XXIV (1968), pp. 15-28.

Steed, Gitel P. "Notes on an Approach to a Study of Personality Formation in a Village in Gujarat." *Village India* : *Studies in the Little Community*. Edited by McKim Marriott, Chicago: University of Chicago Press, 1955.

Stone, Harold. "The TAT Aggressive Content Scale." *Journal of Projective Techniques*. XX (1956).

Storr, Anthony. *Human Aggression.* New York : Atheneum Publishers, 1968.

Thomas, A. T. and Znaniecki, Florian. *The Polish Peasant in Europe and America,* New York. Knopf, 1927.

Thurstone, L. L. *Multiple Factor Analysis.* Chicago : University of Chicago Press, 1947.

Tietze, Christopher; Lemkau, Paul; and Cooper, Marcia. "Personality Disorder and Spatial Mobility." *American Journal of Sociology.* XLVIII (1942), pp. 29-39.

Vernon, Philip E. *Personality Assessment : A Critical Survey.* London: Methuen & Co., 1964.

Wallace, Anthony F. C. *Culture and Personality.* New York : Random House, 1961.

Weiss, Walter and Fine, Bernard J. "The Effect of Induced Aggressiveness on Opinion Change." *Journal of Abnormal and Social Psychology.* LII (1956), pp. 109-114.

Whiting, John W. M. and Child, Irvin L. *Child Training and Personality.* New Haven : Yale University Press, 1953.

Wolfgang, Marvin E. and Ferracuti, Franco. *The Subculture of Violence.* London : Tavistock Publications, 1967.

Yates, A. J., ed. *Frustration and Conflict.* Princeton : Van Nostrand, 1965.

Development

Abernethy, David and Coombe, Trevor. "Education and Politics in Developing Countries." *Harvard Educational Review.* XXXV (1965), pp. 287-302.

Almond, Gabriel A. and Verba, Sidney. *The Civic Culture : Political Attitudes and Democracy in Five Nations.* Princeton : Princeton University Press, 1963.

Almond, Gabriel A. and Powell, G. Bingham, Jr. *Comparative Politics : A Developmental Approach.* Boston : Little, Brown and Company, 1966.

Arendt, Hannah. *The Origins of Totalitarianism.* New York : Harcourt Brace, 1951.

Bailey, F. G. *Stratagems and Spoils.* Toronto : Copp-Clark, 1969.

Banfield, Edward C. *The Moral Basis of a Backward Society.* Glencoe : Free Press, 1958.

Bendix, Reinhard. *Nation-Building and Citizenship.* New York : John Wiley & Sons, 1964.

Bhatt, B. P. and Krishnamoorthy, P. V. "Radio Rural Forums Spread Throughout India."*Radio Broadcasting Serves Rural Development*. Paris: UNESCO, 1965.

Bienen, Henry. *Violence and Social Change*. Chicago : University of Chicago Press, 1968.

Blumer, Herbert. *An Appraisal of Thomas and Znaniecki's "The Polish Peasant in Europe and America."* New York : Social Science Research Council, 1939.

Bowman, Mary Jean and Anderson, C. Arnold. "Concerning the Role of Education in Development." *Old Societies and New States*. Edited by Clifford Geertz. Glencoe, Illinois; Free Press, 1963.

Brayne, F. F. *Better Villages*. Bombay: Oxford University Press, 1937.

Campbell, Angus: Converse, Philip E.; Miller, Warren E.; and Stokes, Donald E. *The American Voter*. New York : John Wiley and Sons, 1960.

Campbell, Angus: Gurin, Gerald; and Miller, Warren E. *The Voter Decides*. Evanston, Ill. : Row Peterson and Co., 1954.

Cantril, Hadley. *The Politics of Despair*. New York: Collier Books, 1962.

Coleman, James S., ed. *Education and Political Development*. Princeton : Princeton University Press, 1965.

Dahl, Robert A. *Political Opposition in Western Democracies*. New Haven : Yale University Press, 1966.

Dawson, Richard E. and Prewitt, Kenneth. *Political Socialization*. Boston : Little, Brown and Company, 1969.

Desai, A. R. *Rural Sociology in India*. Bombay : Indian Society of Agricultural Economists, 1961.

Dube, S. C. "Communication, Innovation, and Planned Change in India." *Communication and Change in the Developing Countries*. Edited by Daniel Lerner and Wilbur Schramm. Honolulu : East-West Centre Press, 1967,

Easton, David. *A Systems Analysis of Political Life*. New York : John Wiley and Sons, 1965.

———. and Dennis, Jack. "The Child's Acquisition of Regime Norms : Political Efficacy." *American Political Science Review*, LXI (1967), pp. 25-38.

Etienne, Gilbert. *Studies in Indian Agriculture : The Art of the Possible*. Berkeley : University of California Press, 1968.

Frankel, Francine. *Annex P : Employment and Income Distribution.* Washington: Agency for International Development, 1969.

Galbraith, John Kenneth. "Rival Economic Theories in India." *Foreign Affairs.* XXXVI. (1958), pp. 587-96.

Gamson, William A. *Power and Discontent.* Homewood, Illinois: Dorsey Press, 1968.

Geertz, Clifford. "The Integrative Revolution." *Old Societies and New States.* Edited by Clifford Geertz, Glencoe: Free Press, 1963.

Graham, Hugh Davis, and Gurr, Ted Robert. *Violence in America: Historical and Comparative Perspectives,* New York : New American Library, 1969.

Grewal, I. S. "Differential Characteristics of Farmers of Predominantly Refugee, a Native and a Mixed Village, Affecting the Adoption of Improved Agricultural Practices in a Block in Ludhiana District of the Punjab State." *Summaries of Extension Research by Post-Graduate Students.* Edited by Aditya N. Shukla and Iqbal Singh Grewal. Ludhiana: Department of Extension Education, Punjab Agricultural University, 1967.

Gumperz, John J. "Language Problems in the Rural Development of North India." *Journal of Asian Studies.* XVI (1957), pp. 251-59.

———. "Some Remarks on Regional and Social Language Differences in India." *Changing Dimensions in Indian Society and Culture.* Chicago: University of Chicago Syllabus Division, 1957.

Hagen, Everett E. *The Economics of Development.* Homewood, Ill. : Richard D. Irwin, 1968.

———. *On the Theory of Social Change.* Homewood, Ill. : Dorsey Press, 1962.

Hess, Robert D. "The Acquisition of Political Efficacy in Pre-Adults" (Mimeo), 1969.

Huntington, Samuel. *Political Order in Changing Societies.* New Haven: Yale University Press, 1968.

Hyman, Herbert H. *Political Socialization.* Glencoe: The Free Press, 1959.

Kahlon, A. S.; Johl, S. S.; Moore, C. V.; Kahlon, S. S.; and Sharma, M. L. *Dynamics of Punjab Agriculture.* Ludhiana: Department of Economics and Sociology, Punjab Agricultural University, 1966.

Keller, Stephen L. *Government and the Agricultural Implements*

Industry. Chandigarh : Department of Industries, Punjab Government, 1962.

Krishna, Raj. "Agrarian Reform in India: The Debate on Ceilings." *Economic Development and Cultural Change*. VII (1959), pp. 302-17.

Lakshmana Rao, Y. V. *Communication and Development: A Study of Two Indian Villages*. Minneapolis : University of Minnesota Press, 1966.

Lane, Robert E. *Political Ideology*. New York : Free Press, 1962.

———. *Political Thinking and Consciousness*. Chicago : Markham Publishing Company, 1969.

Lerner, Daniel. *The Passing of Traditional Society*. Glencoe, Illinois: Free Press, 1958.

———. "Toward a Communication Theory of Modernization, A Set of Considerations." *Communications and Political Development*. Edited by Lucian W. Pye, Princeton: Princeton University Press, 1963.

———. and Schramm, Wilbur, eds. *Communication and Change in the Developing Countries*. Honolulu : East-West Centre Press, 1967.

McClelland, David C. "Achievement Drive and Economic Growth." *Harvard Business Review*, XL, No. 4 (1962), pp. 99-112.

———. *The Achieving Society*. Princeton : Van Nostrand, 1961.

———. and Winter, David G. *Motivating Economic Achievement*. New York : Free Press, 1969.

Marriott, McKim. "Return to Kishengarhi" talk before the South Asia Seminar, University of Chicago, April 9, 1969.

———. "Technological Change in Overdeveloped Rural Areas" *Economic Development and Cultural Change*. I (1952-53) pp. 261-272.

Menefee, Selden and Menefee, Audrey. "An Experiment in Communications in Four Indian Villages." *Indian Journal of Social Research*. VI (1965), pp. 148-58.

Millikan, Max F. and Blackmer, Donald L. M. *The Emerging Nations*. Bombay : Asia Publishing House, 1962.

Myrdal, Gunnar. *Asian Drama*. New York : Pantheon, 1968.

Nair, Kusum. *Blossoms in the Dust*. New York : Frederick A. Praeger, 1962.

———. *The Lonely Furrow : Farming in the United States, Japan, and India*. Ann Arbor : University of Michigan Press, 1969.

Nieburg, H. L. *Political Violence.* New York : St. Martin's Press, 1969.

Pye, Lucian W. *Aspects of Political Development*, Boston : Little Brown, 1966.

———. ed. *Communications and Political Development*, Princeton : Princeton University Press, 1963.

———. *Politics, Personality, and Nation Building*, New Haven : Yale University Press, 1962.

———. and Verba, Sidney. *Political Culture and Political Development.* Princeton: Princeton University Press, 1965.

Rajagopalan, C. and Singh, Jaspal. *Adoption of Agricultural Innovations.* Delhi : Indian Institute of Technology, 1967.

Rogers, Everett M. *Diffusion of Innovations.* New York: Free Press, 1962.

———. *Modernization among Peasants : The Impact of Communication.* New York: Holt, Rinehart and Winston, 1969.

Schramm, Wilbur. "Communications Development and the Development Process." *Communications and Political Development.* Edited by Lucian W. Pye. Princeton : Princeton University Press, 1963.

———. *Mass Media and National Development.* Stanford : Stanford University Press, 1964.

Schuman, Howard. *Economic Development and Individual Change.* Cambridge : Harvard University Centre for International Affairs, 1967.

Spector, Paul; Torres, Augusto; Lichtenstein, Stanley; Preston, Harley O. *Communication and Motivation in Community Development.* Washington: Institute for International Services, 1963.

Streeter, Carroll P. *A Partnership to Improve Food Production in India.* New York : Rockefeller Foundation, 1969.

Taylor, Carl C.; Ensminger, Douglas; Johnson, Helen W. and Joyce, Jean. *India's Roots of Democracy.* New York : Frederick A. Praeger, 1966.

Thal Development Authority. *Handbook.* Jauharabad (Pakistan), 1954.

Tocqueville, Alexis de. *Democracy in America.* New York: Vintage Books, 1945.

Verba, Sidney. "Comparative Political Culture." *Political Culture and Political Development.* Edited by Lucian W. Pye and Sidney Verba. Princeton: Princeton University Press, 1965.

Ward, Robert E., ed. *Studying Politics Abroad,* Boston: Little Brown & Company, 1964.

Index

irt : in relation to